Total Survival

A comprehensive guide for the physical, psychological, emotional, and professional survival of law enforcement officers.

Compiled and Edited by

Ed Nowicki

PERFORMANCE DIMENSIONS PUBLISHING
P.O. Box 502, Powers Lake, WI 53159-0502

Total Survival

A comprehensive guide for the physical, psychological, emotional, and professional survival of law enforcement officers.

Compiled and Edited by
Ed Nowicki

Published by:  **PERFORMANCE DIMENSIONS PUBLISHING**
a division of Performance Dimensions, Inc.
P.O. Box 502, Powers Lake, WI 53159-0502, U.S.A.
Phone (414) 279-3850

All rights reserved. No part of this book may be reproduced or transmitted in any form or by any means, electronic or mechanical, including photocopying, recording or by any information storage and retrieval system without written permission from the publisher, except for the inclusion of brief quotations in a review.

Copyright © 1993 by Performance Dimensions, Inc.
First Printing: January, 1993
Printed in the United States of America

Library of Congress Cataloging-in-Publication Data

Total survival : a comprehensive guide for the physical, psychological, emotional, and professional survival of law enforcement officers / compiled and edited by Ed Nowicki.
    p.   cm.
  Includes bibliographical references and index.
  ISBN 1-879411-18-0 (trade pbk.) : $24.95
  1. Police--United States. 2. Law enforcement--United States.
I. Nowicki, Ed, 1947-
HV8141.T67 1993   92-85340
363 .2' 0973--dc20   CIP

Library of Congress Catalog Card Number: 92-85340
ISBN: 1-879411-18-0 $24.95 Softcover

Dedication

This book is dedicated to the men and women who care enough about their families, communities, brother and sister officers, and themselves to realize the importance of total survival.

Warning—Disclaimer

The information, photos and graphics displayed in this book are intended to assist the law enforcement officer. It is not the intention of the authors, publisher, or any of their agents to encourage persecution of any single person, group, organization, or religion who are free to express themselves under the protection of the First Amendment of the Constitution of the United States.

This book is designed to provide information in regard to the subject matter covered. It is sold with the understanding that the authors and publisher are not engaged in rendering legal or other professional services. If legal or other professional assistance is required, the services of a competent professional should be sought.

It is not the purpose of this book to reprint all the information that is otherwise available to the authors and publisher, but to complement, amplify, and supplement other texts. You are urged to read all available material and to learn as much as possible about officer safety and survival and to tailor the information to your individual needs. For more information, see the "Suggested Reading" section at the end of this book.

Every effort has been made to make this book as complete and as accurate as possible. However, there may be mistakes, both typographical and in content. Therefore, this text should be used only as a general guide and not as the ultimate source of officer survival. Furthermore, this book contains information on officer survival only up to the printing date.

The purpose of this book is to educate, inform, and stimulate thought. The authors and Performance Dimensions shall have neither liability nor responsibility to any person or entity with respect to any loss or damage caused, or alleged to be caused, directly or indirectly by the information contained in this book.

If you do not wish to be bound by the above, you may return this book to the publisher for a full refund.

Introduction

The Concept of Total Survival

by Ed Nowicki

Total Survival is one of the most unique books ever written about the important topic of officer survival. It is not meant to compete with, or to replace, any other books dealing with officer survival. It is meant to be a part of each law enforcement officer's survival library. The importance of officer survival can not be over emphasized. Perhaps the German playwright, Bertolt Brecht, described the importance of survival best in his 1924 play, *Jungle of Cities*. He stated, "It isn't important to come out on top; what matters is to be the one who comes out alive."

The book's title, *Total Survival*, was selected not because it contains "total" information available about surviving the streets, but because true officer survival requires a "total" approach. Officer survival means more than law enforcement officers physically surviving the streets. They must also survive the job, the courts, their families, and other demands placed upon them. That is why it is important to take the total approach to officer survival; the physical, the psychological, the emotional, and the professional.

Virtually all aspects of officer survival are interrelated. If officers can not survive the stress (psychological) of the job, they may be unable to survive the streets (physical) or even to remain in law enforcement (professional). They may have survived an armed confrontation (physical), but accurate and complete reports and testimony are necessary to survive the courts (professional). They may survive seeing humanity at its worst (emotional), but if they must abuse alcohol or other substances in order to cope, this has a detrimental effect on their health (physical) and the job (professional).

Officer survival is also an attitude; an attitude that requires a personal commitment to attain the skills and information necessary to meet the various challenges of law enforcement. This requires individual officers to reach beyond their limitations. It means never accepting defeat and looking at mistakes as learning experiences. If and when mistakes are made in critical situations, it means having the skills and attitude to survive the mistakes. The survival attitude is the winning attitude.

Total Survival was not written entirely by professional writers. Although writing ability was an important consideration in assembling this cadre of contributors, being an expert was the primary consideration for selecting the author of each chapter. A total of forty-five different authors and experts contributed chapters to this book.

A recognized expert on a specific topic developed each chapter since it is difficult for one individual to have all the necessary skills and experience on all the topics. Each of these experts is well known and respected for their knowledge about their chapter. *Total Survival* contains the "best of the best." Each author's expertise was attained through education, training, and more important, experience.

You will find a survival plan within the following pages of this book. This plan provides you with information on how to survive the demands that may be placed upon you. These demands, in one way or another, all relate to your law enforcement duties. You are provided with important information on firearms' tactics and defensive tactics, report writing and stress management, chemical agents and physical fitness. Department policies and personal preference may affect the way you choose to use this information.

There is also no correct way to read *Total Survival*. You may wish to start with the first chapter and continue through each following chapter until the entire book is completed. You may want to selectively read chapters based on your perception of personal importance and interest. You may not want to read certain chapters because you don't care for the author, or you feel strong in your opinions about the topic. How you choose to read this book is up to you.

You may not agree with all of the information contained in these chapters and there may be other alternatives or insights that were not covered by the authors. If this is the case, you were conscious of the fact that you do not agree, so you did actually learn something from the chapter. In fact, many of the authors do not totally agree on some of the information contained in *Total Survival*. Therefore, the proverbial, "There's more than one way to skin a cat," should be remembered while reading this book.

With an open mind and the motivation to learn you will receive the maximum benefits from this book. Your survival is not only important to you, but to your family, friends, brother and sister officers, community, and department. Remember, don't just think officer survival, think *Total Survival!*

Contents

Dedication   iii

Warning - Disclaimer   v

Introduction   vii
The Concept of Total Survival
by Ed Nowicki

Chapter 1   1
Contact & Cover: Field Tactics for Effective Suspect Control
by Steve Albrecht and John Morrison

Chapter 2   8
Body Armor: Advantage for Law Enforcement
by George Armbruster

Chapter 3   12
Off Duty Survival
by Massad Ayoob

Chapter 4   22
Principles of Police Report Writing
by Stan Berry and Dean Berry

Chapter 5   37
The Police Shotgun
by Michael F. Boyle

Chapter 6   49
Law Enforcement Liability: Reflections On Survival
by Michael A. Brave

Chapter 7   58
Dealing With Fear and Danger
by Stephen M. Bunting

Chapter 8   65
Law Enforcement Applications of Chemical Agents
by William E. Burroughs

Chapter 9 74
Tactical Principles and Concepts
by Andrew J. Casavant

Chapter 10 82
Psychological Survival for Police Officers
by Dr. James T. Chandler

Chapter 11 90
Stress of the Gunfight
by Jim Cirillo

Chapter 12 94
Personal Development
by Bill Clede

Chapter 13 101
Police Fitness
by Dr. Thomas R. Collingwood

Chapter 14 119
Burnout in Law Enforcement
by Ed Donovan

Chapter 15 124
Reading the Streets
by Mark S. Dunston

Chapter 16 132
The Law Enforcement Rifle
by Dick Fairburn

Chapter 17 142
Handle Your Handgun Correctly!
by John S. Farnam

Chapter 18 150
The Law Enforcement Attitude
by Neal Fortin

Chapter 19 155
How to Stay On the Team
by Roger Fulton

Contents

Chapter 20   169
Building Searches
by Kevin Gordon

Chapter 21   182
Principles of Officer Survival
by David Grossi

Chapter 22   189
Vehicle Stop Survival
by Harvey V. Hedden

Chapter 23   197
Conducting Field Interviews: Gathering Knowledge Safely
by Dennis F. Jurasz

Chapter 24   203
An Introduction to Defensive Tactics
by Gary T. Klugiewicz

Chapter 25   208
Handgun Retention System
by Jim Lindell

Chapter 26   222
Space, Time, and Distance
by "Coach" Bob Lindsey

Chapter 27   229
Patrol Response to Hazardous Materials Incidents
by William A. May, Jr.

Chapter 28   238
Looking Glass Cops
by Dr. Murlene "Mac" McKinnon

Chapter 29   249
Courtroom Demeanor and Testimony
by David W. McRoberts

Chapter 30   260
Multiple Assailants: A Test of Mind, Body, and Spirit
by Phil Messina

Chapter 31
Methodology vs. Madness: Self-Directed Firearms' Training
by John Morrison
273

Chapter 32
Use of Force
by Mildred K. O'Linn
281

Chapter 33
Management of Aggressive Behavior
by Roland Ouellette
289

Chapter 34
Tactical Groundfighting
by Tracy Robinson and Douglas Chu
298

Chapter 35
Practicing for the Street
by Guy A. Rossi
309

Chapter 36
Ammo Evaluation Basics
by Ed Sanow
318

Chapter 37
Tactical Conditioning for Law Enforcement: The Triad of Strength
by Arthur N. Sapp
330

Chapter 38
The Technicalities of Speed
by Anthony J. Scotti
338

Chapter 39
Compliance Holds
by Larry Smith
350

Chapter 40
Impact Weapon: The Need for Greater Understanding and Function
by Terry E. Smith
360

Chapter 41
Special Purpose Police Firearms
by David J. Spaulding
375

Contents

Chapter 42 — 386
Advice From the Pros: Searching and Frisking Methods
by Brian J. Stover

Chapter 43 — 396
Police Ethics and Professionalism: Dealing with Attitude, Anger, Lust and Greed
by Neal E. Trautman

Chapter 44 — 409
Handcuffing and Officer Survival
by Joseph J. Truncale

Chapter 45 — 422
Crowd Confrontation Management
by John P. Vazquez

Biography — 443

Contact Information for the Authors — 444

Suggested Reading — 448

Suggested Video Viewing — 451

Index — 452

Other Books and Videos Available from Performance Dimensions Publishing — 522

Order Form — 525

"Irrational barriers and ancient prejudices fall quickly when the question of survival itself is at stake."

— John F. Kennedy

Chapter 1

Contact & Cover: Field Tactics for Effective Suspect Control

by Steve Albrecht and John Morrison

It is Friday, September 14, 1984. On a clear and cool autumn night, San Diego Police Officer, Timothy Ruopp, drives his marked white police unit through Grape Street Park, a grassy area built on a hill in a high crime neighborhood.

Grape Street Park is especially noted for its gang-bangers and narcotics' activity. Many of the locals come to the area to park and drink, and blare their radios at one another. This night is no different.

As Ruopp cruises his car through the park, he sees two adult males drinking with, what appears to be, two underage females. He steers his police unit over to their location and parks near their open Mustang convertible. He gets out to investigate further. He questions the males and confirms his suspicions: the underage females were drinking liquor given to them by the two men. He puts the females into the back of his cage car and wearily reaches for his citation book.

He positions himself along the driver's side hood of his police car and begins writing misdemeanor tickets for the two men. He notifies the dispatcher of his situation: two minors and two adults in custody for alcohol violations. No big deal. Just another set of contacts on a long second-watch night.

San Diego Police Officer, Kimberly Tonahill, from her squad hears Ruopp's radio transmission and decides to cover him. She is only a few blocks away from the park, so she aims her car in his direction. Within minutes, she arrives on the scene and sees Ruopp talking with one of the men near his unit while the other man stands near the Mustang.

She parks her car at an angle near the Mustang and gets out to talk with Ruopp. He tells her what he discovered and what he is doing in terms of enforcement. She nods in agreement and walks over to talk to the man standing near the Mustang.

At this point, the other male is near the hood of Ruopp's police unit, signing his citation. The officers are approximately 15 feet apart. Ruopp has his head in his ticket book and is busily writing the cite. Tonahill has her back to him as she speaks to the man near the Mustang.

After talking with the man for a few minutes, Tonahill decides she wants to conduct a quick pat-down on him before he goes forward to sign his citation. He is neatly groomed, wearing wire-rimmed glasses and a black leather jacket. She positions herself behind the male and has him raise his hands away from his sides. When her hands make contact with his jacket, he spins quickly around and forcefully knocks Tonahill to the ground with his elbow.

As she falls to the pavement, he calmly reaches into his jacket, draws a 9 mm semi-automatic handgun from a shoulder holster, and fires several rounds into the prone officer. One of the rounds hits under her arm — an area unprotected by her vest — and fatally wounds her.

The subject then turns and aims his gun at Ruopp, who tries in vain to get behind his police car for cover. Several shots hit the officer in the legs and he is knocked down. As he tries to crawl away, the subject walks over to him and fires two fatal shots into his head.

The subject then opens the door of Ruopp's police car to release the underage females. They run away from the shooter, screaming and bringing the other male with them.

By coincidence and only a few minutes later, San Diego Police Officer, Gary Mitrovich, drives into the park, sees the parked police cars, and drives over to help. He is at first unaware of any problems until he sees the prone officers. He climbs from his car and confronts the subject from behind the Mustang.

The officer and the subject exchange gun fire and Mitrovich is hit in the upper arm before the subject flees. The subject, hit in the leg and the ear, is captured hours later hiding in a nearby drainage pond. Officer Tonahill is dead at the scene, Officer Ruopp dies a short time later, and Officer Mitrovich survives his wound and later returns to full patrol duty.

Too often, it's only after the deaths of police officers that we learn from our mistakes. Sadly, the police profession sometimes waits in a re-active rather than pro-active position, changing dangerous or questionable tactical procedures only after tremendous tragedies. Thankfully, when the art and science of police work evolve positively after the loss of fellow officers, the new techniques and officer survival methods help to make us all better at what we do.

From the San Diego Grape Street Park incident, where two officers were gunned down by a single subject, a police procedure that saves officers' lives has risen above all others to become a shining example of how to do this job safely, effectively, and with a minimum of risk. This street survival procedure is known as "Contact & Cover."

Perhaps procedure is not the correct word. When you understand the founding principles behind Contact & Cover, you'll come to see it more as a way of life. Once you fully understand the method and the reasons why it works, it will change the way you do business out in the streets.

Detective Lieutenant John Morrison and Sergeant Charles Peck of the San Diego Police Department developed the Contact & Cover approach after carefully analyzing previous SDPD officer fatalities. The lessons they learned from these deaths, mixed with their long history as veteran street cops, gave rise to Contact & Cover.

Morrison and Peck created a department-wide training program based on the method. It offered a more positive way to help new and experienced patrol officers learn not only from the Grape Street Park case, but from another subject-officer disarming incident that ended the life of a San Diego Police Officer only five months after the Ruopp-Tonahill incident.

Using his military, SWAT, and street officer background, Lieutenant Morrison refined the Contact & Cover techniques into a descriptive written format and began to educate patrol officers with it. The written training bulletin and the subsequent 45-minute, in-house, training video that followed it served to educate San Diego's entire 1,800-officer force. Within months of its release in late 1985, the Contact & Cover video program became a highly requested item from interested law enforcement agencies all across the nation.

The Contact & Cover concept represents state-of-the-art thinking in terms of police officer survival training. Over the past several years, the idea has become a role model for Federal, state, and a large number of city and county law enforcement organizations. This widespread acceptance of the Contact & Cover techniques should tell you one thing: it works!

There's no secret as to why it is so successful: it makes good sense and it saves officers' lives! This two-officer subject control method allows police officers to take complete tactical advantage during all contacts, from the most normal to the highest risk. Better still, it's easy to train, implement, and follow.

The Method

Contact & Cover is used any time two or more field officers contact one or more unsecured subjects. Examples might include a traffic stop, a field interview, or any potentially violent call, such as a domestic disturbance, a bar fight, a warrant arrest, and any other misdemeanor, felony investigation, or arrest situation.

Contact & Cover begins with a definition of terms: The "Contact Officer" initiates and conducts all the business of the contact itself. This officer has a wide variety of important duties; each that he or she is solely responsible for.

The Contact Officer talks to the subject, writes all of the subject or incident information, performs all pat-downs and searches, gathers any evidence, writes all citations, runs radio checks, notifies the dispatcher of any relevant information, and initiates all handcuffing and arrest movements.

The Contact Officer — usually the officer who started the contact, i.e., made the stop, went to the door, etc., — is the primary investigator and is responsible for the chain of custody and the evidence.

The "Cover Officer" has significantly different duties than the Contact Officer. The Cover Officer's primary role is to protect the Contact Officer by devoting all of his or her attention to the actions of the subject(s). While the Contact Officer deals with the subject(s), the Cover

Officer offers protection to the Contact Officer from a position of surveillance and control.

The Cover Officer watches all subjects, prevents escapes or the destruction of evidence, and more importantly, discourages any assaults on the Contact Officer. Put simply, because the Cover Officer is not distracted by the "business" of the contact, he or she can concentrate on the actions of the subject. The Contact Officer knows the Cover Officer is "watching my back" at all times and can focus on doing a safe, thorough job throughout the entire encounter. However, the Cover Officer's duties don't end with subject surveillance. He or she must be ready to protect the Contact Officer if the subject decides to fight.

Two factors make the subject of successful intervention critical to the Contact & Cover approach: more officers are being killed with their own guns than ever before, and 60% of police officer assaults happen in front of other officers.

These facts should tell you that the likelihood of a subject trying to assault you or kill you in front of your partner is very great indeed. The Cover Officer must know when and how to intervene to protect the Contact Officer. In short, the Cover Officer must establish a "force presence."

When to intervene is usually up to the Contact Officer. If he or she can control the subject with defensive tactics, then the Cover Officer should remain in position and continue to watch the subject. Only if the Contact Officer asks for help with the subject, or is clearly losing the battle, should the Cover Officer join the fight. The reasoning here is crystal clear: the Cover Officer must be in a position to neutralize the subject if he grabs the Contact Officer's gun.

How many times have we heard about a subject who took the first officer's gun away and killed or wounded the officers because both officers were trying to wrestle the gun away? Contact & Cover effectively prevents that scenario from ever happening. If a fight starts and the Contact Officer is disarmed, he or she will know to move quickly out of the line of fire because the Cover Officer will already be in a ready position to shoot the subject.

Establishing the Roles

For the concept of Contact & Cover to work properly, the officers must decide in advance of each call who will play which role. This is not hard to do. Some officers working a two-man unit agree that one officer, usually the driver, will be the Contact Officer for the whole shift. Other officers trade off and switch roles each time they make a new contact. The important thing is to make the decision with your partner or arriving cover unit before you ever leave the station, or before you start the contact.

If other officers arrive on a scene that two officers are already handling, the Contact Officer will give them their own Contact & Cover instructions.

Officers working one-man units automatically become the Contact Officer because they initiate their own activity. Any arriving officers will automatically take the Cover Officer role.

These are not hard-and-fast rules, however. One of the advantages of the Contact & Cover principle is its inherent flexibility. In certain situations, a pair of officers may decide to switch roles during the contact. This may become necessary or beneficial if, for example, the Cover Officer knows the subject from previous encounters or he or she has had special training in narcotics, firearms, or evidence collection, etc., that the first Contact Officer may lack. The officers can easily switch roles in these cases.

The Cover Officer's Arrival

Once a second unit arrives on the scene to become a Cover Officer, the Contact Officer needs to brief the officer on the situation. This communication is critical to the safety of both officers and should take place out of the subject's hearing range.

The Contact Officer will want to tell the Cover Officer as much information as possible, including: the reason for the contact; the subject's crime potential; what the Contact Officer saw or heard upon arrival; any evidence recovered; any information about the subject gathered from a previous contact, i.e., criminal, mental, or violent history; whether or not the Contact Officer has performed a pat-down; if there are any other subjects nearby; and lastly, what the Contact Officer plans to do with the subject.

Once the Cover Officer has heard this information, he or she will want to tell the Contact Officer additional information as well, including: any previous contact with the subject; any suspicious activity the Cover Officer saw while coming to the scene; any important radio information the Contact Officer did not hear; and lastly, a clear signal to the Contact Officer that the Cover Officer will assume the proper cover role.

Positions

In many high stress situations, officers may want to stand right next to each other. This "safety in numbers" idea is dangerous and just a poor idea tactically. Using the Contact & Cover format, the ideal position for the Cover Officer is close enough to get a clear front and peripheral view of the subject and the surrounding area.

Although it's not always possible, the Cover Officer will want to stand in a position that provides some personal cover and that puts the subject at a tactical disadvantage, i.e., against a wall, facing into the sun, etc. The Cover Officer will also want to watch for other subjects in the area, choose a position that cuts off escape routes, and establish a safe background in case the subject starts shouting.

Many officers already position themselves tactically like this during all contacts, so it's not really "reinventing the wheel" to follow these cop-crook positioning guidelines. Just remember that as the Cover Officer, you'll want to be in the best position possible to protect yourself and the Contact Officer from any possible assault, destruction of evidence, or escape by the subject.

Communications

One of the most dangerous times in any contact is when the subject realizes that he or she is about to be arrested. A fight may happen during or after a pat-down, when the subject is ordered to "assume the position," or when the subject first sees or feels the handcuffs.

To prevent problems like this, Contact & Cover Officers should communicate with each other prior to any movements toward the subject. Most departments use 10 and 11-codes or Penal Code section numbers to speed up their radio transmissions and to help officers talk in a secure manner. Take advantage of these codes to communicate safely with your Contact or Cover Officer, telling him or her exactly what happens next.

Other departments rely on specific hand signals to communicate, especially at a distance. One hand signal may mean, "I need immediate help!" "I have a dangerous subject here!" or, "Do not approach; cover me from your car!" Another might mean, "I only need routine assistance from you." Whatever hand or radio signals your department uses, make sure you know them and can use them in a stressful situation.

Many officers use the Contact & Cover technique faithfully. They adapt it to different situations as necessary, but for the procedures to work effectively, **all** officers have to use them, **all** of the time.

A shooting in Miami, FL should reinforce this last fact. In one tragic instance, two Metro-Dade officers were **both** disarmed and shot by a parolee out of prison only ten days. The subject ended up with both police guns and a police car before he was caught.

Do you think these officers would have survived if they had used established Contact & Cover techniques? No one likes to Monday-morning quarterback a police shooting, but we think that if one officer had assumed the role of the Contact Officer and the other the role of the Cover Officer immediately after confronting this subject, one or both of the officers would still be alive today.

Officers who use Contact & Cover say that what they like best about it is, while one officer goes about police business with the subject, the other officer devotes his or her complete attention to covering. That's a comforting feeling.

Reviewing the Basics

Here's a quick review of Contact & Cover principles:

- Officers should decide who will Contact and who will Cover prior to any encounter with subjects.
- The Contact Officer conducts all the business of the encounter, e.g., talks to the subject, conducts all pat-downs and searches, gathers any evidence, writes all field interviews and citations, runs records checks, talks to Dispatch, and finally, handcuffs the subject, if necessary.
- The Cover Officer is there to protect the Contact Officer by establishing a "Force Presence."
- The Cover Officer also discourages escape attempts and prevents the destruction of evidence by assuming the best possible tactical position.
- The officers can reverse roles any time for reasons of expertise, or to reinforce the safety of the Contact Officer.
- The Contact and Cover Officers should use hand signals or radio code language to communicate tactically in front of the subject.

Many criminals have told the arresting officer later, "Yeah, I'd have tried to jump you, but I knew that other cop was covering your ass." Let's try to make this phrase the watchwords for today's street hood.

Practice Contact & Cover whenever the situation arises. Update your code words and hand signals, and use more than just the standard "Code 4" when necessary. Always remember that the other officer is counting on you to perform your role properly.

If you're the Contact Officer, focus your attention on the subject and use good safety habits when you search, cite, or arrest. If you're the Cover Officer, focus your attention on protecting the Contact Officer and establishing this thought in every criminal's mind: "These cops know what they're doing. This is serious business."

Above all else, know that Contact & Cover was designed to help you survive.

About the Authors

Mr. Steve Albrecht is nationally known for his written work on officer safety and tactics. He has been with the San Diego Police Department since 1984, as a regular officer and now as a reserve. He is a member of the American Society of Law Enforcement Trainers and contributes articles to police publications across the country. He is the author of **Streetwork: The Way to Officer Safety & Survival** *(Paladin) and co-wrote* **Contact & Cover: Two-Officer Suspect Control** *(Charles C. Thomas) with John Morrison.*

Mr. John Morrison is a Detective Lieutenant and 24-year veteran of the San Diego Police Department. He is widely known for his work as an officer safety trainer and innovator. He writes a number of columns for various police publications.

George Armbruster

Chief Deputy Armbruster is a career law enforcement professional and currently serves with Lafayette Parish, Louisiana, Sheriff's Department. He is also an active member of numerous law enforcement associations.

Chapter 2

Body Armor: Advantage for Law Enforcement

by George Armbruster

Officer survival is a topic area that has received widespread attention in law enforcement. There are countless schools and seminars an officer can attend to learn the newest and time-tested methods of surviving an attack.

In conjunction with these opportunities, many officers are taught that officer survival is dependent on five areas: mental preparation, physical preparation, tactics, equipment, and shooting skill. All of these areas are vitally important to the overall goal of survival.

Many seminars are conducted that deal with these topic areas individually and/or in conjunction with one or more topic areas. However, there is available to law enforcement technology that crosses into three of these areas on an everyday basis. Soft body armor or ballistic protection has been around for many years but is still not recognized by too many officers as being vital to their safety.

Soft body armor is a piece of police equipment. It plays a vital role in the officer's mental preparation and offers a tactical advantage in conjunction with a wide variety of other skills and actions in law enforcement in the 90's.

Yet, there are many facets of body armor selection that officers are not aware of. Like any other piece of equipment, it must be evaluated thoroughly to meet the needs of the individual and the job assignment the officer is required to perform.

First and foremost, the officer's approach to his or her survival is a mental one. The officer must be willing to examine those areas of the profession that can and/or will cause him or her difficulty. Mental preparation requires the examination of one's weaknesses as well as one's strengths.

There are eight factors to consider in selecting soft body armor. It is important to remember that one factor alone cannot be used to select a vest, since all factors interrelate with one another, making it a "total picture" decision.

1.) **Threat level.** This is the level of protection the vest will provide to the officer. Threat levels are means of determining the threat. Threat Level I is designed to provide protection for .22 and .38 caliber rounds; Level II A, for low velocity .357 and 9 mm rounds; Level II, for high-velocity .357 and 9 mm rounds; and Level III, for .308 rifle rounds. Level IV vests fall into the class of tactical or assault vests and are designed to meet very specific and expected threats.

Approximately 10-20% of the officers killed by firearms each year are killed with their own weapons. This statistic requires that the best rule of thumb to follow in selecting a threat level is to make certain it will provide protection for the specific round the officer will carry in the duty sidearm.

With the recent addition of the .40 caliber and 10 mm rounds, additional research should be conducted to make certain that these rounds are covered by the threat level selected.

2.) **Area of coverage.** The most common vest today offers both front and back protection as well as side protection. There are a variety of combinations available, but one must remember that there will still be "windows," or unprotected areas no matter which selection is made.

3.) **Weight.** An important factor is the total weight of the vest. The more material (higher threat lever, greater area of protection), the more weight.

4.) **Cost.** This question can only be answered by the individual and in only one way, "How much is my life worth?" Remember that this is an equipment purchase that may save your life!

5.) **Tradeoff.** The interrelationship of threat level, weight, and area of coverage is addressed here. The more material in a vest not only adds to the weight, but also results in heat build-up for the wearer of the vest.

6.) **Wearability.** This basically refers to the comfort of the vest. Although soft body armor offers the advantage of increased protection levels, there are the disadvantages of heat build-up and possible discomfort.

The "fit" of the vest can play an important role here. The better the fit, the more comfortable the vest will be, resulting in increased wearability.

The type of climate the officer must work in will also play an important role in the final selection.

Remember, if it is not worn, it offers no protection at all! Custom fit options, usually at additional cost, should be examined completely.

7.) **Psychological factors.** No vest is "bulletproof." Bullet-resistant materials, such as Kevlar, Spectra-Shield and others, won't make any officer invincible. Mental preparation will assist the officer in avoiding the "tombstone courage" syndrome.

8.) **Blunt trauma.** This basically refers to the amount of energy the body will absorb even after the vest stops the projectile. It is gauged, according to standards, by measurements of the backface signature left in the backing material during testing.
   It is important to remember that blunt trauma can be a vital concern to an officer's ability to function, depending on the location of impact.

These eight factors must be evaluated prior to the selection and purchase of a vest. These factors will be interrelated depending on the individual officer and the job assignment. Each factor must be decided upon and then weighted in relationship to the others to reach a final decision.

According to industry standards, each vest and/or vest panel is required to be labeled. This label will state the date of manufacture, the threat level of the vest, and the National Institute of Justice test standard the vest meets. The latest standard is NIJ 0101.03. The officer should inquire about the latest test standards prior to purchasing a vest.

Even after a vest is purchased, the officer must remember that it is a piece of equipment that requires care and cleaning. Regular inspection of the vest should be conducted, and irregularities should prompt return to the manufacturer for a complete evaluation.

Kevlar manufacturer, Dupont, requires a five year replacement policy on its products. Any vest manufactured with Kevlar should be replaced after five years.

As the advancement in technology continues, officers should avail themselves of any new information that affects soft body armor. New materials, improved manufacturing techniques, and changes in ballistic threats will require the officer to re-evaluate his or her soft armor and the protection it affords.

It is important for the officer to remember that many criminals today are wearing body armor while committing crimes. Officers need to address this possibility in their firearms training and develop techniques to combat this.

Law enforcement officers have available to them another advantage in lethal encounters. Soft body armor, combined with proper training and sound tactics, can provide the difference between life and death!

Massad Ayoob

Captain Ayoob of the Grantham, NH Police Dept. recently completed his eighteenth year of sworn law enforcement. He is one of the very few policemen in the country who, though working only part-time, has full command authority over both full-time and part-time personnel. Working full time as Director of Lethal Force Institute, Massad also serves at the time of this writing as National Director of Firearms and Deadly Force Training for ASLET, as a senior research associate for the Center for Advancement of Applied Ethics at Carnegie-Mellon University, and as co-vice chair of the forensic evidence committee of the National Association of Criminal Defense Lawyers. He has several times been a state and regional champion in combat shooting.

Chapter 3

Off Duty Survival

by Massad Ayoob

I guess the reason Ed asked me to do this particular chapter is that, being part-time albeit fully worn, I spend more time off duty than the rest of you. About half the times I've had to pull guns on criminal suspects, I was on my own time. That ratio may be different for **you**, depending on the demographics of your jurisdiction or maybe just the luck of the draw. It was published a few years ago that in New York City and Atlanta, as many as 40% of the police action shootings involved off-duty or plainclothes personnel. A friend on the Cook County Sheriff's Office, Chicago, notes that in his district more than half of the officer-involved shootings take place off duty, as both of his did.

But don't base your strategies on demographics. The next time a brother officer who only wears his gun with his uniform asks you, "How often do off duty cops get shot around here?" you can use the classic reply of Police Instructor, John Farnam. "Same as anywhere else, just once."

Deadly Complacency

Why is the average murdered cop a seven-year veteran in his thirties? Most investigators will answer with one diagnostic word; "complacency." It seems to go double when you look at the officers who lose off-duty engagements.

Consider that, as I write this, three NYPD officers have been murdered in the last twelve months. Only one died on duty. He was shot in the back with a .357 Magnum. For comfort, he had decided to wear only the front panel of his required ballistic vest. Complacency?

The second was shot down on his own time by an armed robber at an ATM (Automated Teller Machine). The third was on an elevator with his girlfriend when two men barged on and pulled guns. Fearing apparently that they'd find his ID and execute him, the young officer went for the off-duty gun on his ankle.

The ankle holster is a suitable choice for a backup gun or a last ditch hideout, but often hopelessly remote from the hand for a fast-breaking reaction situation like this one. The officer was shot several times in the face. Before he died, he managed to shoot each of his killers twice. They were arrested when they showed up at the hospital for treatment.

Would a kid with that kind of courage and aggressive determination have fared better with a fighting handgun in quicker reach? He couldn't have fared any worse.

Dress for Peace, Arm for War

I have never understood why cops who go on duty with service sidearms, backup guns, more ammo on their belts than Pancho Villa, shotguns and/or rifles in the trunk, and perhaps equally armed partners beside them, will change in the locker when they go off duty and arm themselves with a 5-shot .38 snubnose and no spare ammo.

If you **ever** need a powerful gun with lots of bullets, you need it when you're alone. This is why in many departments, where the agency might require a service revolver on duty but does not specify the off-duty gun, seasoned cops will hang up the Police Special after shift and strap on a high-capacity 9 mm or a .45 autoloader. That is particularly true among those who have already been in one or more off-duty emergencies.

Losing the Aura

Law enforcement is an ego-investment profession. That means it's the kind of job that takes over your identity. If you ask the guy or gal in the street what they are, they'll probably say, "I'm a human being." It'll take a second question to elicit their occupation.

But if you ask the same of a physician, an attorney, or a peace officer, the likely reply is, "I'm a doctor." "I'm a lawyer." Or, "I'm a cop."

The first two won't get you killed. The last one, however, bespeaks an attitude that has proved itself lethal.

An overwhelming sense of Duty can take over the decision-making process of an off-duty cop present at the scene of a violent felony. Something that says, "It's my job to intervene in this."

In and of itself, this is not necessarily bad. When it becomes deadly is when a guy or gal with a badge in one pocket and a Chief's Special in the other tries to bite off more than he or she can chew.

Off duty, there's no radio to call for backup. The cavalry won't ride to the rescue — indeed, won't know anything's wrong — until the situation is over and you've survived long enough to get to a phone or command someone else to call 911. You are unlikely to be accompanied by a partner who is trained and armed to the same level as you are. You probably don't have access to a long gun, and are most likely miles away from your ballistic vest.

The inner-city kids say "cops are the biggest street gang." That's because there are half a million of us, we wear our colors, we call each other "bro," and we do not take it lightly when one of our own is hurt. When an on-duty officer broadcasts that he or she is in trouble, the rest of his shift and a few other departments besides will respond with the same furious speed as the elephant herd returning to the Valley of the Lost Ivory.

For the lone, off-duty cop remote from radio communication, that doesn't happen. You're no longer the point patrol for the cavalry that's poised to ride to the rescue in brigade strength.

Instead, now, you're the lone scout . . . and you'll have to survive a skirmish with the enemy before you can make your way back to friendly lines and let the troops know you need reinforcements.

In short, you need to know that the off-duty cop isn't a whole cop anymore. It's a lot safer to see yourself as a highly trained armed citizen, who is carrying a shield and an ID card instead of a concealed carry permit.

Avoid Giveaways, Maintain Surprise

It's bad enough that we can spot scumbags as if by radar, and vice versa. Don't compound the problem by wearing "identifiers" that give you away as a cop.

LAPD officer survival authority, Rich Wemmer, once debriefed a captured gunman who had shot a plainclothes cop during a bank robbery. The nearly-successful cop killer said that he'd known there was a cop before he turned around, and that seeing the man only confirmed it. Wemmer pressed for more details.

The man said, "I heard the keys jingling on his belt. When I saw him, I knew he was a cop."

Wemmer professed skepticism, "Don't janitors and bus drivers also carry keys?"

"Yeah," leered the prisoner, "but only pigs an' screws carry their keys on those little leather teardrop things to keep the keys from cuttin' up their pants, like that guy was wearin'."

You don't need me to tell you that you shouldn't wear your Fraternal Order of Police hat except when you're **at** an FOP function. All the cute cop wear can be funny in a controlled environment like a party open only to card-carrying good guys. "Feel safe tonight: sleep with a cop!" "Just lay down and do what the nice policeman says." "So many scumbags, so little time."

But they also signal your identity as surely as the duty-belt key carrier did for the police lieutenant shot in the bank incident above. Some of your more controversial shirts ("Police brutality: the fun part of law enforcement") will also come back to haunt you if you end up using force that takes you to court.

Polished dress shoes or brogans flash you as a cop. So, in most jurisdictions, does a trouser belt in black basketweave. Does your belt have a brown finish and white stitching on its 1 3/4" edges? In some western states, you look like just another cowboy, urban or otherwise. In most midwestern and eastern states, your choice of leather cries, "Dress gunbelt." Remember, your National Trooper's Coalition belt buckle or your buckle with the S&W logo will send the same message.

When a lone off-duty cop is caught up in an armed felony in progress, particularly one involving multiple perpetrators who may not all be identifiable yet, one of the few things the officer has going for him is surprise. It's not something you can afford to lose. Hang the cute cop hats and T-shirts on the walls of your den or workshop, or donate them as wall-hangers at your favorite cop bar. Don't be wearing identifiers in a moment when your anonymity is the only thing that might keep you alive long enough to take necessary police or survival action.

Off-Duty Backup?

One off-duty cop on the East Coast interrupted an attempted murder in progress. His 5-shot Chief Special quickly ran dry, and the firefight was so intense he couldn't have reloaded even if he'd been carrying speedloaders, which he wasn't. He drew a .25 Colt auto from his pocket and sustained fire, finally overwhelming the opponent, who was wounded and captured. That officer now wears his issue 4" model 10 off duty as well as on, and backs it up with the Chief twenty-four hours a day.

In another off-duty incident in the same metropolis, the cop was hit by two armed muggers on a subway. He knew if he reached for the 4" model 10 in his shoulder holster, the one on his right would cut him and the one on the left would shoot him. When the gunman demanded his money, the officer reached as if for his wallet, but drew instead from his overcoat pocket a hammer-shrouded Colt Detective Special, and put a .38 slug between the gunman's horns, killing him before he could pull the trigger of his Sterling .25 auto. The knife-wielding accomplice fled, only to be captured and sent to prison later.

The department in question both times was New York City. For the last couple of years running, no cop in the City has lost his duty revolver from his uniform holster. Several, however, have been disarmed, **all when off duty or in plainclothes.**

Remember, your guard is down more when you're off duty . . . you're unlikely to have a partner there to peel the gun grabber off you . . . and while security holsters for the duty belt exist in abundance, few have been made for plainclothes carry. Bianchi, Alessi, and Strong Leather respectively offer holsters with a higher than average degree of retention that are suitable for concealed carry.

The backup gun has historically been the final fall-back against a disarm. Another reason to carry one on your own time is the fact that so many of the other off-duty or retired cops you might hang out with don't carry one at all. The feces hits the fan, two trained men are there to deal with it, but only one is armed. Now, the backup gun ceases to be mere spare equipment and gives you true backup, the ability to arm a trained partner.

Vest Off Duty?

It's generally seen as paranoid to wear a vest on your own time unless there's something unusually dangerous going on. But, I can remember when it seemed equally paranoid to wear one **on** duty.

I'll wear a vest off duty when in a high risk area, and often, as a matter of routine in winter. The deep cold of Northern New England requires you to dress in layers anyway. The vest's wind-breaking and insulating properties allow me to wear fewer layers of bulky clothing, giving me more arm flexibility and more comfort in general.

Richard Davis, inventor of the concealable ballistic vest and an officer survival authority, has noted that in winter we are more likely to face criminals with guns in general, and particularly with larger, more powerful, more accurate guns. This is because winter clothing allows them to conceal heavier hardware.

Frankly, the main reason I'm likely to have armor on during the December-February season at home is that this is also the time of year when bozos skid on the ice and snow and crash into your car. Some half of the more than 1200 documented "vest saves" have involved vehicle collisions, which generate far more destructive force than bullets. Docs say the crash that hospitalized me for a week some years ago with a long and painful convalescence to follow, would have seen me walk from the emergency room that day with a few stitches if I'd just been wearing the vest.

In the past four months, two good friends were saved from death by their vests. Randy lost his spleen after his cruiser was T-boned by a truck that busted a red light, but attending surgeons said death would have been certain had he not been wearing his Point Blank. When Bruce's cruiser was struck head on, his Second Chance kept him from being impaled on the steering wheel, and he was back on patrol the next day.

Training Predictable Bystanders

We've all heard the chilling story of the cop who's in the stop n' rob with his kid when the holdup goes down, and the rug rat yells, "My daddy's a policeman! Arrest 'em, Dad!" In one New York City case, a cop on his way to work had dropped into a deli for a pack of smokes and didn't realize a stickup was in progress. Recognizing him, the terrified counterman screamed, "My God, you're a cop, do something!" That officer had good reflexes. He was able to shoot and kill the first perpetrator before the second put a bullet through the off-duty cop's brain.

This tells us that family, friends, and storekeepers or bartenders who know we are cops **should also know what to do if they and we are ever there together when a situation explodes.**

My spouse and children know that in this situation, they are to shut up and not even look at me. If at all possible, they are to discreetly distance themselves from me.

My druggist and the proprietors of my local markets know that if I'm there when a holdup goes down, they are not even to look in my direction. They are to make a clear, audible statement on the order of "Easy with that gun, I'll give you everything you want," and leave the rest to me or any other officer they know to be present.

Avoid Gun Mules

It's a lazy cop who lets his wife or girlfriend carry his gun for him in the purse. There are any number of lethal trick-bags in this practice, including the following:

- Murphy's Law will find her, her bag, and your gun in the ladies' room when the crisis goes down.

- If your wife is anything like mine, you'll whisper "Gimme my gun," and she'll hiss back, What do you mean, **your** gun?"

- X number of untrained relatives will be overcome with fear for their beloved officer's safety should the cop intervene, and will deliberately ditch the gun to prevent a shooting. This leaves the trained officer, the better judge of the situation, totally helpless.

- Accessing a weapon from someone else's purse or fanny pack will never be as fast or as unnoticeable as the practiced act of drawing it from a familiar place on one's own person.

Prevent Mistaken Identity Tragedies

In the shadows and the excitement, a plainclothes cop knows that even he can look like "a man with a gun" to the responding uniformed officer. Some departments in some years have had more brother officers shot by other cops than by the bad guys.

"Color of the day" is an iffy concept at best, and doesn't work at all for a cop who's off for a week and wasn't at roll call to learn the daily color. In the mid-1970s I developed a concept called "the three rings of safety" to prevent this type of friendly fire tragedy, and it has worked safely for every officer who has employed it since, to the best of my knowledge. It goes like this:

- The **"Message"** is the first and outermost safety ring. Once the situation is stable, the officer sends, or causes to be sent, a message to dispatch describing **the situation, and physically describing the officer.** "There's been a robbery, and the officer is holding the robber at gunpoint. The officer is a black male, five-ten, 180, clean shaven, blue jeans and gray sport shirt, holding a silver-colored revolver."

    Of course, this may not suffice. A witness may have flagged a passing sector car before the message was broadcast. The dispatcher may have simply transmitted it as an "armed robbery in progress, man with a gun, there now."

▬▶ Ergo, the second ring of safety, the "**Welcoming Committee.**" If I'm outside my jurisdiction, the incoming officers won't know me from Adam. So, I'll **send a person the officer can trust, who will intercept him before he sees me standing there with a gun, and will repeat the message.**

That person won't be a companion. Armed robbers often use seeded backups or tail-gunners, who pose as customers and serve the function of shooting to death from behind anyone who goes for the cops or interferes with the primary robbery team. My trained companions will be on scene, backing me up with drawn guns, thank you.

The store manager will go to the door. The cops may not know me locally, but if they patrol this sector, they probably know this manager. They'll have less reason to believe they're being lured into an ambush and will be more likely to accept "the message" from this person.

Which door will the officers come to? Will it **be** officers, and not an armed outrider coming in from the getaway car to rescue his scumbag friend from the point of my gun? Solve both problems at once. **Tell the manager, "Lock all the doors, and open them only to IDENTIFIED police!"**

▬▶ The final and innermost circle of safety is what crisis management always comes down to: "**You!**" By that I mean your position, your bearing, and your demeanor. Be in a position where you can see the incoming officers before they see you. This way, you don't get startled at their command and turn toward them suddenly and reflexively in a way they could construe under the circumstances as hostile and representative of a "shoot situation."

If at all possible, have your gun in the holster with your hand on it instead of drawn. The difference between drawing and firing with the hand already indexed, and coming up to fire from low ready, is almost infinitesimal. Try it yourself on an electronic timer and see. "Hand on gun" as opposed to "gun in hand" is much less likely to threaten the responding officer into firing a reflexive shot.

The unidentifiable officer **always has the responsibility to obey the commands of the identifiable officer.** Certainly, your shield should be out and visible, but you know how many phony badges are out there, and how unreadable an ID card is from a distance.

When the identified officer orders you to drop your drawn weapon, do it. Step on the gun so a suspect on the floor can't get at it and, explaining what you're doing, use your foot to slide your gun toward the officer and away from the suspect. If the gun falls flat on its side, it won't bounce; dropped on either end, it will cartwheel, which is highly undesirable. A semiautomatic pistol without a firing pin lock (pre-1980 Colt, pre-MKII Browning Hi-Power, first generation S&W) can go off if dropped. **Your** shot at that moment will have been accidental, but understanding what the responding officer perceives, **his** reactive shot will be intentional.

Badge, Gun, Cuffs

When you carry off-duty on strictly police authority as opposed to an issued gun permit like a civilian's, remember that shield, weapon, and restraints are a triad that should not be separated.

Power and responsibility must always be commensurate. The badge represents the authority, and in an armed felony interruption requires the power of the gun to back it up. Without shield and ID, it can be argued that you're carrying the gun outside regulations.

Similarly, always have restraints on you or nearby. The new generation of folding Velcro restraints are fine for this. It's not so much that you'll be cuffing perpetrators while alone and off duty (though in some circumstances, that may be the least of the available evils); rather, it protects you in court.

The privilege of being armed off duty is tied directly to the concept of being a cop 24 hours a day; the gun is therefore a tool of arrest. However, quick questioning by a skilled lawyer will show that while you may have used a gun as a tool of arrest before, your cuffs have always been your **primary** tool of arrest. Your good faith as an off-duty cop can now be called into question.

If you've been in an off-duty shooting and were carrying a gun but not cuffs, opposing counsel can convince the jury to find against you with the following arguments:

"Gun but no cuffs: he obviously wasn't planning to take prisoners."

"He used his badge to steal a privilege. You citizens here in Illinois can't get a license to carry a gun, but this man carries one. He says it's because he's a cop all the time, but if that were true, wouldn't he have handcuffs too? I submit that he carried the gun, not to protect any of you, but to protect his own selfish and cowardly self!"

"He's a thief, ladies and gentlemen! Here in Florida, you citizens have to pay $140 for the license to carry a gun to protect yourself. He got around that with his badge, even though his failure to carry restraints showed he had no intention of making an off duty arrest, just of shooting his way out of any tight situation. He could have got a permit like yours, but instead, he stole the privilege like he'd steal an apple off a pushcart."

This line of attack, frankly, is one reason the last two departments I've worked for have made a point of issuing a concealed carry permit to all officers. Involved in a shooting, the officer and the officer alone can define whether he acted as an armed citizen or under color of law, especially if the shooting went down when he was outside the community he serves.

Final Suggestions

The forgoing is by no means a complete and total guide to off-duty encounter tactics and procedures. It is designed merely to make the officer begin to think, and to plan for the sort of situations that could involve him or her in crisis while off duty.

Remember that you're a cop eight hours a day, but the felon you face is a scumbag 24 hours a day.

Remember that you work as a cop forty hours a week, and the other one hundred twenty-eight hours, you're on your own.

Finally, remember that if you lose the encounter, you'll be dead for every fifty-two weeks of every coming year.

Stan Berry   **Dean Berry**

Mr. Stan Berry has a B.A. from the University of Minnesota and a M.A. from Yale University. He is the Co-Author of Action Writing for the '90s *and* Business Grammar & Style, *and the Law Enforcement Resource Center's two video series,* Report Writing *and* Writing Skills for Command Personnel. *He is an active member of the American Society of Law Enforcement Trainers (ASLET).*

Mr. Dean Berry has a B.A. and a M.A. from the University of Minnesota. He is the Author of A Workbook of Writing Models; The Officer As Writer; *and* Report Writing and Writing Skills for Command Personnel. *He is the Co-Author of the Law Enforcement Resource Center's two video series,* Report Writing *and* Writing Skills for Command Personnel. *He is also an active member of the American Society of Law Enforcement Trainers (ASLET).*

Chapter 4

Principles of Police Report Writing

by Stan Berry and Dean Berry

Few police officers enter law enforcement to be writers. Yet, an officer's ability to write clear, concise, and understandable reports is often a part of the criteria by which he or she is measured at performance evaluation time. An officer's total effort relative to a given situation is often reduced to a few sheets of paper. The successful resolution of a serious incident may depend upon how well an officer is able to document the event on paper.

Law enforcement personnel agree on the value of a good report narrative. The quality of an officer's report can influence the success of an investigation and the efforts of both the prosecuting and the defense attorneys. In court, the officer's written word can help establish the officer's individual credibility as well as that of the case being prosecuted. The police report is the catalyst which calls the other components of the criminal justice system to action.

To help you make your report narrative (or supplement) as effective as possible, the authors will present four objectives, a list of standards for professional police writing, and three narrative format options, with examples.

Objectives

The authors have four primary objectives in writing this chapter.

1.) To suggest current professional police report-writing standards, thus assuring officers that they are writing their narratives in a current, acceptable style.
2.) To help officers write narratives which are complete and useful to supervisors and investigators and prosecuting attorneys for follow-up activities.
3.) To save time in the writing of police report narratives.
4.) To simplify the reading of reports.

Standards

The standards that follow will help you write clear, concise, and easy-to-read reports.[1]

▭▶ The first standard: **Use the first person pronoun "I" when reporting your actions.** It sets the stage for clear writing. Many officers have been taught to write in the third person pronoun (this officer) when writing police reports because it was felt that somehow that style gave a more impersonal, professional flavor to their reports.[2]

The proper use of "I" or "me" (first person) instead of the writer's formal name or the phrase "this officer" when referring to oneself will produce a report which more effectively meets the needs of the reader. The use of "this officer" (third person) is outdated and self-conscious. It is not a more objective or detached point of view. Using "I" is professional, clear, natural, and unaffected.

▭▶ The second standard: **Use names rather than abbreviations such as V or W.** This standard relates to the goal of making the report easier to read and understand.

When writing reports, you should try to put yourself in the readers' place in order to see the information from the readers' point of view. By doing this, you may discover that a report is not really as clear as it first appeared. For example, certain abbreviations may be standard procedure in your organization, but confusing to an attorney or citizen who is trying to understand them. The authors suggest limiting the use of abbreviations to those which have universal meaning.

▭▶ The third standard: **Use the past tense of the verb as the main verb in most of your sentences.** (Tenses are verb forms which tell whether the action is in the past, present, or future.)

In most report narratives, you should write in the past tense *saw, said, took, handcuffed, told,* and so on which indicates that the events were over when you wrote your report.

When you write your narrative, you are reporting events that happened in the past, so you should use the past tense. When you shift in your writing from the past tense to the present, the reader must adjust mentally and put everything in the past. Also, avoiding the emphatic form (*did* say or *did* see or *did* handcuff, etc.) will make police reports easier to read. Using the emphatic form of the verb, introduced by the word *did* is necessary only when you are trying to emphasize an action. (I did write the report at the end of my

Principles of Police Report Writing 25

shift). If you use the emphatic form before most verbs, you negate its purpose. Again, you should usually use the simple past tense of the verb.

- The fourth standard: **Use the active voice of the verb.** The active voice of the verb tells the reader *who* did the action or made the statement. It is more exact to say, "Officer Able found the knife in the bushes" (active) than to say, "The knife was found in the bushes" (passive). This exactness, of course, is critical in law enforcement reports. Knowing who did the action or made the statement can be crucial to the investigator and the prosecutor.

    When speaking, people use the active voice about 90% of the time. When writing, you should also use the active voice about 90% of the time.

    A simple way to write in the active voice is to put the *doer* of the action before the action. Example: "The chief promoted the officer to sergeant." Here the *chief* is the doer and *promoted* is the action. The chief is doing the action. Hence, the name, *active* voice.

- The fifth standard: **Use factual, rather than opinion, statements.** You are used to dealing with factual information. Every day during the course of your duties, you are forced to gather facts related to the calls you answer or the situations you handle. It becomes second nature and, in serious situations, is pre-empted only by the protection of life and property and crime-scene security.

    It would seem that writing only factual statements when recording actions or the elements of some criminal activity would also be second nature. Yet, when reading reports, one often comes across a statement which is clearly the officer's opinion rather than fact. Nothing can more discredit a report than the presence of opinions, conjecture, and unsubstantiated conclusions.

    As a test, ask yourself whether what you are writing can be verified. Is it open to different interpretations? Statements of fact can be verified or proved, but statements of opinion or conclusions are open to different interpretations. Two types of statements are invariably inferences and therefore not factual: statements about the future and statements which attempt to describe the emotional or mental state of someone.

    A part of writing factual statements is the use of concrete language. Concrete language is factual. It paints a specific picture for the investigator or the attorney as to exactly what the officer saw, heard, was told, and did. Words such as *often* should be replaced with words that describe as closely as possible exactly when.

If you should use an abstract expression such as *appeared intoxicated* in a report, you should then describe the driving behavior — facts — which led to the conclusion.

▱ The sixth standard: **Use simple, professional language.** This includes the use of short, simple words and short sentences. Using short, everyday words is a characteristic of professional writing, whether in business or in law enforcement. It makes writing easy, fast, and natural.

Some officers resist the use of everyday language because they equate simple words with simplemindedness. Nothing could be further from the truth. It is extremely telling, however, when an officer is caught using a "sophisticated" word improperly when a much simpler word would have done the job nicely.

Words such as *left, told, asked, tried,* and *later* are more effective than *exited, advised, inquired, endeavored,* and *subsequently.*

The use of short, simple sentences naturally follows the use of short, everyday words. Writing short sentences is another characteristic of professional writing. The simple sentence is the most emphatic sentence you can write. It makes reading clear and easy and tells the story in a straightforward fashion.

▱ The seventh standard: **Sort ideas for the reader.** This sorting can be done by organizing paragraphs effectively, using bullets, using transitions, and developing narrative formats.

One way of sorting ideas is through the use of properly organized paragraphs. A paragraph should contain only one idea. It is a single unit of thought. A typical police narrative is made up of several "units of thought" and thus may contain several or many paragraphs.

Keeping this single unit-of-thought rule in mind will help you organize your report. It does not, however, tell you how the individual paragraphs should be written.

One way to organize paragraphs effectively is to use a topic or lead-in sentence with supporting details as a way of creating a visual picture for the reader. The lead-in sentence should state clearly the action taken, while the supporting details explain why it was necessary.

Example: I charged the subject with:

❐ Driving under the influence of alcohol.
   M.S.S. 169.121

Principles of Police Report Writing

☐ Speeding. 67 mph in a 40-mile zone.
M.S.S. 169.14
☐ Having an open container of alcohol in a motor vehicle.
M.M.S. 169.122. Sub.2

The action in this paragraph is the charging of the suspect. The supporting details tell the reader the charges brought against the subject. Each of the supporting details is sorted in the paragraph by using hyphens or dots — what the authors call the bullet style of writing.

Nearly as important as the proper organization of paragraphs is the ability to link ideas together, both within a paragraph and between paragraphs. Words or phrases which help guide the reader from one idea to the next are called transitions. Words or phrases such as *first, second, third; on the one hand, on the other hand; for example; in summary*, and so on are examples of transitions. Bullets and numbers are also effective transitions.

Another useful technique to help sort and categorize ideas is the use of structured formats with headings. The use of such a format creates a kind of road map for the writer, as well as for the reader. It visually organizes your ideas into categories which are easy to follow. The authors suggest the following formats for two of the most commonly-written police report narratives, the Offense/Incident Report and the Driving Under the Influence Report.

Offense/Incident Report

Synopsis
Officer's Observations/Actions
Complainant's/Victim's Statements
Witness' Statement
Subject's Statement
Investigation Of The Scene
Evidentiary Exhibits
Disposition

Driving Under The Influence Report

Synopsis
Observation
   Driving
   Weather
   Road Conditions

Pre-Arrest
  Field Sobriety Tests
  Statements
    Driver
    Passenger
    Witness
Post-Arrest
  Vehicle Disposition
  Implied Consent
  Chemical Test
  Defendant's Statement
  Disposition
    Temporary Driver's License
    Citation/Charge Sheet
    Release/Held

A few comments should be made about the use of headings.

- ❏ Most departments can improve the narrative or supplemental section of their reports by using headings to sort ideas.
- ❏ The formats suggested above can be changed, of course, to fit individual department needs.
- ❏ The headings also can be changed to follow the sequence of events of the call.
- ❏ The same heading can be used more than once in a narrative.

The authors have identified three options in the use of headings, depending on the amount of detail in the narrative. These will be discussed later.

Now for a brief explanation of what to include under these headings:

Synopsis

Purpose: A synopsis gives the reader a brief summary of an incident.

Key Points: A synopsis should usually answer four questions:
1. How did you get involved?
2. What incident/crime was investigated?
3. What evidence, witness/es, etc. could you collect?
4. What is the outcome or disposition of the incident?

Officer's Observations/Actions

Purpose: This shows probable cause for further action.

Principles of Police Report Writing

Key Points: Describe what you saw, did, or heard when you arrived on the scene. Be specific. Use factual statements.

Victim's/Witness'/Subject's Statement

Purpose: These provide an essential link in the continuity of the investigations. They can be used in guiding the investigation, as well as for court evidence.

Key Points: Keep in mind two key points when reporting these statements:
- State what they told you they had seen, done, or heard.
- Paraphrase most of the statements.

Investigation of the Scene

Purpose: Describe the activities of any investigation following your initial observations/actions and statements.

These are pertinent activities done in the pursuit of evidence.

Key Points: Describe the activities of any investigation done in the pursuit of evidence. Describe the circumstances of finding any evidence. Keep these key points in mind:
- Document the chain of custody: who found the evidence, where it was found, exactly what it was, how it was identified, and what you did with it.
- Identify the significance of the evidence.

Evidentiary Exhibits

Purpose: List all evidence gathered up to this point.

Key Points: Keep these key points in mind:
- Physical evidence. List all material evidence or seized property, giving each item an exhibit number. Arrange each item in sequence by time and date obtained. Identify the person responsible for collecting the item and its location when collected. Indicate the disposition of each exhibit. Identify the significance of the evidence.
- Document evidence. List documents such as search warrants, affidavits, subpoenas, judicial transcripts, court orders, and so on.

Disposition

Purpose: Identify the particulars of the arrest or the result of the incident.

Key Points: List the location of the subject, along with any charges. If the incident is a crime against property, include the recovery of the property. Identify any follow-up activities.

Narrative Format Options

We suggest three options for writing the narrative section of the report. The one you use will depend on the amount of information you gathered during your initial investigation.

The three examples which follow describe the same incident, an aggravated assault/attempted murder, but are, in this case, written by three different officers. The level of involvement of each officer was different, suggesting a different narrative format for each.

▻ **Option one.** When there is very little information and no need for a narrative, write only a synopsis or a variation of a synopsis.

Synopsis

At about 0945, I responded to a call about a possible aggravated assault/attempted murder in progress. As I arrived at 215 12th Avenue South, I saw several squad cars parked outside. I entered the house and met Sgt. BAKER, Officers CHARLIE and EASY, and Investigator DAVID. Sgt. BAKER told me they had more than enough backup and wouldn't need additional help. I left the residence with no further involvement.

▻ **Option two.** When you have enough information to need a brief narrative section in your report, use the following headings:
   Synopsis
   Officer's Observations/Actions
   Disposition

Synopsis

I heard Dispatch assign some officers to 215 12th Avenue South, where a domestic aggravated assault/attempted murder was being reported by an upstairs neighbor. This neighbor stated that one of the people probably had a gun and was telling the other person not to come any closer, or he would shoot. Since I was near the house, I drove to it.

Officer's Observations/Actions

I arrived at the house before any uniformed officers and informed Dispatch of my location and plan to approach the residence. I:

- ☐ Took a position on the northwest side of the house and was able to listen to the people inside. I determined that my immediate intervention was not needed as there was no discussion of a weapon.
- ☐ Waited for the uniformed officers' arrival and directed Officer CHARLIE toward the front of the house and asked Officer EASY to come to the rear of the house with me.
- ☐ Knocked on the door and a female asked who it was. I yelled that I was a police officer and asked them to come outside. A male said that he would go to the front door and after several minutes Officer EASY and I entered the house through the rear door.
- ☐ Heard the female state that the gun was in a box on the kitchen table.
- ☐ Saw Officer EASY take custody of the male and tell him to remove items from his pockets and put them on the table. He removed some rounds of ammunition, along with a clear plastic container containing white tablets with crosses on them, and a knife.
- ☐ Saw Officer EASY handcuff the male and take possession of the container of tablets along with the other items that were in the male's pockets.

Disposition

I cleared the area, leaving the initial investigation for Sgt. BAKER and the Uniform Division.

> **Option three.** When you have a great deal of information and need a more detailed narrative, use appropriate headings.

Synopsis

In my follow-up investigation of the domestic incident at 215 12th Avenue South, I contacted the complainant, MARY ANN SMITH, and later the victim, SHERRI ANDERSON. This report should be sent to the city attorney's office.

Complainant's Statement

I asked the complainant to tell me if she had heard any part of the conversation which was going on at the time of the domestic. She told me that she:

- ☐ Heard ANDERSON tell RANDY WILLIAMS to get out of the house several times. There was a lot of yelling and bad language between the two people.
- ☐ Became aware of a gun when she heard WILLIAMS yell, "Oh, good! Go ahead and shoot me!" She then heard ANDERSON yell back, "What do you expect me to do, just lie here and let you rape me?"
- ☐ Decided at this time to call police.
- ☐ Heard shortly later a noise that sounded as though someone had bounced against a wall or the floor in the kitchen. She soon became aware that WILLIAMS had been able to get the gun away from ANDERSON. She thought she heard WILLIAMS say, "How do you like having a gun pointed at your head?" At this point she was concerned that WILLIAMS was going to shoot ANDERSON.

Victim's Statement

I contacted ANDERSON and asked her what had happened after WILLIAMS was able to pick the gun off the kitchen table. She told me that he immediately emptied the gun, dropping the bullets onto the floor.

I asked her if WILLIAMS had pointed the gun at her, saying, "How do you like having a gun pointed at your head?" She said that she remembers being very upset at the time, but she does not remember WILLIAMS ever pointing the gun at her.

She told me that she is sorry that the whole incident happened and that she does not want any charges pressed against WILLIAMS.

Evidentiary Exhibits

Case-related forms and documents:

- ☐ Warning and Statement of Rights (RANDY WILLIAMS)

☐ BCA lab report — 878-3210, and receipt

Disposition

A copy of this report should be sent to the city attorney's office. The BCA lab report on the tablets seized by Officer EASY stated the tablets were ephedrine.

It might be instructive to compare a typical original, one-paragraph narrative with a revised narrative using headings.

Offense/Incident Report
(original)

This writer was dispatched to 1234 Second Street at 1500 hours on April 10, 19XX, in response to a possible house burglary. When WTR got to the house, he saw a female standing in the front yard who introduced herself as Patricia Olson, the owner of the house. WTR observed a muddy impression of the bottom of a shoe that was visible on the outside of the door, approximately 6 inches left of the front door handle. WTR observed that the deadbolt was still in a locked position and the inside door frame had been torn from the doorway. Parts of the frame were visible lying on the floor of the entryway. WTR entered the house through the front door. The house appeared in good condition with none of the room ransacked. WTR found the middle drawer of a desk in the master bedroom was open, but the contents did not look disturbed. WTR found the back door to the house unlocked and standing open. WTR called for an evidence technician and protected the scene until Officer Michael Able arrived. The victim said that she arrived home at her usual time from work, about 1500 hours. Upon noticing the condition of the front door, she did not enter but went immediately to a neighbor to call the police. She stated that the only thing that appeared disturbed was the middle desk drawer in the master bedroom. She said a blue and red nylon wallet with $500 was missing. Jane Johnson, 1235 Second Avenue, tel. 222-3190, approached this writer at the scene and stated that she has been at home all day working in her kitchen. She said that at about 1230 hours she saw a male run from the direction of the Olson house across her backyard toward the east. She identified the male as Pete Doe, who lives at 1405 Second Avenue and is a friend of the victim's son. Officer Michael Able, an evidence technician, examined the scene. Officer Able photographed the front door and the master bedroom. He then dusted the front and rear doors and desk in the bedroom for fingerprints. Officer Smith collected a latent fingerprint from the inside door knob of the rear door. He also collected a latent fingerprint from the inside door knob of the rear door. This officer tried to contact subject at his residence, but no one was home at the time.

Offense/Incident Report
(revised*)

Synopsis

I was dispatched to 1234 Second St. at 1500 hours on April 10, 19XX, to investigate a forced entry house burglary. The front door was apparently kicked open, and $500 had been taken from the master bedroom. A neighbor, JANE JOHNSON, identified PETE DOE as a subject, but I was not able to find DOE for an interview. This report is being forwarded to the investigative division for follow-up action.

Officer's Observations/Actions

Upon my arrival, I:

- Met a female standing in the front yard. She introduced herself as PATRICIA OLSON, the owner of the house.
- Saw a muddy impression of the bottom of a shoe on the outside of the door, about 6 inches left of the front door handle.
- Saw that the deadbolt was still in a locked position and the inside door frame had been torn from the doorway. Parts of the frame were lying on the floor of the entryway.
- Entered the house through the front door. The house appeared in good condition with none of the rooms ransacked.
- Found the middle drawer of a desk in the master bedroom open, but the contents did not look disturbed.
- Found the back door to the house unlocked and standing open.
- Called for an evidence technician and protected the scene until Officer MICHAEL ABLE arrived.

Victim's Statement

Olson said that:

- She had arrived home at her usual time from work, about 1500 hours. Upon noticing the condition of the front door, she did not enter but went immediately to a neighbor and called the police.
- The only thing that appeared disturbed was the middle desk drawer in the master bedroom. She said a blue and red nylon wallet with $500 was missing.

Offense/Incident Report
(continued)

Witness' Statement

JANE JOHNSON, 1235 Second Ave., tel. 222-3190, approached me at the scene and said that:

- ☐ She had been home all day working in her kitchen.
- ☐ At about 1230 hours she saw a male run from the direction of the OLSON house across her back yard toward the east.
- ☐ She identified the male as PETE DOE, who lives at 1405 Second Avenue and is a friend of OLSON'S son.

Investigation of the Scene

Officer ABLE, the evidence technician, examined the scene. He photographed the front door and the master bedroom. He then dusted the front and rear doors and the desk in the bedroom for fingerprints.

Evidentiary Exhibits

Officer ABLE collected photographs of the shoe print on the front door. He also collected a latent fingerprint from the inside door knob of the rear door.

Disposition

I tried to contact DOE at his residence, but no one was home at the time. This report is being forwarded to the investigative division for follow-up action.

* *This revision contributed by Officer Tim Heroff of the Rochester, Minnesota, Police Department.*

In conclusion, the authors believe that the ideas presented in this chapter really do work. Some officers resist parts of the program, preferring to cling to their old ways of writing. This resistance is understandable — most of us do resist changes in the way we conduct our jobs.

Yet, the effectiveness of the program was again validated when City Prosecutor Greg Galler recently told Gene Ostendorf, Chief of Police at Oak Park Heights, Minnesota, "The reports are now so good that one public defender asked that I not share them with other law enforcement officers in the area. As the reports cover all aspects of an incident in a systematic way, there are no 'cracks' for the defense to work on."

Stan Berry welcomes any questions about the contents of this chapter or about in-house seminars for law enforcement personnel.

Footnotes

[1] The authors developed this list of "Professional Police Report Writing Standards," patterning them after writing techniques taught by the authors to over 35 thousand professionals in corporations, associations, and public agencies.

These standards were refined for law enforcement personnel after reviewing hundreds of police reports and interviewing dozens of police command personnel, street officers, and city and county attorneys. Also incorporated into the standards is feedback from officers and supervisors in law enforcement report-writing seminars. Richard Gregory, formerly with the Minnesota POST Board and now a Special Agent with the Minnesota BCA, was a continuing mentor during this refinement. Lt. Dave Ericson, director of the Law Enforcement Resource Center and co-author, with Dean and Stan Berry, of the the Report Writing column in *The ASLET Journal*, The Official Publication of the American Society of Law Enforcement Trainers, also contributed to this chapter.

[2] When writing books or chapters of books, authors do usually write in the third person.

Chapter 5

The Police Shotgun

by Michael F. Boyle

A familiar bromide has it that the dog is man's best friend. A convincing argument could also be made that, during those anxious moments, the shotgun is a cop's best friend. The shotgun remains a most effective tool for short to intermediate range lethal crisis management and is typically the only shoulder weapon available to the uniformed patrol officer. It offers stopping power well beyond that of any handgun as well as a better hit potential, especially under high stress conditions. The mere presence of the shotgun has given many a criminal cause to reconsider his behavior and its psychological intimidation value is not overstated.

Of late, the police shotgun is in the midst of a renaissance of sorts. Traditional ideas concerning the weapon system and operator skills are being closely re-examined. The quality of police handgun training has improved dramatically in recent years and progressive trainers have finally begun to give the shotgun the attention it deserves. Along the same line, recent technological improvements in shotguns and ammunition have given the system the first meaningful performance boost in nearly a hundred years. The end result, of course, is a better trained and equipped officer prepared to cope with an increasingly hostile operational environment.

Evolution of the Police Shotgun

Over a century ago, the frontier marshal often relied on a short tubed, Greener double to uphold the law. Both 10 and 12 gauge doubles were popular with lawmen during that tumultuous period. However, with the introduction of the slide action repeaters, the 12 gauge began a dominance that exists to this day. As the doubles that came before, barrels of the new repeaters were kept short for handy deployment and unchoked for greatest disbursement of shot. During World War I, the most popular of the early pump-guns, the Winchester 97, saw significant use by the American Expeditionary Force. Outfitted with a bayonet and a handguard, these "trench brooms" proved so effective in close range combat that Germans protested their use. Sixty years later, the shotgun was used in a similar role in the Vietnam War.

For the better part of this century, the evolution of the fighting shotgun was at a standstill. Despite improvements in metallurgy, safety systems, and ergonomics, there was little improvement in performance over the ancient Model 97. One of the biggest drawbacks were crude sighting systems which were more appropriate for bird hunting than for defensive use. This effectively limited the police smoothbore to short range applications.

Today's officers and administrators recognize the need for a more flexible response with the primary support weapon. Fortunately, the arms' manufacturers have picked up the gauntlet and offer more refined versions of existing designs better suited for defensive use. A small but growing cottage industry of custom gunsmiths are now turning out some very well thought out designs as well.

The Fighting Smoothbore

Traditionally, the police shotgun has been a 12 gauge, pump action with an open bore and bead sights. Barrel length has typically run 18 to 20 inches. If there is such a thing as a universal choice as far as ammunition, it has to be 00 buck. Although not a bad combination, with a little effort we can do much better.

Jeff Cooper once compared the bead sighted smoothbore to a car that only takes first and second gear. Sure it goes, but not too fast. A superior sighting arrangement is a set of rifle sights. Rifle sights, when used in tandem with slugs, extend the practical range of the shotgun 3 to 4 times that of the buckshot stoked smoothbore. Of course, buckshot can still be used and one gives up nothing in the ability to hit quickly at the shorter ranges.

By far, the best rifle sights for the police shotgun are the ghost ring arrangements. A large aperture is fitted on the receiver and mated to a sturdy, wide front blade. The eye will automatically center the front sight in the aperture which, after a split second, seems to disappear (hence the term ghost ring). The set up is very quick and easy to pick up, even in dim light. Ghost ring sights are typically more durable than the fine rifle

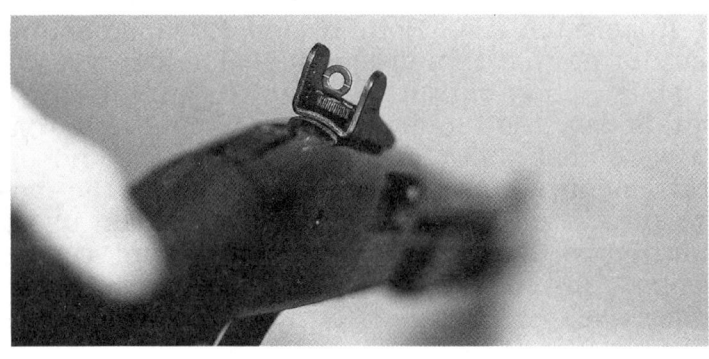

Mossberg offers ghost ring aperture sights as an option in their line of police shotguns.

The Police Shotgun

sights used on hunting shotguns and are better able to hold up to the rigors of patrol. Both Benelli and Mossberg offer them as factory options.

The barrel of the police shotgun should be no longer than 20 inches and 18 inches is even better. The longer the barrel the greater the likelihood of it getting hung up at some inopportune time. Officers who anticipate a preponderance of indoor problems may even want to consider a 14 inch barrel. This could also prove popular with agencies that use down size patrol vehicles. The FBI reports that terminal effectiveness is not compromised to any significant degree with the abbreviated tubes, and handling qualities may be improved.

Contrary to established doctrine, the open choke or cylinder bore is not the best choice for the police shotgun. Guns choked in this manner typically cannot keep all the pellets of a load of 00 buck in the torso of any realistic size target placed just 20 yards away. It does not take a strong imagination to envision what will happen when we factor in the stress and dynamics of a real life encounter. Minimally, the police smoothbore should be constricted to improved cylinder dimensions, though modified is even better. This will not result in any meaningful increase of practical range, but it will better ensure that the pellets strike the intended target.

Pump action shotguns still dominate the scene, but autoloaders are coming on strong. Just as many police administrators have come to recognize the many advantages of the autoloading pistol over the revolver, so it goes with the shotgun. Autoloader advantages include better hit potential while under stress, the ability to fire from odd positions, one hand operation, better use of cover, and ease of manipulation. Sound designs from Remington, Benelli, and Beretta will carve out a bigger piece of the police market in years to come.

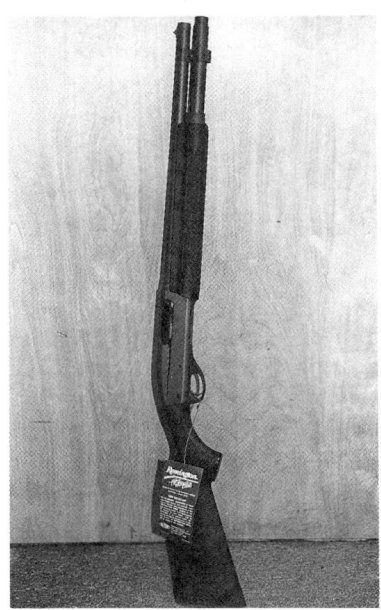
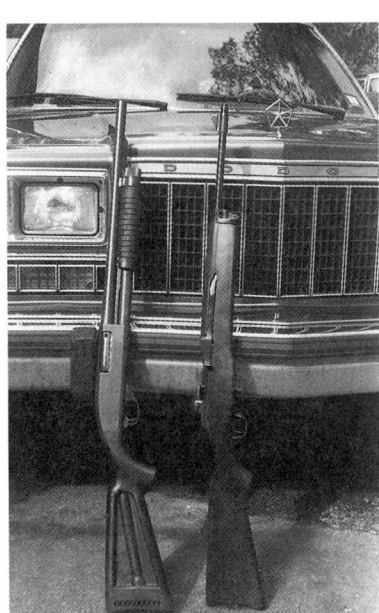

(left photo) Remington has a police version of the 11-87 autoloader. Autopistols have advantages over revolvers and so do self-loading shotguns. (right photo) Agencies are issuing light rifles or carbines such as the Mini 14 (right) to supplement or replace shotguns. Light rifles are better for the smaller statured officer.

Useful Accessories

Currently, there is almost a bewildering array of after market accessories available for the combat shotgun. Some of these will prove valuable, while others are best left to the Saturday afternoon, would-be Rambos. When evaluating accessories, consider whether they improve the overall efficiency of the weapon system. If not, you probably don't need them.

Useful accessories can be grouped into two categories, must have and nice to have. A quality recoil pad clearly falls into the "must have" department. Anything more than just a couple of rounds of buck or slugs is likely to make a negative impression (literally) on even the most dedicated shotgunner. A properly fitted recoil pad goes a long way in turning the smoothbore into a much more user friendly tool.

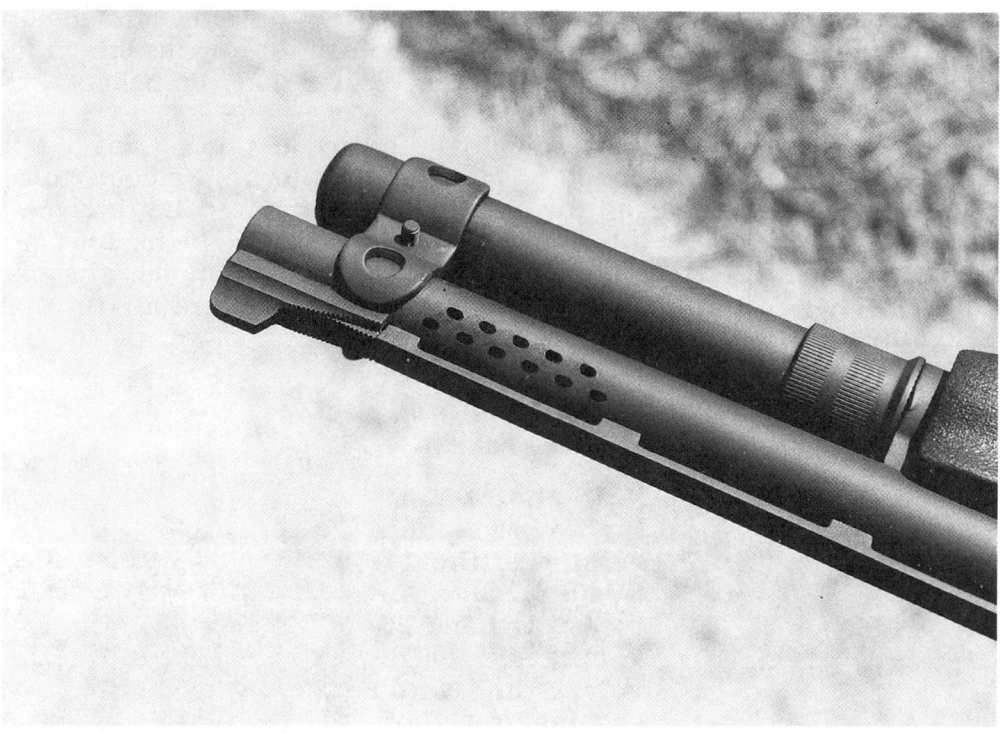

Muzzle climb may be reduced by the Pro-porting process from Magna-Port, Inc. The shooter is then able to get the gun back on target faster.

Another useful accessory are extended magazine tubes. These typically boost magazine capacity from 4 rounds to 6 or 7, depending upon barrel length. Most of the police shotgun manufacturers offer extended tubes as a factory option and Choate offers a variety of models to retrofit to most popular shotguns.

The Police Shotgun   41

Gun mounted shell carriers can be used as an alternative or to supplement extended magazine tubes. Two examples include the leather butt cuffs and the sidesaddle designs. Butt cuffs are affixed to the off-side buttstock and give the officer 5 reserve rounds that are always with the gun. Unfortunately, butt cuffs effectively prevent the weapon from being fired from the opposite shoulder.

A better alternative is the sidesaddle, shell mount which allows one to carry spare ammunition on the left side of the receiver. The earliest designs were made of nylon fabric, but a new design of polymer will hold up much better over the long haul. Combat loading is much easier with the sidesaddle than the butt cuff, and of course the gun may be fired from either shoulder. Both designs, however, guarantee the officer will have extra ammunition if away from the car. They can also be used to store a different type of ammunition than that which is already loaded in the gun. Shell carriers that can be worn on the belt are also a consideration. Safariland markets an inexpensive dual carrier which can be clipped on the sun visor or in the briefcase until needed.

Other accessories include slings and gun mounted lights, and other exotic sighting systems such as lasers. All can prove valuable but, in most cases, these accessories will be reserved for the tactical officer. All nice, but maybe not essential.

One popular add-on best avoided is the folding stock. It tends to amplify felt recoil to very unpleasant levels and if there is a need for a shorter weapon, cutting the barrel back to the magazine tube is the way to go (B.A.T.F. approval required). Likewise, pistol grip shotguns fill a unique niche but they are not flexible enough for general patrol use and should be avoided.

Ammunition That Goes the Distance

The hands down ammunition choice for the police shotgun is 00

All quality buckshot loads contain a buffer which reduces shot deformation and makes for tighter patterns. The buckload on the left contains 27 pellets while the Federal Tactical Buckload contains 9 larger .33 caliber pellets.

Rifled slugs extend the range of the police shotgun. Slugs are also effective in penetrating light cover.

buckshot. The standard 2 3/4" load holds nine .33 caliber pellets and has a muzzle velocity of 1300 fps.

Magnum loadings containing 12 identical size pellets are also available, but in reality, offer little real world advantage since they generate more recoil and do not pattern as well. Number 4 buckshot (twenty-seven .24 caliber pellets) is a distant runner up and some agencies have settled on 1 buck which splits the difference between pattern density and pellet size.

Buckshot delivers superior stopping qualities against unarmored human targets within its limited range. When the multiple pellets simultaneously strike an adversary, it often results in neural shock and rapid incapacitation, even when non-vital areas are hit. Smaller pellets lose energy quicker and even the large 00 pellets run out of gas at relatively modest distances. The 1986 Miami FBI shootout illustrated that buckshot is often defeated by even light cover.

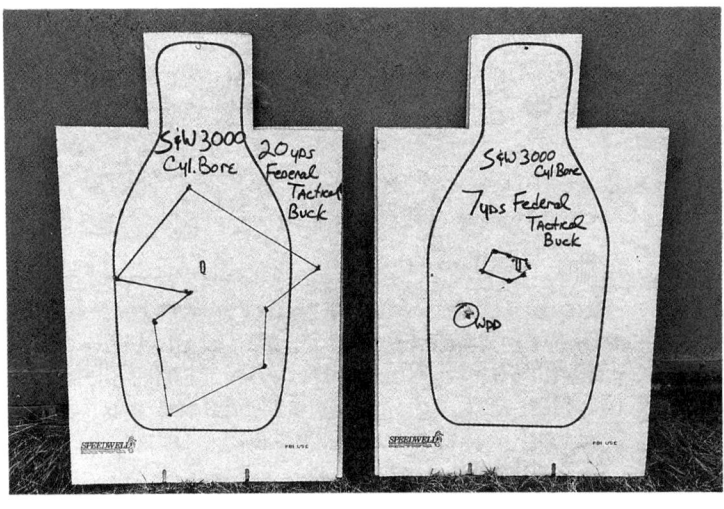

Shotguns should be patterned with duty loads to understand the strengths and limits of the system. Even under ideal conditions 20 yards is the limit for the cylinder boregun. Federal H1 32001 loads pattern tighter than conventional loads.

The Police Shotgun

No matter how you slice it, buckshot is a very erratic performer beyond 20 yards. This is especially true when fired in cylinder bore, police shotguns. The good news, of course, is that most police encounters take place well inside this distance.

Granted, officers usually have no control over their issued equipment. They should, however, be cognizant of the fact that 20 yards is about the limit that one can place most of the pellets on the target under the most ideal conditions. Beyond that range, pellets are likely to miss the target entirely and this presents serious moral and legal responsibilities in populated areas. At extended distances, placement of pellets in the torso becomes a matter of luck rather than skill.

Two buckshot loads stand out as being a cut above. Winchester offers the XM257 4 buck load in their Ranger line. This extra hard shot delivers a significantly tighter than usual pattern and would be the choice if close range problems are anticipated. Federal has also gotten into the act with their H132 00 Police Tactical Buckshot round. Loaded to only 1145 fps rather than the traditional 1300 fps, the Tactical Buck load is easier on the shooter and patterns are significantly tighter as well. Buffered, copper plated shot is used to tighten up the pattern and makes the H132 00 the best general purpose police buckshot load available.

Number 4 buck delivers better pattern density than 00 buck, but at the expense of less penetration. It is best reserved as a special purpose load. Shotgun is a modified Remington 870 by AdvanTac Systems.

To effectively employ the shotgun in intermediate range scenarios, rifled slugs are a must. A rifle sighted shotgun loaded with slugs can be effective out to at least 100 yards and can defeat various types of light cover, including automobile bodies. Unfortunately, these very same obstacle penetrating properties can also contra-indicate their use in certain environments. They do, however, warrant a very serious look as they allow the shotgun to be used in an expanded role.

Speciality rounds include ammunition for breeching locks, gas delivery, flechettes and less than lethal missiles. Typically, these rounds are only accessible to tactical officers.

Learning to Live With the Shotgun

Some law enforcement training programs devote considerable time and effort to handgun skills' development only to provide a cursory familiarization with the shotgun. This often takes the form of firing a dozen or so rounds on some unrealistic course of fire. The programs do not address such vital issues as firing reflex, manipulation skills, or tactical considerations. As a consequence, many officers never develop the skill and confidence needed to become comfortable with the shotgun. On a hot call, these officers are apt to leave the shotgun locked in the rack when, in fact, it could be the best tool for that particular scenario.

The biggest obstacle to overcome in shotgun training is fear of the gun itself. Without a proper foundation in the fundamentals, shotguns loaded with buckshot and slugs can be rather unpleasant to shoot. Firing the shotgun at the police academy is just as likely as not to be the recruit's first experience in firing any type of long gun. If this experience proves to be negative, it will no doubt bias his opinion towards the shotgun for the rest of his career.

No weapon in the police armory is as unforgiving of negligent gun handling as the shotgun. Finger remains outside the trigger guard until ready to fire.

The Police Shotgun

Proper stance, hold, mount, and manipulation skills should be assimilated before the first shot is fired. Significant time should be devoted to dry fire drills where the shooter practices mounting, getting a sight picture, manipulating the trigger, and cycling the action. Loading skills in both administrative and combat scenarios should be addressed, as well as conditions of readiness.

High assault position may be used for problems at arms length. Buttstock is pinned between the upper arm and torso.

Muzzle depressed position is used when scanning for threats or when covering a subject. The gun is placed in a low ready position with the muzzle pointed just outside the feet for building searches.

After the new shooter has demonstrated competence in dry fire practice, the serious work can begin. Initial live fire drills should be done with light birdshot loads. Remember, we are trying to instill positive training experiences with the shotgun. There is no better way to discourage a new shooter than to have him run 50 rounds of buckshot through his shotgun in short order.

Shotgun training need not be complicated to be effective. Initially, drills can be designed around the firing of single, double, and multiple shot bursts. Emphasize reloading a round as soon as possible for each round fired. Shooters can work out of a variety of ready positions and drills can become more complex as skill level increases. These could include use of cover, tactical movement, multiple targets, and transition to handgun. Limit the duration of the drill to the ammunition in the gun, plus one reload. This lends a sense of realism in that the officer is unlikely to carry more ammunition and equally important, it makes for happy shoulders.

An effective method of combat loading is illustrated here. With the action open, the shooter cups a round in the off hand and drops it into the loading port on the carrier. The round is chambered when the shooter runs the slide forward.

For more advanced shooters, buckshot and slugs can be used in training scenarios as well, but be careful not to over do it. Reactive targets such as steel plates, pepper poppers, or even bowling pins are great confidence builders and provide instant feedback. For both new and experienced shooters, they are light years ahead of paper targets. Targets which do something often capture the shooter's undivided attention and prevent focusing on the less pleasant aspects such as recoil. Save the paper for qualification and patterning.

Advanced training with the shotgun should be conducted with uniforms and gear worn on duty. It is much better to find out about limitations of movement on the sterile environment of the range than in the hostile real world. One unexpected benefit is that with proper gun mount soft body armor acts as a recoil shield. Even stout buck and slug loads are relatively tame with a Kevlar buffer. For the last touch of realism, courses of fire can begin with a vehicle dismount while removing the shotgun

The Police Shotgun

from the rack. Proper use of cover, and manipulation skills as well as marksmanship can be evaluated.

Equipment will always play second fiddle to the trained officer who understands the strengths and limitations of the weapon system. A skilled operator, even when equipped with a plain vanilla police shotgun, has the means to prevail against overwhelming odds. The confidence that comes with this knowledge will allow him to perform, even his more routine duties, to a higher standard.

Recommended Reading

The Defensive Shotgun, Techniques and Tactics by Louis Awerbuck, SWAT Publications.

Police Shotguns and Carbines by Brian A. Felter, Prentice-Hall.

Police Shotgun Manual by Bill Clede, Stackpole Books.

Recommended Video Tape Viewing

Tactical Shotgun Techniques by Video Phenomenon, 2437 Albany Ave., West Hartford, CT 06117.

Combat Shotgun Modifications

AdvanTac Systems, P.O. Box 62, Manahawkin, NJ 08050.

Useful Accessories

Gun Mounted Lights:
Laser Products, 18285 Mt. Baldy Circle, Fountain Valley, CA 92708.

Plastic shell holders, slings:
Safariland, 1941 S. Walker, Monrovia, CA 91016.

Extended magazine tubes, lights, sidesaddle shell carriers:
Adventurer's Outpost, P.O. Box 70, Cottonwood, AZ 96326.

Extended magazine tubes, stocks:
Choate Machine & Tool Co., P.O. Box 218, Bald Knob, AR 72010.

About the Author

Mr. Michael F. Boyle is a Lieutenant with the New Jersey Department of Environmental Protection and an active member of the American Society of Law Enforcement Trainers (ASLET).

Chapter 6

Law Enforcement Liability: Reflections On Survival

by Michael A. Brave

Introduction

Officer survival includes physically surviving the incident, but it also includes surviving the incident's legal aftermath. Law enforcement liability can no longer be considered as an after thought to the incident.

Liability is most often thought of as the civil litigation consequences of officers' actions. However, liability actually encompasses:

- officers' survival at the scene;

- the liability associated with the mental, emotional, and psychological survival of the incident's aftermath;

- the liability of administrative sanctions for violation of department policies;

- the liability associated with criminal law violations; and

- civil tort and Federal civil rights liability.

Liability could be thought of as accountability. If officers act incorrectly in the performance of their duties, they could face administrative sanctions, criminal prosecution, and civil forfeitures. If an agency acts incorrectly by having unconstitutional policies or customs, or by being deliberately indifferent to the rights of citizens in the training and supervision of its officers, then liability (accountability and getting into trouble) can flow to the governmental entity of which the agency is a part.

One way for officers to stay out of trouble — and avoid liability — is to act professionally in the performance of their duties. Acting professionally means acting reasonably with deliberate forethought based upon a solid framework of knowledge, training, and guidance, and treating those with whom they come into contact with respect, dignity, and compassion.

Nearly everything a law enforcement officer does in the line of duty can lead to some form of liability. An officer can:

- ☐ violate a person's constitutional rights by making an unlawful stop, frisk, or arrest;
- ☐ use unreasonable force;
- ☐ violate a person's privacy rights;
- ☐ fail to protect someone the officer placed in jeopardy; or
- ☐ conduct a pursuit in a negligent manner.

This chapter is not intended to be an all encompassing legal treatise on law enforcement liability. Rather, it is written to provide a basic non-legalistic understanding of law enforcement liability and to provide some insight into managing the liability associated with an incident. This chapter will only briefly touch on the tactical, survival liability aspects of an incident and the personal emotional and psychological liability associated with the trauma of an incident.

Officers at the Incident or Directly Involved

Officers' liability stemming from an incident (use of force, pursuit, arrest, etc.) can take many forms, including administrative sanctions, criminal prosecutions, and civil liability. Officers can be held accountable to their agency for violations of policy. If during the course of an incident officers violate policy, the officers may be reprimanded, suspended, terminated, or suffer other employment sanctions.

Officers can also be prosecuted criminally if their actions violate criminal statutes. Officers can commit assault, battery, false imprisonment, excessive force, and other criminal violations. If the officers' actions are not privileged (self-defense, defense of others, lawful detention or arrest, etc.), then the officers' actions may violate criminal law and they may be prosecuted for their criminal behavior. This criminal prosecution can be at the state level, the Federal level, or both. At the Federal level, officers can be criminally prosecuted for violation of a person's constitutional rights (18 U.S.C. §§ 241-242) and other statutes.

Officers' actions can lead to lawsuits in civil court. Depending on the jurisdiction, officers may be sued under state civil law for negligence, intentional torts, and/or harm to dignitary interests. There are four criteria that must be met before officers can be found liable for negligence.

The officers must:

1.) first have a duty to the injured person;
2.) breach that duty;
3.) be the proximate cause of the person's injuries; and
4) cause the person to suffer actual damages.

Intentional torts include:

- assault
- battery
- false imprisonment
- intentional infliction of emotional distress
- trespass to land
- trespass to chattels
- conversion

Officers can harm a person's dignitary interests by defamation, violating the person's rights to privacy, or initiating wrongful legal proceedings, such as malicious prosecution or abuse of process. Officers can also be sued in both their official and personal capacities. In their official capacities, officers are being sued as officers of their department. In their personal capacities, officers are being sued in their private capacities.

Officers may also be sued under the Federal civil rights statutes (42 U.S.C. §§ 1981-1988).

A person's constitutional rights include:

- freedom from unreasonable searches and seizures (seizures includes the use of force)
- right to privacy
- protection against self-incrimination
- freedom to petition the government for redress of grievances
- protection from denial of counsel
- right to freedom of assembly and association
- right to be free from cruel and unusual punishment
- right to medical attention (when in custody)
- freedom from verbal abuse and harassment (by officers)
- right to protection under the due process clause
- right to be free from deprivation of property without due process of law

Agency Executives, Supervisors, and Trainers

Just as officers can be held accountable, agency executives, supervisors, and trainers can also be held accountable if directly involved in the injury causing conduct. In addition, they can also be held accountable for Federal civil rights violations if they are "deliberately indifferent" in the screening, hiring, training, direction, supervision, discipline, and/or retention of the officers, and this deliberate indifference results in the officers violating someone's constitutional rights. Deliberate indifference could be thought of as simply not caring.

An example of deliberate indifference is if an agency executive gives an officer an electronic restraining device (ERD) and does not provide the officer with any policy, training, or guidance. The officer illegally uses the ERD as a torturing device on a person (victim) who is COC (contempt of cop). The victim could allege that the agency executive was deliberately indifferent to the victim's constitutional rights through negligent direction (not issuing the policy), negligent training (not providing adequate training), and negligent supervision (not providing the officer with adequate guidance).

The Employing Governmental Entity

The law enforcement agency itself is not a viable defendant in a lawsuit. It is the employing governmental entity (state, county, city, or municipality) that can be held accountable if the entity has an unconstitutional policy or custom that was the driving force behind the constitutional violation. Unlike the private sector, governmental employers cannot be held liable purely for employing a tortfeasor, unless state law permits the entity to be held liable.

An agency's deliberate indifference can also equate to an unconstitutional policy or custom. It is this deliberate indifference that can also lead to Federal civil rights liability.

Basic Precepts-Realities of Liability

When thinking about liability, or taking appropriate action to eliminate it, officers need to examine the management of liability in three distinct phases:

1.) pre-incident liability avoidance;
2.) incident liability control and management; and
3.) post-incident damage control

Before looking at the three phases of liability control, officers should consider the realities of the circumstances surrounding a liability generating incident. First, officers must remember that during prosecution or litigation everything is subject to be discovered by the opposing side. Anything officers say, write, or express can be discovered, and will probably be misconstrued by someone, maybe even the judge or the jury.

When officers become involved in a litigation, they quickly learn who their true friends are, as opposed to those who cannot stand the heat. The officers may find that their fates rest with the political mood surrounding the incident fallout. If a politician is up for re-election and can make political progress out of the officers' prosecution, the officers may find themselves indicted on criminal charges.

Other outside factors may also have a strong influence on the officers' fates. If the officers are involved in a cross-racial shooting, the officers may find their futures are manipulated by minority special interest groups.

Officers' futures may also be at the mercy of fallacies of our legal system. Most people believe that a person can only be tried in a court of law once for the same offense. Ask the four officers involved in the Rodney King case whether they now believe in double jeopardy. The truth is that double jeopardy is attached to the sovereignty and there may be more than one sovereignty: Federal, states, and/or Indian Nations.

Officers are held accountable for the law they are presumed to know. Give officers a test on the legal principles of criminal procedure, Federal civil rights, and constitutional law, and it will become strikingly apparent that officers usually do not know the law. This lack of knowledge or understanding is the primary underlying cause of liability.

Before being confronted with a liability generating incident, officers should remember to plan for the worst and hope for the best. Officers can have their lives, and their families' futures, destroyed by not taking the liability stemming from an incident seriously. Many officers have committed professional suicide by failing to actively battle the liability aftermath of an incident. Some of the realities include: the truth of the incident may not be provable (by the officers) or is in fact irrelevant, and witnesses may intentionally lie, omit the truth, not want to get involved, or inaccurately perceive the incident.

After an incident occurs, the officers, their agencies, and their administrators may be placed under microscopic scrutiny by the prosecutor, the courts, the community, the media, special interest groups, and others. The officers must be ready to defend themselves when confronted by these groups.

Pre-Incident Liability Avoidance

Liability can be avoided by acting professionally. Professionally means being well trained, acting with intelligence and common sense, and being reasonable, respectful, and compassionate. Officers should act according to all applicable standards regulating their conduct. These standards include Federal law, state law, and departmental policy in compliance with documented training according to supervisors' lawful direction and manufacturers' specifications.

If officers act out of panic (not to be confused with controlled fear), anger, frustration, jealousy, retaliation, malicious motive, with reckless disregard, or in an outrageous manner, their actions may become questioned. Their actions may be construed as improper and in violation of governing standards.

Incident Liability Control and Management

At the incident officers must first be sure of the lawfulness of their actions. Before officers take any action, they must have legitimate authority — be within their jurisdiction and acting in conformance with agency policies. Officers can make **Terry** stops, but they must first have reasonable suspicion. Officers can make a lawful arrest, but they must first have probable cause. In using force, officers must use only reasonable and necessary force, and not unreasonable, excessive, or retaliatory force.

While the incident is evolving, the officers should try to get consent for their actions from the people confronted. The officers should try to get this consent even if they have legitimate authority to complete their desired actions. The officers may have legitimate authority to search a car subject to the lawful arrest of the driver, or to search the car subject to a lawful motor-vehicle inventory policy. However, the officers would still be well served by acquiring consent to search the vehicle from the driver or the owner prior to the search.

If the totalities of the circumstances permit, the officers should reconsider their actions and, if possible, use the least intrusive or minimal means of accomplishing their lawful objectives. If the officers need to retreat, through de-escalation, creating distance, or awaiting backup without compromising fulfillment of their lawful objectives, the officers should strive to do so. It is not always a disgrace to retreat.

Also, if time, distance, and the totality of the circumstances permit, officers should try to give violators reasonable time to comply with lawful commands. It is better to give the violator time to comply rather than to escalate the confrontation before the violator has had a reasonable opportunity to submit.

In dealing with citizens, subjects, violators, and others, officers should attempt to treat everyone with respect, even if they don't deserve it. Sometimes called the "Beverly Hills Syndrome," officers should treat everyone as though they were dealing with a resident of Beverly Hills. If officers use racial slurs, remarks, or derogatory statements, the officers uttering the remarks may find themselves in trouble for the disrespectful statement. If officers use racial slurs while they are using force, the officers may find themselves accused of using unreasonable force because of racial animus.

In addition to showing respect, officers must also be cognizant of citizens' privacy interests. Citizens and violators have a right to their privacy in medical issues (HIV/AIDS), to be free from ridicule, and to be free from dissemination of private matters (e.g., sexually explicit video tapes).

After violators are under control, officers may wish to attempt to defuse the violators' anger and frustration by allowing them the opportunity to regain their self respect and dignity. By talking and explaining to the violators the reason for the officers' actions and the role the violators played in escalating the confrontation, the officers may be able to lower their frustrations.

Post-Incident Damage Control

After an incident, officers can substantially limit their potential liability through damage control. The extent of the damage control will vary with the severity of the injuries or damages caused during the incident. The higher the severity of the incident, the greater level of damage control implemented.

If the incident is severe enough, such as a shooting or pursuit ending in death, the officers should:

- protect the integrity of the scene;

- not discuss the details of the incident;

- strongly consider not giving a statement (written or oral) unless upon the valid order of a superior and upon advice of personal counsel;

- expect to be treated like a criminal; and

- after a shooting, expect to have their firearm confiscated.

After a potentially life-threatening incident, officers should foresee the potential for emotional and psychological trauma to have a negative effect upon them and act accordingly to minimize the negative impact of the trauma.

The Prosecution or Litigation Has Commenced

Once the administrative sanctions, criminal prosecution, and/or the civil litigation has commenced, the affected officers must have competent legal representation and actively manage, or at least monitor and record, the events.

Once the prosecution or litigation has commenced, the officers have many factors to consider:

- ☐ Who is controlling the litigation?
- ☐ Who has final settlement authority?
- ☐ What is the width and depth of the litigation (who are the defendants)?
- ☐ Beware of conflicts between defendants.

In choosing an attorney officers should consider many factors. The officers should consider who is actually going to perform the work on their case. Is it the seasoned senior partner of the law firm or the new associate? Even though the officers may talk to the senior partner, a new associate or even a law clerk may do most of the work on their case.

How accessible is the attorney? If the officers cannot reach their attorneys, or the attorneys do not timely return phone calls, then the officers will be very frustrated with the flow of the proceedings. If the attorneys do not return the calls from their clients, then how will the attorneys manage the litigation? How hard will it be for other parties to the litigation to contact the attorneys?

What level of law enforcement knowledge do the attorneys have? Are the attorneys experienced and knowledgeable in law enforcement litigation or are the officers going to pay (by the hour) for the attorneys' education? In the same light, veteran law enforcement attorneys should have a well developed law enforcement litigation library. Attorneys new to law enforcement litigation will probably have to acquire a competent library, which will probably be paid for by the officers.

The officers should be aware of the fees they are being charged. They also should have entered into a detailed retainer agreement with the attorneys that spells out the fee parameters in unambiguous detail.

Lastly, the officers should make sure that their attorneys have adequate levels of malpractice insurance. Many law firms and attorneys do not have malpractice insurance. If the attorneys commit malpractice and the officers suffer from the malpractice, then the officers need to have the ability to acquire a collectible judgment from the attorneys. This may only be possible if the attorneys have adequate levels of malpractice insurance. Also, if the attorneys do not have malpractice insurance there is probably a good reason. The attorneys have been sued in the past and cannot afford insurance, or the attorneys are new and inexperienced and cannot afford malpractice coverage. In any event, the officers should only engage attorneys who have malpractice coverage.

Once the officers have chosen their attorneys, the officers must also take a knowing, active role in monitoring the litigation. To that end, the officers should have included in their retainer agreements that the attorneys will timely provide the officers with copies of every document pertaining to the litigation. The attorneys should also provide a monthly, written update on the litigation, and provide all advice to the officers in writing. The officers should maintain a complete litigation file, including detailed conversation notes. The officers' files are necessary because the law firm could be ravaged by fire, the attorneys may not be reputable, or they may not keep a complete file. The officers may have to change lawyers on short notice and may experience difficulty in acquiring the former attorneys' complete files.

Conclusion

The key to surviving and managing law enforcement liability is professionalism. By acting professionally in all their actions, officers can

Law Enforcement Liability

effectively avoid the vast majority of liability. If officers are confronted with liability, they can still manage the liability and effectively use damage control measures to minimize the potential negative ramifications.

About the Author

Mr. Michael A. Brave is a Senior Account Executive, Senior Associate, and staff member of the Law Enforcement Division of Gallagher Bassett's Institute for Liability Management. A licensed attorney in Wisconsin and Minnesota, Mike is admitted to, among others, the U.S. Supreme Court. He is also a (patrol) Sergeant, training Officer, FTO, and legal adviser to a Wisconsin police department. He is on the National Advisory Boards of the Police Law Institute, the Jail Law Institute, Defense Training International, Inc., and the Defensive Tactics Institute, Inc. He is also on the Executive Committee of the Legal Officers' Section of the International Association of Chiefs of Police and is a consultant to the Law Enforcement Legal Defense Manual.

As a certified instructor in several facets of deadly force, many non-lethal and less-than-lethal programs, and several law enforcement driving programs, Mike has presented many law enforcement risk management programs across the country. Mike has been a litigation consultant and an expert witness in law enforcement use of force and pursuit driving cases.

Stephen M. Bunting

Mr. Bunting is currently a Captain with the University of Delaware Police. He is an eighteen year veteran of law enforcement and has spent the last twelve years with the University Police. He is a Monadnock International Instructor, a Counter-Assault Systems International Instructor, and a Monadnock Straight Baton International Instructor. In addition, he is certified to instruct firearms, defensive tactics, and officer survival. During the past 14 years, he has trained thousands of officers from agencies of all types including Federal agencies, numerous state police agencies, countless city and county agencies, and officers from foreign countries. He is a Founding Director and current Executive Director of the American Society of Law Enforcement Trainers and a member of the Monadnock PR-24™ Training Council Advisory Board. Captain Bunting is a frequent lecturer to police recruits on coping with fear and danger in the police profession.

Chapter 7

Dealing With Fear and Danger

by Stephen M. Bunting

The young police officer picked up the microphone and answered his call sign to hear the radio crackle in response, "Go to 11th and Vine, officer in trouble, shots fired, respond Code 3." He tried to answer with a 10-4, only to hear his voice utter a high pitched unintelligible sound. The officer could hear his heart pounding in his chest, his breathing was heavy, and his fumbling fingers had a difficult time returning the microphone to its holder.

This young police officer was experiencing, physiologically, the same thing that Neanderthal man did when suddenly confronted by a dangerous beast. Our bodies are equipped with a mechanism that, when activated, prepares the body for extreme activity, thus enhancing the likelihood of survival. While man has evolved and changed in many ways, this mechanism has remained almost unchanged over the course of the history of mankind. It has had many names over time, including the "Adaptation Theory," the "Emergency Reaction," the "Survival Mechanism," and the "Fight-Flight Response." Currently, the Fight-Flight Response is in vogue and is the term that will be used here.

Vesalius first discovered and documented the Fight-Flight Response in anatomical drawings during the sixteenth century. Those anatomical drawings identified a few of the physiological changes that occurred in the body. Today researchers have found over 150 such changes. Much of the pioneering research was done by Dr. Walter B. Cannon of the Harvard Medical School during the early 1900's. His book, *Bodily Changes in Pain, Hunger, Fear, and Rage*, stands today as an authoritative text on the subject.

Police officers should consider the Fight-Flight Response as their "survival mechanism," for that is truly what it is. When humans function normally, without threat or fear, they are primarily under control of the cerebral cortex, which is the main thinking portion of the brain.

Bodily Changes

Located between the cerebral cortex and the spinal column, among other things, is the hypothalamus. The hypothalamus is very small compared to the cerebral cortex and serves to regulate the autonomic nervous system. This system is an internal regulatory system and has two opposing, or counter-balancing, branches known as the parasympathetic and sympathetic branches.

Normally the parasympathetic branch dominates, but when an animal, in this case man, perceives a threat or danger, an amazing process takes over. First the cerebral cortex passes primary control to the hypothalamus. The hypothalamus activates the sympathetic branch of the autonomic nervous system, and at nearly the speed of electricity, the body undergoes dramatic changes that prepare it for extreme physical activity. In short, the activation of the sympathetic branch prepares the body to fight or run, therefore the name Fight-Flight Response.

The body's survival mechanism shifts into high gear. Many things happen to the body, and they happen simultaneously. The heart rate soars, causing blood pressure to rise as the arteries have not yet had time to dilate. This increases the blood flow or energy to various locations of the body. Breathing becomes rapid and the bronchi dilate. This provides additional oxygen to the blood, which in turn fuels the muscles once they reach an aerobic state of function. The blood vessels in the large muscles dilate supplying them with oxygen rich blood. In addition, glycogenolysis is stimulated in the liver, which releases glycogen or sugar into the bloodstream for added fuel. The upper body undergoes an increase in muscular tension; this can be observed as a rise in the shoulders, muscular twitching in the neck, and clenched fists. So far these changes have prepared the large muscles for extreme physical activity associated with fighting or running.

Additional changes occur. As the blood flow is enhanced to the large muscles, it is diverted away from other areas of the body. The brain receives less blood; the organism is seeking only to survive and therefore has a reduced need and ability to think or reason. The officer relies upon trained responses and reacts to the environment in a manner designed strictly to survive. The officer can't think or reason clearly; actions occurring while in this survival state must be viewed accordingly. No person sitting in judgment of an officer's action should do so without first thoroughly understanding this process; this includes administrators, internal affairs investigators, judges, juries, prosecutors, and defense attorneys.

Diminished blood flow also affects other areas, such as the viscera (digestive organs) and the capillaries in the skin. An officer doesn't need the blood flow in the digestive organs when the organism is threatened. When the capillaries in the skin constrict, they allow blood to be used for more important things, such as the fueling of the large muscle groups. The added benefit to survival is, the body bleeds less if injured due to the minimal amount of blood near the surface of the skin.

Changes not necessarily associated with preparing the muscles for extreme physical activity also occur. For instance, the pupils dilate which enhances vision in shadows and dark areas. The lens of the eye flattens to allow enhanced far vision and hearing also increases. Another effect is, the anal sphincter will constrict for obvious reasons. Thus the term "pucker factor," sometimes used in police circles, is an actual part of the

Fight-Flight Response system.

The goose bumps that officers often experience raise the hair follicles. When Homo sapiens were much hairier than the modern day version, the raised hair follicles made the body look larger and more intimidating. The raised hair follicles are very sensitive to slight air currents, giving the body an early warning mechanism, especially to the rear where vision does not cover. Dropping a book next to a cat graphically demonstrates this phenomenon.

Other things happen as well. The body experiences a decreased sensitivity to pain. Pain is not necessary for short term survival. The officer can therefore withstand physical attack and continue to respond in order to survive. The officer must realize that the Fight-Flight Response occurs in the body of the opponent also, and the opponent is less sensitive to pain. Defensive tactic techniques performed must be done with full explosive power initially. The officer must train knowing this; how the officer trains is how the officer responds!

Perceptual Distortions

Many officers have heard that they develop "tunnel vision" and "auditory exclusion" during times of high stress and danger. This seems to conflict with the mention earlier of increased vision and hearing capabilities. What really happens is that the officer focuses on the threat. Often, all other sights and sounds are excluded. Recollections of details of the actual threat are greatly enhanced, yet other visual stimuli are excluded and perceptual errors result. Persons posing a threat are perceived as much taller, heavier, and uglier. Knives with two-inch blades grow to six or twelve inches. Twenty-two caliber barrels become forty-five caliber. This happens to trained observers and novices alike.

Perceptual distortions of time also occur due to a phenomenon called "tachypsychia." Some police officers experience a sensation of slowed time, while others experience the opposite. Officers, witnesses, and victims who have survived life threatening experiences are not lying when they report these seemingly exaggerated or incorrect accounts. They are simply victims of perceptual distortions.

Understanding the Adrenal Dump

Another function triggered by the sympathetic branch is the secretion of adrenal compounds into the bloodstream. Many of the things that happen to the body were thought by many to be from the adrenal dump. Not so, at least not initially, for if police officers had to wait for adrenal compounds to activate their survival mechanisms, officers would most likely not survive the wait. It is the nervous system that fires the Fight-Flight Response immediately; the adrenal compounds sustain and augment the same changes caused by the nervous system. The nerves can only "fire" so many times before they must recharge. Thus the nerves start the process and the powerful hormones from the adrenal dump sustain it. Once the adrenal compounds are in the bloodstream, they diminish very slowly and further cause the body to have a tendency to relieve this state through aggression. This is a major factor contributing to many cases involving the use of excessive force by officers. Many high-speed chases and other similar high charged incidents results in officers relieving this hormonally influenced state through aggression.

When officers understand that these changes in their body are to be expected, there are several important things to consider. They must first understand that what is happening is a normal reaction to an abnormal situation. Many things happen that enhance their ability to survive, while many things happen that impair their normal functions.

Police officers experience impaired cognitive function or the ability to think. They must overcome this by high-repetition training. A physical skill must be performed 3,000 to 5,000 times before it can occur without conscious thought in a crisis. Thus officers must practice survival skills, both physically and mentally, to be adequately prepared. They must mentally rehearse responses to life-threatening situations and have backup plans as well.

Fine motor skills involving eye-to-hand coordination suffer during the Fight-Flight Response. Skills, such as operating levers and buttons on an auto pistol, inserting live rounds into a revolver cylinder, some defensive tactics and handcuffing skills, and operating knobs, buttons, and switches inside a patrol vehicle, all fall into this category. Yet, gross motor skills are enhanced by the extra energy available to the large muscle groups. Skills, such as stunning techniques, kicks, strikes, blocks, and other similar techniques, are delivered with intensified power and force.

As the muscles tense in the upper body and neck region, the muscular tension affects the normal function of the vocal chords. Further, a decrease in salivary response (dry mouth) occurs. The net result is that the voice may squeal in an unexpected manner leaving officers feeling somewhat inferior! Strong vocalization skills are necessary to overcome this limitation. Officers should practice during training to shout loudly commands, such as "Get back," "Get down," "Drop the weapon," etc. How officers train is how officers will respond.

Police officers must understand that the increased auditory and visual focus and acuities are directed toward the threat. Again, they know this as tunnel vision and auditory exclusion. These bodily responses are good. The officer's total attention is focused on the threat. What if there are multiple threats? Officers are likely to miss other threats with disastrous consequences. Scanning the environment continually is a skill that must be practiced in training, and at all other times, for it to work when the Fight-Flight Response is triggered. A good firearms' training program teaches officers to scan for multiple threats to avoid falling into the tunnel vision trap.

Officers must understand that the Fight-Flight Response is triggered often during police work, and that, more times than not, officers neither fight nor flee! What happens when a high-speed chase ends and

Dealing With Fear and Danger 63

the subject gives up peacefully? Because of the high adrenal state and the tendency for this state to be relieved through aggression, the result, far too often, is the excessive use of force and claims of police brutality. What can officers do?

Harness the Power

In cases where the threat or fear is sudden and requires an immediate response, officers must act immediately, harness the power of the Fight-Flight Response and couple it with trained responses. Survival is the immediate priority and the only concern. In cases of responding to hot calls, operating a vehicle in a high-speed chase, having to think clearly in volatile situations, and other similar functions, officers must exert self-control before they can control others. How do officers do this? They can't control bodily functions such as heart rate, arterial dilation, pupillary dilation, adrenal secretions, etc. Yet, there is one physiological function over which officers can exert conscious and intentional control. That function is the rate of breathing.

Police officers can use a technique known as autogenic breathing to control their respiratory rate. They do this by breathing intentionally in a slow, deep, rhythmical manner as follows:

- Sit in a comfortable position and remain quiet.

- Keep eyes closed.

- Beginning at your feet, deeply relax all muscles.

- Become aware of your breathing. Breathe easily, in through your nose and out through your mouth.

- Maintain a passive attitude for 10 to 20 minutes.

Officers must practice this control technique thousands of times and during times of "normal" function in order for it to work in a crisis. Slowing the rate and manner of breathing interrupts the stress-feedback loop in the body and has a tendency to bring the body back slowly to a more normal level of function.

Today's officers must understand the body's survival mechanism, or the Fight-Flight Response. This knowledge enables them to recognize that they are responding normally to abnormal situations. Officers know that certain enhancements and limitations occur, and that they can harness and make use of the added strengths and work to overcome the weaknesses.

At times when immediate survival is not threatened and control is needed, officers can overcome the effects of the Fight-Flight Response with the autogenic breathing technique. Thus, they can function better during the extreme stresses of police work.

The results of this knowledge and ability to exert some control over the Fight-Flight Response are officers who can survive life threats, or who can function more professionally in less threatening crises and are less likely to be targets of brutality claims.

Bibliography

Benson, Herbert. 1976. *The Relaxation Response.* New York: Avon.

Cannon, W.B. 1929. *Bodily Changes in Pain, Hunger, Fear, and Rage.* New York: Appleton.

Lorenz, Konrad. 1966. *On Aggression.* London: Methuen.

Remsberg, Charles. 1986. *The Tactical Edge.* Illinois: Calibre Press.

Storr, Anthony. 1968. *Human Aggression.* New York: Murray.

Chapter 8

Law Enforcement Applications of Chemical Agents

by William E. Burroughs

One often overlooked, but very important member of the weapons' arsenal, is the chemical agent munitions supply. Historically, agencies began to stockpile a wide array of munitions in the 60's and 70's in response to the threat of riotous activity. Much of that ordnance is still in inventory in agencies throughout the country. For one reason or another, the material is not serviceable now and has long since seen its expiration date for application. To compound the problem, very little training, if any, was given to support the tactical application of these agents. When the law enforcement mission changed in the 80's, and again in the 90's, an attempt was made to find an effective use for the chemicals in indoor tactical situations and in personal defense. This has proven useful, but there are some major considerations.

First of all, there is the type of chemical agent to be used. Currently, there are three classifications of agents available to the law enforcement community. The oldest and most used is Chloroacetophenone or CN. This agent is classified as a lacrimator due to its tearing effect on the eyes. The second agent is Ochlorobenzylidene Malononitrile or CS. Due to its painful effects on the body, CS is classified as an irritant. The third agent is Oleoresin Capsicum or OC. Classified as an inflammatory, it works on the mucous membranes and surface capillaries, causing difficulty in breathing and an inability to see because of the involuntary closing of the eyes.

The agent CN is a solid compound consisting of colorless crystals. To date, it is second only to Brobenzylcyanide in its strength as a lacrimator. It is practically insoluble in water and is not affected by moisture. CN is listed as having a very low vapor pressure which is the key to its function — evaporation. The higher the temperature, the higher the evaporation rate and the more persistent and aggressive the agent will be. During periods of cool weather, however, more agent will be required to saturate the same area because of the reduced rate of evaporation.

The particulate cloud created by a Pyrotechnic CN munition is readily identifiable to the senses of sight and smell. A faint, blue tint will be noted in the cloud at its point of origin. Your sense of smell will detect a characteristic Apple Blossom odor. In its micropulverized form, evidenced by a blast or expulsion munition, CN is very persistent in its effects on the human body. Liquid application of highly refined CN in the form of an aerosol is extremely effective with immediate results.

Exposure to the agent CN, in any of its deployed forms, will show full symptomatic effects in 2 to 5 seconds. The symptoms are a profuse watering and partial closing of the eyes, irritation to the upper respiratory tract, and a burning and itching sensation on the skin, particularly on moist areas of the body. It is important to note that increasing the exposure dosage beyond that which is computed to be incapacitating does not increase the severity of the symptoms.

The agent CS has the notoriety of being much more effective than CN due to the severity of the symptoms experienced. Many favor CS over CN for safety considerations in deployment. The compound itself is a white, crystalline solid seen in the form of free flowing crystals. CS is an extremely stable chemical and is only slightly soluble in water. The stability of this chemical makes it difficult to decontaminate if an inappropriate method of deployment is used, particularly indoors.

The symptomatic effects of exposure to CS with incapacitating effects will be experienced within 20 to 60 seconds. Symptoms begin as a burning sensation in the eyes followed by copious tearing, sneezing, profuse nasal discharge, skin irritation, and an involuntary closing of the eyes. The agent also acts as an irritant to the upper respiratory tract. Of interest to the tactical officer: if the dosage is increased or the time of exposure prolonged, the symptomatic effects become more severe. Advanced effects include the sensation of having a heart attack, as well as a self-induced panic. Nausea and vomiting are experienced by those heavily contaminated.

A pyrotechnic munition using CS will burn at the source and a pepper-like odor will be detected. Munitions using a micropulverized loading of the agent will more quickly incapacitate, but will also be more difficult to decontaminate. Aerosols require a direct application to the eyes in the form of a stream or inhalation in the form of a mist in order to be effective.

The agent OC is a relative newcomer to law enforcement in the area of subject control. Its documented effective use has spearheaded national acceptance of the product. OC is deployed as a microparticulate solid suspended in a liquid carrying agent. The solid is actually the synthesized irritant element of Cayenne Pepper. The agent is an organic, non-enduring compound that is easily decontaminated.

OC becomes airborne through either aerosol use or liquid loaded breaching projectiles. The agent is dependent upon a misting effect or the immediate evaporation of the carrying liquid to effectively contaminate the breathable oxygen surrounding the subject. The result of this area saturation is an observable series of symptomatic effects that give the officer a tactical advantage in control. These symptoms include an inability to breathe in deep lung breath which is required for sustained aggressive physical activity, and an involuntary closing of the eyes caused by a temporary swelling of the capillaries in that area. A heightened sense of pain accompanies skin contact and is noted as the subject attempts to rub off the contaminant.

By comparison, CN and CS provide law enforcement with the means of subject control that is physiological (pain) and psychological (fear). This type of control is best applied to rational thinking individuals who respond to pain and can reason what is happening to them. OC works in much the same way, but additionally affords the officer the means of control over those who have a high tolerance to pain or who are irrational in their thought processes. OC works to temporarily restrict the airway limiting breathing and redirecting the aggressor's thought process toward the ability to breathe.

The appropriateness of the use of these agents is dictated by each tactical situation. As a rule of thumb, however, pyrotechnics should be used outdoors with liquids and expulsion munitions applied indoors. The most frequently selected agent for a tactical mission has been CS. The reasons are many, but the most important seems to be the aggressive activity of the agent in incapacitating those exposed. In a confined space, CS can readily induce panic behavior if the adversary is unable or unwilling to escape the contaminated field. This could precipitate behavior not consistent with what the tactical team may be set up to control. Further, the use of CS indoors presents some major decontamination problems if delivery amounts are not calculated, or if the deployment method is incorrect. The effects of CN and OC are more predictable from one person to the next and are not as heightened as they are in the advanced stages of CS exposure. CN and OC are also more readily decontaminated and lend themselves to indoor situations where confined areas are the norm and evacuation of the surrounding property is not appropriate.

Chemical agents are delivered on target by the use of grenades, projectiles, dispersers, and aerosols. Each one of the delivery systems used may deploy the agent in any one of three physical states. The first is in the form of a solid which is seen in the case of a pyrotechnic or burning type munition. Contained inside the munition is a pyrotechnic mixture and a microparticulate form of the agent. The pyrotechnic mixture must contain a fuel or carbon source to generate heat and enhance the burning rate, and an oxidizing agent to advance the burn. The fuel used in munitions of this type is a form of sugar, usually lactose. The oxidizing agent is potassium chlorate. These materials are compressed into a cake or pellets under high pressure. The uniformity of the mix contributes to a controlled burn rate and temperature that can reach 800 degrees Fahrenheit. With temperatures this high, it is necessary to include a carrier such as nitrocellulose in the mixture to ensure the agent is transported into the atmosphere before the heat oxidizes the agent. CN and CS are available in munitions of this type.

The second physical state is observed in blast or expulsion ordnance. In these munitions, a micropulverized powder or dust version of the agent is either mixed with, or coated by, a buoyant carrier such as silica aerogel, diatomite, cab-o-sil, or magnesium oxide. The carrier serves to keep the agent airborne longer to enable the contamination to spread over a wider area. Again, CN and CS are agents for the ordnance.

The last physical state is in the form of a liquid loaded into an aerosol or disperser. Here a microparticulate agent is mixed with a solvent to suspend the agent in solution. The solvent not only aids in the transmission of the agent, but also degreases and sensitizes the area. There is also an evaporative or drying agent present that helps to keep the chemical airborne and aids the dispersal rate. All of the agents, CN, CS, and OC, may be delivered by liquid.

The officer in charge of disseminating the agent must now make a determination as to the method of deployment for the given situation. Pyrotechnic munitions should be used in outdoor situations where the dangers of fire and asphyxiation are reduced. With the indoor use of any pyrotechnic, the immediate venting of the exposed area must be considered to limit the asphyxiation hazard and reduce obscuration. The munitions themselves should have a burn time of no longer than 15 seconds with no observable external flame.

Expulsion munitions are useful in confined spaces outdoors and in any indoor area where the presence of the micropulverized agents pose limited decontamination problems. Again, select a munition size closely approximating calculated amounts for incapacitation.

Liquid loadings are more diverse. Aerosols are used for personal defense, apprehension and control; dispersers are employed for riot control and area coverage; and liquid loaded projectiles are applied in barricaded situations.

From a tactical perspective, enough agent must be deployed outdoors to insure that the target area is contaminated. Further, the supply will need to be replenished and a new target line formed as these munitions expire to keep the area saturated and to prevent the reforming of groups of rioters. The intent is to sweep the area clean through initial deployment, tactical movement, and follow-up procedures.

A common tactical error made during indoor applications is to not wait a sufficient length of time for the agent deployed to permeate the entire contained airspace. Without complete saturation, the officers will not be working with the full effects of the agent. Raid tactics that use dynamic entry are better suited to the application of distraction devices than to chemical deployment.

Prior to releasing any chemical agent, it is necessary to compute the actual amount needed. From a liability standpoint, this is crucial to the agency and the deploying officer. The following is the means for quick computation regarding how much agent to use, given the parameters of the incapacitating dose versus the lethal dose. This information is applicable to CS and CN only and is intended to serve as a guide for the selection and use of an agent. No incapacitating or lethal values have been established for OC.

Facts Necessary for Computation

1.) Median lethal dosage (LCt_{50}) for **CN** and **CS**
   CN: 14000mg-min/M^3 **CS**: 25000mg-min/M^3

Law Enforcement Applications of Chemical Agents

2.) Median incapacitating dosage (ICt_{50}) for **CN** and **CS**
   CN: 20mg-min/M^3 **CS**: 10/20mg-min/M^3

3.) Conversion of the gram weight of the agent in the selected munition to milligram weight
   Multiply gram weight by 1000

4.) Compute the volumetric size of the room
   Compute by multiplying length X width X height

Procedure

▭▶ **Step 1** Compute the volumetric size of the space to be exposed (cubic meter measurement)
Example: 9' X 8' X 10' = 720FT^3
720FT^3 divided by 27 = 26.66YD^3
26.66YD^3 divided by 1.31 = 20.35M^3

Note that 27 is the divisor in step two as there are 27 cubic feet per cubic yard. In the final step, 1.31 is the divisor to convert cubic yards to cubic meters.

▭▶ **Step 2** Convert gram weight of chosen munition to milligram (mg) weight
Example: 75 grams X 1000 = 75000mg

▭▶ **Step 3** Compute incapacitation and lethal amount for calculated volumetric size
Example: 20.35M^3 X 20mg-min/M^{3^3} = 407mg
20.35M^3 X 14000mg-min/M^3 = 284900mg

▭▶ **Step 4** Compute the actual number of munitions to be delivered
Example: (Divide the answer in step three by the answer in step two)

Incapacitating Calculation
407mg divided by 75000 = 0.005

Lethal Calculation
284900 divided by 75000 = 3.80

Since you cannot deliver a portion of a selected munition, to achieve the results that you expect, you will always round your answer up. The delivered amounts for the above would then be 1 to incapacitate and 4 to create a lethal environment. By computing both the lethal level and the incapacitating level, the deploying officer is provided with a practical range of application that is flexible and safe.

This range is also important when computing outdoor applications where wind, weather, and mechanical turbulence can play havoc with your deployment. Use a ceiling height of 30' for all outdoor computations, leaving only length and width to be measured to complete the volumetric calculation. The controlling influences of wind speed and direction, and thermal and mechanical turbulence can be effectively plotted inside this dimension, but not beyond. The figures generated are applicable for initial deployment. Resupply must be calculated if the dimensions change during the sweep. If the dimensions do not change, resupply occurs at the same initial deployment rate. While the threat of lethality from the toxic effects of the agents themselves can be shown by mathematical computation, very few agencies have enough agent to accomplish the task. Death is not instantaneous if an individual finds himself in a computed lethal field. Exposure must remain constant at a lethal level for a period of no less than ten minutes.

Deaths have occurred in the past from the use of chemical munitions, but it is extremely difficult to place the responsibility on the toxic effects of the agent. However, death can occur from improper deployment. For example, the utilization of a pyrotechnic munition in a confined space could potentially lower the oxygen level in the area to below 19%. This dramatically increases the danger of asphyxiation.

To date, no known deaths are attributable to the exposure of the agents CS or OC. There have been a very small number of deaths in which the agent CN was a factor. Death was not immediate, but took place at a time well after the initial exposure. The reasons cited for the deaths have been listed as Broncho-Pneumonia and Acute Pulmonary Edema.

Having made the determination on agent selection, method of deployment, and concentration amounts, you must examine the parameters of proper and sound tactical application in a variety of settings. Let us examine outdoor considerations first. Wind speed and direction must be taken into account to ensure proper saturation of the targeted area. Wind direction is an intangible that cannot be controlled and may prohibit the use of the agent. Wind speed, however, is a variable we can deal with. Optimum wind speed for area saturation is from 5 to 7 mph. This is observed as a steady, light breeze. During still conditions, more agent will have to be deployed closer to the target area to achieve the desired results. When the wind is blowing faster than 7mph, more agent will need to be deployed further away from the target. During ideal wind conditions, observe that the lateral spread of the agent will occur over one fifth of the distance it has to travel to reach its objective. The faster the wind, the less the dispersion.

Another consideration is the area in which the agent is intended for use. It is advisable not to use a chemical agent around hospitals, retirement homes, secondary schools, or mental institutions. In the case of the first three, what you are trying to avoid is irritation to individuals who may have existing respiratory problems or their respiratory systems are

Law Enforcement Applications of Chemical Agents 71

sensitive due to being in their formative stages. Chemical munitions should not be used in or around mental institutions or on the mentally deranged. You cannot predict what the response to the exposure will be. Chemical agents are designed to be used on rational human beings. The idea is simply that once a rational individual is exposed and becomes uncomfortable, reason will indicate his submission or departure. Not so with the mentally unstable. There could be no response, an extremely violent one, or anything in between.

Factors that also influence outdoor use are the size and temper of the crowd. Dispersal of the crowd is probably your best approach, given manpower considerations in trying to make arrests. Photograph the crowd and arrest the agitators at a later time. In dispersing the crowd, keep in mind that you must provide an avenue of escape for them. Your initial deployment of the agent should start them in a planned direction with continuing resupply providing them with no alternative but to comply. The most common tactical errors made outdoors are warning the crowd what you are going to do if they do not disperse, and then failing to use enough agent to accomplish the mission. The approach of just giving them a "taste" to see if they will comply is a crucial mistake. Hit them quickly, hit them hard, and follow-up to secure the area.

Mechanical turbulence in the form of trees, buildings, and vehicles can play havoc with your deployment. Objects of this type can impede agent dispersal, prevent it from getting to the target area, or cause it to swirl aimlessly about. Here is where an inert smoke munition comes in handy. By deploying smoke, you will get immediate visual feedback regarding the dispersal pattern of your live agent. Do not hesitate to use smoke in any area where the mechanical objects present could influence the rate of dispersal. This is vital for the tactical officer.

Indoor considerations are much more complicated. Generally, apprehension is of paramount importance. Considering the possible presence of a hostage, selection of the type of agent, length of time to incapacitate, and method of dissemination are ruling factors. Appropriate for use indoors are munitions that function by expulsion, liquid loadings fired from a shotgun, 37 mm or 40 mm weapon, and specially designed aerosols. Decontamination is much easier with any liquid loading. If a hostage is present, however, chemical type and deployment method must not cause panic on the part of those exposed. If there is no hostage, CS should be used in computed amounts to limit resistance.

The easiest and safest means of saturating a building is to do it from a distance with liquid projectiles fired from a shoulder weapon. These projectiles are effective both in accuracy and penetration out to 300'. When contaminating a building, first determine where you want your adversary to exit. Saturate all other areas of the building adjacent to the room occupied by the subject and expose his or her escape route last. This way you won't be playing a dangerous game of hide and seek. You can channel where you want the subject to go and who awaits his/her arrival.

Computations for agent levels must be made for individual rooms and not for the building as a whole. Based upon the length of time for symptomatic effects of the agent to occur, and knowing the size of the area, make sure you wait for the agent to act before entering. Using proper deployment techniques, it is rarely necessary to send in an extraction team. If the individual has not exited after your waiting period, you should presume that the person has protected themselves or has been overcome. Continued delivery of the agent or a change of type of agent is inappropriate. Dynamic entry techniques using K-9, stun munitions, and extraction teams should be employed.

Ideally, an evacuation of the people not required at the scene is a must. To enhance your tactical edge, have the ventilation system shut down and the water turned off before deployment. You want to isolate the person as soon as possible and eliminate the possibility that he or she might protect themselves. In a barricaded situation, do not advise your opponent of what you intend to do. You must use surprise to your benefit. Coordination of all units is the key to success.

The greatest uses of chemical agents by law enforcement are personal defense aerosol projectors. The sad part is that most of them are not personal defense oriented, but rather a game to be played. Good examples are spraying dogs and cats, spraying contact areas to secretly expose your friends, and emptying a canister on an arrestee. These problems can be traced back to a lack of training. Since this is a weapon, officers should be trained and regularly tested regarding their knowledge of the weapon, their proficiency in its use, and the agency's use of force policy. Aerosol weapons are intended to be used in one on one applications inside ten feet. They are only used to give the officer a tactical advantage over an adversary to reduce the likelihood of physical injury to anyone during the arresting process. Under no circumstances are these devices to be used to inflict punishment.

The best agents to use in an aerosol are those with an immediate effect upon contact. When dealing with individuals at close distances, it is imperative to gain the advantage quickly. Application must be to the proper area and in the proper amount. Many officers complain that aerosols don't work. Generally, the people found resistant to the immediate effects of the agent are drunks, dopers, and the mentally deranged. None of these individuals has a properly functioning sensory system that will allow them to detect and act upon what is being done to them, at least in terms of CN or CS exposure. The use of OC loading would eliminate the problem. The alternative is another level of controlling force that may result in soft tissue damage.

The training technique for the proper use of an aerosol is quite simple. First is the selection of a target area. You want to expose the mouth and nose by direct contact with either CN or OC. By exposing an individual at these locations on the body, you will insure that they experience the full range of symptomatic effects. In the case of CS, this area is appropriate if the delivery system is a mist. If it is a stream, the area directly beneath the eyes is targeted. The old idea of spraying the chest of an individual does more to contaminate the officer than anything else.

Next is the technique for delivering the liquid to the target area. While holding the device in one hand, begin to spray off the shoulder of the individual in an arcing motion, and continue to spray to the opposite shoulder. This takes care of any movement on the part of the individual to avoid the spray and gives the officer a pattern to follow. The application should last no longer than 1 to 2 seconds. If this technique is used, the officer will see the mist or stream contact the facial area of the subject. Once the officer is sure of contact, no further application is necessary. If the agent is going to work on this individual, it will do so with the singular amount applied. Any more will be excessive. For this reason, it is important to teach subject control methods in conjunction with the aerosol.

Officers employing weapons of any type against the civilian population must be able to show the reasonableness of their actions. They must know where the use of chemical munitions lies in the force continuum. When available, chemical agents are used prior to the use of impact weapons. Further, trainers are well advised to have an understanding of the medical implications of exposing the population to agents of any type. From a historical perspective, there has been no evidence to substantiate claims that the agents cause cancer, TB, Asthma, elevated blood pressure, or birth defects. There is also no supporting information to claim any ocular damage or disfigurement of the skin. All in all, these less than lethal devices work very well for what they were intended, and when used by those properly trained.

Special Thanks to Damon Wilson and Terry Thorpe of Def-Tec Corporation, Rock Creek, OH 44084, and John English of Federal Laboratories, Sattzburg, PA 15681.

Bibliography

Swearengen, T. 1966. *Tear Gas Munitions.* Springfield, IL: Charles C. Thomas.

Crockett, Thompson. 1969. *Police Chemical Agents Manual.* Washington, DC: IACP, Police Standards Division.

Jones, Eugene. 1976. *Law Enforcement Chemical Agents and Related Equipment.* Santa Cruz, CA: Davis Publishing Company, Inc.

About the Author

Mr. William E. Burroughs is currently the Assistant Director of Training for SIGARMS Academy in Exeter, NH. Prior to this position, he was the Training Coordinator for Smith & Wesson Academy in Springfield, MA for nine years. He has his MBA from Western New England College in Springfield, MA and his BS in Criminal Justice from Radford College in Radford, VA.

Andrew J. Casavant

Mr. Casavant is President of Midwest Tactical Training Institute, and an adjunct faculty member of the University of Illinois Training Institute. He is currently a part-time police officer and SWAT Team member with the City of Freeport, Illinois. He has served with several police departments from 1974 to 1984 as patrol officer, sergeant, and SWAT Team Leader. He is a Major in the Army Reserves specializing in Military Police Special Operations.

His articles have appeared in The Police Marksman, Tactical Edge, The ASLET Journal, and other law enforcement magazines. He is also on the National Advisory Board for The Police Marksman and a consultant to the National Tactical Officers Association.

Chapter 9

Tactical Principles and Concepts

by Andrew J. Casavant

An understanding of tactical principles is essential for everyone involved in law enforcement, but particularly for those confined to daily street and tactical operations.

The Relationship

Tactical teams are a necessity due to the lack of strategy and tactics on the part of most patrol officers. Our current non-strategic use of patrol units to respond to high risk situations keep our SWAT teams in business. Our patrol units, by their typical calvary charge tactics, sometimes create more problems than they solve.

Police officers are slowly becoming more aware of the risks associated with their work and beginning to look for ways to minimize the risks. Is there a relationship between teaching strategy and tactics and the minimizing of risks to officers? Officers trained to think tactically show that risk is minimized in proportion to the quality of what is taught and the regularity with which officers are exposed to such training throughout their careers.

Is there a relationship between the teaching of strategy and tactics to police officers and the minimizing of successful civil litigation involving officers receiving such training? Again, the relationship is not only real, but is proportional to the quality of that which is taught and the regularity with which officers are exposed to that training.

An officer who is philosophically in tune with a strategic approach, who can develop, modify if necessary, and execute a proper tactical plan, will generally solve most enforcement situations without resorting to the use of unnecessary force.

Why We Are Failing

What is meant when we talk about the proper teaching of strategy and tactics? Have we not taught tactics for years to our police academies? Is that not what we are doing when we teach vehicle stop procedures, building search procedures, or procedures for responding to crimes in progress? This type of training, as it is typically delivered today, has little to do with the teaching of strategy and tactics. More important, it fails to develop the ability to think tactically.

Instructors who provide students with "school solutions" are setting them up to fail when circumstances are different from those visualized by the developer of the procedures. Officers using school solutions become dogmatic thinkers unable to assess a situation and "let the circumstances dictate the tactics."

The Objective of Strategy

Strategy can best be viewed as a philosophy. The definition of philosophy is a "system of principles for the conduct of life." Thus we can view strategy as a system of risk minimizing principles for conducting our law enforcement lives. It is a mind-set that is constant whether on or off the job.

The objective of strategy is "to diminish the possibility of resistance." This objective is obtained through the use of two of the basic elements of conflict management, "movement and surprise." Movement allows an officer to gain an undetected tactical advantage, thus achieving the element of surprise resulting in minimal resistance on the part of the opponent. It must be understood that all movement is done to achieve surprise, otherwise, it is wasted effort.

Since we can count on resistance in some instances, officers must be able to overcome that resistance quickly and totally with little or no risk to themselves or others. Can this be done? Studies of human psychology tell us that most human beings are risk aversive. Many decision models in business are based on this knowledge. In other words, raise the risk level beyond what the individual is willing to bear and a change of behavior will occur. Humans almost always recognize and respond to various levels of risk. Raise that level and a solution with little or no resistance is probable. When an officer develops a tactical plan based upon such knowledge the potential for resistance is minimized. If the resistance goes down, the amount of force required to overcome that resistance goes down. If an officer is required to use less force, the probability for injury goes down, and along with it the potential of liability.

The advantage created by this type of tactical thinking starts a domino affect in favor of the officer. Constant thought must be given to living one's law enforcement life by the philosophy of "diminishing the possibility of resistance through the application of proper tactics." This may mean a complete reorientation in doing our jobs and a different way of thinking and living.

The Objective of Tactics

For the officer who thinks strategically, demonstrated by the creation of a tactical plan which minimizes risk, there can be but one objective — the creation of an advantage for himself and a recognizable disadvantage for his opponent. Just gaining the advantage is not enough. The opponent must recognize the disadvantage or they may resist. Hopefully this advantage will be announced at the officer's choosing, thus bringing into play the strategic element of surprise leaving little doubt as to where the advantage lies. Again, knowledge of risk aversion becomes an important factor in risk-minimizing activities.

Strategy enables the officer initially to deploy using the elements of "movement" in an effort to achieve the second element of "surprise." Tactics apply to risk minimizing actions during actual engagements. Building search and vehicle stop techniques certainly fall into the purview of tactics. It would appear that strategy as a philosophy is more closely related to initial response and deployment, while tactics are more related to actions which occur subsequently.

Can strategy and tactics be so clearly defined as to create a clear line between the two? Probably not, other than as definitions. One clearly relates to the other as to render such attempts futile. Philosophy (strategy) cannot be separated from actions (tactics). The intent is to merge the two concepts together into a few axioms which seem to apply in most circumstances. The result is to meet the stated objectives of strategy and tactics which diminishes the possibility of resistance through the application of a properly developed and executed tactical plan. This results in the creation of an advantage for the officer and a recognizable disadvantage for the offender.

The Principles of Conflict Management

In order to develop sound strategy and tactics, officers must have an understanding of the basic building blocks of strategy. These nine principles have governed all conflict for thousands of years. *The Art of War,* written by Sun Tzu, the Chinese military historian and strategist, has developed into the most prestigious and influential book on strategy ever written. It is the study of organizations in conflict at every level. Its aim is invincibility, victory without fighting, and overwhelming strength through the understanding of the physics, politics, and psychology of conflict. Police officers are involved in internal and external conflict and the proper application of these principles will most certainly give them the advantage.

These principles are: Objective, Offensive, Mass, Economy of Force, Maneuver, Unity of Command, Security, Surprise, and Simplicity. A brief description of each principle is intended to provide a framework for thinking, but the officer must let circumstances dictate the appropriate actions. Suffice it to say that these principles are the building blocks of all strategy and they should be viewed, not as a definition, but as a way of thinking.

1.) **Objective:** This principle addresses the direction of strategy and is the path for all actions taken. It states that actions should be directed toward a clearly defined, decisive, and obtainable goal. This is accomplished by setting time limits, the means, and the ramifications of the actions pursued. It is by far one of the most important of the principles because it determines the direction one will take. If you're not sure where you're going, you will never know if you arrived there!

2.) **Offensive:** When the opportunities come, seize them, retain them, and then exploit them to your advantage. The offensive is directed at the mental attitude of an officer, as well as his actions.

3.) **Mass:** This principle states that we need to deliver all of our power at the decisive time and place. When dealing with street level situations, a two to one advantage is necessary.

4.) **Economy of Force:** Use only what you need, no more and no less. This is difficult to do as our society has a "more is better attitude."

5.) **Maneuver:** As an element of strategy, it has but one purpose; to gain the element of surprise.

6.) **Unity of Command:** This principle is divided into two levels, tactical and logistical. At the logistical level, only those items necessary to conduct the operation should be carried or used.

At the tactical level, the offenders are our unity of command; our actions or inactions are determined by their actions or inactions. They will determine how much force to use, and they will determine the outcome.

7.) **Security:** This principle refers to undetected movement. Since we are after surprise, the opponent must never acquire an unexpected advantage. Deception is the primary tool in maintaining security.

8.) **Surprise:** Officers should always do the unexpected. They should be predictably unpredictable. They must go up against the offender at a time, a place, or in a manner that the offender is unprepared for. This will help the officers achieve the advantage. Surprise can be either partial, where the offender reacts, but the reaction is ineffective, or total, where no reaction at all is allowed.

9.) **Simplicity:** This is the common thread that binds all the others together. Keep your plans and actions simple, for even the simplest ideas become very complicated actions during combat.

Tactical Planning Principles

▸ **Undetected Movement:** Since surprise is the key to placing your opponent at the disadvantage, thus reducing resistance, this is a crucial principle to understand and execute. In fact, it is by far the most important, for it allows us to apply the other planning principles.

Whenever an officer responds to a call, the first act is to observe what is going on. Being able to observe is critical to

Tactical Principles and Concepts

a successful conclusion. More problems are caused by the knowledge that the police have arrived. This allows the offender to prepare defenses. Violations of this planning principle have forced financial institutions to implement policies requiring employees not to activate silent alarms until the offenders have left the premises. This is, of course, due to the reasonable fear that the police will arrive and cause more serious problems.

Movement to the scene as an element of strategy requires undetected movement. This allows the offenders to conclude their activities and depart without the knowledge that they are under surveillance and that a plan is underway to effect their arrest. This should minimize risk to victims and facilitate the offender's apprehension through the element of surprise.

Undetected movement may require that an officer locate himself further from the scene, rather than ignore the principle and pull up to the front door. In fact, the whole concept flies in the face of current police actions which normally require high visibility.

Optical aids such as binoculars are an essential piece of patrol equipment. They allow officers to stay at a safe distance and observe. Small, roof prism binoculars are inexpensive and very effective. Other weapons might be considered in lieu of the handgun due to this type of deployment.

Undetected movement has to do with more than just not being seen. It also covers the area of noise discipline and the effective use of lighting to conceal oneself. This requires practice and all officers must have a thorough understanding of those elements in order to approach and remain undetected.

Needless to say, application of this principle will require much modification in the way most officers currently do their jobs. However, if nothing more tactical than this is done, we could significantly reduce injuries to both officers and the public.

- **If You Can See Them, They Can See You:** This basic truth has always been important to officers who want to remain undetected. There are numerous examples of officers who failed to understand this simple principle. The officer killed by Charles Whitman, the "Texas Tower Sniper," provides a most poignant illustration. The officer, observing the tower from a cement wall, was looking through a 12" hole in that wall, at a very tiny, pin like figure of Whitman several hundred feet above him. Whitman, who was observing the officer through a scoped rifle, had a perfect view and made a head shot on the officer.

Taking this principle one step further to allow for the

height or lighting advantage, you would have to include the following statement, "Even if I can't see you, I must assume that you can see me." Whoever occupies the high ground has the advantage, and whoever has the darker of the two environments has the advantage. So remember, to look up and take to the shadows to give yourself an edge.

Once you have violated the principle of undetected movement, the offender takes charge and you can now only react to his plan.

Closer Is Not Always Better: The typical response of officers to in-progress calls is to get right on top of the building. This is due in large part to previous training in which officers were taught to "corner" the building. That is exactly what they do. It is interesting to note that no building has ever escaped from the police, only people have.

This principle is affected in three major areas. Much of this is learned by officers during defensive tactics training when they are constantly reminded to STAY AWAY! Take that same thought and apply it to a tactical situation. You would want to stay away because it is much safer. Getting close is dangerous and the odds against you go up. Eventually you will have to get in close, but try to do it on your own terms after you have had time to observe and assess.

Staying further away also allows you to react. Again, this is nothing new. If you stand close to someone, they can hit you faster than you can react, since action is always faster than reaction. Staying away also allows you to see more. The closer you are the more narrow your vision. Move away and your vision widens. The reason officers have to do the "quick peek" is due to the fact that they cannot see. The quick peek doesn't cure that. Only moving away from the item you are behind will allow you to see more, safely.

It is not difficult to see why closer is not always better. It is closely tied to the principle of undetected movement.

Make Or Let Them Come To You: Violations of this critical principle is usually preceded by violations of one or more of the previously discussed principles. Officers tend to get themselves into positions that require split-second decision making, thus giving the offenders the advantage.

Application of this principle requires that officers overcome the aggressive nature most of them exhibit when they think, or feel, that they have to go to the offenders. When we go to the offenders, they have the advantage, especially if they know we are coming.

Officers who operate with this principle in mind will think tactically, thus bringing into play the two elements of strategy, movement and surprise. This should minimize re-

Tactical Principles and Concepts

sistance, but if resistance should occur, it will be the police officer who is ready and waiting, and not the offender!

Any time that you must go to the offender, the risk to you goes up. This is especially true during patrol operations where your uniform and equipment may not be suitable to stealthy movements. It is much easier to lie in wait, and let the offender enter your area of operation.

Knowledge of Terrain: Perhaps the "knowledge of terrain" is as much related to strategy as it is to tactics. Certainly, no one has studied the art of combat without understanding the importance of knowing the "lay of the land."

If you review the previously stated principles, you will discover that optimal application of any of them is dependent on the knowledge of terrain. How could you move undetected without knowing the terrain? How could you know that they could possibly see, you even if you couldn't see them, unless you had knowledge of the terrain?

Knowledge of terrain goes much further than just knowing your beat. Knowing your beat is a rudimentary understanding of this principle. However, other important tactical considerations must be taken into account if you are to grasp this principle. Cover, concealment, and lighting are all very important, if you are to exploit the knowledge of terrain.

Walking these areas in both daylight and darkness will provide the kind of information you need to make proper deployment choices without violating one of the other principles. Study the terrain from the only point of view that counts in law enforcement — the offenders. Go into that convenience store and see what they will see if they are looking for you, because they will be! The knowledge of their terrain will make a difference on how you might deploy next time. Count on it!

There you have it! These five principles form the basis for developing tactical plans that give the officer the advantage. All strategic planning is guided by the nine principles of conflict management. The tactics or actions for deployment, such as those mentioned, must be part of the officers thinking.

This thought process will create plans that place the offender at a recognizable disadvantage while giving the officer the advantage. The officer that integrates these into his behavior will always be able to "let the circumstances dictate his tactics."

How hard will it be to change the behavior of today's officers? The answer lies with you. You are responsible for your safety and for your actions which have a direct impact on the safety of others. Thinking tactically is the most powerful weapon at your disposal. Use it and you may not have to resort to other weapons to solve law enforcement problems.

Dr. James T. Chandler

Dr. Chandler is an individual contractor in the areas of training, seminar presentation, writing, speaking, and personnel management consultation. His last full-time assignment was as Chief State Police Psychologist for the Illinois State Police. Dr. Chandler's book, Modern Police Psychology, began distribution in the Spring of 1990.

Chapter 10

Psychological Survival for Police Officers

by Dr. James T. Chandler

In 1960, an officer had a gun thrust in his face. The trigger was pulled, but the gun misfired. He became highly upset, even hysterical, at the scene. "No way would I react like that," you say! Are you sure?

Psychological survival in law enforcement involves physical, mental, emotional, and social components, and have both short and long term aspects. A significant weakness in any of these areas can destroy an officer, let alone a career.

Psychological survival is a professional skill, like pursuit driving or the proper use of a gun. While there are inherited and experiential factors involved, psychological survival strength needs to be enhanced by deliberate education and training.

Before retiring as a police psychologist, the author evaluated many officers for the potential of psychological survival. For example, we needed to know who could handle the mental and emotional stresses of those considered for assignment to tactical response, hostage negotiation, child abuse, and peer counseling duties.

This chapter will review some of the areas a police psychologist assesses in reviewing the psychological survival potential of an officer. Let's make that officer **you.**

Psychological Strength and Physical Conditioning

First, psychological strength is strongly tied to physical conditioning, and to personal health in general. Proper physical conditioning not only makes one less physically vulnerable, but more important, raises mental confidence levels.

Have you ever described your basic training as something you are glad you experienced, but something you would not want to do again? What you probably value from your rookie training is the realization that you have more of the "right stuff" than you had previously believed.

Military and law enforcement basic training programs traditionally push cadets to their physical limits. These procedures also significantly increase their ability to withstand future mental and emotional pressures, and as a graduating cadet might say, "What else can they do to me?"

Many officers, however, develop life styles after basic training that tear down many of the gains achieved. To give one example, the ability to resist the negative mental and emotional effects of stress, burnout, and trauma is severely hampered by a lack of proper sleep.

Officers who display pride in getting by with a few hours of sleep a day, who fail to attain proper rapid eye movement (REM) sleep because of the effects of alcohol, or who remain on hostage scenes without sleep for too many hours, significantly reduce their potential for psychological survival.

Similar examples of self-defeating physical life styles include poor nutrition, strength training without a built-in endurance factor, physical conditioning fanaticism, and a lack of a proper weight control program.

For purposes of this chapter, however, let us assume that you have no obvious weaknesses in the area of physical conditioning or personal health (a big assumption, right?). In any event, we assess you as at least normal as to the physical ability to face stress.

Psychological Strength and Mental Conditioning

We next assess your mental conditioning, including your control of basic thought processes and your possession of proper psychological survival information. We are essentially appraising your ability to concentrate under stress, and to accept and properly apply scientific knowledge of psychological survival.

Do you have difficulty concentrating on complex tasks under high stress? Does your crisis behavior seem to follow the rule: "When in trouble or in doubt, scream and shout and run about?" Do you react with "no-brainers" in tough situations?

We would want to determine if you have gained sufficient information about the aspects of physical and psychological survival through attendance at presentations like the *Street Survival* series put on by Calibre Press.

Have you completed any college courses in behavioral psychology? Have you attended, and taken seriously, in-service programs in law enforcement stress? Have you learned to separate fact from fantasy about stress, burnout, crisis, and trauma in policing?

Unfortunately, there are reporters, police academy instructors, novelists, police officers, and even psychologists who "know" police work is more stressful than all other occupations. This myth continues to flourish in law enforcement circles in spite of considerable research to the contrary.

Are you aware of these prevailing and harmful myths, such as the myth that suicide, alcoholism, and divorce are higher in our profession than in almost all others? If not, such negative myths can become self-fulfilling prophecies, significantly increasing your feelings of psychological vulnerability and undermining your coping abilities.

Are you familiar with the problems of self-destructive behavior in law enforcement? Your psychological survival odds are dramatically reduced if you possess an insatiable pursuit of excitement. This life-style leads to a degree of risk-taking that exceeds reasonable boundaries of safety, survival, and self-preservation.

We know that law enforcement stress reactions are more a function of personality traits than on-the-job experience. The rigid, cynical, "John Wayne" type officer is more likely to suffer from the effects of a stressful incident than more flexible, positive, and mature officers.

"John Wayne, Jane Wayne, or Wyatt Earp" behavior creates needless physical danger. However, the real danger of this behavior pattern, as seen in this police psychologist's practice, is the inevitable **psychological** burnout that results.

In his younger days, before assuming the deck and conn on a destroyer, the writer was taught to review the steps necessary to perform a "man overboard" evolution. Do you mentally rehearse the steps required in successfully handling at least one crisis situation prior to going on duty?

If assigned desk duty, have you mentally worked out the procedures necessary to handle a walk-in with a gun? If you are assigned telecommunications duties, do you routinely rehearse the steps required for an "officer needs help" situation **before** sitting at the console?

We might ask if you, on a regular basis, rehearse the steps required following a computer "hit" while on patrol, or if you mentally rehearse the steps for proper CPR periodically.

Many of you have imagined, and some have experienced, a situation culminating in the use of deadly force. We have been trained to rehearse mentally what we should be doing, for example, if the bad guy's gun starts moving in our direction. Issues such as body positioning, available cover, and distance factors come to mind.

How many of you, however, continue the mental rehearsal of that scenario? After shooting a perpetrator, are you clear what your next steps are, or will you just "wing it?"

When do you use the radio — before or after checking the condition of those involved? What do you say (or not say) on the air? Would it be wise to work out some wording beforehand? How will you sound on tape if a law suit results — like someone in control or like Mickey Mouse?

What steps are necessary to preserve evidence and to make adequate preparation for a resulting court case? Who do you trust to come to the scene to protect your rights after a critical incident?

Do you have knowledge of an acceptable mental health professional who understands police work? How about an attorney? Have you had enough contact with them so you are not strangers? Which of your peers will remain calm and objective? Which department administrators will be the most helpful?

What does your department's public relations directive require if you are approached by the media immediately after the incident? What conscious control over your appearance and behavior will be necessary?

Are you familiar with recommended steps for getting through the first night after a critical incident? At what point do you demand the right to sleep, so as to avoid foolish actions or statements.

I hope the point has been made that a repeated mental rehearsal of proper action in the minutes, and indeed hours, **following** a critical incident are at least as important as rehearsal of actions prior to such incidents.

All too often, proper actions during a crisis are outweighed by improper actions that follow. A controlled, one-step-at-a-time approach has been found to be the most effective method of handling post-crisis situations.

Now let us assume that you are mentally prepared to handle psychological stresses, that you practice good thought control and have gained sufficient knowledge of stress reactions. What about emotional preparedness?

Have you experienced, and successfully handled, a sufficient number of emotionally-charged situations? Are you familiar with both normal and abnormal reactions following crisis situations? Are you really sure you know what behaviors are abnormal under severe stress?

The writer has found that some degree of previous emotional trauma better prepares an individual to handle and survive crises. Thus, when an officer states he or she has had a "bad life," the response has often been, "Congratulations — you should be able to handle police work." It is as if the body and mind say, "I've been here before and survived — I can do it again."

However, too many or too severe life crises can mean officers have reached a point very near to their limit. A crisis then, especially one similar in nature to previous ones, can cause officers to "crash and burn." It is these individuals the writer often attempted to screen out of high stress or dangerous duties.

The mental rehearsal of optimistic statements, such as, "I will remain in control," instead of, "I'll try not to lose control," has proved to be an effective approach in handling crises. The concentration, then, is on eliminating the cynical and pessimistic thought process too often revealed by law enforcement veterans.

In addition, individuals who effectively handle crises are adept at a process called "reframing," in which they deliberately change their frame of mind when they find it to be negative. They can readily change a "half-empty" attitude to one of "half-full."

Access to Psychological Counseling

If you have a winning mind-set prior to a traumatic incident, there is less likelihood that chronic symptoms, such as depression or anger, will result. However, a sufficiently severe situation, such as the murder of a fellow officer, or too many crises in succession, can overtax the emotional resources of any officer.

The question then becomes, does the officer have access to appropriate psychological counseling services? Returning to the situation involving the officer reacting to a gun stuck in his face, the man missed no seriously consider what role you should be assuming in our profession. Have you noticed that high speed chases, lights, and sirens have lost their charm? Should you be backing off and avoiding as much trauma as possible? Haven't you paid your dues? Don't you owe it to your family?

Over time, our survival resources decrease, not only from the natural aging processes, but also from varying degrees of professional burnout. Please consider retiring from this exciting, but stressful, profession at your earliest opportunity. Save your remaining psychological survival resources for a new profession — that of retirement.

How does one sum up the topic of psychological survival for police officers? First, make sure you have the necessary physical, mental, emotional, and social elements in your life. After that, keep repeating to yourself and to others: **"I know how to survive, I can survive, and I will survive."**

Jim Cirillo

Mr. Cirillo is a 22-year, veteran police officer of the New York City Police Department, five years of which was spent in the Stakeout Squad. Prior to the NYPD, Mr. Cirillo was Chief of Firearms' Training with U.S. Customs for four years, and then with the Federal Law Enforcement Training Center for ten years.

Jim was in 17 direct armed encounters and receives many requests for consultation. He recently had patented a new bullet for law enforcement with radical expansion properties.

Chapter 11

Stress of the Gunfight

by Jim Cirillo

I'm sure unseasoned law enforcement officers wonder how they would react in a gunfight. In that moment of truth a miraculous reaction manifests itself.

Many of you have heard stories of a woman of normal size lifting an automobile off her child who was run down, or of other amazing feats that appear to be impossible? When we hear these stories, we tend to disbelieve them. I no longer disbelieve. As a result of participating in several gunfights, I have learned that we are capable of superhuman feats when placed under stress.

If you turn a corner and walk into a gunfight, you will react as you were trained — and these are key words — "as you were trained." If you were properly trained, you should be diving for cover. This is at the top of the survival tactic's list. Drawing your weapon should follow. You will probably survive your first gunfight, if you react with reflex as you were trained.

A reaction called fear may appear: butterflies in the stomach; a wobble in the knees; and a feeling of disbelief. You may feel stress, physiologically and psychologically. This occurs as a post syndrome reaction to the gunfight. This is normal. Before, you had too many defensive physical things to do to protect yourself. Now that your mind is free from thinking of physical defense, you realize just how close to death you came. I have spoken with many fellow officers who also experienced this phenomenon.

If prior to your first gunfight, you have moments to expect that gun play is imminent, it can be most horrifying. This happened to me during my first gunfight. It was evident by the actions of the four males who entered the establishment I was staking out, that an armed robbery was about to take place. In those terrifying moments, I wondered, "Will I fail?" "Will I be killed?" Self doubt and fear grab you.

A feeling of intense weakness came over me. I felt as though my limbs were coming apart and my bones had melted. I mentally cursed myself for feeling so much fear. When three of the robbers produced weapons and placed them to the heads of the cashier and manager, I knew that despite my fear, I had to challenge the gunmen before any harm came to the cashier or the manager.

As I popped up from concealment to make my challenge, I experienced a miraculous phenomenon. My pistol sights came into view as clearly and precisely as though I were at one of the many pistol matches I had attended. My mind proceeded to commit the gunmen into blurs of a color-coded scenario. Blue and Black melted into Gray as two of the gunmen jumped behind the cashier, who was wearing a gray shop coat. My pistol sights quickly shifted to gunman Green. I dared not fire with the cashier acting as a shield for Blue and Black. Green had crouched down and was running toward Gray to use her as cover. At that moment, a white object appeared in Green's raised arm. I asked myself, "Is he raising a white handkerchief in an act of surrender?" At precisely that moment, I heard a shot and saw a blaze of fire emit from my pistol barrel. I felt the revolver bucking in my hand, not once, but several times, and I questioned myself as to who the hell was shooting my weapon? Green disappeared.

I shifted my attention to Blue and Black who were partially exposed on both sides of Gray. I fired on Blue and Black with intention. They were still armed and heading for the exit. Gray was frozen in her tracks and did not duck down as she was previously instructed to do. Blue and Black, as well as Green, were now out of view.

According to the manager, all of this action took only three to four seconds, which I found hard to believe. To me, everything appeared to be happening in slow motion. As the smoke cleared, I found Green dying near the cashier.

I was relieved to find that what I thought was a white flag of surrender was actually a nickel-plated revolver with one shot expended. The bullet was found lodged in a can of Planters Peanuts just in front of my position behind the Planters Peanuts display! I was also relieved that I had at least been able to stop one robber. Ten minutes later, over the police radio came information that two males dressed in black and blue clothing were apprehended in a doctor's office seeking medical attention for several bullet wounds.

I could not comprehend how I was able to take out three gunmen when I was so consumed with fear prior to the gunfight. I also dared not speak of the strange phenomenon when I felt that someone else was shooting my revolver. Later, I understood that this miraculous reaction, that probably saved my life, was from the subconscious.

I remembered that I had felt a similar reaction on several occasions in police pistol competitions. Once, as I walked off the firing line, everybody started to congratulate me. I wondered why. I had not realized that I shot an outstanding score or that others had been shooting in competition next to me. It was the subconscious taking over due to the stress induced by my desire to win, or not to lose, the competition. I realized that whenever I was under a great deal of stress during competition, I almost always shot a near record score, even beyond my best practice scores.

The shots I made during my first gunfight were so precise and quick that consciously I have not been able to duplicate them at a range on paper targets. The noted firearms' instructor, Colonel Jeff Cooper, has developed this gunfight into his program and calls it the "Cirillo Drill." I believe Ray Chapman, another notable firearms' instructor, is the only man who has been able to achieve this feat successfully on paper targets.

I do not wish to convey to the reader that these reactions are unique to rare individuals, or to me. I am normal. In fact, I consider myself to be — if not a coward — not brave beyond the average person. Throughout my life, I knew many people bolder and braver than me, and I always admired their self assurance.

How then was I able to perform such a feat? From the first day my weapon was given to me, I was afraid of it. I shot it from every conceivable position I could think of — one hand, two hands, and weak hand — and each time I shot, it was with great fear. I knew I must learn to shoot the weapon well as my life or someone else's may depend on it. I practiced diligently and frequently.

The subconscious mind had committed all the practice into my memory banks like some super computer. When my conscious mind went haywire from stress, the infallible subconscious mind came forward to save my skin. If you are one of those blessed, self-assured people, your conscious mind will probably serve you as well as my subconscious mind did in my first gunfight. Once self confidence is achieved by successful performance in succeeding gunfights, most of the stress factors will disappear. By the fourth or fifth gunfight, the most you may feel is slight excitement, but that first one is the tough one!

Train yourself well and assure yourself with the knowledge that the fear and stress of your first gunfight will be overcome with your ability enhanced by the subconscious.

It is your subconscious mind that allows you to catch a falling glass, even when your conscious mind is occupied elsewhere. An example would be, if suddenly an object were thrown at you when you least expected it, you would automatically block it without any conscious thought. First, conscious thought would have to be registered in the brain. Then, the brain would have to prod the conscious mind to move the arms and hands to block the object. All of this conscious thought requires reaction time which would not be fast enough to block the flying object, unless you were previously aware that it was coming.

The subconscious is there to protect us. It knows that it must act faster than the conscious mind can react. From infancy on, we were taught that objects flying in our direction could harm us. We were probably even hurt by some. Now this information is filed away in our instant reaction computer, "the miraculous subconscious."

In all of my firearms' courses, I strive to program my students' subconscious reactions I know they may need if (God forbid) suddenly confronted with the moment of truth. To the reader I say, "Practice every chance you get and escalate the stress of the course gradually until your confidence and ability increase. Get a buddy, and each of you design firearms' training courses that are unknown to the other. Push each other to react instantly, and watch how, as the stress builds, the subconscious mind comes forth to help you achieve that which would be difficult with the conscious mind alone.

Bill Clede

Mr. Clede is a former law enforcement officer and nationally renowned law enforcement journalist and author. He is extremely knowledgeable in the various microcomputer applications for law enforcement. He is also an active member of the American Society of Law Enforcement Trainers (ASLET) and the International Association of Law Enforcement Firearms' Instructors (IALEFI).

Chapter 12

Personal Development

by Bill Clede

There is little practical difference between a police officer and any other person, but that word "practical" is significant. Cops are people, too. We suffer the same hurts and have the same marital problems. Law enforcement isn't the only stressful profession. Police officers are not unlike others who must complete rigorous training and meet requirements for continuing in-service training.

Since we are trained to do a job requiring a high level of personal integrity and diverse performance, police officers really are held to a higher standard by society than untrained civilians. Civilian professionals are trained in specific fields. Engineers and doctors are experts in their fields, but what is the police officer's field, really? Law enforcement, sure, but what does that mean?

A police officer is expected to deal with people ranging from a felon with no regard for human life, to a little old grandmother who didn't see the stop sign. We're expected to arbitrate a marital dispute and break up a riot. We must exercise judgement to immediately recognize whether the guy running out of the store with a shotgun is a crazed criminal, scared kid, or the store owner chasing the perpetrator.

Training

Your chief doesn't want you to expose the department to liability, yet he expects you to do your job. He also knows that he must provide you with training.

In Leite v. City of Providence (1978), the court decided that the town, and not just the police officer, could be held liable if the plaintiff's injury resulted from non-existent or grossly inadequate training and supervision of the police department.

Popow v. City of Margate (1979) applied the Leite decision to the type of training provided. Margate's officers received basic training at the state police academy and in-service firearms' training on the range every six months. The case concerned the fatal nighttime shooting of an innocent bystander by a police officer in a residential community. Range training provided no instruction in shooting at a moving target, night shooting, shooting in residential areas, or any other shooting decisions. Evidence was presented that the chief considered the rules of firing on residential streets a matter of common sense, not requiring detailed explanations. The court held that to be "grossly inadequate" training and found for the plaintiff.

Whatever your employer's training budget, and you can be sure it's not enough, you are judged by what you do and how you act. It's in your own interest to get training on you own, even if it is not provided.

Personality

I'm convinced, it takes a special kind of person to be a police officer. Aside from the stamina to endure verbal abuse, you must remain alert during hours of monotonous patrol, yet react quickly when you need to. You must be able to switch instantly from a state of near somnambulism to an adrenalin-filled struggle for survival. You must learn your patrol area so well that you can recognize what's out of the ordinary. You are a part of your business community. And after all that, you must remember that you are the personification of your town, city, and state. The image of your area is perceived by visitors on the basis of the image **you** project.

It takes initiative, effective judgment, and imagination to cope with the complex situations that you must face — family disturbance, potential suicide, robbery in progress, gory accident, or natural disaster.

Police officers must be able to size up a situation instantly and react properly, and even make a life or death decision in some cases. You need mature judgment to determine whether an offender should be warned, ticketed, or arrested. You need self-restraint to use only the degree of force justified by the circumstances.

You need the initiative to perform your functions while your supervisor is far away. Yet, you must be able to be part of a strike force team under the direct command of a superior when called upon. You need to take charge in chaotic situations, but avoid alienating participants or bystanders. You must be a helpful influence when crowds gather, yet be able to single out and placate an agitator trying to cause a riot.

Police officers must have curiosity tempered with tact, yet be skillful in questioning people, ranging from a traumatized victim to a suspected perpetrator. You must be brave enough to face an armed criminal, yet gentle enough to help a woman deliver a baby; cope with the stress of a deadly assault, yet remain alert on patrol during the wee hours when everyone else is asleep. You must maintain a balanced perspective in the face of exposure to the worst side of human nature, yet be objective in dealing with the public.

As if all this isn't enough, police officers must be adept in a variety of psychomotor skills: operating a vehicle in emergency situations; using weapons properly under adverse conditions; and maintaining their own agility, endurance, and strength in applying techniques to defend themselves while detaining a subject with a minimum of force.

Then, when it's all over, you must be able to explain what happened — in writing, to someone who wasn't there, in such a way that there's no opportunity for misunderstanding, and document your actions so you can relate your reasons years later.

Attitudes

The public's attitude toward police officers is influenced by the individual's family life, past experience in school, present environment, and encounters with police officers.

Your own attitude determines the respect you get as a police officer. If you act like a professional, others will see you as a professional.

Career Development

The professional development of its officers is a concern of every police department. Many send officers to outside courses that help them develop into more valuable employees. You may have to argue, cajole, and stubbornly persist in submitting applications, but opportunities are there. Professional development is a key factor in anyone's success, but it won't just come to you. You need to work on it through your entire career.

A trainer I know told me about a college police officer he came to know quite well. The officer attended many of the trainer's courses on his own. He paid his own way. That officer paid attention to career opportunities. He applied for the job of chief in a neighboring state, and got it.

It Depends On You

Few people in today's work force have active professional development agendas. You need to have a future vision. What conditions and requirements do you expect will face your field in the future? Projecting that, identify what you must do to fit into that picture.

> **Know yourself:** Recognize your own levels of knowledge and skill, career stage, professional and organizational contributions, competency strengths, and the knowledge and skills

you want to develop. Ask those who have worked with you to help you assess yourself.

- **Have a system:** What are the top professional challenges you'll face in the next five years? Who else will be facing these issues, or who will have a useful perspective on them? Seek associates who will be helpful in developing your own skills. Attending conferences or professional associations puts you in touch with others who have similar interests. You learn not only from the seminars, but even through conversations beside the swimming pool.

- **Develop a plan:** Define your goals. Set reasonable short-term intentions. Plan what you need to do to meet those aims. Then review and revise your plan every year.

- **Develop learning skills:** Continually improve your ability to listen, concentrate, read, think, explore ideas openly, and generate innovative ideas. You can learn from surprising sources, but you need to think critically to recognize and control your own biases and blind spots.

Promotions Are Earned

Department policies, and possibly a union contract, spell out the exact procedures for promotions, but once all except the top few candidates are eliminated, how is the final decision made? Very likely the subjective opinions that your superiors passed on as recommendations to the boss. Everything you do from day one, your performance on the job, influences those opinions. Do you arrive for work on time? Are you eager to learn? Do you find things to investigate when you're on patrol? Do you seek training on your own?

Many students in police training courses are not sent by their employers who pay the bill. They are conscientious officers who foot their own tuition to get training.

A positive job attitude is the willingness to slosh through a swamp after a subject, to accept onerous assignments and do them with a professional effectiveness, to back up your partner in the face of danger, to plan a patrol so you're likely to be in the right spot at the right time, and to seek every opportunity to improve yourself.

An officer's professional performance is the basis for the effectiveness reports that a supervisor writes. The completeness of reports, judgment in exercising the duties of your office, and relationships with the community can all influence a supervisor's opinions when they are asked to evaluate you.

Document What You Do

If you've been in police work any time at all, you know the job isn't completed until the paperwork is done. (I shouldn't have to explain that familiar cartoon.) Well, it holds true for your career advancement.

Of course your department maintains records of every course **they send you to**. They maintain records to show the state they've met the requirements of in-service training, but are they as diligent in maintaining records of other training you've received? What about the course you attended on you own? If you reported it and filed a copy of your certificate, perhaps a secretary got around to entering it into the computer. I snuck a peek at my training records once. I was aghast at the inaccuracies and incompleteness. What can you do about it? Maintain your own records.

You are the one who needs proof of training. Keep your original certificates in your own file. Give the department a machine copy. Make a list of every course, with dates, summary, and ratings conferred, if any.

What about other training? Isn't reading this book training? This is a study project. Read the book. Make note in your training records that you read it and when you completed it. Remember, you're going to have to remember all these details years from now, and explain it to someone who wasn't there, in terms that leave no room for misunderstanding. I don't care if what you read was a Joseph Wambaugh novel. *The Onion Field*, for example, could influence an action you take in the future. Make note of it.

The more items you can list in your personal training record, the more credible is your claim to knowing what you're doing. When you go for Sergeant, you take a test. Then you endure the oral board. They know what score you got on the test. That doesn't matter any more, but you might be able to slip in the comment that you found particularly interesting a certain part of the book on how to be a great sergeant. Without even telling anyone you read the book, the board members might think, "Gee, this guy is really working at getting promoted."

Your personal training record might serve you in ways you didn't think of when you started it.

Suppose a friend of yours has Epilepsy, and because of that, you read up on the subject and learned better how to help your friend when he has a seizure. Make note of it. Who could possibly care that you've become familiar with a malady that affects many people?

You're in court. You're called to the stand. The obnoxious drunk who tried to remove your paternal instincts testifies that he's an Epileptic and was having a seizure at the time. Since you have some knowledge on the subject, **and can document your training**, you suddenly become a qualified witness instead of just a poor cop who's in over his head.

I spent too many years behind the badge to not recognize our penchant for being something beyond an ordinary citizen. We are! That doesn't mean that what we are doesn't influence the job we try to do. Remember, I said cops are people, too. When you get on a witness stand, you are what you can show yourself to be. You **can** be a firearms' expert, forensics expert, domestic dispute expert, or any other kind of expert your interests take you. All you have to do is show credentials to prove your expertise.

Your credentials are your training record — the department's if **they** are trying to show your qualifications — your own if the department's records aren't up to date.

Chapter 13

Police Fitness

by Dr. Thomas R. Collingwood

Why Be Fit?

The unique physical performance demands on the police officer needs to be accounted for in designing a Physical Fitness Program. For the past fifteen years, the Cooper Institute for Aerobics Research has been involved in developing physical fitness programs for public safety agencies. From this experience, many trends have been noted which help define the need for fitness.

National Trends

General national trends: Physical fitness is viewed as a public health issue. It is **not** a fad. For the American society as a whole, fitness is being institutionalized, with a massive expansion of worksite, home, and recreational programs. Specific national goals have been set because the value of fitness has been proven.

The U.S. Department of Health and Human Services through the Healthy People 2000 report made specific recommendations regarding the health habits of the American population. Examples are as follows:

- Reduce to no more than 15% the proportion of people aged 6 and older who engage in **no** leisure-time physical activity.

- Reduce coronary heart disease deaths to no more than 100 per 100,000 people.

- Increase the proportion of work sites offering employee sponsored physical activity and fitness programs as follows:

Worksite Size	2000 Target
50-59 employees	20%
100-249 employees	35%
Greater than 750 employees	80%

Physical fitness definition: There is a growing consensus that physical fitness is defined as the following:
1.) aerobic power
2.) strength
3.) flexibility
4.) body composition

These factors are recognized as having a bearing on disease risk and maintenance of physical performance capacity.

A Physical Fitness Rationale for Police Officer Fitness

Physical fitness is now viewed as being job related for the police officer. Research conducted by the Cooper Institute has focused on assessing the job relatedness of fitness. Generally, the following police officer profile is found:

- Lower fitness and work capacity compared to the general population.

- High incidence of early retirement and disability for lifestyle related diseases (heart disease, back problems).

- Higher than average health risk for heart disease and cancer (high blood pressure, high cholesterol, high percent fat).

- High levels of reported stress.

As a consequence, the goal for law enforcement fitness is to change lifestyles to improve these fitness and health profiles. The justification for law enforcement fitness is three-fold: 1) physiological readiness, 2) health risk reduction, and 3) psychological control.

Physiological readiness: Fitness is shown to have a bearing on an officer's readiness to perform strenuous activity. In terms of physiological readiness, underlying fitness factors have emerged from the Cooper Institute research to include the following:
1.) aerobic capacity
2.) body composition
3.) upper body strength
4.) trunk strength
5.) lower back flexibility
6.) agility
7.) leg power
8.) anaerobic power

These fitness areas are shown to account for or predict officers' performances of a variety of physically demanding job tasks (i.e. pushing a car, dragging a body, foot pursuit, self-defense, etc.). As such, they have construct validity for being job related.

Health risk reduction: In terms of risk reduction, a major rationale is for physical activity to serve as a preventive and rehabilitative activity for improving known health risks of police officers. There are mixed results regarding the mortality of police officers versus the general population. However, some research indicates a higher than average risk for death due to heart disease. Data specifically reflective of police officers indicate that lower levels of risk are associated with higher levels of fitness.

Physical fitness is a risk factor for many health and occupational problems. By effecting health status, studies show that absenteeism and injury rates can be reduced by fitness program participation. Since police work is not demanding enough to maintain fitness, an activity program is required. When programs are applied, an increase in fitness has a favorable impact on lowered cardiovascular risk.

Psychological control: Part of being trained and being fit is having more physiological and psychological control of your body. This has specific implications for managing stress. There are three major purposes that a physical program can be used for to prevent or reduce stress:

- **Increased fitness.** A physical program can directly: a) build up adaptive energy, b) make the body more efficient so less adaptive energy is needed to meet stress situations, c) serve as protection by keeping the body strong and flexible to reduce physical tension, and d) positively affect many physiological and emotional factors related to stress.
- **Release.** The physical exercise can provide a release of tension and serve as a modified fight-flight reaction.
- **Relaxation**. The physical program can provide a healthy diversion from day-to-day stress and provides a sedative effect through physical fatigue.

Maintaining fitness also has implications for controlling the use of force. With all the concern expressed by the media and administration over the use of excessive force, the maintenance of fitness can serve to help deal with that problem.

A Personal Rationale

All of the foregoing rationale points are but a professional justification for mandatory fitness as it pertains to your job as a peace officer. However, experience confirms that getting on an exercise program is a **personal** decision and commitment. Consequently, a personal rationale needs to be developed.

There are a variety of benefits of exercise. So whatever the reason, it is important that you define **your** reason to be fit.

Survival: You may or may not have defined a personal reason for exercise. Regardless, there is a **very major reason** to exercise, and that is survival.

From a health perspective, research indicates that fit people may live longer, but more important, the quality of life is better. With lowered disease risk, one can expect to get more out of life, not just more life.

From a job perspective, fit individuals survive both physical traumas (gunshot wounds) and cardiovascular traumas (heart attacks) at an increased rate. If individuals are more physically fit, they are more capable of performing critical physical tasks, whether in foot pursuit or forceful arrests.

From a psychological perspective, fit individuals are better prepared to handle the stress of the job, whether they be family disturbance calls, rotating shift work, or marital problems.

To be fully performing police officers with some positive job satisfaction, they must be prepared, physically and mentally, to perform the job. The key word is preparation or readiness. Fitness is a survival skill; it makes one **ready**.

Developing a Fitness Program

Designing and starting a fitness program follows a certain sequence. As an adult, it is not just a question of getting some jogging shoes and sweats and going to the gym. There are four steps to setting up your program.
1.) Health and medical screening
2.) Fitness assessment
3.) Fitness goal setting
4.) Designing your exercise prescription

Health and Medical Screening

Due to the prevalence of certain health problems, such as heart disease and hypertension, it is necessary to be screened to insure that exercise can be performed safely. The general recommendation is to obtain a physical clearance before starting a program, especially if you are middle-aged or older (> 40), male, sedentary, or overweight. One method to see if a medical checkup is required is to answer the following questionnaire:

Readiness Questionnaire

If any of these items are answered "yes," it is suggested you get a medical check-up.

___ Yes   1. At the time of your last medical examination, were

___ No   you advised of any medical problems or limitations

Police Fitness

on your fitness duty?

___ Yes
___ No
2. Do you frequently suffer from pains in your heart or chest?

___ Yes
___ No
3. Do you often feel faint or have episodes of severe dizziness?

___ Yes
___ No
4. Has a doctor ever told you that you have heart trouble?

___ Yes
___ No
5. Has a doctor ever told you that your blood pressure was too high?

___ Yes
___ No
6. Has a doctor ever told that you have a bone or joint problem, such as arthritis, that has been aggravated by exercise or might be made worse with exercise?

7. Do you have any of the following medical conditions? (check if you do)

___ Muscular disorder

___ High blood pressure or use of medication to control blood pressure

___ Heart disease

___ Asthma

___ Seizure disorder

___ Significantly overweight

___ Alcoholism

___ Anemia

___ Lung disease

___ Liver disease

___ Kidney disease

___ Diabetes Mellitus

___ Sickle Cell Anemia

___ Gastrointestinal Ulcer

___ History of heat stroke

Fitness Assessment

Once you have screened yourself for participation, the next step is to assess your fitness level. If you have been training regularly, then you can take the full fitness assessment. If you have not been exercising for several years, then you just need to take the "starter" assessment which is a simple one mile walk test developed by the Stanford Heart Disease Prevention Program. To take the test, do the following:

- Measure a one mile distance. Use your car odometer to mark a course in length.

- Warm-up for approximately 5 minutes before you begin your walk. Do side bends, walk stretches, arm swings, and walk.

- Walk one mile as fast as you can without feeling any signs of discomfort. Maintain a brisk, steady pace. Using a stopwatch or a watch with a second hand, record your time to the nearest second.

- After you take the test, compare your results to the following scale:

Male		**Female**	
Age 20-30	Age 40+	Age 20-39	Age 40+
18:00	19:00	18:30	19:30

Your goal is to walk the mile at or below the times provided for your age group. The results of the walking test provides a rough index of aerobic fitness with your one-mile time representing the minimum level.

If you have been on a physical activity program for several weeks, then you can take the full fitness test battery. There are five tests: 1) Body Mass Index (body fat), 2) Sit and Reach Test, 3) One Minute Sit-Up Test, 4) One Minute Push-Up Test, and 5) Twelve Minute Run/Walk Test. The procedures for testing are as follows:

You need to have a fitness coordinator or physician conduct an

Police Fitness

assessment of body composition. Normally, it is done by skinfold calipers or underwater weighing. A rough assessment can be provided by doing your own body mass index.

Body Mass Index: This is an indication of the appropriateness of weight in relation to height.

1.) **Equipment:** A weight scale and a measuring tape.
2.) **Procedure:**
   a) Determine body weight in pounds.
   b) Divide body weight in pounds by 2.2. This will give your body weight in kilograms.
   c) Determine height in total inches.
   d) Divide height in inches by 39 to get height in meters and tenths.
   e) Apply the following formula: KG/h^2 = weight in kilograms divided by height in meters squared. This will be your index score.

Sit and Reach Test: This is a measure of the flexibility of the lower back and upper leg area. These areas are important for performing tasks involving range of motion and in minimizing lower back problems. The score is in the inches reached on a yard stick.

1.) **Equipment:** A box and a yardstick on the box with a 15" mark at the edge.
2.) **Procedure:**
   a) Warm up slowly by practicing the test.
   b) Sit on the floor or mat with legs extended at right angles to the 15" line on the box.
   c) The heels touch the near edge of the box and are eight inches apart.
   d) A yardstick is placed between the legs and rests on the box with the 15" mark. Shoes are off.
   e) Slowly reach forward with both hands as far as possible and hold the position momentarily.
   f) The distance reached on the yardstick by the fingertips in inches is recorded.
   g) The best of three trials is considered as the flexibility score.

One Minute Sit-Up Test: This is a measure of the muscular endurance of the abdominal muscles. This is an important area for maintaining good posture and minimizing lower back problems. The score is in the number of sit-ups completed in one minute. This test should be performed on a mat or carpeted surface.

1.) **Procedure:**
   a) Start by lying on the back, knees bent, heels flat on the

floor.
b) A partner holds the feet down, or wrap them under a chair.
c) Perform as many correct sit-ups as possible in one minute.
d) In the up position, touch the elbows to the knees and then return to a full lying position before starting the next sit-up.
e) Score is total number of correct sit-ups.

One Minute Push-Up Test: This is a measure of the muscular endurance of the upper body extenders (deltoid, triceps, pectorals), and is an important area involving a pushing motion. The score is the number of push-ups completed. There is a regular push-up and a modified push-up for females.

1.) **Regular Push-Up Procedure:**
 a) Start in the front, lean, and rest position.
 b) Lower the upper body until the chest touches the floor, then push up again.
 c) The back must be kept straight and in each extension up, the elbows should be locked out.
 d) Rest in the up position.

2.) **Modified Push-Up Procedures:** (This is the female test.)
 a) Start in the front, lean, and rest position, but place the knees on the floors with lower legs and feet tilting up.
 b) Lower the upper body until the chest touches the floor, then push-up again.
 c) Rest in the up position.

Twelve Minute Run/Walk Test: This is a timed run to measure aerobic capacity or cardiovascular endurance. The score is in miles and tenths.

1.) **Equipment:** A stopwatch or clock with a sweep second hand, and a 440 yard track marked in tenths.

2.) **Track or Course Layout:**
 a) 12 minute run/walk course — a course can be set up in any configuration by placing markers at 1/10 mile in a lap. Another option is to get in a car, drive a course, and mark off each 1/10 of a mile.
 b) 440 yard track — the 12 minute run needs to have a marker at every 88 yards. That represents 1/20 of a mile.

3.) **Procedures**:
 a) Warm up.
 b) Mark the time you start.
 c) Run as fast as you can in 12 minutes.

d) Record distance in miles and tenths at completion.

Fitness Goal Setting

The fitness assessment scores only represent what is called a **raw** score. You need to compare that score to a norm to see how you compare. The following chart has the norms that are recommended for police officers by age (decade) and sex.

	Fitness Standards Chart							
	Male				Female			
Test	20-29	30-39	40-49	50-59	20-29	30-39	40-49	50-59
%Fat Raw	17.4	20.5	22.5	24.1	23.7	24.9	28.1	31.6
Body Mass Index Raw	26	26	26	26	25	25	25	25
Sit & Reach Raw	17.5"	16.5"	15.3"	14.5"	20.0"	19.0"	18.0"	17.9"
1 Min. Sit-Up Raw	40	36	31	26	34	27	22	17
1 Min. Push-Up Raw	36	27	21	15	26	21	15	13
12 Min. Run Raw	1.50	1.45	1.37	1.29	1.29	1.25	1.17	1.10

The goal should be to gradually improve to reach these standards. If you are already performing at these levels, the goal is to at least maintain these levels.

Designing Your Exercise Prescription

The exercise routine is a "game plan." It is a formally structured program that, if designed correctly, will allow you to reach your fitness goals. For an exercise routine to be effective, it must meet certain requirements. To achieve a threshold of training in a fitness program, remember F I T:

▸ Frequency: Regularity of time spent to improve fitness (how

often one exercises — days per week).

▸ Intensity: Effort required to improve fitness (how **hard** one exercises).

▸ Time or Duration: Length of time spent in a single workout to improve fitness (how **long** one exercises).

In order for the training program to work, it must meet certain training thresholds and it must be specific to each fitness area.

Threshold of Training			
Component	Frequency	Intensity	Time
Aerobic Power	Minimum of 3 times per week, year round.	Raise resting heart rate (HR) to target HR (60-80%).	Exercise at target HR for at least 20 min.
Strength	Minimum of 2 to 3 times per week, year round.	Use 40-60% of maximum resistance (how much you can lift if weight training) for each muscle group. During isotonic calisthenic exercises, use own body weight for resistance.	Complete 10-25 repetitions in each set. Do 3-5 sets.
Flexibility	Minimum of 3 times per week, year round. Daily stretching is preferred. Stretching should be used before and after vigorous exercise.	Move each joint through its maximum range of motion by static stretching.	Stretch muscle slowly to the point of tension and hold 15-30 sec. Repeat 3 times.

Aerobic Capacity or Cardiovascular Endurance Prescription

For cardiovascular changes to occur, the body must be forced to perform work so that large amounts of oxygen are consumed. The amount of oxygen consumed is determined by the frequency, intensity, and duration of work as well as the mode of exercise. Activities using a large amount of muscle mass will force the body to use more oxygen than activities using small amounts of muscle mass.

Heart rate training is a good method that can be applied to any aerobic activity. Heart rate during aerobic exercise is **usually** a reliable reflection of how much oxygen is being consumed (high HR usually indicates high oxygen consumption). So monitoring exercise during activity can insure the intensity is correct. To develop a heart rate training program, you need to use the Heart Rate Training Form.

Heart Rate Training Form

Factor	Very Poor & Poor Low Fitness Level	Fair & Good Average Fitness Level	Excellent & Superior High Fitness Level
Frequency (Days/Week)	3	3 or 4	5
Duration (Mins. at THR)#	10-20	15-30	30-60
Intensity (% HR Reserve)	60	70	80
Mode* (Type of Exercise)	Walk, Swim, Cycle	Cycle, Walk, Jog, Run, Swim	Jog, Run, Swim Cycle

#Target heart rate.
*Other activities may be used provided they meet the criteria for aerobic exercise.

    A. Fitness level (low, average, high) _____
    B. Frequency (3, 4, or 5 days/week) _____
    C. Duration (10-20, 15-30, 30-60 minutes) _____
    D. Intensity (60, 70, 80%) _____
    E. Target heart rate range _____
    F. Type (walk, jog, run, cycle, swim, other) _____

The procedure for setting up a program is as follows:

    A. Current level of cardiovascular fitness is determined by an aerobic power test such as the 12 minute run.
        1. Low = below 1/10 of a mile on the standard.
        2. Middle = within 1/10 of a mile on the standard.
        3. High = above the standard.
    B. Frequency, Intensity, Duration, and Mode guidelines based on current cardiovascular fitness level are found on the chart.

C. Calculation of Target Heart Rate:
1. Determine predicted maximal heart rate: 220 - age.
2. Subtract resting heart rate in beats/minute from predicted maximal heart rate. This is called the heart rate reserve.
3. Multiply results of step 2 by desired intensity range from the chart.
4. Add resting heart rate back to the results of step 3. This is the training heart rate zone.

Strength Prescription

Strength pertains to the ability of a muscle or group of muscles to generate force. Absolute strength is the maximal amount of force that can be generated during one maximal effort, and dynamic strength (muscular endurance) is the ability of a muscle to contract repeatedly over time. Separate strength training prescriptions are required, depending upon whether the goal is absolute strength or dynamic strength.

The overload principle says that in order for adaptation (physiological change and improved strength) to occur, the muscle must be challenged to performing more work than it is used to performing. The muscle can be overloaded by using more resistance or by performing more repetitions. In other words, a specific workload is defined for a specific goal.

- If the goal is absolute strength, the workload is defined in terms of using greater resistance with fewer repetitions.

- If the goal is dynamic strength, the workload is defined in terms of using less resistance, but more repetitions.

These basic principles of specificity and overload define the underlying principles of any strength training program. If using weight equipment, more variety of training techniques can be applied.

The most efficient way to increase strength is with weight training. However, if weights are not available, a calisthenic routine can develop muscular endurance. The resistance is always the same — body weight and gravity.

The procedures for setting up the circuit are as follows:
1.) Select exercises.
2.) Determine how many of each exercise can be performed in one minute.
3.) Week one — your routine should consist of the selected exercises. Perform the maximum number of repetitions determined in the previous step. Rest approximately 30 to 60 seconds between each exercise.
4.) Week two — cut the number of repetitions for each exercise in half and perform two sets.
5.) Successive weeks — increase to three sets and add additional

repetitions each week.
6.) Frequency should be three times a week. Allow a day between workouts.

Major Exercises

Toe Raises — (Calf Muscles) — With your hands on your hips and standing erect, raise up on your toes as high as possible. To make it a little harder, place a two-inch board under your toes.

Modified Knee Bends — (Thighs) — With your feet shoulder width apart, your toes pointed straight ahead, and your hands on your hips, squat until your thighs are parallel to the ground. Keep your back straight.

Sit-Ups — (Abdominal) — From a position of lying on your back with knees bent at a 90 degree angle and your hands and fingers interlocked behind your head, come up to a sitting position. As you do so, touch your left knee with the right elbow and alternate knee touches thereafter.

Walrus Calisthenic — (Lower Back) — Lie on the floor on your stomach. Push up with hands to full extension from the abdomen.

Arm and Shoulder Flexors — (Chin) — Use the underhand grip. Beginning from a hanging position with the arms straight, pull up until your chin is above the bar. Return to the hanging position.

Flexed Arm Hang — (Alternative to Chin) — For this exercise, use the underhand grasp and place your body in a position with your chin above the bar (as you would if you had just completed a chin-up). Hold this position for as long as possible.

Chair Dips — (Arm Extensor) — With your back to the chair, grasp the sides of the chair seat (make sure the chair is stable), and slide your feet straight out. Lower yourself as far as possible and push yourself back up.

Full Push-Up — (Arm and Shoulder Extensor) — With your toes on the ground, lean forward and put your hands on the ground about shoulder width apart. Keeping your back straight, lower your upper body to the ground and back up again.

Modified Push-Up — (Alternative to Arm and Shoulder Extensor) — Same as Full Push-Up, except these should be done with your knees on the ground, not your toes. Don't forget to keep your back straight.

Flexibility Prescription

Flexibility pertains to range of motion and can serve many purposes, such as the following:

- Reduce muscle tension.
- Assist in the coordination of movement.
- Prevent injuries.
- Make strenuous activities less of a shock.
- Help to saturate the tissue with oxygen.
- Increase circulation.

Due to the effects of stretching, it is recommended as part of a general warm up and cool down program, as well as a program specifically for its own purpose, to develop range of motion.

Stretching Activities

Most stretching exercises can be classified into two basic categories:

- **Active stretching:** This involves repeated fluid and ballistic type movements. They should not be jerky and they are not meant to be exhaustive or painful. The general purpose of stretching is to provide general warm up and cool down. The specific movements tend to be specific to the type of activity, such as movements that may relate to running.
- **Static or sustained stretching:** This involves one slow stretching movement and the holding of the stretch for approximately 15-30 seconds. It involves gradually moving into the stretch with gentle pulling for relaxation. This is the preferred technique for increasing range of motion and avoids jerky movements that may lead to injury.

The general prescription principles for stretching involve the following:

- **Frequency:** As often as one wants to do it (it can be daily).
- **Duration:** Duration is as long as someone wants to perform the stretching activity. There are no set limits.
- **Intensity:** The intensity that is recommended to increase range of motion is to do both active and static stretching.

Active Stretching Exercises

Head Rolls — Roll head slowly from side to side to a comfortable position.

Shoulder Rolls — Rotate shoulders clockwise, then counter-clockwise to warm muscles.

Upward Reach — Alternate each arm by extending upward over the head and across the body while placing your opposite hand on your hip. Bend sideways at the trunk to an easy point of tension.

Side Reach — Repeat the process described above, but reach from side to side.

Static Stretching Exercises

Achilles Tendon Stretch — (Calf and Achilles Tendon) — Stand in front of a wall approximately three feet away. Keeping your feet flat on the floor, place your hands on the wall and lean forward as if you are doing a push-up. You should feel your calf muscles stretching. Execute slowly and hold for 15-30 seconds.

Sit and Reach — (Low Back and Hamstring) — From the seated position, and with your legs straightened in front of you, bend over slowly. Try to touch your toes moving your head toward your knees. Hold for a count of 15-30.

Walrus Stretch — (Low Back) — From a face down, lying position, place your palms on the floor shoulder width apart. Raise yourself to your elbows, bending at the waist, keeping your head up. Hold for 15-30 seconds.

Shoulder Stretch — (Shoulder and Upper Body) — With a partner positioned behind you, have him pull your arms together while they are straight, keeping your arms parallel to the floor.

Putting the Exercise Plan Together

The exercise bout sequence should consist of three basic phases:

1.) Warm up.
2.) Intense exercise (aerobics or strength training).
3.) Cool down.

Sometimes participants like to do all the exercises in one bout in which there are five phases:

1.) Warm up.
2.) Aerobic exercise.
3.) Aerobic cool down.
4.) Strength training.
5.) Cool down.

Depending upon your schedule, only three days may be available. If so, doing aerobics and strength building in a five phase workout makes sense. Some participants do six days a week — three for aerobics and three for strength. It is up to you.

Exercise Safety

It is important to be aware of basic safety factors before beginning an exercise program. Following safety guidelines will allow an enjoyable program with a minimum of injury and soreness. The major safety and prevention factors are: environmental conditions, clothing and equipment, water, awareness of warning signs, and warm up and cool down.

Environmental Conditions

Hot Weather: The body cools itself primarily with the sweating mechanism. When sweat evaporates, the skin's surface is cooled, and this helps regulate the internal temperature. If there is a high concentration of moisture in the air (humidity above 70 percent), the body's sweating mechanism will be hindered, because the sweat will not evaporate so readily. If this occurs with prolonged exposure to extreme heat, dehydration followed by heat exhaustion or heat stroke can occur. Under these conditions, it is wise to exercise in the morning or evening when it is cooler. To keep your body hydrated, drink plenty of fluids throughout the day and wear light, loose clothing to allow air circulation. Fit individuals should allot 7-14 days for gradual acclimatization to hot weather.

Cold Weather: When exercising in the cold, make sure you wear adequately warm clothing, but do not overdress. Instead, dress in layers which can be progressively removed as your body temperature increases from the exercise.

Altitude: If you are exercising at an elevation of 5,000 feet or more, or at any elevation higher than you are accustomed to, your performance will be affected. When moving into an area of higher elevation than you are used to, you may find it helpful to reduce your exercise intensity and duration for 7-10 days. This will allow your body time to acclimate to the new environment.

Clothing and Equipment

Shoes: When shopping for the right shoe, always take the time necessary to select one that fits good, is well-padded, is made of quality material, and is right for the job. Wearing the right shoe will help prevent foot, leg, and lower back injuries.

Clothing: Wear light, loose fitting clothing made of natural fibers to promote air circulation and to aid in the evaporation of sweat. Do not wear plastic or rubberized clothing when exercising in hot weather.

Water

Do not trust your thirst. You should drink 6-8 eight-ounce glasses of water per day on normal days, and more on hot days.

Awareness of Warning Signs

If any of the following occur, stop exercising, and consult a physician:
1.) Abnormal heart action.
2.) Chest pain.
3.) Abnormal shortness of breath in combination with chest pain.
4.) Sudden pain or numbness in any part of the body.
5.) Pain or heartburn in the upper abdomen.
6.) Temporary loss of speech or vision.
7.) Extreme dizziness, sudden loss of coordination, or cold sweat.

Sticking With a Program

Maintaining a fitness program is not always easy. The assessment and detailed exercise and nutrition plans are only the first steps. A separate program is often needed to "stick" to the fitness plan. To avoid "slippage," use the three R's of program maintenance: Reviewing, Recycling, and Reinforcing.

- **Reviewing**: This involves maintaining a Fitness Log of how well you maintain the exercise plans on a weekly basis.

- **Recycling:** This involves reassessing fitness status on a regular basis to see if improvement occurred, and if program modifications are needed. It is easy to reassess yourself every 16 weeks. However, you may retest yourself at any time.

- **Reinforcing:** This refers to a formal motivation plan. Build in a reward for participation to keep motivated. Attending exercise and health promotion classes and using fitness videos are examples of methods to keep your interest up.

Bibliography

American College of Sports Medicine. 1990. *Guidelines for Exercise Testing and Prescription.* Philadelphia: Lea and Feberger.

Boyce, R., Jones, G., and Hiatt, K. 1991. "Physical Fitness Capacity and Absenteeism of Police Officers." *Journal of Occupational Medicine.* 11: 33: 1137-1145.

Collingwood, T. 1990. *Fit for Duty* (Video tape and manual). Northridge, CA: Medina Productions.

Collingwood, T. 1988. "Implementing Programs and Standards for Law Enforcement Physical Fitness." *Police Chief.* 55: 4: 20-24.

Collingwood, T. 1980. "Stress and Physical Activity." *Police Chief:* XLVII (2): 25-27.

Cooper, K. 1983. *The Aerobics Program for Total Well-Being.* New York: M. Evans.

Williams, M., Petratis, M., Baechle, T., Ryschon, K., Campain, J., and Sketch, H. 1987. "Frequency of Physical Activity Exercise Capacity and Atherosclerotic Heart Disease Risk Factors in Male Police Officers." *Journal of Occupational Medicine.* 29: 7: 596-600.

Dubrow, R., Burnett, C., Gute, D., and Brockart, J. 1988. "Ischemic Heart Disease and Acute Myocardial Infarction Mortality Among Police Officers." *Journal of Occupational Medicine.* 30: 8: 650-654.

International Association of Chiefs of Police. 1977. *Physical Fitness Programs for Police: A Manual for the Police Administrator.* Washington, D.C: Government Printing Office.

U.S. Department of Health and Human Services. 1991. *Healthy People 2000.* Washington, D.C: Government Printing Office.

About the Author

Dr. Thomas Collingwood is the Director for the Institute for Aerobics Research in Texas. Dr. Collingwood has an M.S. in Exercise Physiology and a Ph.D. in Psychology, and has authored over 6 books and 100 articles in the field. He has trained and certified over 4000 police fitness instructors, and designed programs and standards for over 50 public safety agencies. Dr. Collingwood is a Special Consultant to IACP and is on the President's Council on Police Fitness.

Chapter 14

Burnout in Law Enforcement

by Ed Donovan

Causes of Burnout

Most of us enter the law enforcement profession with high ideals and unrealistic expectations. We want to do a good job, get the bad guys off the street and make a difference. We put on badges and guns, and the uniform of the day for our respective agencies. We go to work and hope to make a dent in the drug wars, and to curb the holocaust of deaths of the youth of America. Too soon we find out that we are outnumbered in all arenas.

We are facing, on a daily basis, a more violent society than ever before in history due to drugs, poverty, unemployment, and the rapidly increasing homeless. Criminals not only out number us, but they are better equipped than we are. They have free lawyers and crisis counselors. They have walkie-talkies, beepers, faster cars, and better guns, and without rules and regulations on when they can use them. We are constantly being policed by our departments, the public, and the media.

Most agencies are short handed. They have had layoffs, cutbacks, and budget cuts. They have stopped hiring officers, and have no money for the necessary continuous training of the officers they have now.

We are bombarded with lawsuits for negligent retention, negligent hiring, negligent training, and most of all, for "police brutality" with the recent Rodney King case in Los Angeles. It has become open season to sue officers from all over the country. In some departments, they are even going back as far as five years to investigate past allegations of excessive force.

We are expected to be all things to all people — cop, lawyer, juror, doctor, psychiatrist, social worker, ambulance driver, firefighter, plumber, veterinarian, locksmith, and every other conceivable occupation. We are routinely given new directives and policies by our departments, but we can't possibly keep up with the incessant demands placed upon us by our departments, ourselves, and the public without paying a price. As public servants we are acutely aware that we can't meet these demands, but somehow we feel that we should be able to. The training we receive at local, state, and Federal police academies does not adequately equip us to handle the diverse requirements of today's police work.

Effects of Burnout

There have been enough studies completed over the past decade to show that law enforcement is a highly stressful occupation. To quote just a few: there is a relatively high rate of cancer, suicide, and heart disease among law enforcement professionals, Vena (1985); police have a suicide rate far above the national average, Alymyer (1980); three-fourths of the heart attacks suffered by police officers are due to job-related stress, Territo (1981); in the Creek v. Wyoming, WY Sec. 1982 finding, no exception exceeds that of police officers in combined mortality ratios' — law enforcement is the most stressful occupation that can be found, and; the suicide rate among law enforcement personnel is higher than that for other occupations, (Fell, Richard and Wallace, 1980). Socialist, Leanor Boulin Johnson, of Arizona State University studied the link between work and family stress among police officers and their spouses. She concluded that police as an occupation was high in alcoholism, family violence, divorce, and suicide.

The fact is that police chiefs are being sued, fired, resigning, and dying on the job, and some are even committing suicide. Although with the knowledge of these overwhelming statistics, there are still some police administrators out there who say that there is no stress on the job. This cave man attitude among the brotherhood prevents many police officers from seeking professional help, and they will eventually burnout.

With the daily witnessing of all the pain society inflicts on itself, we begin to put up walls to shield ourselves from being emotionally overwhelmed. For fear of ridicule, we tend to live by the unwritten rule of suffering in silence and never speak about all that passes before our eyes to others outside our profession.

We become cynical and pessimistic. We start to withdraw from society. We isolate ourselves and only socialize with other officers. We become paranoid. Soon it becomes a we — they world; us against them. This breeds negativism, alcoholism, and divorce. Many of us start to police our own families. We become over protective, or cold and callous to the needs of our families and loved ones which are major contributors to the high divorce rate in law enforcement.

We begin to lose our love and passion for police work. We feel we have little or no control over the job we have to do. We start to live with the evil we see as part of reality. With all this frustration and sense of helplessness, the job becomes less important. Other issues take top priority, such as overtime, pay details, involvement with the unions, studying for promotions, and our other jobs.

All of this leads to burnout. Burnout can be defined as a state of emotional and physical exhaustion when we work with the public over long periods of time under extremely stressful and demanding conditions.

The late Dr. Hans Selye of the International Institute of Stress, the foremost authority on stress, defined stress as the "non-specific response of the body to any demand made upon it." He further told me that it wasn't the stress that is coming at you. It is the way you handle it that determines how stress will effect you. What is stressful to one person will not bother another.

Dr. Selye described the General Adaptation Syndrome (GAS) as the fight-flight response. First there is the alarm stage, where the perceived danger, such as a radio call, sends automatic signals to the brain. Resistance falls far below normal and stress levels are secreted more abundantly. Then we put into effect our defense mechanisms with body chemicals which cause rapid breathing, clammy hands, and a nauseous feeling in the stomach. This is the body reacting to a threatening situation and preparing itself for flight.

When the body senses the danger is over, it will go back to normal, depending on the intensity of the stressful event. If left in this stage of resistance for too long, we then enter the stage of exhaustion which leads to disease and burnout. Too often in police work, we remain in a state of exhaustion for long periods of time, unaware that we are even affected by it. Exhaustion causes lapses in coordination, errors in judgment, and our reflexes and muscles don't respond. Over a period of time, we become less effective and a danger to ourselves, to the public, and to the officers we work with.

Burnout leads to the abuse of alcohol and pills, gambling, overeating, sexual dysfunctions, insomnia, back and neck problems, high blood pressure, heart attacks, depression and anxiety attacks, and many other psychosomatic illnesses.

There are signals the body gives out to tell us that we're burning out: when we don't want to go to work and begin to hate our jobs; when the frustration makes us say, "Why Bother?" "No one gives a damn." "What's the use;" or we are tired and depressed all the time with a negative attitude about everything.

We are constantly sick with colds and the flu. We have chronic diarrhea or constipation, stomach disorders, chest pains and hyperventilating, trouble breathing, and pains going out our arm. We can't sleep, or oversleep and still feel tired. We become accident prone, both on and off the job. We're constantly at war with the department and getting into trouble, and have an abnormal amount of civilian complaints. We are unhappy with our family life.

We have thoughts that we are going crazy and are afraid others will find out the way we feel. We think of suicide and are afraid to tell anyone for fear they will think us weak. We want to quit the job and run away, or count the days till retirement.

This is the life of very lonely, wounded officers, but they can be restored to the very system that recruited them. They can become productive officers once again for their departments, the public, and their families.

Preventing Burnout

The first step in preventing burnout is to train all new recruits in stress management. They must be taught coping skills to better handle the stress they will face while on and off the job. A department supported "confidential" counseling program for all employees and their family also says the department cares for its personnel.

There are many things that you can do individually to combat burnout. First and foremost, you have to get out from behind that badge you love. Get rid of that rigid image that says, because you are society's problem solver, you are not supposed to have problems. Ask for help. Getting help is not a sign of weakness; it is a sign of strength. It takes much courage to ask for help.

Ventilate. Learn to talk to a concerned person about what's bothering you. Don't hold it in. If you do, it will eventually eat you. Drink alcohol in moderation, and do not self medicate or abuse prescription medicine.

Find outlets to relieve tension, such as hobbies, movies, television, skiing, fishing, dancing, building models, or anything you enjoy that keeps your mind relaxed and away from your job and life's problems. This gives you a chance to recharge your run down batteries and restores the energy you need to handle stress.

Learn a good relaxation technique. My favorite is biofeedback, but there are others just as good. Meditation and yoga use visual imagery.

Make a physical fitness program part of your life. Try to find a combination of exercises, and don't rely on just one. Try jogging, brisk walking, boxing, weight lifting, aerobics, bicycling, or anything that will get your heart pumping for twenty minutes, three times a week.

Get enough sleep. Maintain a healthy weight for your physique. Avoid smoking and have regular check ups by a doctor that knows you. Take mini vacations, or just escape from your job every chance you get.

Socialize with the rest of the world and get to know that everyone in it isn't a maggot. There are decent hard working people, like yourself, in all walks of life, but you'll never find this out if you only socialize with other officers, or don't socialize with anyone.

Work with kids, whether it is in sports, or in school or community activities. This helps you to make a difference, and to see that all kids aren't bad. Put humor in your life, and I don't mean the callous humor we use as a defense mechanism. It is often hard to grasp that the crisis of today can be the joke of tomorrow.

Don't take yourself too serious, and don't try to tackle all of life's problems at once. Learn to accept what you cannot change. This will help change your negative thinking into positive thinking.

As I learned in A.A., plan for tomorrow, but live in today. Try to help another person in trouble. The rewards are never-ending. When all else fails, try God. Faith is the strongest tool on the face of the earth for handling stress.

There are many reasons for police departments to have stress management programs. The biggest reason is that it costs money to have troubled employees. Absenteeism, accidents, injuries, civilian complaints, lawsuits, replacement of overtime, disability pensions, bad publicity, and low morale are but a few reasons why departments should be taking care of their personnel.

Every department has an obligation to the officers they hire, and their families, to implement stress management programs. Burnout costs all law enforcement agencies their most valuable assets — well trained officers with years of experience.

About the Author

Mr. Ed Donovan is a retired police officer from the Boston, Massachusetts Police Department. He is currently the Executive Director of the International Law Enforcement Stress Association in Massachusetts and a consultant, lecturer, and author specializing in "Stress in Law Enforcement."

He has been interviewed by U.S. World & News Report, Newsweek, and Time, as well as many others. He has also made several appearances on radio and television, including the ABC Special "The Shattered Badge," the HBO Special "Cops Behind the Badge," the Oprah Winfrey Show, the Phil Donahue Show, and Good Morning America.

Mark S. Dunston

Mr. Dunston is the Director of the North MS Law Enforcement Training Center and a Captain with the Tupelo, MS, Police Department. He serves as State Director for the prestigious American Society of Law Enforcement Trainers (ASLET). He has trained law enforcement officers from several Federal, state, and local agencies, and the U.S. Military. Mark is a member of the Police Marksman Advisory Board and sits on several law enforcement advisory committees. He is Certified by the International Association for Identification as a Senior Crime Scene Analyst, and has had numerous articles published in law enforcement periodicals and journals. Mark's first book, Street Signs, is a critically acclaimed book on identification available from Performance Dimensions.

Chapter 15

Reading the Streets

by Mark S. Dunston

From forty-five mph to zero in what felt like less than a second; out of the car and the chase was on. The young drug dealer stretched out ahead with long, light-footed strides; a not so young police officer on his tail. The cool, wet weather that had been in the area for the past few nights made the sidewalk slick. In obvious need of a new pair of felony fliers, the rock star-turned-would-be-track-star lost his footing and fell face down on the cold, abrasive pavement.

The running was over, but the race continued for the contents of the young man's mouth. The officer grabbed furiously at the young man's throat, and yelled for him to spit out the crack cocaine he was trying to swallow. Failing in his attempt to destroy the evidence, the young now thoroughly exhausted drug dealer gave it up, and out popped two tiny, white rocks.

To the uninitiated, these tiny, white pebbles would seem to be just that, rocks, but the officer knew exactly what they were. He had, after all, observed the drug dealer doing business with a female in a car that was parked by the curb. He also knew that the subject had been previously convicted of the same crime.

How did the officer know? What did he see that tipped him off that the guy was holding crack cocaine in his mouth? Amazed, Officer Brad Baker, a new officer on his first day of field training, couldn't even get out of his seat belt before his partner had the subject on the ground. The only assistance the new officer could render was to pick the guy up off the sidewalk and take him to the patrol car.

Once at the vehicle, Officer Baker began to search the young drug dealer. Pulling back the sleeves on his pro football team jacket revealed a large, ominous tattoo; a gang tattoo.

The tattoo was a large heart and wings with a large "G" in the middle. Although Officer Baker found it interesting, his partner found it a good sign of identification and told him that this young man was going to be a problem. As his partner explained the meaning of the tattoo and that the wearer was in the wrong neighborhood, Officer Baker found himself amazed, once again. How did his partner know this?

The knowledge of how to read the streets is as essential to the survival of officers as knowing how to operate their weapons. The training of officers involves teaching them to use their everyday tools; firearms, intermediate weapons, and patrol cars. What is overlooked is the tool that officers cannot survive without — awareness. Being alert to the possibility of a crime being committed is not just luck, it is the ability to look and listen to the streets.

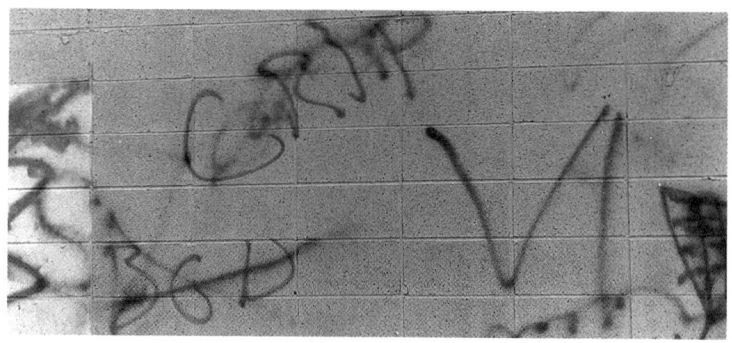

Graffiti indicates that this area was infiltrated by BGD's, Vice Lords, and Crips at one time.

To learn to read the streets, curiosity is the first necessary element; being curious enough to go that one step further. For example, the officer inquires as to what business a subject has behind a shopping mall after hours and receives a vague answer, such as waiting for a girlfriend or relative. Upon further questioning, the subject cannot tell the officer the girlfriend's or relative's full name or place of employment. This is where curiosity comes to play. Sometimes although the officer has established that the subject is fabricating the story, the officer leaves the answers at that.

What separates a street smart officer from an officer who has no desire to pursue a criminal? Curiosity. The officer who ultimately beats the criminal is the curious officer with a desire to discover the who and why. The street smart officer's interest is sparked by the lies in the subject's story content. This is the officer who observes spray painted graffiti on walls and takes the time to interpret its meaning.

The graffiti before him could reveal gang activity, pending violence, or activity that has already occurred. Curiosity causes the officer to note the symbols and words in his notebook for future reference.

Gangs

What was once considered to be a big city problem has become a nightmare for small communities throughout the country. Gangs that were once dismissed by officials as just a bunch of kids now have the capability to terrorize entire neighborhoods. Ignoring the problem did not produce positive results for they did not just go away as was hoped.

Extortion, narcotics' trafficking, and violence are all part of the business that give gang members their power. How can street smart officers effectively control this type of crime in their area? They can't just throw their hands up in despair and walk away. There must be an answer.

Reading the Streets 127

Acquiring the ability to look at a given situation and see below the surface is a trait the street smart, curious, officers possesses. They have actually taken the time to exit their patrol vehicles and talk to the players on the street. They know the face, the name, and the game each are playing. Who are the crack dealers? Who are the hustlers, the users, and the potential informants?

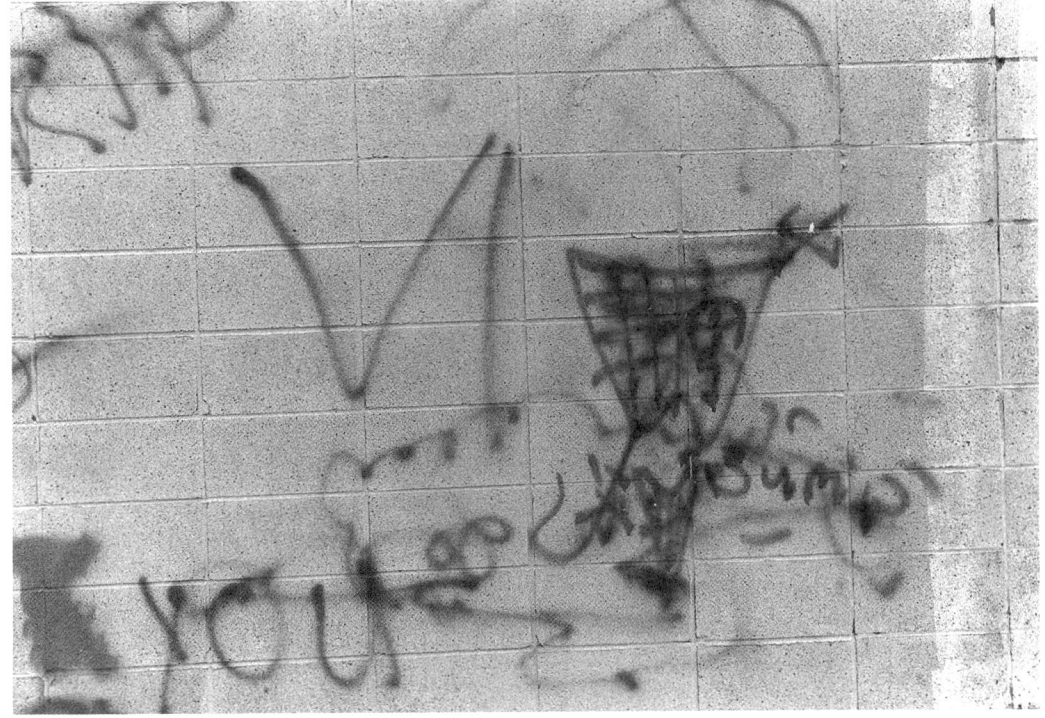

A big part of "reading the streets" is being able to interpret gang graffiti.

Often you hear uniformed officers complain that it's not their job to develop informants, and to know who does what and how on the street. This is just not so. Officers working a beat or district can solve a considerable amount of crime by taking the time to get out of the car and find out who is playing street games. Who is selling drugs, and who will tell them about it? Just as the officer in the beginning of the chapter knew who the violator was, that he was a crack dealer and a gang member, so can the curious officers.

Tattoos

Part of knowing the street entails knowing how to identify the subject when no information is given. Tattooing is one means of identification that can be beneficial to the curious officer. Many tattoos are harmless in nature. Remnants of a long night of drinking while on leave from the service has left quite a few people pondering their choice of body art.

A tattoo can very well be a form of identification, or a warning to those who know its meaning. Prison tattoos, for example, can inform officers that the person confronted has been incarcerated. If the officers fail to recognize the advertised threat, they could pay with their lives.

Often the crude tattoos found on violators were not acquired in prison but the product of craftsmen on the street. Followers of the doctrines of black street gangs from places like Chicago and Southern California have been identified by their affiliated tattoos. Tattoos that identify the wearer as a member of a volatile street gang are valuable resources to the street smart officer. Skinheads and others with criminally motivated white supremist beliefs can be found to display their association with tattoos. Some tattoos may also be simply a representative of personal feelings and not affiliated with any particular gang.

Those who involve themselves with the trappings of the occult may reflect their belief through the use of tattoos. One good indicator of adolescent involvement in the occult is the use of self-mutilation and self-tattooing. Many times, the curious officer will find these occult related tattoos engraved on the left side of the body. Why?

Historically, literature has shown that the right is the path of good and the left the path of evil. Therefore, tattoos may be placed on the left arm, left leg, and so forth to depict the person's association with evil. Most gangs also have a "side" they revere as theirs. For example, the Black Gangster Disciples and other Folk gangs identify the right side as their side.

Many times, these subtle identifiers are localized. A certain color, saying, tattoo, mode of dress, and even sports brands have different meanings dependent on the location of the wearer. An investigator once told me of a young, white female who was sitting with a group of young people at a fast food. They were involved in the occult. The young lady was wearing an ankle bracelet, which had attached to it beer can pull tabs. When he asked her the meaning of the pull tabs, she replied that they indicated the amount of sexual activity a person had been involved in. She had many pull tabs.

Every area of the country seems to have different slang expressions; terms for drugs, sex, violence, and even code words for the police. In one part of Florida, the terms "Bo Brown" and "99" are quick warnings for the approach of police officers. Elsewhere the term "Five-O" is used when "undercover" officers are seen in the distance.

The streets have a language all their own, and just as dialects and accents change with national languages, so does the language of the streets. In some parts of the country, people may look strangely at those with the nickname of "Skeeter." They may be embarrassed to find that this moniker is a street term for semen.

Think of all of that time we spent in freshman English and composition class just to be forced to rethink the language of the streets.

Drugs and Crime

Every evening, the local or national news has at least one tale of a violent crime directly related to illegal drugs. News? No, not really. How many times can officers faced with the battle every day stand to hear someone on television with no front line knowledge of the "drug war" say that we are winning the war on drugs?

For a long time, drug trafficking was confined to heroin and marijuana. The heroin problem was not experienced by smaller rural agencies. It was strictly a big city problem. Marijuana, however was available everywhere. Before much could done about existing drug problems, the arrival of cheap, smokeable cocaine hit the streets.

Our nation has found itself in a drug market flooded with abusers from all walks of life and ethnic backgrounds. The addicting affects of crack know no racism; anyone is welcome. With the demand for the product come the supply and the suppliers.

The image ingrained in society's mind of what a drug dealer looks like was eradicated. The figure of an older, dirty freak selling drugs to children was quickly replaced with children selling drugs to children and children selling drugs to adults. Most of the time the sales from children are for adults who know how the youth justice system works. Using kids is good business. There is very little overhead and they are eager to work, especially if they also hit the pipe.

The spread of the popularity and abuse of crack throughout rural America can be attributed to several factors, but one strong factor is the quick cash that comes from the crack market. In the South for example, a young person from a small, depressed community might have been sent to a larger city to reside with a relative due to the financial restraints on the family. This young person might become involved in the crack trade. If they are smart and stay off the pipe themselves, they might see the cash potential of the product.

Thinking they are hot shots in the big city can lead them to think they can "own" their neighborhoods back home. Once they return to their home towns, they already have a product, a strategy, and a marketing plan. Now law enforcement officers in the smallest of towns have to deal with the problem of crack.

Indicators of drug use that may be overlooked by some include the crack itself. Ranging in size from a sliver to a slab, the rock can be obtained in shapes from flat and thin to fat and square. The most common appears to be the pebble shaped rock that is readily available on the street. Crack has also been found secreted in every imaginable location on the body. Its design allows for quick destruction of the evidence when a police officer approaches.

Paraphernalia for the smoking of crack can be found in a vast array of products. Take for example, the need for a pipe. Remember when the pipes you found in a subject's possession were for the smoking of marijuana or hashish? They were available in all sorts of fancy shapes and sizes, and were made from wood, brass, clay, or whatever was stylish. It seemed that just about every teenager in wood shop was trying his hand at craftsmanship.

Just as the substance changes, so does the paraphernalia. Often, items used by violators have been overlooked because of their routine appearance. The beverage can has become a favorite disposable pipe. So has the use of any item that can hold the rock in one part, and allows the smokers to inhale the ignited drug without completely destroying their face with the flame; plastic bottles, bathroom tissue rollers, aluminum foil, and the list continues.

Easily overlooked items, such as this soft drink can, fulfills the requirements of a disposable crack pipe. Tiny holes are punched in the dented portion of the can and the burning crack is inhaled from the original opening.

Other indicators found in the vicinity of crack use include the remnants of entirely burned packs of matches and disposable butane lighters with their "heads" removed. In order to get the desired effect of fast, hot flames for the ignition of their rock, smokers use the whole pack of matches at once or take the regulating head off a lighter. The result is, once again, disposable pieces of equipment.

With the abuse of drugs come crime, and with crime comes danger for society and its protectors. We see the overt dangers of violence towards police officers, but the hidden dangers of items such as razor blades, hypodermic needles, and body fluids are just as dangerous. A quick frisk of a subject for weapons can leave an unsuspecting officer cut by a concealed razor blade or syringe. Regardless of the obvious injury that can be incurred, what of the dangers of accidentally injecting a mind altering substance? More than one law enforcement officer has been pensioned out because of accidental ingestion of drugs such as PCP or LSD.

Many life threatening diseases can be injected by the prick of a used needle. The street smart officer finds alternatives to reaching into a subject's pocket with a bare hand. The use of various probing devices can be employed. Even a ball point pen can be used to feel for injurious objects.

The rule of "look before you leap" has never been more true than when searching a person or vehicle. Taking the time to look safely into an area at a distance or with a mirror can save an officer a great deal of pain. Whether the injurious object was deliberately placed there to injure an officer, or was completely accidental, the results are the same.

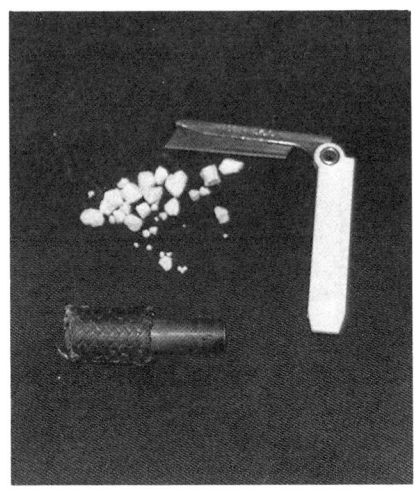

Paraphernalia, such as this straight edge and metal crack pipe, can be hazards for an officer searching a subject.

room, he or she should stop to observe the doctors and health care professionals who are dealing with the wounded. Often, the officer will see the doctors and nurses wearing rubber gloves, face masks, and even goggles to prevent the introduction of infection and body fluids.

Do they need protection more than the law enforcement officer? They certainly do not come into much more contact with the subject or victim than the officer does. It is obvious then, that the street smart officer should wear the same items when confronted with medical emergencies, or the search of arrestees. The combination of progressive training and thinking will aid street smart officers in performing their duties safely and effectively.

Most of what the street smart officer sees on a tour of duty is routine and mundane. Yet, often enough, for those few fast, furious, and frightening moments an officer sees and feels more than the average citizen will experience in a lifetime. These are the moments that make an officer feel that if he or she were to blink, he or she would die in the dark. Instead of blinking, the street smart officer keeps both eyes and ears open. His or her sense of smell and touch are heightened and tuned to the surrounding environment. The street smart officer is aware of the importance of his or her sixth sense; the feeling that something is wrong.

While many police officers possess advanced degrees, nothing can take the place of their ability to feel, see, and listen to the streets. Perhaps there should be a special lambskin created specifically for the street smart police officer. Printed on the front would be the price the student paid in time, stress, and dedication. Only after a curriculum of the sights, sounds, and smells of society's darkest moments, can a student be awarded this degree. And never should the graduate, the street smart officer, forget those who fell short of their degree.

Dick Fairburn

Mr. Fairburn has his B.S. in Law Enforcement Administration. He is a graduate of the Illinois State Police Academy (Class Valedictorian), a graduate of the American Pistol Institute (Gunsite), and has over twelve years of law enforcement experience. He is currently Chief of Police with the Upton, WY, Police Department and is involved in terminal ballistics research of handgun and rifle ammunition. He is a technical adviser for Police magazine, a member of The Police Marksman National Advisory Board, and has had more than 50 articles published in Police, The Police Marksman, SWAT, Law and Order, and Law Enforcement News.

Chapter 16

The Law Enforcement Rifle

by Dick Fairburn

While some U.S. police agencies have long had rifled arms in their arsenals, the common issuance and use of such weapons is relatively new to most agencies. The shotgun has been the most common long gun used as a step up from the sidearm on the use of force continuum. A major disadvantage of the police shotgun is that the multiple pellets of a buckshot load must be accounted for after the trigger is pulled. Few shotguns will keep all pellets on target past 25 yards. With rifled slugs the shotgun can deliver a very powerful hit out to 50 yards, perhaps to 100 yards, or maybe even a bit further in the hands of a good shooter. In reality, the shotgun offers much more power but little gain in range over what a good shooter can expect from his sidearm.

A rifle, on the other hand, can deliver more range and more accuracy than is available from any handgun. While rifles do not offer the crushing power of a load of buckshot or a rifled slug, the wounds produced can be impressive. Many agencies now provide officers with a choice of the short-range effectiveness of the traditional shotgun, or the medium to long-range precision of a rifle.

Police rifles can be divided into three general categories with some degree of overlap between. These general categories are: the Sniper Rifles, the Assault Rifles, and the Patrol Rifles.

Sniper Rifles

The primary mission of a sniper rifle is precision. When these rifles are used, either as a stand-alone option, or as a part of an overall Special Team operation, their mission is the near-surgical delivery of deadly force. Such a use prevents the injury of innocent hostages and minimizes the risk to officers on the scene. Using a SWAT team for a forced building entry always involves extreme danger, so the chances of ending the situation by having the sniper "reach out and touch someone" is too valuable to overlook.

The primary attribute to a sniper rifle is practical accuracy. Practical accuracy means more than just good grouping ability. The rifle must be able to place the all-important first shot from a cold, clean barrel in exactly the right spot. Most police sniper rifles today are chambered to fire the .308 Winchester cartridge and are based on bolt-action designs, commonly the Remington Model 700 or the Austrian Steyr series. Another, smaller segment of the sniper rifle group is based on the U.S. Military's M14 or M16 self-loading, gas operated actions.

The rifles based on the M14, with its 7.62 mm x 51 mm NATO chambering (.308 Winchester), approximates the Army's M21 which is an accurized M14 with telescopic sights. The M16 based sniper rifles use special barrels and hand guards to derive maximum accuracy from their 5.56 mm x 45 mm round (.223 Remington). The military branches have all adopted bolt-action rifles for the bulk of their snipers, proving a large magazine capacity is not especially important in a weapon of this type.

The prices of these rifles can vary widely, and their accuracy potential does not always relate directly to their price. Often the Remington Model 700 Police rifle will produce accuracy so good that it would be difficult to tell the difference between the factory built rifle and a custom built one that may cost 5 times as much.

We need a rifle that can consistently hold a 5 shot, 1 minute-of-angle (1 inch) group at 100 yards. This is a more difficult standard to meet than many braggarts would suggest, but it can be done by unmodified factory rifles firing factory ammunition. Some rifles can cut this accuracy level to 1/2 inch or even less, but it is doubtful much difference could be seen under field conditions. The primary benefit of a "one hole" gun is in the confidence it gives its user, and that confidence can be extremely important to the successful use of the weapon.

Sniper rifles are always fitted with some type of telescopic sight. Some truly excellent sniper scope designs have surfaced in the last few years from several manufacturers. Unfortunately, many of these scopes seem to be designed by someone that does not understand the mission of a police sniper rifle. We have no need for a scope with a high, fixed magnification and range-finding reticles geared for shots out to 800 yards. The average police sniper shot is estimated to take place at about 75 yards. For this reason, a variable scope can often be the best choice.

A fixed power scope should be either a 6 power or 8 power. Some 10x fixed-power scopes may not focus clearly at 50 yards or less and some sniper situations will be at these close ranges. If your locale suggests the need for longer range precision, then more magnification may be appropriate. The variable scopes in the 3x-9x, 3.5x-10x, and 4x-16x range can serve as excellent police sniper optics. They offer enough magnification for almost any long range situation, while allowing adjustment to a lower magnification for the more common close shot. When these scopes are high-quality, they will be reliable and accurate.

The scopes with 50 to 56 mm objective lenses are very bright under limited light conditions, and make an excellent choice for a sniper package. Such scope sights are also available with self-illuminating reticles, but if the target is visible enough to identify, the normal reticles should be visible as well. These telescopic sights must have reliable adjustments and many snipers prefer a target-style adjustment in minutes-of-angle rather that the ones with complicated range-finding reticles. An expert sniper will already know where his bullet will impact at a given range.

The Law Enforcement Rifle

Assault Rifles

The next category of police rifle is the assault rifle. While these are occasionally used as sniper rifles in highly accurate models, they more commonly overlap into the patrol rifle category. The definition of an "Assault Rifle" is a nebulous and highly political matter. This type of rifle will generally consist of a small, self-loading rifle chambered to fire an intermediate-power cartridge and is fed from a magazine holding 20 rounds or more. You will note that many of the weapons the media call assault rifles do not fit this definition. If the weapon fires a pistol cartridge in a semi-automatic action, the definition of assault rifle may stretch to cover it. But, if the pistol cartridge is fired from a fully-automatic action it is more correctly called a sub-machine gun. If the weapon fires a full-power rifle cartridge then it is more correctly called a battle rifle.

Officer with AR15 shows a realistic position when firing an assault course. The cover several yards in front allows him to fire from this kneeling position.

In the U.S. the most common rifles that fit into the assault rifle category are the M16 series, the Ruger Mini-14 series and, to a lesser extent, the Steyr AUG. These rifles will be called upon to perform reliably under the worst police conditions and only tried and true military arms are rugged and reliable enough for this purpose. In the U.S. these rifles are most often chambered for the 5.56 mm x 45 mm (.223 Remington) round. Both Ruger and Colt are producing assault-type rifles chambered for the 7.62 mm x 39 mm former Warsaw Pact round. These short .30 caliber rifles should also do an excellent job.

Another photo of the assault course. Here, the officer has an H & K 91. The targets have been moved and he uses the post as a rest for a long shot.

U.S. police agencies normally assign these rifles as the general purpose long guns of their special teams. In this role these rifles are often the select-fire (fully automatic) versions, though the logic of using these rifles in the automatic mode is subject to debate. In analyzing SWAT type operations it seems that most of the actual shooting is done by sniper rifles, sub-machine guns, and shotguns. The assault rifle, however, is the logical choice for arming the bulk of the special team members.

In situations where special teams may be assigned to more rural duties, the battle rifle can be an excellent alternative to the assault rifle. These larger rifles, with their hard hitting rounds, can do a better job when a police team moves into a setting more like a military unit would expect.

The Law Enforcement Rifle 137

Patrol Rifles

While the pure function of the assault rifle may be limited to special police operations, these rifles are commonly seen filling the role of the next category, the patrol rifle. Where the sniper and assault rifles can be defined by describing the rifle itself, the patrol rifle is more of a "use concept." A patrol rifle can be any rifle that will accomplish the role it may be called upon to perform. So, lets define just what a patrol rifle's mission is.

We need a rifle of compact dimensions that can be mounted easily in a patrol vehicle. This rifle must fire a cartridge capable of inflicting a serious wound out to at least 100 yards, preferably further. The weapon must be rugged and reliable, and be of a repeating action type. Accuracy standards for a patrol rifle would be geared towards its anticipated short to medium range use, from the muzzle to perhaps 150 yards. Since we are not discussing sniper performance here, a rifle that will produce consistent 4 inch, 100 yard groups under field shooting conditions will suffice. It would be nice to have a patrol rifle that can produce groups as tight as our sniper rifles, but we really don't need that level of accuracy. As you can see, many assault type rifles fit this description nicely, but other designs do also.

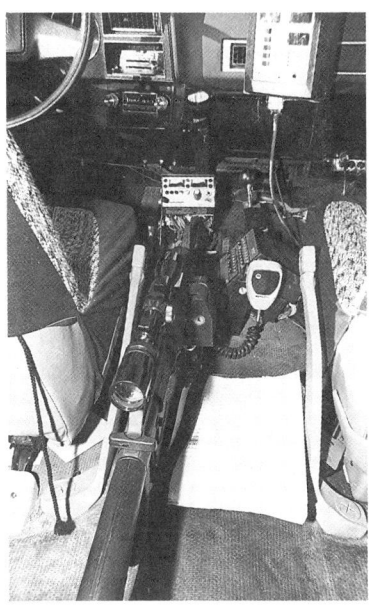

(left) A variety of patrol rifles from left to right: U.S. M1 (Garand) .30-60; Colt AR15 .223 Remington (5.56x45mm); Winchester Mod. 94 .356; Browning Mod. 92 .35 Magnum. (right) An AR16 is secured in a modified shotgun rack between the seats of a Blazer type vehicle. They are no harder to mount than shotguns.

The first element to be considered for a patrol rifle is the caliber. Some experts recommend a carbine chambered for the duty sidearm cartridge. This concept has some obvious advantages for training and logistics, but problems develop when the sidearm caliber is 9 mm Parabellum or .45 ACP chamberings. These two cartridges do an excellent job in handguns, but are not very impressive when fired from rifles. For example, when a 9 mm or .45 carbine is sighted to strike point of aim at 50 yards, it will drop from 8 to 10 inches by the time it has reached 100 yards. These carbines are not suitable for use much beyond 75 yards. Therefore, many experts do not think they make good patrol rifles.

Those sidearm rounds that are "magnums" can do a good job as patrol rifle cartridges. The .357 Magnum makes an especially nice cartridge for a light carbine. A typical 158 grain JHP load will have a muzzle velocity of about 1250 feet-per-second from a 4 inch revolver barrel, but can reach 1750 f/s from the 18 to 20 inch barrel of a carbine. The other magnums, the .41 and .44's will also gain much power and can provide good hits to beyond 100 yards with power to spare. Another handgun round that might qualify under this "magnum" rule would a full-power load in the 10 mm Auto. Since no carbines have yet been produced in this caliber, we will have to wait to see what they will do.

The next level above the magnum handgun rounds is the intermediate rifle round. These are generally the same rounds we find in assault type rifles, the .223 Remington and the 7.62 x 39. Another cartridge we must consider simply because there are many rifles around to fit it, is the .30 U.S. Carbine load. This round has an almost universally bad reputation from its military career, but testing with the 110 grain soft point load suggests it may give at least minimal performance as a patrol rifle.[1] The carbines that fire this load vary a great deal in quality, but if you have a good one, and are willing to consider 100 yards as your maximum range, the .30 Carbine can suffice. The .223 Remington (5.56 mm x 45 mm) and the 7.62 mm x 39 mm (.30 Russian Short) are both proven rounds. A small step above the power level of the 7.62 x 39 is the very common .30-30 Winchester cartridge. The heavier bullets of this round place it in the bottom range of the full-power rifle rounds, but with light bullets it gives performance similar to the 7.62 x 39.

The last category of rifle rounds would the full-power rifle cartridges, most commonly seen as the .308 Winchester (7.62 mm x 51 mm NATO) or the .30-06 Springfield. Any rifle cartridge beyond the power level of these two military rounds is more than we need for a patrol rifle. In fact, these two .30's may be over powered for many urban situations, where over-penetration can be a concern.

If you already have a rifle chambered for one of the intermediate rounds, you have a fine patrol rifle that may also do double duty as an assault rifle. If, however, you don't have a good patrol rifle and cannot afford something like a Colt H-Bar, don't be afraid to look elsewhere. Define your needs by the situations you can reasonably expect to face and select a cartridge that will handle the problem. Then select an inexpensive, but reliable rifle that will handle the cartridge.

Perhaps you already have an old Winchester or Marlin lever-action chambered for the .30-30. You're in business. Have the rifle checked by a gunsmith to make sure it's sound, fit it with an aperture sight for better practical accuracy and buy as much ammunition as you can afford. Investing your money in practice ammunition will give you a better end result than spending several hundred dollars for a fancy rifle that you cannot afford to train with. The point here is that almost any action type can fill your needs. Lever actions, pump actions, semi-auto actions, or even bolt actions will do the job.

We need a magazine capacity of at least 5 rounds, but the types of situations in which you might use a patrol rifle make a 30 round magazine a bit superfluous. You should carry some spare ammunition either on your person or on the rifle. The average police pistol shooting situations remain at the 3 shot level. With the increased hit potential and power of the patrol rifle, 5 rounds would seem plenty, though more would do no harm.

The primary limit to your choice of a patrol rifle will be departmental policy. If your administrator is willing to consider your ability to hit, instead of departmental uniformity, your choices are wide open. If the department insists on uniformity you are forced to either comply or to encourage the agency head to purchase and issue rifles.

Ammunition selection is an important part of the rifle package. Since most U.S. sniper rifles are chambered for the .308 Winchester, your decision here is easy. While this may sound one-sided, the ammunition of choice is the Federal 168 grain match load. Similar rounds are loaded by Winchester, Remington, and others, but few can equal the amazingly consistent performance of the Federal load. The Federal load will give excellent accuracy and terminal performance. The 168 grain Sierra Bullet used in these loads normally fragments upon impact but can over-penetrate on body shots.[2] A 150 grain match load may be available in the future to correct the over-penetration where it could be a problem.

If you use a .223 Remington caliber sniper rifle, your ammunition selection is more difficult. Federal makes a 69 grain match load which gives good terminal performance,[3] but many rifles don't seem to shoot it really well. This bullet is extremely long and requires a rifling twist of at least 1-turn-in-9 inches (1/9) to group it well. Since most bolt-action rifles in this caliber have rifling twists of 1/10 or 1/12, their lack of gilt-edge accuracy with this load is understandable. Most 50-55 grain soft point loads use lightly constructed bullets which may not produce reliable results on body shots.[2] The Federal 40 grain "Blitz" load should be avoided since it has been known to disintegrate in flight, especially from the fast twist (1/7 inch) barrels.

Research is on-going to develop a duty-grade expanding bullet load for the .223 Remington. Until then, Ball (full-metal jacket) ammunition gives reliable terminal performance if it will shoot well enough from your rifle. The 60 grain soft point load from either Hornady or Black Hills Ammunition is a marginally acceptable all-around soft point load. Winchester loads a 64 grain power point that gives very good terminal performance, but it requires at least a 1/10 rifling twist to give good accuracy. We can only hope the on-going developments will soon result in a top notch expanding bullet performer in this caliber.

Assault rifles will often do their best with military-grade Ball ammunition, but expanding bullets are preferable. Ammunition selection for the .223 (5.56 mm) rifle has been covered. In the 7.62 x 39, the 125 grain soft point loads will give the best effectiveness, but terminal performance varies quite a bit from brand to brand,[3] so check your load in gelatin or water. Ball ammunition for the 7.62 x 39 tends to penetrate a lot more than the .223, so its use must be evaluated carefully.[2] In the .30 Carbine, only the soft point round should be considered, though Ball ammunition will provide more penetration when cover must be defeated.

In patrol rifles the choices can be more varied. Those using the calibers already covered need read no further. For those using magnum handgun rounds, choose the full-weight jacketed hollowpoint loadings for your caliber. In the .357 Magnum this would be the 158 grain JHP, with the .41 Magnum it is the 210 grain, and in the .44 Magnum, choose the 240 grain loads. Choose carefully since the greatly increased velocity from the carbine can blow some JHP's to bits. With rifle rounds from the .30-30 on up, ammunition selection becomes far less critical. These rifle rounds are designed to hunt big game so they possess plenty of power for people. With these .30 caliber rounds, select a soft-point bullet weighing from 125 to 180 grains and you can expect good performance.

Some terminal testing may be in order to see if your round will over-penetrate. Most of these expanding rifle bullets show from 12 to 18 inches of penetration at muzzle velocity, which matches our needs almost perfectly.[2] At the reduced velocities that come with longer range, these loads can penetrate more than they do at the muzzle, so watch your background when they are employed in populated areas.

One of the most important elements of police rifle use is training. We can touch briefly on the subject here, but it is too complex for much detail in this limited examination. The first step in rifle training is to realize that rifles are different than handguns and shotguns. For that reason most police firearms' trainers are not properly equipped to teach the rifle. A police rifle instructor should be an experienced rifle shooter and should also attend an instructor school designed specifically for rifle training. Currently, the NRA is the only major organization offering a Police Rifle Instructor school. This course will teach you the basics of rifle marksmanship instruction to equip you to teach officers that will be handling all types of police rifles. It is especially good at teaching the shooting positions and record keeping needs of precision shooters.

The instructor fires from the sitting position with a sling on an NRA Rifle Instructor Course.

An officer using any type of rifle should receive a basic training course in the use of their particular rifle. In the case of the patrol rifle, this can be as little as 24 hours if the shooters are already familiar with their rifles. Snipers need more training, at least 40 hours which must include methods of concealment and covert movement. Records must be kept of all rifle training and many agencies require their snipers to record each shot fired from their rifles.

As with training in handguns or shotguns, it is important to spend enough time and to shoot enough ammunition to become intimately familiar with the weapon. With rifles we must train for both rapid shooting at close distances and the slower, more precise style of shooting needed for longer ranges. The training should use sensibly sized targets, practical shooting positions and at least some of the training should be off the formal range. These sessions must emphasize a combination of marksmanship, tactics, and scenario-induced stress.

Another photo of the NRA Rifle Instructor Course. The instructor fires from the prone position with a sling and a coach assists. The rifle is a stainless steel Ruger Mini-14.

The various rifles add an important element to law enforcement's arsenal. With proper selection and training these rifles will help us greatly in our war on crime. With poor equipment choices or inadequate training these rifles can get such a bad reputation that their use might be severely limited. It is important that we use these weapons wisely and well. You might need one to save your life someday!

Bibliography

[1] Fackler, M.L., Bellamy, R.F., and Malinowski, J.A. *The Wound Profile Illustration of the Missile-Tissue Interaction.* The Journal of Trauma. 28: 21-29.

[2] Roberts, G.K. 1991. *Introduction to Wound Ballistics, 2nd Ed.* U.S. Navy, Naval Station. Treasure Island, CA and California Department of Justice.

[3] Fackler, M.L., Roberts, G.K. 1992. "Failure to Expand: Federal 7.62 x 39 mm Soft Point Bullets." *Wound Ballistics Review.* (Winter): 18-20.

John S. Farnam

    Mr. Farnam is one of the world's top authorities on defensive shooting and tactics. He is a combat veteran of the Vietnam War, a major (retired) in the U.S. Army Reserve, and a police officer with many years of practical experience. In addition, Mr. Farnam is an acclaimed and prominent author, lecturer, expert witness, consultant, and professional firearms training specialist.
    Through Defense Training International, Inc., John conducts defensive firearms' training seminars nationally and internationally. He teaches the latest defensive techniques to police departments, Federal and state agencies, and foreign governments. John's dynamic teaching style, superlative communications skills, courtroom savvy, and considerable personal experience have made him the dean of defensive shooting and tactics' instructors.

Chapter 17

Handle Your Handgun Correctly!

by John S. Farnam

It is amazing to see even ostensibly experienced police officers routinely handle their sidearms with incorrect and often dangerous techniques. If we, in the law enforcement business, are to cut down on our own handgun accidents and, by example, cut down on gun accidents in general, all of us must have a solid foundation in correct manipulation of the weapon.

Colt/Browning System Autoloader

These weapons are properly carried with the hammer cocked, a live round in the chamber, and the manual safety on. The first and all subsequent shots are fired from a cocked hammer. Typically, the trigger need only move 1.5 mm (.06 inches) against a resistance of 2.3kg (5 lbs.) to release the hammer and discharge the weapon. The center of the pad of the trigger finger should lie on the center of the trigger. The triggers on Colt/Browning System autoloaders should be narrow, and may be grooved as long as the grooves are not sharp.

During firing, the correct grip must be maintained. Thus, the strong-side thumb must push the manual safety off (down) during the draw, and must remain on top of the safety, maintaining continuous downward pressure as the weapon is fired. If the right thumb gets under the manual safety during firing, the weapon's recoil may force it back up (on), thus making the weapon temporarily unfirable. This also means that fingers and thumbs must be kept above the slide-release lever. If a finger or thumb is positioned under the slide-release lever, the weapon's recoil may force the slide-release lever upward, locking the slide to the rear while there are still rounds in the magazine. Conversely, if finger pressure is inadvertently applied to the top of the slide-release lever, the slide may not lock to the rear when it is supposed to, that is, after the last round is fired. The slide, of course, should lock to the rear when the last round is fired. This is to remind the operator that the weapon is empty. Obviously, the slide should not lock to the rear when there are still rounds in the magazine.

In defensive shooting, the trigger finger must be able to make contact with the trigger as the target is tracked. The operators must be able to touch the trigger in anticipation of shooting, and then, at the last moment, be able to decide not to shoot. They must also be able to hold the weapon on someone with their finger making light contact with the trigger. They must be able to be ready to shoot for several minutes with every confidence that the weapon will not discharge, until or unless they want and need it to do so.

When holding a Colt/Browning System autoloader on a subject, the trigger finger is properly in light contact with the trigger. The manual safety is on and the strong-side thumb rests on top of it, ready to push it off. If you must fire, the safety is pushed off and the trigger is pressed. However, if there is already sufficient pressure on the trigger, pushing the safety off will discharge the weapon. In extreme circumstances, this may be necessary and prudent, but it is generally advisable to get into the habit of firing the weapon with the trigger, not the safety lever. You may have to push the safety off and back on again several times during the confrontation, all the while keeping your finger in light contact with the trigger. Therefore, with the Colt/Browning System autoloader, we teach you to disengage the safety first, and then, with the trigger finger, make contact with the trigger. Take up the slack and carefully press the trigger straight back in one smooth motion, all the while keeping the front sight on the target. When the weapon discharges, contact is re-established immediately and the scenario repeated, if necessary.

Some heavily involved target shooters suggest that when the Colt/Browning System autoloader is held in the fire position, the trigger finger should be slightly out of contact with the trigger, and "poised" just in front of it. They contend that the shooters can then simply "bump" or "slap" the trigger gently when they want the weapon to discharge. As with so many other "advanced" techniques developed by naive contest shooters, this procedure is counterproductive in defensive shooting. The problem is that this technique requires a super light trigger (less than 1.3kg). A "bump" forceful enough to release a legitimate 2.3kg defensive trigger will invariably "bump" the front sight right off the target.

Double-Action Revolver

Here, the center of the trigger should lie in the first joint of the trigger finger, not on the pad. You need that much finger on the trigger in order to have sufficient strength to pull it through smoothly. It is necessary to concentrate on the front sight and hold the weapon steady during the entire trigger pull. When the weapon discharges, the trigger must be allowed to return all the way forward to its original resting position. The sight picture must be immediately re-established, and trigger pressure may then be started once again for the next shot.

The double-action revolver's trigger itself should be smooth (no grooves) and narrow, if the weapon is intended for defensive use. Wide, sharply grooved target triggers and triggers equipped with "trigger shoes," are a liability in defensive shooting. When shooting in the trigger-cocking mode, the trigger finger must actually slide slightly across the face of the trigger during the trigger pull if the muzzle is to remain stationary. A grooved trigger tends to adhere to the finger as soon as contact is made. When the trigger finger is not permitted to slide smoothly across the trigger face, the trigger finger forces the entire weapon to move during the trigger pull, and the sight picture will be disturbed.

A revolver chambered for the 357 Mg cartridge will also chamber and fire 38 Spl cartridges. The same is true for 44 Mg/44 Spl. This is claimed by many to be a great advantage of the 357 Mg revolver, since 38 Spl ammunition is less expensive than 357 Mg ammunition. However, there are some problems with this practice. Shooting a lot of 38 Spl practice ammunition in a 357 Mg revolver deposits lead, soot, and bullet lubricant on the inside of the chambers everywhere ahead of the mouth of the 38 Spl case. The subsequent chambering of the longer 357 Mg rounds is nearly impossible until the contamination is removed. This condition can be more than just a nuisance. If you have been shooting 38 Spl practice ammunition in your 357 Mg revolver, you will have to clean the weapon before you leave the range. Otherwise you will be forced to load it with the under powered practice ammunition for the trip home, since you will not be able to get your 357 Mg rounds in it.

Another problem is the hot gases associated with bullet launch eventually cause spalling on the walls of the chamber. The chamber will gradually be ringed with tiny spall marks where the bullet comes off the 38 Spl case. When the longer 357 Mg's are then fired in the same chambers, the brass will expand into the spall ring, making extraction difficult and eventually impossible. What all this means is that shooting a lot of 38 Spl's (especially +P's) in a 357 Mg revolver will eventually ruin the weapon for 357 Mg rounds. As a solution to the problem, you can do one of two things. Simply dedicate the weapon to 38 Spl and do not bother with 357 Mg rounds, or shoot only 357 Mg rounds in it, both for practice and for duty. The 357 Mg practice ammunition is becoming fairly common and is available from most commercial ammunition re-manufacturers. It is only slightly more expensive than 38 Spl practice ammunition, and it is worth it.

The bullets on some of the more powerful revolver reloads are not properly crimped and, when chambered, they can jump forward under the recoil of other rounds being fired. Sometimes they jump forward far enough to protrude beyond the front face of the cylinder. This condition will obviously seize the cylinder as it attempts to rotate, producing a frozen gun. Therefore, test a particular brand of reloaded ammunition before acquiring large quantities of it.

Trigger-Cocking Autoloader

In this case, the trigger movement for the first shot will be similar to that of a double-action revolver. As with a double-action revolver, the first joint of the trigger finger lies in the center of the trigger. Hence, a defensive trigger-cocking autoloader should have a smooth, narrow trigger, similar to that on a defensive double-action revolver, and for the same reasons.

With trigger-cocking, self-decocking autoloaders, such as the Glock, every trigger press is exactly the same, since the gun decocks itself with every shot. The second and all subsequent shots (until the weapon is decocked) are fired from a cocked hammer. A trigger-cocking, manually-decocking autoloader has two distinctly different trigger pulls; one for the first shot and another for subsequent shots. It is usually inadvisable to shift finger position after the first shot. Such finger shifting is time-consuming, distracting, and clumsy. Instead, continue to use the first joint position, but reduce the pressure. For the second and subsequent shots, the trigger will, as mentioned above, be in a position near the rear of the trigger guard. This position only requires 1.5 mm (.06 inches) of movement against 1.8kg (4 lbs.) of resistance to release the hammer and discharge the weapon.

In all fairness, some people have had success shooting the trigger-cocking autoloader via the finger tip position for all shots. If you can do it consistently well, there isn't any reason not to. However, most people do not have sufficient size or strength in their hands and fingers to make this maneuver work. Needless to say, mastering this type of handgun requires a lot of correct practice.

All trigger-cocking autoloaders are properly carried with the hammer down on a live round, full magazine inserted, and with safety (if the weapon has one) off. I do not recommend carrying the trigger-cocking autoloader with the safety on as a general practice. The act of taking the safety off during the draw is awkward and dubious for most people, even those who claim they can do it reliably. Fingers should also be kept above the slide-release lever, the same as with the Colt/Browning System autoloader, and for the same reason.

Follow Through

You often hear instructors describe the "Crunch, Crash, Bang Syndrome" when talking about trigger-cocking, manually decocking autoloaders. They are describing a common occurrence when new shooters are introduced to these handguns.

The first shot requires what seems like a long, agonizing trigger pull. This is the "Crunch." New shooters often put too much muscle on the trigger, pulling the muzzle down or heeling the shot off to the left. For the next shot, the trigger is now in its rear position, and requires much less movement and pressure. Inexperienced shooters will put as much pressure on the trigger as they did for the first shot. This is the "Crash." The gun will discharge prematurely, mightily surprising the shooter. The shot predictably goes way wide, because the sights were not yet on target. After thus squandering the first two shots, the astute shooter finally settles down and gets a hit with his third shot. This is the "Bang."

Handle Your Handgun Correctly! 147

The point is that every time the trigger finger leaves contact with the trigger and returns to the register position, the gun must be immediately decocked (and immediately re-enabled in the case of the two-stage decocking autoloaders). This is an absolute necessity, because the trigger must be repositioned to where the trigger finger expects to find it. There is really no viable alternative. As long as the shooter keeps firing, and his finger is thus in continuous contact with the trigger, the trigger's location within the trigger guard is irrelevant. However, when trigger contact is lost, as it will be when the trigger finger returns to register, decocking is necessary. The alternative is to inherit a high probability of missing with the next shot and maybe even wounding yourself.

The sight picture and stance must be re-established immediately after discharge. Do not turn to jelly the instant the hammer falls. Since you do not know the exact moment the hammer will be released, hold your position steady before, during, and after the hammer falls. Maintain your stance and sight picture for at least three seconds after the last discharge and be prepared to shoot again, should it become necessary. When you are satisfied that it is safe to reholster, lower the weapon from eye level, keeping your arms affixed in your shooting stance. Move your head left and right to see if there is anything that escaped your notice. It does not suffice to merely shift your eyes; you must move your entire head. Tunnel vision will thus be broken, and you will be able to notice things on the periphery of your vision. This may also be a good time to reload.

As you lower the weapon from eye level, the trigger finger automatically comes off the trigger and returns to register. With autoloaders, particularly the Colt/Browning System, when the trigger finger comes off the trigger, the pad should find its place where the front of the trigger guard joins the frame. Do not put your finger on the right extension of the slide stop pin, as you might inadvertently push it in, causing the weapon to instantly disassemble itself. Also, as you lower the weapon from eye level, the manual safety (Colt/Browning System autoloaders) is re-engaged. Then the thumb is immediately repositioned back on top of the safety, ready to push it off again. With trigger and squeeze-cocking autoloaders, the weapon is decocked at this time. With manually decocking, trigger-cocking autoloaders, the weapon is decocked by manipulating the decocking lever with the strong thumb only. Neither the trigger, nor the hammer, is touched during decocking. Self-decocking autoloaders (often erroneously referred to as "double-action" only by the unenlightened) of course, automatically decock themselves every time the slide goes into battery.

"Decocking" is a process necessitated by the trigger-cocking feature on a slide-cocking autoloader. The gun is correctly carried with the hammer forward and a live round chambered. Pressing the trigger draws back and subsequently releases the hammer, firing the chambered round. With autoloaders, which feature two-stage manually decocking with the trigger finger in register, the strong thumb pushes the decocking lever down and then immediately pushes it back up (it springs back up by itself in the single-stage decocking autoloaders). The lever should not stay in the down position for more than an instant, because pushing the lever down not only decocks the weapon, but sterilizes it as well. Since holding a sterile weapon in one's hand in the middle of a threatening situation is not a prudent thing to do, the safety/decocking lever is in the down position only long enough to decock the weapon. It is then immediately pushed back up, re-enabling the gun.

During the cycle of operation on manually decocking autoloaders, the consequent movement of the slide ejects the expended case, chambers a fresh round, and recocks the hammer. After the first shot, the shooters are always holding a gun with its hammer cocked (until the last round is fired and the slide locks to the rear). If the shooters desire to stop shooting and reholster their gun prior to the last round being fired, they are presented with a problem. The gun cannot be safely carried or holstered with the hammer cocked. The hammer must be safely lowered. The safety/decocking lever is there to permit the shooter to quickly, safely, and conveniently lower the hammer without the danger of firing the gun accidentally.

There are four sets of circumstances when any trigger-cocking autoloader should be decocked:

- prior to holstering;
- when holding a subject at gun point;
- prior to moving with the gun in hand; or
- any other time the trigger finger loses contact with the trigger.

Holding a cocked, trigger-cocking firearm on a subject for an extended period of time is an invitation to tragedy. There is not sufficient trigger movement or spring resistance to assure total control over the gun. Any sudden or loud sound that is sufficient to engender an involuntary spasm in the shooter's hand will cause the gun to discharge unintentionally, with tragic and appalling results.

In addition, users of these guns (trigger-cocking autoloaders) have learned how to move their trigger finger quickly from register to trigger contact, but only when the trigger is in the forward position as it would be when the weapon is decocked. If the user tries to fire suddenly with a cocked weapon when his finger is in register, the trigger will not be where his finger has trained itself to expect it. What often happens is the finger falls through the empty space within the trigger guard and ultimately slams into the trigger (in its unfamiliar rearward position), often with sufficient force to cause an accidental discharge.

With any trigger-cocking autoloader, when the trigger finger loses contact with the trigger, immediately return the trigger to where the finger expects to find it. Thus, if the users try to move with the hammer still cocked and their finger in register, when they suddenly have to shoot again, they will probably fire long before their sights ever reach the target, for the exact reason depicted above. Their first shot will certainly not hit the intended target. It may strike the ground several meters in front of them, or it may strike their leg, knee, foot, or groin.

Handle Your Handgun Correctly!

In Summary

The pistol is drawn and brought up to eye level and the decision has been made to fire. As the gun reaches eye level:

- Hit the breaks! Don't try to fire before the sight picture has been confirmed.
- Confirm that the sights are on target and that the sight picture is correct.
- Establish finger contact with the trigger.
- Start rearward pressure while holding the pistol steady, or track the target if it's moving.
- Wait for the gun to discharge.
- After the gun discharges, hold the trigger all the way to the rear and immediately recover and re-establish a correct sight picture on the target.
- Hold the gun steady as you let the trigger up until you catch the link. Let it up no further.
- Assuming additional shooting is necessary, immediately start rearward pressure on the trigger again.
- Repeat the cycle as many times as necessary.

Remember, there are two things which distinguish a professional gunman from an amateur. **We don't have accidents, and we don't miss!**

Neal Fortin

Mr. Fortin is a thirteen-year veteran of law enforcement. He has been a uniformed police officer, security supervisor at a maximum-security facility, and currently serves as a plainclothes investigator. He has received two citations for personal courage, five letters of commendation, and ten other awards for his work contributions. Neal writes the "Police Locker" column for Combat Handguns and is a contributing editor and writes the "Training Tips" column for Guns & Weapons for Law Enforcement.

Chapter 18

The Law Enforcement Attitude

by Neal Fortin

"Why did you become a police officer?" This is a question every police officer will be asked at one time or another. More often than not, the answer is just a shrug of the shoulders.

"Why did you become a police officer?" is a difficult question to answer mostly because the question is steeped in prejudice and misconceptions. No one asks a doctor, a teacher, or a garbage collector why they entered their career path. Yet, young people who announce their intentions of becoming police officers are often bombarded with arguments that the ambition is a waste of time and intelligence.

Certainly, other jobs would be more rewarding in public respect and finances. Police officers, by and large, have above average intelligence. They could have become successful businessmen, executives, and engineers.

Most police officers are dedicated individuals who heroically shoulder the demands of the job, often at great personal sacrifice. Many put in hundreds of hours of uncompensated overtime to solve cases simply for the personal reward of serving justice.

The work is often hazardous and always demanding. Officers are spit on, stabbed, shot, and beaten. At any time, a fellow human being may try to extinguish an officer's life with no more concern or remorse than someone swatting a mosquito.

Not long ago in my jurisdiction, an AIDS infected prisoner smeared officers with his feces, and then tried to slash them with his, sharpened, talon-like fingernails. Yet, an officer must accept this abuse like a martyr and display the self restraint of a saint.

Stepping onto the witness stand in the halls of justice, police officers discover that the rules of decency and the laws of slander and perjury don't apply to defense attorneys. The officers must endure the foulest of accusations, lies, and insults. They must learn to take it or lose their credibility and their cases. Is it any wonder that police officers tell so many jokes about attorneys?

Typically, even the worst criminals have more rights than police officers. For example, if placed under internal investigation, officers often find that the law revokes their Fifth Amendment rights. Bitten by a known drug addict, an officer's risk of infection by hepatitis or AIDS often has less merit in the court than the addict's "right" to refuse a blood test.

Citizens often blame police officers for the lawlessness on the streets, yet the officers must stand by as criminals have their wrists slapped by the courts. Criminals are paroled, sentences are suspended, and felonies are plea bargained down to meaningless misdemeanors for the sake of expediency.

Officers arrest repeat offenders only to have the courts release them on meaningless bail. It is not uncommon to re-arrest the same criminal three or four times before the original charges ever come to trial. Building new, additional charges against the same criminal can result in a multimillion dollar lawsuit against the police department, and the arresting officer individually, for discrimination and harassment.

Police officers have to experience things that no human being should ever have to. A baby is dipped into a pot of boiling water because "he wouldn't stop crying." A 68-year old man murders his wife because she wouldn't make him a peanut butter sandwich. A four-year old baby is sexually assaulted and murdered through sadistic torture. A teenage murderer grins in the back of the patrol car as he enjoys the ride, and gleefully asks, "Hey, can you guys turn on the siren?"

Police officers see the cold, reptilian recesses hidden in mankind that many civilians cannot believe, and even trained psychologists have a difficult time imagining. The officer must live with memories of the gore and inhumanity that sear the human soul.

Police officers must battle becoming cynical about the whole human race. Their friends and loved ones tell them, "You've changed," and the officers lack the words to explain why. One of the most powerful means of coping is humor, but civilians often misunderstand the sometimes bizarre, black humor of the police officer.

It is easy to divide the world into two camps; the initiated and the uninitiated; those who understand and those who never will. So when someone asks, "Why did you become a police officer?" or "What's it like to be a police officer?" describing the experience can seem hopeless.

Silence is easier because of the prejudices about the police that society holds true. The word "police" often conjures up images of slow witted, fat men, who like to drive fast, shoot guns, and push people around. Hollywood and television feed these misconceptions and create other unrealistic images of police work and the police.

Prejudice against the police is one of the last unchallenged bias in our society. Among some groups, it is fashionable to openly display this prejudice, and some even take pride in public display of their bias, mistaking prejudice for reasoned thought.

"Police are on a power trip," goes a common refrain, but these words really reveal more about the speaker than anything about police officers. A great many people have hang ups about power, and have difficulty dealing with authority. What the public usually mistakes for a "power trip" is command authority, often learned the hard way; on the streets. Becoming a police officer is the best school of assertiveness training in the world. A police officer learns — must learn — command authority to do the job and stay alive.

Another cruel fabrication says that police are closed minded. This false perception springs also from the demands of the job. Officers learn early to develop a built-in bullshit detector. They survive by trusting themselves and by trusting only the things that have been proven to work. They must learn these things, or they don't live long.

There is a saying that an idealist is someone who knows that roses smell better than cabbage, so they proceed to make rose-petal soup. The "closed minded" cop comes along and bursts their bubble. "I don't care how good roses smell," the cop says, "Cabbage soup tastes better."

Americans like to view themselves as free thinkers and candid speakers, but actually large segments of our society abhor candor. Just listen to virtually any politician, business executive, or bureaucrat. Our society floats in euphemisms, Orwellian newspeak, and double talk.

Most groups and organizations shelter dogmas or sacred cows, where all candid speech is quashed. Among the police, however, plain speaking and assertiveness are not in short supply. Like the little boy in the fable who says the king has no clothes, a cop is often the one to speak his mind bluntly, even if it means saying things no one else likes to hear.

As a reward for their candor, police are accused of being opinionated. Though commands are expected to be carried out with military-like fidelity, no group speaks their minds more freely. Such candor is just one of the reasons police are interesting people to be around.

The public's prejudice sometimes overflows into physical and verbal abuse. In some ways, the psychological abuse is the hardest to take. For example, police officers are reviled with every foul name in the book, not just by criminals, but by businessmen and other citizens. Often officers are scorned simply because they had the gall to stop a citizen for drunk driving or some other traffic violation. Officers expect such prejudice and abuse from criminals, but it is much harder to take from citizens, people they think of as their people.

Rather than "Why did you become a police officer?" a more poignant, penetrating question might be "Why do you stay?" Victories along the way help, and being the instrument of justice can be satisfying. The system may be frustrating and slow, but justice often has a way of catching up. Experienced officers learn the truth in the saying, "What goes around, comes around."

My favorite example of justice catching up occurred when I was sued for 32 million dollars for discrimination. I had brought three different sets of criminal charges against the same defendant, lapping him while he was out on bail for each of the previous charges. After listening to the defendant's absurd accusations in civil court, I stood by smiling, as he left the civil court only to be arrested in the hallway by brother officers on the fourth set of criminal charges I had brought against him.

The idea of fabricating false charges, fairly common to Hollywood, is absurd to seasoned officers. They know, that like a dog that returns to its own vomit, criminals return to their criminal ways. Officers only have to be patient. "What goes around, comes around."

Many of the satisfactions of the job have nothing to do with criminals. An example is responding to a call that a baby had drown in the bath tub and arriving on the scene to find the child blue and apparently dead.

A single experience of bringing a child back to life with mouth-to-mouth resuscitation makes everything else worthwhile. Other sources of pride are as simple as walking down the street in uniform and seeing the look of relief and security on the face of an elderly lady. Times like this make the officer feel ten feet tall.

Underlying it all, officers stay on the job out of a faith that it is right, important, and good. They believe in justice and have faith that right and good must and will triumph in the end. They believe that protecting the innocent is the noblest calling.

"Hokey ideals," the cynics in our society say, as though belief in goodness and justice are childish playthings mankind should outgrow. Skepticism is healthy, but cynicism is a destructive hoax the mind plays on itself. When cynicism mocks belief in justice and the right and good of law enforcement, the civilian and police officer alike need a reality check.

Law enforcement is the thin blue line that preserves our civilization against anarchy. If you have any doubts about this, rent a copy of the movie, *The Road Warrior*, not as entertainment, but as a documentary of a world without law. In a world without law enforcement, you can be sure the neo-Nazis and KKK types won't fill their idle time by opening soup kitchens for the hungry. And, the Spawn of Satan and Mutant Moron street gangs won't amuse themselves by building shelters for the homeless.

The good men and women of law enforcement hold our world together. They shoulder a demanding job so others can sleep soundly at night; so gentle souls may be poets, and children can laugh and play. Police officers are guardians of everything that is good in our society.

New officers often begin their careers with an image of themselves as Blue Knights. As the cub officers mature, their self image changes and matures, but the best retain their faith in all that is good and right about the job. Often, once their faith dies, officers don't last long. They quit or transfer to jobs where they can mark time, oxen-like, until retirement, or they quit inside. They become limp and leaden eyed; a part of their spirit dies.

Even with today's increasing threats — teams of criminals, heavier firepower, fortified crack houses, and a new ruthlessness — bullets are not the greatest risk police officers face today; stress is. Stress kills more police officers than all the guns, knives, and bludgeons combined.

Loss in the belief that the job is right, important, and good contributes greatly to stress, and maintaining faith is a survival skill. In order to maintain faith, officers must seek out good people; people who support them and their values: loved ones, family and friends, especially those outside the job.

Due to society's prejudice, and because there is no simple way to describe law enforcement work to the uninitiated, too often law enforcement officers shy away from trying to explain the profession. It is healthy to end at least some of this self-imposed silence. Otherwise the public's fascination with police work will feast on unrealistic potboilers and Hollywood inventions.

Ending the silence is the only way civilians will understand the

The Law Enforcement Attitude

profession, and the only way to break down the walls created between police and civilians. It is only way to communicate the well-deserved pride in the good and the right of the job. Silence implies shame, and law enforcement is a noble calling which needs no excuses.

Theodore Roosevelt pitied the poor spirits "who neither enjoy much nor suffer much, because they live in the gray twilight that knows not victory nor defeat." Much honor belongs to the men and women of law enforcement who experience both victory and defeat; who are actually in the arena; and who, through sweat and blood, spend themselves on a great and worthy cause.

Anyone who chooses a career in law enforcement can be proud of their contribution to society. For certain, special kinds of people, no career is more satisfying. Everyone should be proud of the good men and women who answer this call.

Roger Fulton

Mr. Fulton is a retired New York State Police Captain. Throughout his career, he received commendations for his performance in virtually every aspect of police work, from saving lives and arresting dangerous criminals, to designing innovative training programs for officers at all levels.

He holds a Master's degree in Criminal Justice and is a graduate of the FBI's prestigious National Academy. He is the author of the book, Common Sense Supervision, *and writes a regular column for a national police magazine. His work has received national and international attention.*

Currently, he is the driving force behind Knight Management Corporation, an Albany, NY based training and consulting firm which he founded in 1986.

Chapter 19

How to Stay On the Team

by Roger Fulton

When a police officer is killed in the line of duty, everyone is concerned. The aftermath usually includes steps to prevent a similar occurrence. New procedures are installed, additional training programs are put in place, and there is an increased awareness of the career-ending dangers faced by every officer.

Most police careers don't end through the hostile action of a deranged criminal, however. Many careers end prematurely as the result of disciplinary actions, stress-related illnesses, burnout, or off-duty conduct problems. Yet, because these career-ending issues are less dramatic, there are no emotional hues and cries for specific programs to prevent them.

Too often, it is up to individual officers to learn, on their own, how to survive these potentially career-ending problems. Once aware of the pitfalls, most experienced officers are quite adept at avoiding them. Most will learn to work comfortably within the system, with a minimum of stress, until they choose to retire. Those who don't learn the lessons can lose their careers, families and, all too often, their self-respect and dignity.

As a police officer, there are four major areas where you must maintain reasonable relationships, or risk the chance of your career getting into serious trouble or ending prematurely. They include: Dealing With the Department, Dealing With Coworkers, Dealing With the Public, and the most important area, Dealing With Yourself. Each area has several potential problem situations to avoid. Many require specific action, or inaction, on your part. Others simply require that you use good common sense in your dealings to avoid the problems entirely. In each case, survival is up to you!

Dealing With the Department

"Do your work with your whole heart and you will succeed — there is so little competition."

— Elbert Hubbard

In dealing with all levels of your department, a good attitude is your greatest ally. You can take a bitter, anti-management stance in all matters and constantly be in a state of high stress, or you can adopt a cooperative attitude, do what is expected of you, follow the rules, and keep your blood pressure at a reasonable level. It's up to you!

Loyalty

Are you loyal to your department? After all, the department probably provides you with a pay check for your family, health insurance, life insurance, and other fringe benefits. The check is always there on time, and you have job security.

Are you always there on time? Are you out sick only when you can't or shouldn't work? Do you do an honest day's work for an honest day's pay?

Loyalty is a two-way street. Both you and the department owe a certain degree of loyalty to each other.

Keeping Your Boss Happy

Bosses essentially have the same goals that you have. They want to come to work, do their job to the best of their ability with a minimum of hassle, and go home at the end of their shift.

In order for both of you to achieve these mutual goals, you have to cooperate by doing what is expected of you. The greatest areas of conflict between officers and their bosses include incomplete or missing paperwork, cars out of their sector, not answering the radio, and embarrassing the boss by not keeping him or her informed of a critical incident.

Conflicts between officers and their bosses are always counter-productive. Nobody wins except the criminals. Therefore, do what is required to get the job done so you can both go home in a good mood.

Second Guessing Management

All of the various levels of management in a police organization have different pressures to deal with and different information on which to base their decisions. As an example, consider a decision that each patrol car will be required to run an extra 20,000 miles before it is replaced. To the patrolmen, that makes their job tougher with unreliable vehicles. To the Sergeant, it means more maintenance requests and record keeping. To the Chief, it is a way to keep from laying off patrolmen due to budget cuts.

Understanding that management tries to do the best it can with what it has can make some decisions more palatable. This is not to say that you shouldn't protest through channels if the decision presents a safety hazard, but most don't.

Fighting every decision with a "them versus us" mentality is counter-productive, and will cause you a great deal of stress. Since many management decisions are based on information which you may not have access to, accept the change and save yourself a lot of aggravation.

Is Your Department Proud of You?

Your department exists to "protect and serve" the public. When this is done properly, the residents know it and convey their feelings to the politicians, the Chief, and to other high ranking officials.

If the public receives abuse of authority, arrogance, and excessive force from the members of the department, they will convey that message to the same people, except much faster.

When the members of a department act professionally, the department gets a reputation for being professional. Then you can be proud of your department and they can be proud of you.

Dealing With Coworkers

"No man is an Island, entire of itself; every man is a piece of the Continent, a part of the main."
— John Donne

Working in harmony with other officers, civilian personnel, specialized units, and other departments and units have become routine in police departments. This interaction can be enjoyable, but there are some career damaging pitfalls that the knowledgeable officer needs to avoid.

Relationships With Other Departments

Fire trucks at the scene of a fire are blocking all lanes of traffic. Who is responsible for traffic control, the police department or the fire department? When you are assigned to assist the highway patrol with a high speed chase, who is in charge of the pursuit if the patrol car spins out? The answers to these questions and dozens of others should be clear in your mind before the incidents occur. However, there will occasionally be a question that arises which hasn't been thought out beforehand and needs an immediate, on-scene solution.

The key in such cases is to approach the situation rationally with your counterpart, or the person you believe is your counterpart, in the other unit. Cooperation and rational thought, not egos and territorialism, will give you the best solution.

Keep in mind that if a conflict cannot be resolved at the scene of an incident, it will become a major political conflict to be decided the next day by people who weren't even at the scene. When the finger pointing and accusations are all over, you may be upset at the decision. You may also end up being perceived as part of the problem.

Being knowledgeable about interagency arrangements, and keeping a clear head when conflicts do arise, will help your career and make it easier for those who work with those other agencies in the future.

Safety First

"Let's wait for our backup," your partner says, as you arrive at a burglary in progress call at a closed bowling alley. As the senior member in the car you announce, "No, we're going in now. We can't wait all night for them." If someone gets killed or injured, you will be severely criticized. Even if tragedy doesn't strike, your partner may perceive you as a "hotshot" who doesn't care about his safety. Simple logic dictates that two officers can't search a whole bowling alley and cover all of the exits at the same time. Between the two errors in judgment, who will want to ride with you in the future?

Remember that everyone should have the same goal, going home safe and sound.

New Employees

Historically, veteran police have been cool toward "rookies." Somehow it was felt that they must earn their acceptance as police officers by surviving in critical situations. True, new police officers must exhibit courage and competence on the job, but why must they be treated poorly before they ever face such a situation?

If you think back to when you were a "rookie," wouldn't it have been helpful if someone had given you a hand at "learning the ropes." You would have felt more at ease, more confident, and would have viewed yourself as part of the team.

Police work is interesting because you never know who might become your supervisor in the future. Imagine your surprise when your new precinct commander is the "rookie" you pulled all the dirty tricks on a few years ago.

Gossip and Rumors

When you walk into a courtroom in America, there are only certain things you can say about the defendant and his actions. You must present hard evidence to support your case. You cannot convict someone solely on hearsay or gossip. You cannot express an opinion unsupported by facts, and you cannot present rumors of criminal activity by the defendant as evidence.

If you can't do that to a defendant, then why would you do that to a coworker? Many careers have been damaged by unfounded rumors or gossip. Occasionally, justice prevails, and the one who was spreading the untrue rumors becomes the victim of their own venom, and their career becomes the one in trouble.

Your best bet is to avoid gossip, rumors, and those who insist on spreading them.

Sexual Harassment

In recent years, sexual harassment has become a sure fire way to ruin your career quickly. However, many officers don't know that their actions or words can be interpreted as sexual harassment. Therefore, they unknowingly get themselves, their supervisors, and their departments into serious trouble.

Although it is recommended that all officers attend a formal program on sexual harassment prevention, a few guidelines are set out here to aid officers who haven't had access to such a course.

Part of your supervisor's duties is to guard against the words or actions of officers that make the workplace a sexually oriented or distasteful place to work for female employees. Some of the actions which female employees might find sexually oriented and distasteful include:

- Exposure to sexually oriented letters, phone calls, or printed materials.

- Touching, in any form.

- Unwanted sexual advances, or unwanted and repeated requests for dates.

- Questions about sexual activities.

- Off-color jokes or gestures.

You can rest assured that if your department, or any of its supervisors, is charged with allowing sexual harassment in the workplace because of your actions, you will probably face some form of disciplinary action. Depending on the severity of your infraction, your actions could tarnish your career, or put you in the unemployment line. Forewarned is forearmed!

Romantic Relationships

Ted and Sally were assigned to the same precinct on the same day. They were immediately attracted to each other. Over a period of time, they began dating and developed a steady relationship. Unfortunately, the relationship ended after 3 months with a very nasty argument over Ted's involvement with his ex-wife.

Even though the relationship had ended, both officers were constantly reminded of the incident several times a week as they passed in the halls, or were assigned to the same shifts or special details. Their bitterness toward each other was still apparent to their supervisors and coworkers months later. The sergeants felt they had to rearrange schedules to avoid assigning them to the same car or detail. That inconvenienced other officers. Their coworkers felt they had to be careful about mentioning one when the other was present. Mercifully, Ted finally received a transfer he had requested months before to an administrative unit at headquarters.

Ted and Sally's personal involvement had caused months of problems in the precinct, and certainly didn't help their careers. Although some relationships which start at work have happier endings, many others end, as in this example, with lingering problems.

Carefully consider the possible consequences before getting romantically involved with one of your coworkers.

Dealing With the Public

"When a man assumes a public trust, he should consider himself as public property."
— Thomas Jefferson

Police work is an amazing occupation. Where else can you have so much power over other people's actions and freedom in such a short time? In addition, an experienced police officer is given a brand new car and all kinds of modern equipment, and is sent out among the public with little, if any, direct supervision. Police officers are given wide discretion to resolve conflicts and handle problems as they see fit, often under very loose guidelines. Yet, their decisions and actions can affect citizens' lives for an eternity.

With so much public trust, there is always a danger of abusing the power, the freedom, or the lack of direct supervision. Keeping the phrase "to protect and serve" in mind will help you keep your perspective about your position. In addition, here are a few other hints which will help you maintain your professionalism and avoid unnecessary problems with the public.

Looking the Part

Most citizens, not trained in observation techniques, might ask the question, "What do police officers look like?" with an answer like, "You know them when you see them." When pressed for details, they will describe the police officer that they are most familiar with.

Would a citizen describe you as "Clean, neat, always sharp. His shoes are always shined and his hair is always trimmed. He looks like a policeman!"

Does appearance really matter even though you can get the job done? Absolutely!

The public expects a police officer to look good. After all, you are America's finest. They have respect for and confidence in a well-groomed officer. They don't even need to know your name, as long as you look as though you know what you're doing. Even the criminal element has some respect for a well-groomed officer.

However, "looking the part" isn't just grooming. It is the attitude and demeanor you exhibit that makes all eyes look toward you. It makes many potentially combatant persons think twice about attacking you, and makes others listen carefully to what you say. It's knowing that you are confident in your ability to handle the situation and resolve the conflict to the satisfaction of all parties.

When you look good, you feel good. When you feel good, you are good, and that is what you should convey to others.

Customer Service

In many areas of the United States, citizens can choose the police agency that they want to respond to a non-emergency incident. They can choose between their town or village police, the county sheriff's department, or the state police. Some housing developments have their own private police who only work with public sector agencies when they have a serious crime committed, such as a homicide or armed robbery. There are now more private security employees than there are public security employees. Projections are for even more private security positions in the future.

All of this leads up to a word the private sector has lived with for years, but that the public sector is still just learning. That word is "competition." If your department cannot provide the level of service your "customers" demand, you may find your budget slashed, or in extreme cases, your department abolished.

You and your colleagues must answer calls promptly and courteously to guard against such an eventuality. You must address the problem and resolve it to the satisfaction of all parties. When crimes have a chance of being solved, you must exhaust all leads during your investigation. In general, you must provide the best possible service to the citizens you serve, or someone else will.

Not In Your Job Description

What does a policeman's job entail? Some argue that the police should be dedicated solely to fighting crime. Yet repeated analysis of their actual duties show that they spend only a small portion of their time in crime related activities.

The term "to protect and serve" has many advocates, but exactly what does it mean? President John F. Kennedy may have said it best when he stated, "Every society gets the kind of criminal it deserves. What is equally true is that every community gets the kind of law enforcement it insists on."

In a large city, a patrol car with two officers is dispatched to take a pack of matches to an elderly citizen's apartment so she can light her stove for heat. In a suburban area, a deputy sheriff is dispatched to get a snake out of a citizen's living room. In a remote desert location, a state trooper drives forty-five miles to let residents without phone service know that their son has been in an auto accident and is in the hospital.

The duties of a police officer are defined by the citizens they serve. To leave the "service" out of "to protect and serve" would be to eliminate the need for many officers.

Officers who insist that only criminal matters are worthy of their attention are destined for problems throughout their careers.

Respect and Dignity

A blue Camaro runs a red light in front of you. After a short pursuit, you hit your lights and the Camaro pulls to the curb. The driver claims he left his license at home and you ask for his name and date of birth, and you return to your car to check with the computer.

The dispatcher advises you that the name given is an alias for the individual who is wanted for several armed robberies and a homicide. You immediately request assistance. All of your training pays off and you arrest the subject without incident. You recover a loaded, 9 mm handgun from under the front seat. You learn later that he was a four time loser and knew he was facing life if he was arrested again.

When the defendant is in jail and the excitement subsides, you reflect on the incident. "If he knew he was going away for life, why didn't he try to kill me?" you ask yourself. "He would get life if I arrested him and he would get life if he killed me. What did he have to lose?"

The answer may be that you didn't provoke him. You asked for a license, and when he gave you his explanation for not having it, you accepted it. In essence, you treated him with the dignity and respect due any respectable citizen. Then, consistent with your training, you followed a reasonable procedure to protect yourself and to check out his license.

As a police officer, you can take away a man's car, his livelihood, and his freedom, but don't ever take away a man's dignity. It is the last thing many of them have, and they won't give it up to anyone.

If you fail to heed this warning and force him into a position where his dignity is in danger, you may unwittingly be providing him an opportunity to get it back in the future. After all, cop-killers are viewed with special regard in prisons.

The Little Things That Count

Police work has its rewards when you arrest a dangerous criminal or make a large seizure of illegal drugs. But, some of the best rewards come from helping regular citizens overcome, what to them, is a major problem in their life.

An out-of-state family on vacation has a property damage accident — routine for you, but devastating for them. A quick transport to the bus station gets them on their way again. A word to the garage ensures that their car will be driveable when their vacation ends in a week.

Then you "capture" a nine-year old boy who ran away from home with his dog, his teddy bear, and his favorite sweatshirt. It's rewarding to see his parents' faces as you deliver him safe and sound after his four hours of freedom. It's also nice to let the parents know that he's not the first nine-year old to run away. He's just the first one this week.

It's normally a tough job, this police work. However, you can realize many of the rewards and you can control much of the stress, for you and the public, if you just take the time to think about it, and put it in the proper perspective.

Dealing With Yourself

"Beware of no man more than thyself."

— Thomas Fuller

Do You Know Your Job?

Are you technically competent to perform your duties, or are you marginally competent in several areas? Have you kept up-to-date on changes in the law, or are you relying on your academy training from years ago? Do you understand your obligations at a domestic complaint? Do you know when you need a search warrant to arrest a wanted person in someone else's home?

From firearms training to Supreme Court decisions, changes are constantly occurring. Keeping up-to-date with your job is a necessity. After all, how would you like to go to a doctor who had not learned anything new since he graduated from medical school — fifteen years ago?

By the same token, people don't want to deal with police officers who aren't competent, who violate rights, and who don't know the details of the laws they are hired to enforce.

Your department may provide some of the training necessary, but you should take some of the responsibility as well. Virtually every industry has trade magazines, books, and newsletters that keep their members advised of changes in the industry. Police work is no exception.

Law enforcement in the United States has several good magazines available, hundreds of good books, and a host of newsletters which can help you learn new skills and keep current in all areas of police work. But, you must take the initiative to gain the knowledge that is available.

Don't be like the officer who arrested an individual for public intoxication two years after the state appeals court ruled the statute unconstitutional. In addition to the embarrassment, the lawsuit irritated everyone and put the officer's career, and his pocketbook, in jeopardy.

Where Are You Headed?

What is your goal? Do you want to be the Chief of your department, or are you content to be a patrolman and work with people at the street level?

The best thing about police work is that those kinds of options are available to you. If you want to advance, hard work and study can usually get you there. Yet, if you choose to remain a patrolman, there is pride and prestige in the position.

Your decision is an individual one that only you can make. However, whichever direction you choose, be sure that you work at being the best patrolman, sergeant, lieutenant, captain or Chief that you can be. To be less is to invite burnout and cynicism into your career. Both of these are the beginning of the end for your career and happiness.

Off-Duty Conduct

This area ranks near the top of the list when it comes to careers ending before retirement.

Maybe the power of the office makes individuals feel that they are above the law. Maybe officers who repeatedly survive against adversity feel that they are invincible. Maybe the stress of the work tends to cloud their judgment.

Whatever the reason, the fact remains that many officers ruin their careers, or lose their jobs entirely, through their off-duty conduct.

Often, the incident is alcohol related; a traffic accident or an incident with an off-duty gun. Sometimes, it's a domestic situation which escalates out of control. It may be any type of bizarre behavior which cannot be predicted in advance of its occurrence.

The fact remains that if you are to control your own destiny in your career, you must be able to control your off-duty conduct. If you can't, you may be destined for the unemployment line.

Your Health

Police work is demanding. It requires mental and physical fitness to withstand the stress and unusual hours. It requires patience to endure hours of inactivity, and the ability to spring into full action in seconds. It requires emotional stability to face the highs and lows of human successes and tragedies.

Although police work can take a heavy toll, you can control many of the factors that contribute to that toll. Staying physically fit is protection against physical injury, as well as a mechanism for reducing the mental and emotional stresses of the job. Maintaining physical fitness also allows you to continue to "look the part" and to maintain your command presence throughout your career. When being considered for promotion, your physical fitness can contribute to additional points on several of the grading scales.

If you want a successful and rewarding career, you must overcome the stereotype of the overweight, out of shape, doughnut eating, coffee drinking, cigarette smoking, police officer of years' past. Those types of officers still alive are fortunate, since the enemy from within has probably done more damage than the enemies from without.

In short, take control of your physical well-being and maintain a positive and healthy lifestyle. It will greatly increase your personal, as well as your professional, performance over the years.

The Last Secret

Following the procedures and avoiding the pitfalls that have been discussed in this chapter can lead you in the direction of a healthy, happy, and successful career in police work. However, there is yet another secret that will help you to survive against all odds.

You can draw on it at any time. It is well known by successful persons in many industries. It has a great deal of therapeutic value and is a valuable weapon. To be without it is to languish in a world of darkness and human tragedy. To have it is to enter the bright world of life and to laugh at adversity.

What is this magic? It is the maintenance of your sense of humor. When all else fails to make sense, humor enters and makes logic immaterial. It turns tears into laughter in both children and adults. It puts a happy face on the worst of tragedies. And it makes you feel better!

This book was written about survival in a different profession. All of the "street smarts" presented will help you toward that end, but your sense of humor will see you through some of the most difficult times — those when you are alone with your own thoughts and experiences.

Good luck and continue to "protect and serve" the public, yourself, and your career.

Chapter 20

Building Searches

by Kevin Gordon

One of the biggest errors that police officers make concerning building searches and approaches is the officers' own outlook. When discussing building searches, many officers automatically think of a building in which there is a hidden, possibly armed subject, such as a burglary in progress. Certainly this is a concern, but a proper building search covers many different areas; the approach to the door, room entry, hallway entry, stairway movement, etc. Proper building approach should be used on all calls; at a family disturbance, alarm calls, tavern disturbances, and so on, and not just on burglary or "suspect present" calls.

Most officers are familiar with the Relative Positioning Concept as it applies to an individual. By expanding this concept, it can be used just as easily for building approaches, building searches, traffic stops, etc. For those not familiar, here is a brief overview.

As the illustration depicts, there are five positions around the subject. These are: Inside Position; Position 1 (Interview Position); Position 2; Position 2 1/2 (Escort Position); and Position 3.

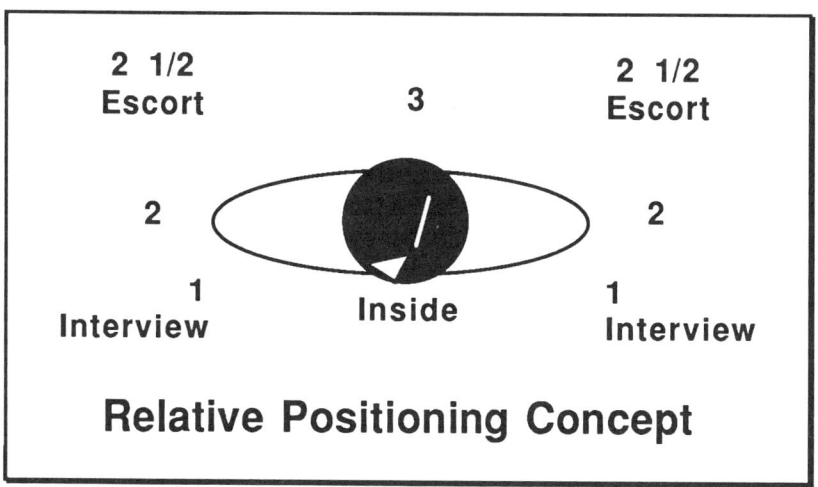

▶ **Inside Position:** The area directly in front of a subject. This position is the most dangerous for the officer, and should be avoided.

◀▬▶ **Position 1:** The area in front and to the side of a subject. This is the typical interview position and is used for the approach.

◀▬▶ **Position 2:** The area directly to the side of a subject. This position can also be used to approach a subject.

◀▬▶ **Position 2 1/2:** The area behind and to the side of the subject. This is the Escort Position and the position an officer should use when arresting a subject.

◀▬▶ **Position 3:** The area directly behind the subject. This position is primarily used for approaching violent offenders, and for such techniques as neck restraints.

The concept is simple, effective, and easily retained. It quickly and effectively teaches officers to stay out of the inside, to talk or interview from 1, and to arrest from 2 1/2. With a little creative thinking, relative positioning can also be applied to a scene.

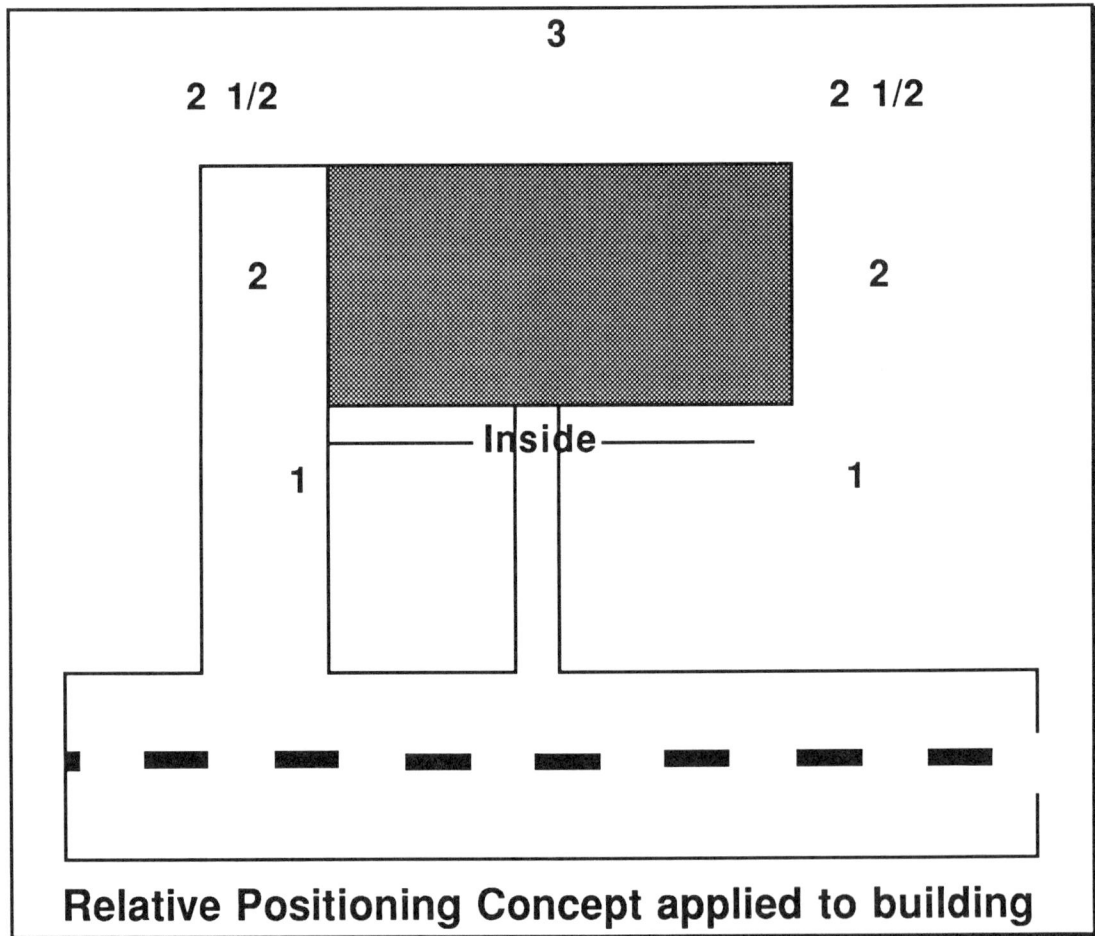

Relative Positioning Concept applied to building

Building Searches

Building Approach

A safe building search begins on the initial approach. Plan a safe approach, don't just arrive. Scan the area upon drive up. The subject could easily have moved since the dispatcher gave the call. Check the obvious places, but also check under cars, on top of roofs and porches. Try to stop the squad at least one house prior to the house in question. This is not always possible as the house numbering systems in some towns were instituted by drunken apes. If the house numbers go from 710 to 948 and they are next door to each other, you may not see it in time. If you cannot stop just before the house, then drive past it and stop. The main point is not to stop directly in front, thus staying out of the Inside Position.

Try to park on the same side of the street. This will keep you from having to run across an open street if you need to return to your squad. Don't just rush up, spend a few seconds at your car to look and listen. Remember, caution is the key. Despite how minor the call, there is always one gun present, that of the officer.

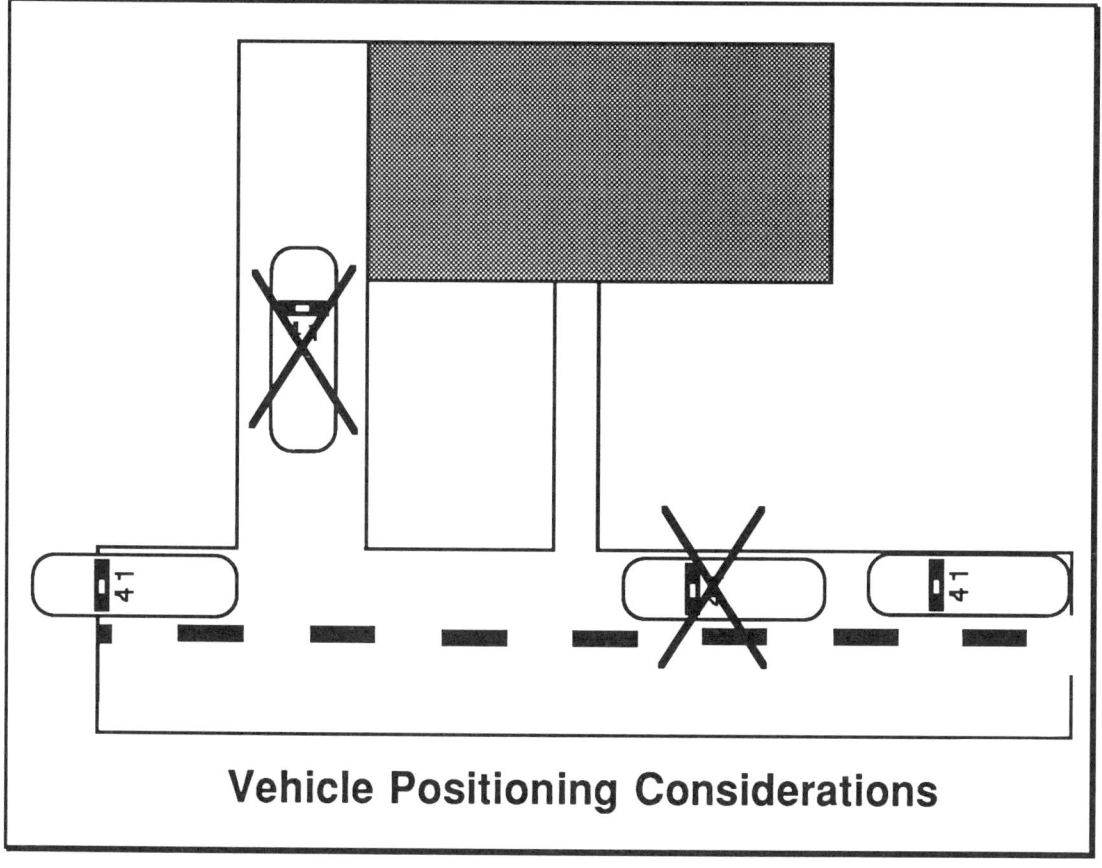

Vehicle Positioning Considerations

Concerning actual building approach, the type of deployment used is often called "invisible deployment." Some call it "star-trekking," which means you are suddenly transported there. It simply means to approach quietly, although it is not easy to be invisible in full uniform and squad car. Approach at an angle to the scene, and do not use the expected means of approach. For example, do not use the sidewalk or approach straight across the front yard. Skirt the front of the house and stay out of the Inside Position. Approach from Position 1. Common sense goes a long way.

On the approach, watch the areas around doors and windows. Officers are aware they can be shot through a door, but forget that they can also be shot through a house. If the house is like most subdivision homes, the biggest thing the round has to penetrate is 3/4" plywood. Some homes are just Celotex and siding. Although it has occurred, it would be unlikely to be shot through the wall, but don't accept concealment as cover. Keep your awareness level up.

Basic recognized styles of deployment are coordinated and diagonal. Coordinated deployment should be used during room entries and so forth. This is when one officer moves and the other one covers. It is coordinated in that no one moves without the other one knowing about it.

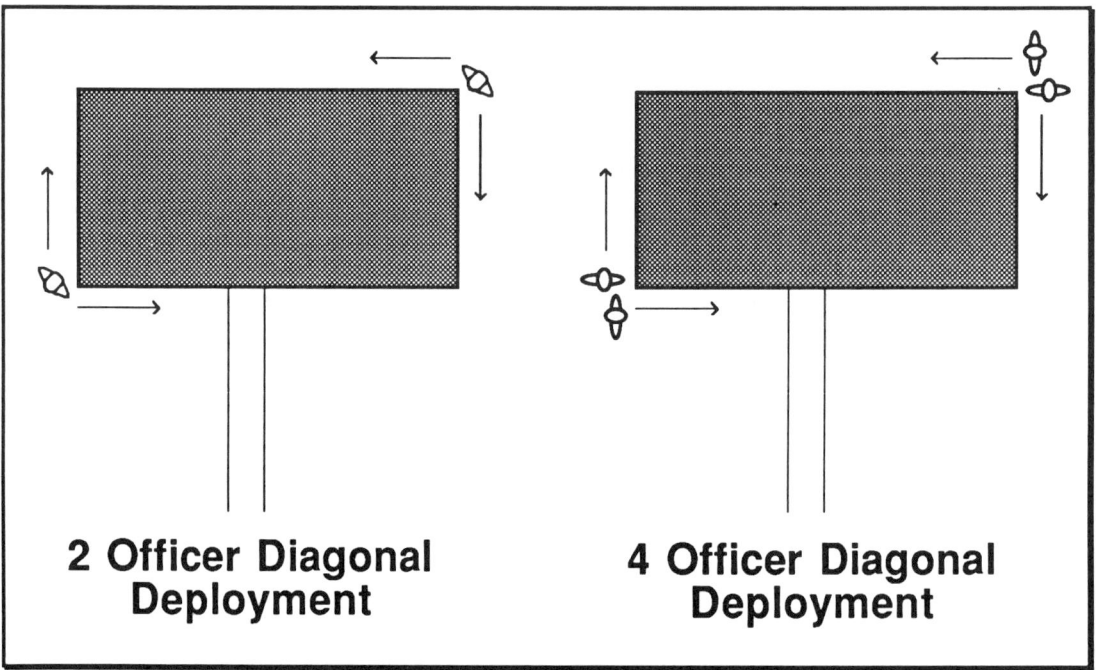

2 Officer Diagonal Deployment

4 Officer Diagonal Deployment

Diagonal deployment is used on the exterior of the building. One officer is stationed at a corner and the other officer is positioned at the opposite corner, diagonal from the first. This allows two officers to cover the entire perimeter. For example, one officer can watch the south and west sides and the second officer can watch the north and east sides. This can be used on a building search, burglary, robbery, etc., and modified to meet the need. Using the Relative Positioning Concept, the first officer would be at Position 1 and the second officer would be at the opposite corner at Position 2 1/2.

If sufficient manpower is available and the situation warrants it, four officers can be used. This is similar to the two man positioning, except two officers are positioned together. Instead of one officer securing the south and west, and the other securing the north and east, one officer secures the south, one the north, one the west, and one the east. Although this positioning is referred to as "at the corners," it is not necessary for the officers to stand physically at the corners. They should be in positions where cover is available and which still allows them view of their responsible area. Using either the two or four-man diagonal deployment eliminates cross fire problems and allows the sealing of escape routes.

If the position is to be held for some length of time, such as a barricaded subject, it is better to use two officers at each corner. The mere fact that someone else is present, someone to converse with if nothing more, will make the length of stay go much quicker. In addition, any officer who has been assigned to secure such a position at 2:00 a.m. in a dark alley, knows very well how this can effect the thoughts. Like it or not, things that go bump in the night still startle. When you start hearing things, seeing shadows, and wondering if possibly "Freddie Krueger" does live, you'll appreciate the uniformed company.

Consider weapons before the approach. Was the shotgun carried to this building search? Why? It might be difficult to use a shotgun in the interior of this building. This doesn't mean the officers should always leave the shotgun behind. Then again, they don't always have to bring it either. Each case may be different. The option is yours. Decide in advance whether you are to bring the baton or not. Some officers treat the baton just like the service weapon if it is there. Other officers bring a flashlight and baton, or just a flashlight. Again, it is your choice, but know before the actual approach. At the front door of the building is not the time to wish you had brought or left something.

Remember, the baton is not just for use as an impact weapon. It can be used to hold doors open, knock on doors, throw doors back, etc.

Another important element of a safe search is the principle of movement. If you are moving, there should be a purpose. Do not move aimlessly, but move to go from A to B. Consider having the weapon out. If officers are searching a building because they believe a subject is hidden there, why are their guns holstered? Unfortunately some department policies require a holstered weapon on a building search. These policies should be reviewed, because weapon readiness is an important tactical consideration.

Also, carry the weapon in a depressed pistol position, provided a threat is not immediately present; in which case the weapon would be on target. The weapon should be carried in the lowered position versus the Hollywood, "up in the air by the head" carry. If carried in the up position, and it is necessary to throw the weapon down to the on target position, the weapon will naturally go too far, ending with the weapon pointed slightly down. Coming on target from a depressed position prevents this.

Also an accidental discharge in the up position can cause you temporary or permanent hearing loss, blindness, etc. Expended rounds, whether accidental or intentional, must come down somewhere in either position, but depressed is a much safer option. Some officers still believe in the "cocked and locked" theory, but weapons can be accidentally fired too easily if cocked, especially under stress conditions or if startled.

If the shotgun is carried and it suddenly becomes a liability, don't just set it down. Disable it at least. Some officers believe in removing the end cap. Others place one handcuff through the port and the other secures it to a stationary object to prevent theft. Use your imagination.

Be in control, and this includes the environment. Control both light and sound, and be aware of the ostrich effect. Just because one officer sees or hears something, this does not mean the other officer did. Tell each other what is seen or heard, and talk with each other as often as necessary. To prevent making any noise, many officers enter a building without ever speaking with their partner. Once that door opens it is likely the subject knows where the officers are anyway. Better to whisper than to keep completely silent.

Control your noise, especially useless noise, such as the countless keys on your gun belt. Are all those keys really necessary or can they be kept in the car? Turn those wrist watch alarms off. When officers approach a dark room to search an area, and a wrist watch alarm suddenly starts playing the Charge of the Light Brigade, this will send the pucker factor skyrocketing. Also, it is not always necessary to search a building in total darkness. If it is an advantage to turn on the lights, then turn them on.

Before entering the building, decide if entering is necessary. Is there sufficient assistance? In theory, it is best to start your search from the top down. If you do this you can flush a hidden subject out. If working down to up, you are forcing the subject into a corner. As stated, in theory, because it is often hard, if not impossible, to search up to down.

What was the subject's entry method? What will be yours? Windows are a very dangerous entry point. Check those windows. Maybe you have never been in the building, but you can get the general layout by a quick walk around. The smallest window is probably the bathroom. The one with the most curtains is probably the living room, etc. This is not fool proof, but it is better than entering unprepared.

If possible, never enter alone. The correct tactic is never, but if only one officer is working and the next town will not send backup for a building search, what choice do you have? If backup is available, although a little time away, wait. If backup is 20 minutes away, why not wait 21 minutes? Remember the old axiom, "Fools rush in where wise men fear to tread." Waiting makes more sense than walking into more than you can handle.

Door Approach

Most officers know not to stand in front of a door (the Inside Position). Get in the habit of standing to the side (Position 1) on all calls,

Building Searches 175

no matter how minor. Being human, we sometimes do silly things. When knocking on doors, officers sometimes stretch across and knock on the center, the most common place to knock out of habit. Knocking on the very edge does just as well and keeps the arm out of the doorway also. Check the door. How does it open? If the hinges are visible, the door opens toward you. If the hinges are not visible, then it opens the other way.

If it is necessary to cross a doorway, use a "leap technique." This is simply moving across the doorway as quickly as possible. Don't try to do two things at once. If the object is to move, then move. If the object is to look, then look. Don't combine the two.

With one officer on either side of the door (opposite Position 1), one officer opens the door and throws it to the other officer (opening out, such as a screen door). However, this is not an absolute. In some circumstances, due to the door type, position of the door, or items around the door, the officers may elect to both be on the same side. The point is, despite where you stand, you should be there because you determined it was the best location, not because you just ended up there.

The interior door is pushed open by one officer and pushed hard so it goes all the way back. Look before entering. Tell the other officer what you can see and vice versa. There is no reason to rush in and run head on into a lamp just because no one took a couple of seconds to communicate. Look in the door crack to see what is behind the door.

Room Entry

To look into a room, there are three basic methods that allow visibility without putting officers in the "fatal funnel" of fire. These are the "Quick Peek Technique," the "Slicing the Pie Technique," and the "Mirror Technique."

The Quick Peek Technique is just that, a quick peek into the room. The officer positions himself or herself at the side of the doorway with hands on the wall or floor, depending on which gives more support and balance. The officer, keeping the rest of his or her body away from the opening, quickly peeks into the room, exposing his or her face to eye level only and returns to a safe position. The first look should be taken from somewhere else than normal height, preferable below chest level. If someone is waiting to shoot as soon as they see a uniform, they will normally be on target stomach height or above. Most officers prefer the first peek to be 12 to 18 inches off the ground.

This technique can be performed more than once if necessary. Each peek should be at a different level than the first one, or the next peek can be done by an officer positioned on the other side. If on the first peek an armed subject is spotted, obviously you won't even consider a second peek. Use verbal commands, retreat, and respond to this situation like it is, a barricaded subject.

With the "Slicing the Pie Technique," the officer is upright, the feet are spread in a Weaver type stance, and the weapon is on target. Standing about 3 feet or so back from the doorway, the officer slowly moves in an arc outward. Figuring the initial position as 0 degrees, the end position would be about 90 degrees.

This technique is used by one or two officers. Each should go no farther than 90 degrees, never actually entering the open space of the doorway. Try this sometime with an officer standing at the end of a hallway, for example. Most officers are surprised at how much of the "subject" is visible before the subject can see the searching officer. Often it is possible to see his or her entire shoulder area down to his or her foot, but don't get carried away in a real life situation. It is only necessary to see enough of him or her to realize that he or she is there, then assume a cover position.

The "Mirror Technique" is just that; simply using a mirror to see around corners, etc.

Some claim the greatest threat to an officer during a room entry is other officers. This can be all too true, but communication will solve most of this. Know when and where the officer is moving. Any officer, who at sometime has been the point man on an entry and suddenly realized that the other officer's weapon was pointed at his or her back, will take this to heart. Be aware of shadows and silhouettes, and turn those lights on or off, whichever helps. Shadows can indicate what is around the corner, but shadows can also tell the subject where the officer is. An example of the proper use of silhouettes is when an officer is standing in a dark doorway that faces a lit street, the officer will most probably be visible. If the officer steps back a few feet, he or she will, for all purposes, disappear.

Officers should be able to see each other at all times. If one loses sight of the other, they have spread the search out too far. Some trainers and departments believe officers should leave their hats on during building searches. This allows the officer to determine who the other officer is by the hat's silhouette. I find this ludicrous. If you have to use the hat to find other officers, you've already lost control of the search. By using proper techniques, there should be no doubt where or who the officers are.

If you must wear the hat, be aware of the brim. It will go around a corner before the officer, exposing his or her position. Certainly the hat can be turned around to prevent this, provided it has a brim on one side only, not a "smokey" or cowboy type. Usually, the hat should be left in the squad. Unfortunately, many departments require it to be worn. Of course many departments require the wearing of a tie, but not a vest. One must wonder where are their priorities.

Know in advance which method will be used to carry the service weapon and the flashlight. There are several techniques, but they are all based on the same concept; the gun and light should be pointed in the same direction at all times.

The weapon should not be pointed north when the subject is spotted south with the flashlight. The few seconds it takes to get on target count. There are various methods of carry, experiment with them and

Building Searches

see which one works best. These methods include the gun hand on top of the flashlight hand, or the gun hand can be placed over the flashlight hand in an X formation. In this technique, the flashlight is carried in side hold fashion to allow access to the switch. Another method places the gun hand next to the flashlight hand, and both hands are pressed tightly together moving as one. Another method places the fists together with the flashlight held slightly upwards to clear the barrel of the weapon. The final method, a variation of the X formation, places the flashlight directly on top of the gun hand.

All of these are good methods, provided they work for the officer. Only you can figure out which method works best for you. These methods force the officer to point the weapon where it is needed. A proper flashlight hold also allows the flashlight to be turned on or off as needed. This not only allows the officer to be on target the moment of discovery, but it also reminds him or her to keep the weapon off his or her partner. Remember to use the push button "signal" switch on the flashlight. It is not always necessary to use the continuous beam.

There are several entry methods to a room. Each instructor calls them by a different name, but the name means nothing. The whole point is to make officers aware that there are other ways to enter a room than just to walk in. They are referred to as the X pattern, the diagonal, the reverse X, the wrap around, the fish hook, etc. As long as the officers know what they plan to do, they can call them whatever they want.

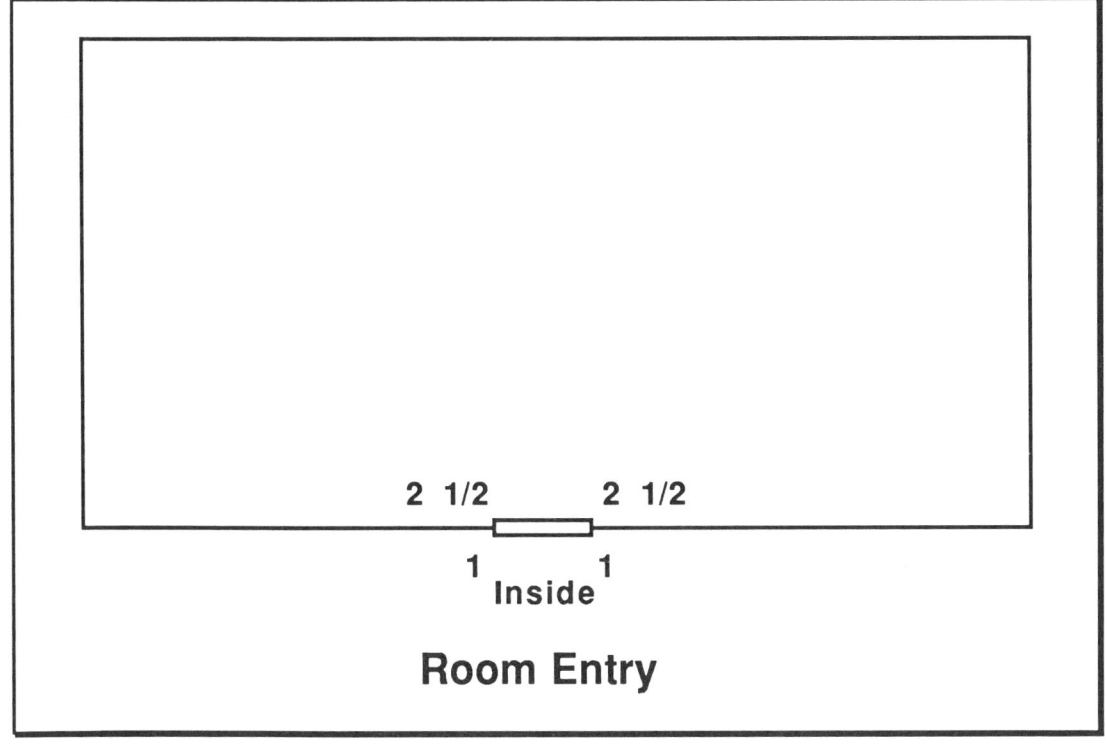

Room Entry

Most of the entry methods start with one officer on each side of the doorway. After using a leap technique to cross the doorway, and a quick peek or other technique to view inside, the officers decide to enter. One method has officer #1 enter first, going low and securing one side. Officer #2 enters on the command of the first officer (1 moves A to B, 2 moves C to D). A similar method has both officers enter the same manner as before, but the difference is they enter together as compared with officer #1 securing the area first before #2 enters. They count 1, 2, 3, 4. At 3 the first officer enters and at 4 the second officer enters. This counting prevents a doorway collision.

Another method has the first officer enter diagonally, bounce off the door jamb, and go in the opposite direction (A goes to D). The wrap around method is used when a solid wall is present on one side which allows movement to only one side. One officer stays out and covers (at C) while the other officer wraps around the jamb (A to B). These methods and others are described in various tactical books, but most involve one simple element; you move from Position 1 to 2 1/2.

Regardless of the method, entry should be quick. Scan the whole room. Many dangers of entering a room quickly are prevented by the previous view into the room. Again, communication plays a part and when the room is viewed from the outside, tell each other what is seen.

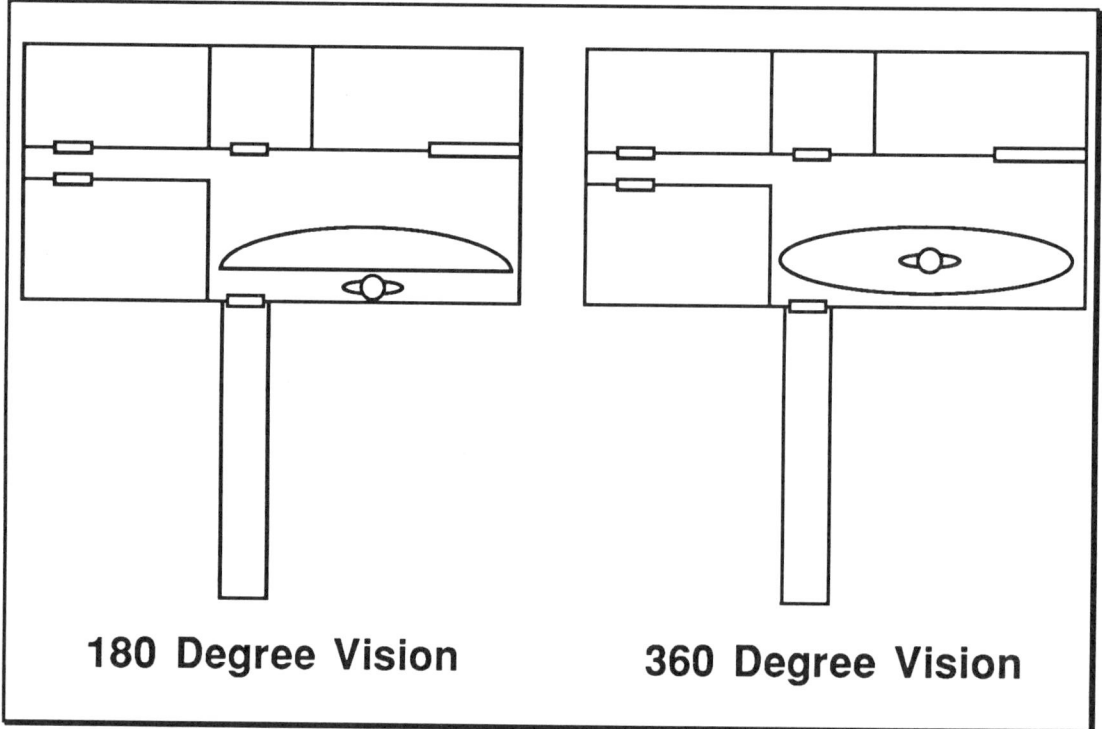

180 Degree Vision   **360 Degree Vision**

Enter fast and begin checking the perimeter, keeping your back to the wall. This allows you to use 180 degree vision rather than trying to

Building Searches

cover 360 degrees which is impossible. Your peripheral vision allows you to see 180 degrees. Once inside, some officers like to keep low, others stand normally, your option, but know in advance. If staying low, some officers use the duck walk to go forward and back and the crab walk for side to side movement. Both are good tactics, but no matter how good of shape the officers are in, the knees will make them forget everything else really quick. To somewhat eliminate this, after each step an officer should rest on the down knee for a brief second. Keeping each knee off the ground continually is what brings on the pain.

Using the Relative Positioning Concept, visualize the center of the room as an individual. Search from 1 to 2 to 2 1/2 and then to 3. An officer will be doing this on each side. One will move while one covers. Don't shine that flashlight at random, even with the proper weapon placement. This is what causes officers to light up their partners. If something suggests someone is behind something or hiding in a closet for example, challenge them. Officers may not be positive a subject is hiding there, but if a subject is, he or she doesn't know for sure if the officers know.

Consider searching the perimeter of the room first. This normally places officers near cover items. Don't forget to look up as well as down. Remember the goal is not to locate evidence, there will be time for that later, the goal is to locate subjects. Don't pass an area unless it has been secured. If a subject is located, secure him or her and continue the search for other subjects; the one plus rule.

Look around things as compared to over things; for example, a couch. When looking over, the basic human anatomy exposes your hair and forehead down to your eyes to a hidden subject before he or she is visible to the officer. Looking around has the advantage of more cover and a better opportunity to retreat quicker.

Hallways are dangerous and extreme caution should be taken. The subject does not have to be a good shot to hit an officer in a hallway. Scan the area before entering. Again, control the environment, turning on or off lights, whichever helps. Have an escape plan in mind. Keep the principle of triangulation; one officer moves while the other covers with the subject area forming the third angle of the triangle (also called L deployment).

The first officer should stay low while the second officer stays high. This prevents either from criss-crossing lines of fire. Move tactically as before. Don't allow the gun to go around a corner before the officer. Remember, if it is necessary to look, then look. If it is necessary to shoot, then shoot. If it is necessary to move, then move. Don't try to do two things at once.

Secure each room and then move on to the next. Hallways are dangerous and it often takes three officers to handle them safely. If a door is locked and it must be passed, remember, it was not previously secured. Also stop occasionally and just listen.

Stairways are no fun to say the least. If it is necessary to go down a set of stairs, exhaust all other options for checking first. Try using basement windows for an interior visibility check. Take your time. Some officers like to slide down on their rears, one step at a time. Others like to go down prone, one step at a time, on their bellies. Some prefer a slow upright descent; each case is different. If the stairs are the open type, there is the additional problem of being vulnerable to an attack from under the stairs. There is no sure way, so use caution. One officer covers while one moves.

As far as going up a set of stairs, avoid rubbing the walls. This telegraphs your position. Again, one officer moves while the other covers. Make sure the moving officer does not end up in the line of fire of the cover officer. If there is a landing, such as in an apartment building, it usually requires three officers for effective cover; one to move, one to cover the immediate threat area, and one to watch the landing area. When in doubt, back it out. If needed, get more help regardless of how long it takes to get it. Use K-9 if available in your area. Hurrying is not worth your life.

Conclusion

From the initial drive up, walk up approach, exterior search, interior search, to the final securing of the scene, take your time. Keep partners informed of what you see or hear. Think before acting; common sense prevails.

Building searches are dangerous. Many officers believe "if they want to get ya, they will." As long as the officers are the searchers and the subjects the "searchees," the officers have the disadvantage. The key is to think and plan. If you are asked how you search a building and you reply, "I walk in and look around," you are on borrowed time. Regardless of what style or methods you use, they should be used because you have determined they work best for you or are best for the situation.

Building searches will continue to be dangerous. They may pay us to put our life on the line, but they don't pay us to give it away.

About the Author

Sergeant Kevin Gordon is an eleven year officer with the Cahokia Police Department assigned to the Patrol Division as the Training Supervisor, holding the rank of Sergeant. He is an International Instructor in the Monadnock PR-24™, the Monadnock Straight Baton, a National Trainer with CAS-Expandable Police Baton, and an Instructor Trainer in a variety of areas with PPCT Management Systems

He also serves as one of four Directors for the Belleville Area College Police Academy and is an Adjunct Instructor for the Belleville Area College Administration's Justice Program, specializing in practical application, tactical concerns, and patrol procedures.

Sergeant Gordon is the founder of Crime Fighters Institute, a

Midwest based law enforcement and security training institute, and operates as the Director. Crime Fighters Institute, known by many as "CFI", supplies training to security and law enforcement personnel and agencies, provides civilian training blocks in self-defense, rape prevention, firearms safety, etc., and has a retail supply shop offering uniforms and a complete line of law enforcement and security gear.

David Grossi

Mr. Grossi is the Senior Instructor for the Calibre Press, Inc. Street Survival® Seminars. He has over twenty years in law enforcement and has served as a patrolman, undercover narcotics' investigator, detective, sergeant, and lieutenant. He retired in 1990 as Commander of Firearms Training for the Irondequoit Police Department in upstate New York.

Mr. Grossi has written dozens of articles on officer survival, use of deadly force, and critical incident aftermath for numerous police publications. He has testified nationally as an expert witness in both State and Federal Court in criminal and civil matters. He holds a Bachelor's degree in Police Administration and is an FBI National Academy graduate. He is a Vietnam combat veteran having served with the Rangers in 1969 before entering law enforcement.

Chapter 21

Principles of Officer Survival

by David Grossi

It has been said that "GOD LOVES COPS." He must, because He so often lets so many of us get away with things that should have gotten us killed.

Officer Survival is a much more complex topic than it used to be. Survival today means, not only physical survival, but emotional and legal survival as well. We're talking about "Professional Survival."

The topic really is all inclusive, and a well developed program on Officer Survival has to include all of these elements.

It amazes me that so many Officer Survival programs focus only on street tactics, such as building searches, felony car stops, shooting skills, and defensive tactics. This is great and surely needed with the Officer Assault stats steadily on the rise, but a complete Officer Survival program MUST include psychological and legal survival factors as well.

What I hope to address in this chapter, are concepts for "street cops" to understand, absorb, and apply to their everyday routine in the field. Specifics on the many different areas touched on in these next few pages, will appear elsewhere in this book.

Physical Survival

As any well-trained officer knows, the criminal community is getting younger and younger every day. Penal Codes across the country are re-codifying their statutes to allow for Criminal Court trials of juveniles beginning at the age of 9 or 10 years old. Heretofore, that arena was reserved for persons 16-18 or older. Recent stories in the newspapers have reported children ages 5 and 6 selling crack cocaine for their parents, who themselves are minors. Juveniles ages 15 and 16 are flying across the country to set up crack distribution networks.

The evidence is in that criminals are definitely getting younger. But YOU, the street cop, are always going to age . . . and unlike fine wine or cheese, you ARE NOT going to get better with time. Even incarcerated criminals are given regular physical fitness regimes and diets regulated by the government to include the four basic food groups . . . no McDonalds or Taco Bells for our nation's felons!

Now for 21 or 22 year old rookies, this may not bother them too much. However, 10 or 15 years of doughnut shop lunches or greasy spoon suppers, coupled with a dose of Father Time, can make for some interesting street encounters.

So when we talk about physical survival, not only do we have to include the basic standards, such as firearms, defensive tactics, batons, weapon retention, chemical agents, and tactical training, but we also have to touch on the wellness aspects of our physical well-being. This, however, is not an area that most street cops want to discuss.

Physical survival, as part of "Professional Officer Survival" must address physical fitness and training as well as tactics. Not only should you practice your psychomotor skills to the point of mastery, such as firearms, defensive tactics, batons, and the like, but that training must include the added element of realism. Realistic firearms' training, confrontational baton simulations, role play scenarios, and other dynamic training sessions must be a staple in today's law enforcement curriculum. Physiologists tell us that after 20-30 seconds of all out fighting, you will experience a significant depletion of energy. I can best describe it as "sucking your diaphragm through your throat." So aerobic training is a must, as well as flexibility and strength training. Dynamic simulations in your other physical skills will add that element of realism to your training.

To stay on top of the game with the best chance of winning physically on the street, you have to prepare for every type of physical attack that might be launched against you. This means being in the best shape you can be in, the best shot you can be, and as expert with your equipment and tactical responses as possible.

Court cases have mandated that police training be realistic, relevant, and specifically job related. One such case is *Popow v. Margate* 476 F. Supp. 1237, 1246 (1978) from New Jersey which touched directly on firearms training. Another, more recent case, decided by the U.S. Supreme Court that has added a new, more stringent look at police training was *Canton v. Harris* 109 S. Ct. 1197 (1989). With these legal concerns in mind, classroom training shouldn't stop in this physical survival realm.

The total package of professional survival include Use of Force Continuum updates, and chemical, electronic, and canine considerations. Also, periodic court cases dealing with training, search and seizure policies, reasonable suspicion, stop and frisk tactics, and non-lethal force options must be included in professional survival.

Surviving physically means more than just winning a street fight. It means having the advantage before the encounter in every aspect; equipment, tactics, knowledge, fitness, and attitude!

Emotional Survival

In my department, as well as through contacts with numerous other agencies across the country, it is becoming more and more common to hear of officers retiring on Stress Disability pensions. Why? Because many of these officers couldn't handle the emotional stress of the

Principles of Officer Survival

street experiences they encountered.

Let's take shootings as an example. Nationally, it has been estimated that 70% of officers who are involved in a shooting situation leave law enforcement within 5 years. A study conducted in the Boston area, revealed that 80% left within 2 years of being involved in a shooting. While some would have retired anyway during that time, many left as a direct result of not dealing effectively with the emotional trauma they experienced. Mind you, these only reflect shooting situations. No one really knows how tragic this loss might be when you factor in the non-shooting type of emotional trauma.

This again is an area that most Officer Survival programs totally ignore or don't feel comfortable addressing. Agency's policy and procedure manuals are replete with "Sick Policy" mandates that require officers who have blown sick to report to the police physician for medical clearance before reporting back to duty. Most never even consider psychological treatment for their employees who have routinely handled suicides, fatal MVA's, SID's deaths, and child abuse calls by the dozens for protracted periods of time.

Progressive agencies rotate their "deep-cover" narcs as part of their "integrity" or "temptation" policy. Few consider periodic rotation for their Honor Guard officers who routinely respond to officer funerals, those who handle child abuse cases on a regular basis, or accident bureau guys who have to "tech" fatalities everyday.

I worked undercover for many years with an excellent narcotics' cop. This officer lived every aspect of the job during our period of deep-cover assignment. He led the Task Force in number of buys, arrests, weight, and quality, and always managed to parlay every buy into a larger score. After our "surfacing" was ordered and the assignment was concluded, this officer crashed . . . emotionally and psychologically. He could not make the adjustment back to the real world. While all of us knew what was happening to him, none of us really knew what to do about it. A great law enforcement future was snuffed out at the age of 43 from a massive heart attack. I also remember a training officer of mine who swallowed his own off-duty revolver after a fire destroyed his home.

What these officers, and a lot more from across the country lacked, were the tactics for coping with the stress of the job . . . critical incident stress as well as cumulative stress, from years of on-the-job experiences that we've all learned to suppress over time. Trying to suppress these emotions is like trying to hold acid in a Dixie Cup. It's not going to work. Sooner or later, it's going to eat through.

Recognition of the effects of this stress, either by one's own self examination or through the help of a peer or spouse, is usually the first step in ensuring emotional survival. In many departments, informal self-help groups are forming to foster a better understanding of the Police Stress phenomenon. In larger, more progressive agencies, police psychologists are on staff, or department appointed counselors can respond to the scene to begin helping officers cope with the stress of a "heavy" job.

My experience over the last 21 years working with training and networking with over 60,000 cops, especially with the Street Survival®

Seminars, has taught me that normal, routine job assignments can be just as dangerous from an Officer Survival standpoint as SWAT, tactical units, bomb squads, undercover, vice, or robbery stake-out duty.

Administrators must become aware of the emotional needs of their officers. Smart administrators can add years of productivity to every officer in their departments by supplying them with access to knowledgeable stress counselors on a "need be" basis. Not only are the officers going to benefit emotionally, but the departments will get the officers back on the street quicker.

A mandated policy for consultation with a competent police psychologist after any high stress situation, or after any protracted period of time in a high stress unit, like those areas mentioned previously, has to be implemented to ensure the emotional survival of today's law enforcement officer. If a chief is going to pay out $125 a head for a 10 minute visit to the police physician after an officer misses 2 days of work in a row, then he or she can pay out the same bucks for consultation with a police psychologist after a violent child abuse investigation, or after several SID cases. I'm familiar with one cop who was the first responding unit on four consecutive nights to four fatal MVA's. It began to take its toll on him when his squad members began calling him "The Angel of Death." On the fifth night, he again was the first responding unit to another fatal MVA. After a while, he began to really believe that he was the cause of these accidents and that he could prevent a fatal accident by NOT responding to the call.

A smart, perceptive supervisor, would have recognized the danger and called the officer in to see how all this was affecting him. Many times, these dangers go unnoticed for what they really are.

If your department doesn't provide these services, or the option isn't available to you from within your agency, seek professional counseling on your own. Someone from another agency may have a resource for a knowledgeable mental health professional. Perhaps the "shrink" that does the pre-screening for police applicants in your area can be a start for you. You wouldn't let a physical injury go without treatment, would you? The same is true for emotional injuries.

Legal Survival

Perhaps the most ignored area of Officer Survival is in the legal realm. Academy curriculums and in-service training programs are saturated with lesson plans on vicarious liability, civil rights, and constitutional issues. Chiefs of police and sheriffs have legal advisers within "hot line" reach when the Notice of Claim or Lawsuit comes down. Very rarely is the street cop trained on how to protect HIS or HER rights, or even what his or her rights are! My experience has been that this is usually an area that the PBA or FOP addresses.

Many agencies are perfectly content to grow their "mushrooms" in the dark and feed them manure from time to time, so most street cops won't become too educated in the ways of the legal world of IAD hearings, legal counsel, and self incrimination. While a two-day rookie can tell you what the *Miranda* case was all about, many 20 year veterans have never heard about *Garrity,* although the *Garrity* case was decided by the U.S. Supreme Court way back in 1967. *Garrity v. New Jersey,* 385 S. Ct. 493, arose out of New Jersey and had a major impact on Police Rights of Self-Incrimination. Most cops just think their Fifth Amendment rights went down the toilet, along with leisurely meals or sincere "thank you's."

When legal trainers talk about the prospect of an officer counter-suing an assailant civilly for assault, administrators usually shudder at the thought. What many police officers don't know is that they have substantial rights in legal confrontations. There is nothing in the police job description that says we have to be blue punching bags for people we meet on the street. It's just that for the most part, departments either intentionally keep those rights a secret, or just don't bother educating the officers in these areas. Also, most officers think that the department's legal adviser or municipal attorney will automatically protect or cover them in the event of a lawsuit. When a lawsuit comes down, however, and the involved officer, chief, department, and municipality are named, if one lawyer is handling the case, and that lawyer has a decision to make about whose interest he's going to protect, who do you think is going to get hung out to dry?

Legal precedent has been set in many states, that when an officer is sued, and both the agency and officer are named, the department HAS to provide the officer with separate counsel. One such case is *Dunton v. County of Suffolk,* (NY) 729 F 2d 903. Officers do not lose their constitutional rights just because they pin on a badge. The old "Code of the West" mentality that you give the bad guy the first punch, or have to beat him on the draw, has been fostered by agency legal beagles or administrators that want to keep individual street officers from exercising their inherent constitutional rights, for fear that officers will begin suing offenders on a regular basis.

Conclusion

In summary, the entire arena of Officer Survival has changed drastically in the last decade, especially over the last several years. Back 20 or 25 years ago, Officer Survival simply meant not getting killed on the street.

Survival on the street still needs to be emphasized and reinforced through comprehensive training programs. These programs should stress building search tactics, vehicle stop procedures, foot and vehicle pursuits, and psychomotor skill development principles, such as weapon retention, defensive tactics and batons, as well as a complete firearms' training program. The Principles of Officer Survival have to touch an officer in a more non-conventional way than heretofore recognized.

Professional survival means physical survival, emotional survival, and legal survival. They must all be linked together with a complete program of constant education and awareness, coupled with a desire and a will to stay alive! In other words, keep "it all" intact!

Remember, it's not ONLY education and awareness . . . it's also keeping ahead of the offender threats that are out there today. That's the real payoff. Staying one step (or more) ahead of the "bad guys" in knowledge, skills, physical ability, equipment, tactics, and ATTITUDE! This is the true essence of Officer Survival.

Chapter 22

Vehicle Stop Survival

by Harvey V. Hedden

Buried among other local news, the Chicago Tribune article was simply titled, "Cop Killed in Routine Traffic Stop." However, the title was a misnomer, because it is the so-called routine traffic stops that kill more officers than those that are known to be dangerous.

The problem with vehicle stops is that they are performed so often without any danger that a routine is established. Officers become unaware of potential threats and assume cooperation and compliance on the part of the subjects. Each year about a dozen officers are surprised to discover that they were wrong, for the last time. Like so many other situations, tactics and equipment cannot compensate for unawareness. A discussion of officer survival needs to reiterate the possible dangers of vehicle stops in the hopes of encouraging officers to be more alert.

As performed, unknown risk traffic stops violate a number of basic tactical principles. Most often, officers stop subjects and know almost nothing about them until after the initial contact. The subjects who ran a stop sign may be fleeing the scene of a much more serious crime. When stopped, they may assume the officers know what they have done and may therefore look for the first opportunity to attack the officers. The officers may be more concerned with reducing the time they are out of service.

The officers leave the cover of their squads to approach the subjects' vehicles, also lethal weapons. When contact is made with the subjects, intelligent officers will try to maintain control of the subjects' movements and in particular their hands. During the transaction of the stop, the officers may be distracted by the drivers, their licenses, other passengers, other traffic, contraband, or other criminal evidence in the vehicles which make them vulnerable to attack. The subjects — would be killers — may use the opportunity to retrieve weapons from a myriad of potential hiding places in the vehicles within easy and inconspicuous reach. The officers' reactions — attempting to draw, aim, and fire — will inevitably be slower than the subjects' attacks. Survival in vehicle stops will depend upon the officers' abilities to detect danger, reduce the tactical advantages of the subjects, evade the attacks, and use appropriate force to defend themselves.

Officers face varying threat levels in performing vehicle stops. The unknown risk traffic stop is the most common and is typified by the stop of traffic subjects. High risk traffic stop tactics are employed when there is reason to believe the subjects may be armed or try to resist. High risk traffic stops are treated much like barricaded gunmen. Tactics used will emphasize the use of time, distance, and cover.

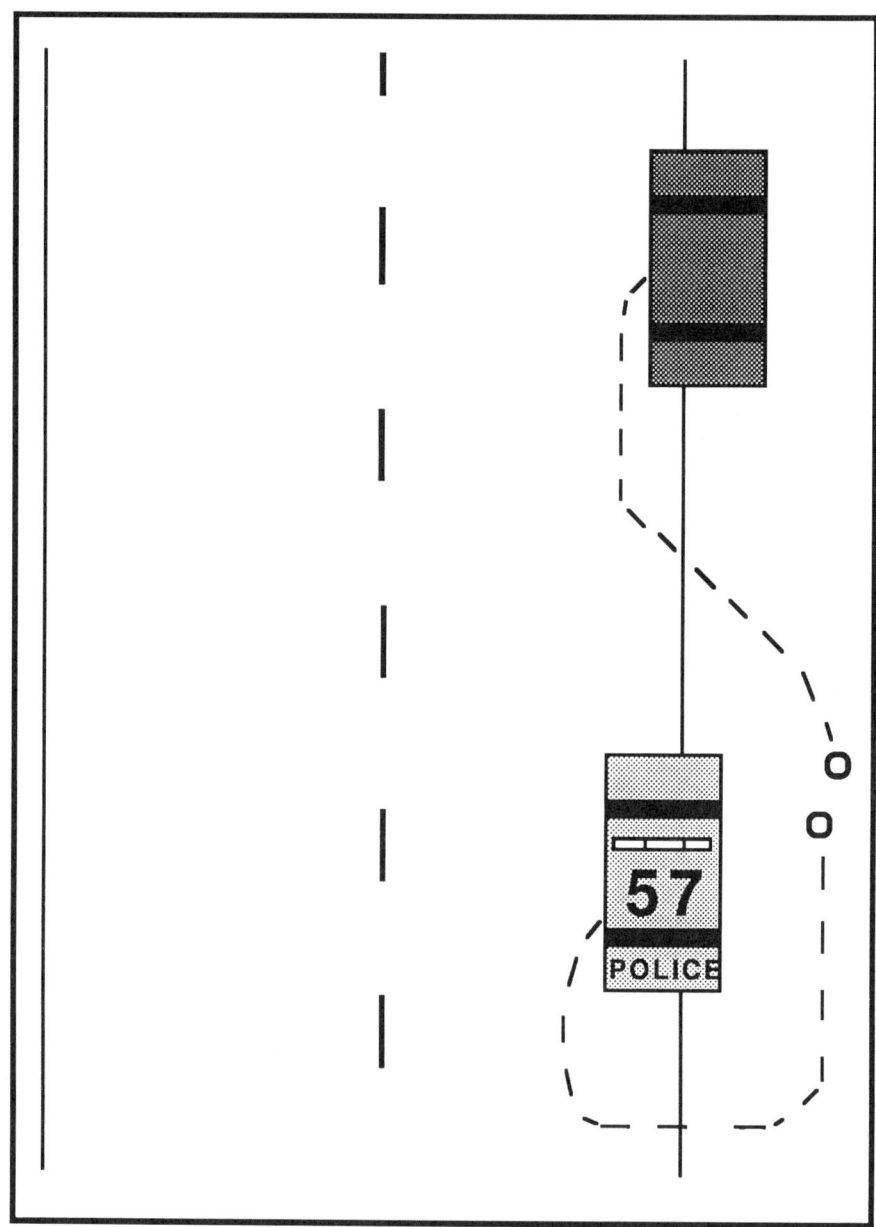

Figure 1: Subject is ordered out of the vehicle.

Anticipating danger, the officers will use assistance from other officers, have weapons in hand, and will not approach the subjects' position of cover and concealment in the vehicles. Control of the inner perimeter around the stops will reduce interference and distractions. The subjects will be ordered out of their vehicles to a position where they can be safely controlled and secured (see Figure 1 on page 190). When officers resist the temptation to rush the vehicles and physically force dangerous subjects from their vehicles, the high risk traffic stop rarely results in officers injured or death.

In the field, officers may stop vehicles for offenses from equipment violations to murder, and for a variety of crimes in between. To be prepared for the street, officers should possess a large repertoire of tactical options to choose from to adapt to each situation. No one tactic should be relied upon for every situation. Just as tactical planning is critical to every traffic stop, officers must be flexible and adaptive to changing situations and escalate their tactical advantages when needed.

Although high risk traffic stop tactics are safer for the officers, we cannot place the subjects into prone positions. At the lower end of the threat assessment scale, our tactics need to be discreet and covert, particularly in today's political climate. Escalation will be predicated on our observations and assessment of danger. In all cases we need to emphasize control. Control of the subjects, the passengers, the vehicle, other traffic, and our own actions are important to our survival.

Every day, there are thousands of uneventful traffic stops, and they begin with the observation of the subject. Be certain of the true nature of the problem. Is the driver speeding, DWI, or fleeing? Ideally, try to get the license plate number before activating the lights and siren. Interviews conducted with subjects who fled, indicate that when the squad is close enough to read the plate, there is a reduced chance the subject will flee, thereby avoiding a pursuit. If possible, run the plate for wants and registration to begin developing information about the subject.

Even if there are no wants, you or other officers may have some knowledge of the registered owner. In-house computer data bases may be queried, and you may be able to check for wants and the driver status of the subject prior to the stop. Throughout this phase, you should be communicating what you are doing; your intention to stop the vehicle for fail to yield for example. Watch the vehicle for unusual movements and actions.

When you believe you have sufficient information about the offense you observed and the vehicle, you need to consider the location of the traffic stop. It should not present a traffic hazard, but permit easy view of traffic in both directions. Consider avoiding areas with high pedestrian traffic, areas that back light you, or alleys that provide an easy escape route for the subjects in the vehicle. When communicating your intention to stop, remember to provide a full description of the vehicle and its occupants, the nature and location of the stop, and the assistance you require. If you determine backup is needed, you may wish to delay the stop or wait to approach the vehicle until cover arrives. You may wish to use your public address system to position the subject's vehicle to your own tactical advantage. An example is having a van park next to another vehicle so that the passenger side doors are unusable.

As you initiate the stop, make certain you and your weapon are clear of your seat belt in case of a sudden attack. Many times, even simple traffic violators have suddenly stopped their car and ran back toward the squad. If you cannot direct the driver back into the vehicle with your public address system, consider using the squad to escape by either backing up (carefully), or driving away. On several occasions, subjects have charged the officers' squads to try to kill them before they could access their weapon.

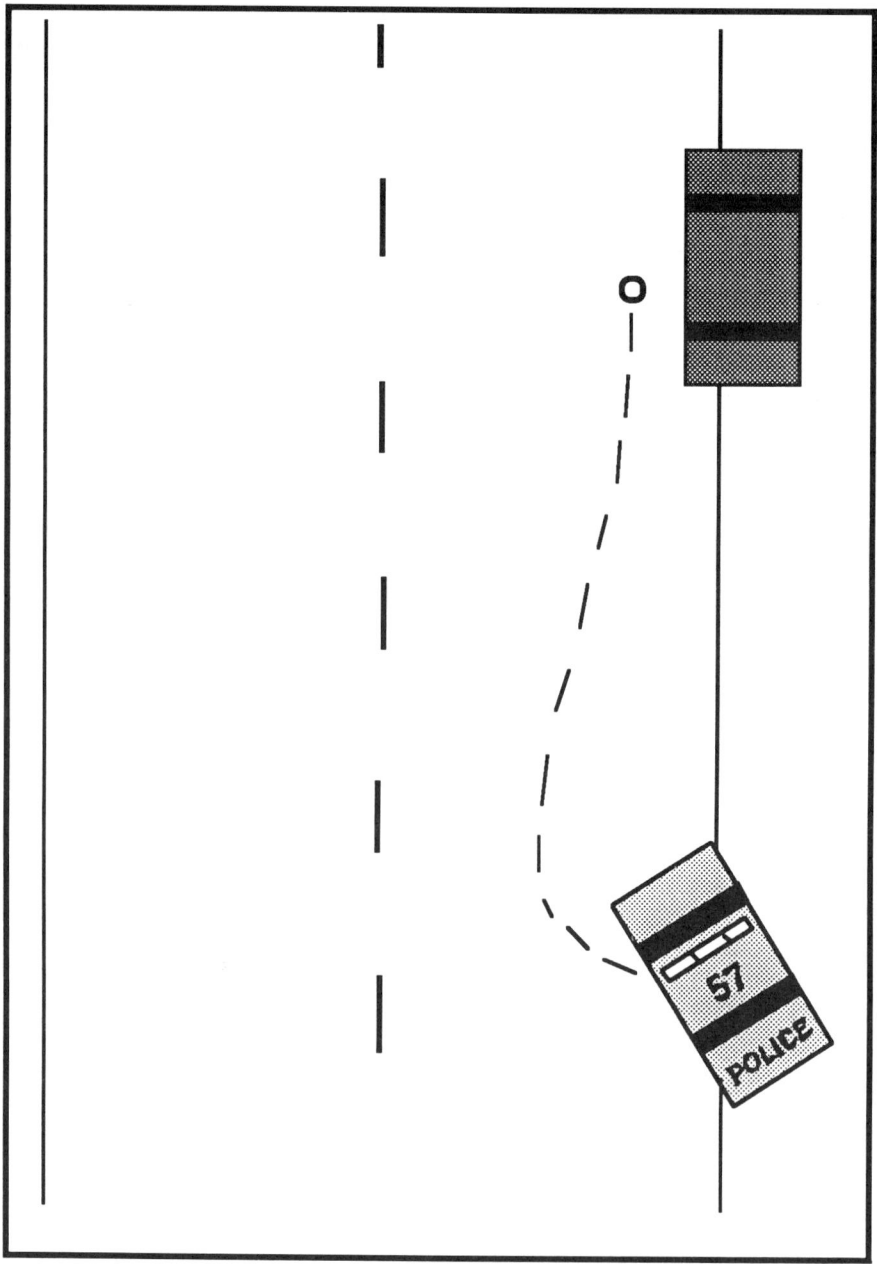

Figure 2: The squad is at a 45 degree angle for better cover.

Vehicle Stop Survival

Your public address commands should be calm and authoritative, and identify your department if necessary. Your requests should include a fair helping of "Please sir . . ." when possible to gain driver cooperation.

Remember, others may be watching you. Other reasonable requests would include: turn off the engine and radio, face forward, turn on the dome light, and place the hands where they can be seen, like on the steering wheel. If the occupants fail to comply, ask yourself why.

Your squad's position is also important. Position the unit at least one to one and one half car lengths behind the subject's vehicle. The traditional stop position also offsets the squad 3 feet into the traffic lane to provide better cover for the officer and some safety from traffic while contacting the subject. The wheels are turned to the left to provide extra ballistic protection and in case your squad should be rear ended.

Some departments are now canting the squad at a 30-45 degree angle away and to the left of the violator to provide better cover (see Figure 2 on page 192). The down side of this tactic is the loss of headlight beams directed at the subject's vehicle, and in the case of a two-officer unit, less cover for the passenger officer. Use your lights even during the daytime to reduce the subject's visibility of your squad. Consider using flashers, instead of rotating lights after the stop has been affected to help conceal your movements. Do not use your dome light.

Among the most significant threats to officer safety in traffic stops is from the traffic itself. More people (including law enforcement officers) are killed in traffic accidents than homicides. Patrol officers have a higher exposure to this danger than the general public. Only last year this writer's department lost a deputy during a field interview with a drunk driver, the most significant contributor to accident fatalities. While our primary concern is the subjects and their vehicles, we must also be on guard for other traffic.

In the unknown risk traffic stop we would next approach the subject's vehicle. Keep in mind that over half the officers killed in these stops die during approach and initial contact with the subjects. Considering the tactical advantages the vehicles afford the subjects, why do we approach the vehicles at all? Some officers feel the vehicles protect the subjects from oncoming traffic, and protect the officers from assault by the subjects. More likely we do it because we want to see what the subjects have inside their vehicles that might mean additional charges based on plain view or other probable cause.

In approaching an occupied vehicle, maintain control of the subject's movements through verbal commands. As you approach, also be ready to escape. Sometimes lateral movement behind the subject's vehicle makes for a more difficult attack than simple retreat to your squad. As you approach, look for altered license plates, signs that someone is hiding in the car, a trunk that might be ajar, and other cues to danger. When you reach the vehicle, check trunks or rear hatches to insure they are secure, and check the back seat for hidden occupants and weapons. Once you advance beyond the rear bumper of the subject's vehicle, your escape route becomes more limited. Check these rear portions thoroughly, but quickly, so that you can reach the driver's door sooner. Never pass a door that is occupied by passengers, even if it appears that they are asleep.

Your position at the driver's door should afford you a good view of the subject's hands (see Figure 3 below). It should also permit you to receive the driver's license and registration. Stand close enough to the vehicle so that the driver will have to turn around to attack you, but not so close that you are unable to draw your weapon. Your weapon side should be on the far side of the subject. Your holster should be snapped, but your body should conceal your draw if necessary.

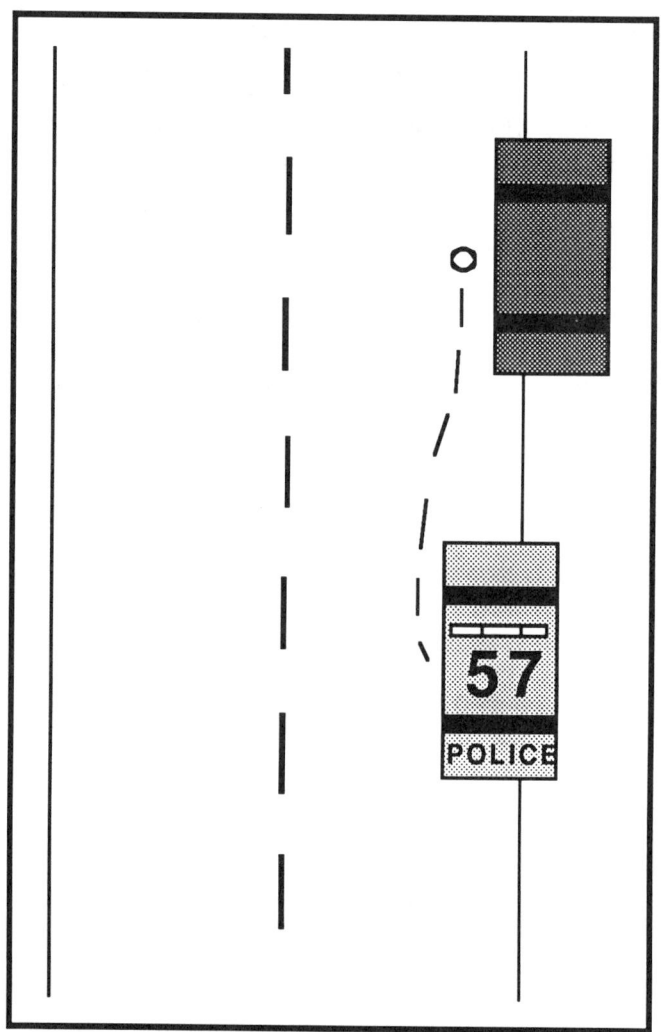

Figure 3: In the unknown risk traffic stop approach the subject's vehicle.

Consider your body angle with relation to your vest coverage, particularly if it lacks side panels. Your gun hand should not be used to conduct the business of the stop, but ready to defend you. Besides conduct-

Vehicle Stop Survival

ing business, your non-gun hand can also be used to deflect weapons thrust by the subject towards you. If you detect a weapon being drawn, tell the subject not to move. If possible, change your location so you won't be where the subject left you. Pushing the weapon towards the roof may give you time to draw your weapon. If you have something in your non-gun hand, drop it or throw it into the face, particularly the eyes, of the subject to help buy you time to draw. If you must shoot, try for a 90 degree angle to avoid rounds being deflected from the target.

During contact with subjects, direct them as to how to produce their wallets. Reaching for a handgun in the waistband is easily disguised as reaching for a wallet. Avoid reaching into the subjects' vehicles. Officers have been injured and killed by subjects who grabbed their arm or rolled up the window and took them on a quick, fatal trip. Avoid reading the license and registration while at the vehicle, thereby losing control of subjects' hands.

It is often best to secure their driver's licenses and registrations before explaining why they were stopped. Some officers will then explain the violations to the drivers and ask them to wait in their vehicles while citations are written. Many officers precede this by asking the drivers if they know why they were stopped. A subject may admit to the offense and during one of this writer's stops, the subject also admitted to concealing stolen property (Miranda warnings generally do not apply to traffic violations which are civil forfeitures in most cases).

Knowing what is going to happen is crucial to the subjects' short term mental health. Traffic violators may argue vehemently if they believe you are flexible or aren't sure of the violation. If they believe you are going to write a ticket, they may elect not to aggravate the situation or waste time. The officers can still elect to change their minds and issue a warning. A fleeing bank robber you stop for speeding may be happy to receive only a citation.

Returning to the squad, it is important to continue to watch the vehicle. You may, if necessary use your tactile senses to feel your way around your unit while watching the subject. Writing a citation in the unit offers protection from the elements, concealment and cover, access to communications, and a means of escape. It is difficult, but very important, to maintain periodic contact with the subject's vehicle. By writing high on the steering wheel you may benefit from peripheral vision in detecting threats from the vehicle. It is preferable, however, to look up at the vehicle after every entry on the citation.

When you return to the vehicle, again be observant and cautious. For some subjects a traffic citation can mean a significant change in their lives which they may wish to fight or even kill over. Practice handling the paperwork without, or with very little, use of your gun hand. Make the driver reach outside for the citation. When you direct the subjects to leave, watch them until they have left the area. It's also a good idea for you to leave the area to complete your paperwork, finding an area where you can observe anyone approaching you. Officers have been attacked by disgruntled subjects who returned to the scene of the stop.

In two officer stops, the second officer assumes the "cover position" in such a way as to be able to observe the subject and the vehicle's occupants. Some officers split up the vehicle into left and right halves for areas of responsibility. Consistent with the concept of contact and cover, only one officer should run the business of the stop. There are stop situations in which a cover officer is very important, but not always used. During DWI (DUI) stops, concentration on the field sobriety test can distract officers from other occupants and traffic. Further, many of these subjects will resist the officer when advised they will be arrested. Vehicle searches have resulted in officer deaths when a lone officer tried to contain the occupants and search for evidence. Anytime an arrest is anticipated a partner is a valuable survival asset. Don't assume compliance on the part of the subjects.

Certain situations call for a modification of unknown risk traffic stops. Vehicles containing multiple occupants, vans, semi-trucks, and other such situations present additional hazards to the officers trying to approach the subject's vehicle. After losing two officers in van stops, the Kentucky Bureau of Police Training began instructing officers to call the drivers of vehicles out of their vehicles and behind the squads where the field interviews would occur.

Other departments have used adaptations of this stop, conducting interviews with the drivers placed by the center of the front bumper while the officers use the hood area as lunge barriers. Other officers perform these interviews on the sidewalk. This is certainly preferable in situations where there is concern about the vehicle's occupants, but not enough cause to initiate high risk traffic stop tactics. It is much more difficult for subjects to attack officers without the vehicles providing cover. The only thing the officers give up is the opportunity to examine the interiors of the subjects' vehicles.

In each case, the officers will need to assess the risks and determine the most appropriate tactics for the situation. Of the thousands of traffic stops performed in a career, only a few may be truly dangerous. Unfortunately, those will be difficult to predict so officers must be always alert to the unknown dangers involved in what is often incorrectly referred to as the "routine" traffic stop.

About the Author

Sergeant Harvey V. Hedden serves as a supervisor of a multi-jurisdiction narcotics enforcement unit with the Kenosha County Sheriff's Department in Wisconsin. He has a B.S. in Psychology and Political Science from the University of Wisconsin. He has taught around the country on topics of officer safety and survival, and he is a professional photographer.

Chapter 23

Conducting Field Interviews: Gathering Knowledge Safely

by Dennis F. Jurasz

The windshield wipers methodically fight to remove the cold, dark rain, and your thoughts are on your children having to walk to school in this weather. With your daughter's pretty face etched on your mind, you mechanically check the front's of the stores in the shopping center. You have checked this center a thousand times, but at 5:37 a.m. this morning, your body, and not your mind, is doing the checking.

Not to worry; after all these years of police experience, flags will go up and bells will ring if there is anything wrong. As you reach the end of the shopping center and turn left to glance down the alleyways behind the stores, a dark figure steps out from the cold, wet shadows. Instantly, you are thrown back into reality! The flags are waving and the bells are ringing! Where did he come from? What is he doing here at this hour? Is he alone? I should radio for backup! Where the hell am I?

This beast is called a Field Interview, and it never seems to occur in broad daylight or when you're ready for it. How it is handled, however, can be the difference between going home safe and winning the case, or getting hurt and letting a criminal walk.

Police are, and should be, suspicious by nature. This is what they get paid for; to ask questions and to catch "bad guys;" but where do they get the authority to stop people and ask questions? Just what gives them the right?

Hundreds, if not thousands, of cases have come out of courts all across this great country that pertain to what is called a "Stop and Frisk." Every state has a law or statute that grants police officers the right, if not the obligation, to stop suspicious individuals.

Most of these laws read something like . . . "police officers may stop a person in a public place . . . when the officers reasonably suspect that such person is committing, has committed, or is about to commit a crime . . . and may demand name, address, and an explanation of the person's conduct. If the officers reasonably suspect that they are in danger of physical injury, they may search for a weapon or any instrument, article, or substance readily capable of causing serious physical injury."

Case law from every state and the Supreme Court is never ending on this subject, and officers must be familiar with the case law that regulates their actions. This is a great tool for law enforcement, and officers must know how and when to use it so it will not be taken from them in these liberal times.

Field Interviews are contacts with the public that should not be confrontational in nature. This theme holds true in most every police department policy across the country. The Rochester Police Department's policy in New York insists that their officers "Remember to be firm, be courteous, be neat, and take the time to explain." Across the land in California, the San Bernardino County Sheriff's Department's policy states, "The most important communication aspects for police officers must reflect command and courtesy." Officers must be courteous, but they must also be aware of officer safety.

Field Interviews are conducted on individuals that are on foot, and officers must be aware of the hazards of approaching them. When, where, and how to stop individuals must be taught, just like every other survival skill. Survival is no accident. An evaluation of the entire scene should be done prior to the stop. Officers who are aware of what they are getting into are much better suited to handle the situation than officers who are surprised. Surprise often translates into injury!

Before approaching the individuals, officers would be wise to evaluate the following approach factors:

- **Why is the stop being made?** Just what is the problem with the individuals that has drawn the officers' attention. Remembering the law or statute that gives officers' permission to "Stop and Frisk" will help answer this question. Something was WRONG in the first place. What was it?

- **Individuals' Appearance.** Are they injured? Are they under the influence of an intoxicant or hallucinogenic? Officers must always be asking themselves, "What's wrong with this picture?" "They just looked as though they were up to no good," is not a good enough answer for the court. Officers must be able to articulate why.

- **Individuals' Actions.** Are they running? Are they looking for an escape route? Are they shifting from one foot to the other? Are they nervous? Why?

- **What neighborhood are the officers in?** Is this a high crime area? Is this an area that has no crime? Do the individuals belong here? Why don't they? Are the individuals committing, have committed, or about to commit a crime? Can the officers safely conduct a Field Interview at this location? Is backup needed? What are the lighting conditions? Is there a crowd, and is it friendly? Will the crowd remain friendly if an arrest is necessary?

- **Knowledge of the individuals.** Have the officers arrested these individuals before? Are they known to carry weapons? Are the individuals drug users or dealers? Are they on pa-

Conducting Field Interviews 199

role or probation? Every time these individuals were arrested in the past, they fought with the officers. Will they fight this time?

Officer safety questions must always be answered first! Being good officers mean being good warriors. This does not mean that officers are looking for war, but it does mean that they have the ability to recognize danger. They know when to call for backup, or when to retreat from the scene to get reinforcements. Officers should be made aware that they are not on suicide missions. Some very smart street officers invented a powerful tool that all officers should use; it's called "backup!"

After the approach factors have been evaluated and are determined to be satisfactory then the contact is made. Remember, this is a "close encounter of the deadliest kind!" How the officers close the gap to the individuals may very well mean the difference between living and dying. Now is the time to be 100% focused; watch — no distractions! What is the best way to close the gap? Let's take a look at some proven methods of closing the gap to the individuals:

- **Rule One must always be that officers NEVER initiate a FI while seated in a vehicle!** All stops should give the advantage to the officers and no defensive tactics' course teaches subject control from inside a vehicle. Only if the FI turns into a deadly force situation should the option of the "Flying Ford Takedown" be considered. This is not an acceptable FI technique.

- **Upon leaving their vehicle, officers should approach the individuals from either the front or the rear of the vehicle, the rear being better.** Attempts should always be made to keep the majority of the vehicle between the officers and the individuals. Any metal may stop or deflect incoming rounds. The vehicle will, if a sudden physical assault should occur, afford a time factor to the officer by forcing the individuals to come around the vehicle. The Japanese have a word for this created space; they call it "Suki," and it means, "Time equals distance and distance equals time." Advantage — Police!

- **Once outside the vehicle, the encounter should begin at the bottom of the Force Continuum.** This encounter is an interview, and not an interrogation. Command presence, non-verbal skills, and verbal skills are the areas that officers must hone to achieve better and safer FI's.

Most jurisdictions define the degree of intrusion that police put on individuals. This usually ranges from "consensual encounter" to "detention" to "arrest."

In "consensual encounters," various case law state that individuals must remain totally free not to cooperate, and be free to leave. This means officers may not restrain or exert any authority over the individuals. An example of this would be where the officers ask to talk to the individuals and the individuals say they are late and walk away. The officers then walk away with the individuals and "chat" with them. Convincing the court that the encounter was "consensual" is an area of concern for the officers. Were the individuals "free," or did the encounter become a "detention?"

The fact that the officers approach individuals, call out to them to "Hold it," shine a spotlight on them, or ask the individuals in a non-coercive manner, "if" they would step over to the side and talk to them, does not constitute a "detention."

A "detention" starts when officers begin demanding answers to questions, use harsh tones, begin giving orders, or draw and display some type of weapon. Even the turning on of emergency overhead lights can be considered a detention. Detentions can, and at times, must be done. However, the governing factor is that the officers had "reasonable suspicion" that, as the law says . . . such individual is committing, has committed, or is about to commit a crime. If and when these suspicions are confirmed, then, and only then, does the "arrest" process begin.

Verbal directions should be courteous, and hand jesters friendly. Verbal directions like, "Hey you," or "Come here," or the ever popular jester of the "thumbs in the belt" should be avoided. Officers need to remember — this in not a confrontation!

Officer safety demands that close attention be given to the:

- **Palms of the hands.** To watch the hands alone is not enough. Many street-wise, knife fighters can palm a blade or razor. If, when closing the gap, the individuals put their hands in their pockets, and the officers are close enough, the hands should be trapped in the pockets! This can be done by pushing the individuals' elbows toward their pockets and securing their forearms. The uncontrolled hand must never be ordered out of the pocket! That hand went into the pocket for a reason; why? If both hands of the individuals go into their pockets, trapping their right hands will give the officers an approximate 90% chance of securing the weapon. Only an estimated 10% of the population is left-handed.

- **Shifting of the feet and/or shoulders.** This is the fighter's platform! Just as officers get into a defensive stance, so do individuals. The feet moving shoulder width apart, and the strong foot moving back should be indicators of danger to the officers. Shoulder shifting, or the dropping of the shoulder, occurs just before a punch is thrown.

- **Shifting of the eyes.** The individuals may be looking for an escape route, or are "target glancing." Target glancing is the quick peek at objects the individuals are interested in. Looks at the officers' chins may indicate a punch is coming, or the staring at the officers' guns may be the beginning of a gun grab. If the individuals are looking at the officers' guns, the officers should say to the individuals, "Don't look at our guns. Look at us!" By the officers telling the individuals not to look at their guns, the individuals know the officers are aware of the threat and can deal with it. The individuals also know that the officers will not be taken by surprise. The officers are alert and prepared for any trouble.

- **Bulges in the individuals' clothes or repeated "touches."** Bulges are one indicator of weapons. Off-duty officers know the problem of trying to conceal handguns. The bulges just don't go away. Remember, small weapons, small bulges. Repeated "touches" or "security taps" are the same moves officers make to "check" to ensure that they still have their weapons. Forearm or elbow touches to the gun butt or belt area (is there a gun under the jacket?), a tap of the individual's foot to the opposite ankle (an ankle holster or knife in the sock?), a pulling up of the pants (a gun stuck in the waistband pulling the pants down?), are indicators of concealed weapons. How many of these indicators can the average officer detect? Watching off-duty officers will point out dozens of them!

- **Behavior.** This includes all of the kinesiological cues that the individuals are giving. It translates into the "I just knew they were dirty" testimony. Being street smart and knowing these cues in today's society is not enough. Officers may be winning the battles on the street, but by not being able to articulate these cues, both in writing and in direct testimony, they may be losing the war in the courtroom.

The location of the encounter has been checked, the vehicle has been positioned properly, and the initial "look" at the individuals has been done. Now it's time to close the gap and finally talk to the individuals, but how?

The Defensive Stance or Interview Position is one in the same. Feet are shoulder width apart, the body is bladed 45 degrees to the individuals with gun side away, the head is up, and the hands are in front of the chest. From this posture, officers can talk, write, defend, and control, and can use an aerosol, or a PR-24™, or they can fire a sidearm. This is a solid base to conduct business from. Ideally, the officers should be 4 to 6 feet from the individuals, however, officers do not live in an ideal world. If this distance is shortened, then the officers' reaction times are shortened.

FI's should, in the best circumstances, be conducted with more officers than individuals. This is the best case scenario, however...

If dealing in a one-on-one situation, the officer should not, relating to relative positioning, be in the individual's inside position. The officer should attempt to get to the individual's outside, or the 2 1/2 Position (the Escort Position).

In a one officer, multiple individual FI, the officer should have backup! If the stop must be made and backup has not yet arrived, then the officer's contact should be with the "person-in-charge." By addressing and controlling the leader, the officer will stand a better chance of controlling the situation until help arrives. The individuals must never be allowed to surround the officer. If this is attempted, the officer needs immediately to disengage from the FI and get help! This is not the place for "Tombstone Courage." Standing ground will only end in an officer injured.

Having individuals "assume the position" against a wall or car is a method used to help control their movements. This position should *never, never,* be used to handcuff or search from. It is far too easy for the officer to be assaulted or disarmed! If one of the individuals has to be cuffed or frisked, then verbal commands can be used to direct the individual into a free standing position away from the others. Use the individual as an obstacle for the others to maneuver around. Also, by having the individual between the officer and the others, the officer's peripheral vision should pick up any movement from the others.

Having two or more officers at the scene allows for the principles of "Contact and Cover" to come into play. The contact officer performs all interviews and frisks, and the business of the stop, while the remaining officers provide cover. Whenever multiple officers are involved in an incident, all officers must remain alert to the possibility of crossfire, and the "laser rule" of muzzle control must be followed.

Once having controlled the FI physically, the information gathering can begin. Information can be as little as name only, or as comprehensive as social security numbers and employer's name and business address. The FI Card can be as complete as an agency likes it to be. Always remember that the court will decide at what point the information gathering has gone from a "consensual encounter" to a "detention." Having gathered all this information, the agency must have some means of sorting and categorizing it so that the information can be useful. Plotting criminal activity and being aware of the individual's movements is the goal of FI Cards.

FI's are necessary and useful tools of law enforcement, but even under the best circumstances they can become deadly! Always stay alert and practice good, proven techniques!

About the Author

Mr. Dennis F. Jurasz is a police officer with over 17 years experience, 15 of which has been as the Assistant Team Leader for the North Tonawanda, New York, Police Department's Emergency Response Team, and 6 years as their Physical Force Instructor.

He is a member of numerous national training staffs: Monadnock PR-24™ Training Council, Inc., NLETC, CASCO, and ASLET.

He is certified by the FBI and the State of New York as a Defensive Tactics' and Firearms' Instructor. He has also written numerous articles and is a National Advisory Board Member of **The Police Marksman***.*

Chapter 24

An Introduction to Defensive Tactics

by Gary T. Klugiewicz

The Problem With Defensive Tactics' Training

If someone were to ask me what's wrong with law enforcement defensive tactics' training, my answer would have to be, "It is the way the training is conducted." Although the training available is getting better, at best, this training is still incomplete. At its worst, defensive tactics training is deficient to the point of being negligent. No matter what's wrong with the training, there are some positive steps officers can take to protect themselves physically and legally. To understand how to do this, we must examine exactly what's wrong with the defensive tactics' training available to officers. The problem is that officers are not trained to answer the basic questions necessary to use force effectively and justifiably.

Many officers are instructed in a wide range of defensive tactics' techniques. They know "what" to do, but not "how" to do them. The techniques are either too complex, or insufficient time is spent on building the psychomotor skills necessary to perform these techniques in the real world.

Often the officers are not trained "when" to perform these techniques, "who" they are justified in using them on, or "where" they will have to use them. And after the confrontation is over, they do not understand "why" they had to use physical force in the first place. No framework has been developed to assist them in the decision making that must accompany any use of force.

Therefore, many officers have a difficult time making the transition from the classroom to the real world, because they have not participated in high level, structural simulations. They learn, to their dismay, that it is not enough to do the right thing, but they have to be able to explain to a jury why they did the right thing. Failure to do so leads to a situation where they discover that "F-O-R-C-E" has become a five letter "F" word.

One way to ensure that all the bases are covered is to make sure that officers understand the rules of the game. Begin by building a strong theoretical foundation with an introduction to defensive tactics. This foundation will provide officers with a vehicle for explaining "what" they are trying to accomplish; "how" they are trained to use force; "when" the use of force is appropriate; "who" this force may be used on; "where" this force is to be used; and after the fact, "why" the use of force was necessary.

Basic Premises of Defensive Tactics' Training

An introduction to defensive tactics begins with a clear understanding of the two basic premises that guide all defensive tactics' training:

- Any use of force has to be based on a system of verbalization skills coupled with physical alternatives.

- The purpose of all defensive tactics training is to establish control.

Once an officer understands these two premises, responding safely and effectively in a justifiable manner is much easier.

The first premise makes it very clear that officers must develop their communication skills, as well as their physical force responses. Verbalization skills include:

- The officers' physical presence; their professional appearance and body language
- What the officers say; the actual words used
- How the officers say it; their tone of voice

Being physically able to restrain subjects is only part of the solution to potentially resistive or assaultive subjects. Officers must first attempt to get subjects to comply with verbalization skills, or be able to show that the use of verbalization skills was not possible based on the subjects' actions as in the case of sudden assaults. Failure to do so may result in a determination that the officers used excessive force.

Situations that require the use of defensive tactics are by their very nature dangerous, high stressed, and dynamic. For this reason, many officers react to these situations by

- Saying nothing; remaining totally silent, often not even breathing.
- Saying things that are inappropriate; shouting hostile or even obscene remarks at subjects that may poison the officer's case.

To prevent the initial problem of not saying anything, officers should practice verbalizing appropriate verbal commands along with the correct physical force option. What officers need to remember is that verbalization is a psychomotor skill that must be practiced just as much as the physical components of defensive tactics' techniques. Officers' verbal-

An Introduction to Defensive Tactics

ization must take place before, during, and after the use of force. For example, in the case of the use of a baton technique against an assaultive subject, the proper way to practice the appropriate response would consist of:

- **Crisis Intervention.** When the officers arrive on the scene, they should begin to try to diffuse the situation before it is necessary to resort to physical alternatives.

- **Verbal Warnings.** As subjects become more agitated, officers should issue verbal warnings, such as "Stay back."

- **Initial Verbal Commands.** As subjects begin to assault the officers, the officers should perform strikes to the subjects' arms to prevent them from grabbing or striking the officers while issuing verbal commands, such as "Move back."

- **Secondary Verbal Commands.** If the strikes to the arms don't control the subjects, strikes should be performed to the subjects' legs with verbal commands, such as "Get down on the ground."

- **Additional Verbal Warnings.** When the subjects are on the ground, the officers should command the subjects to "Stay down." This tells the subjects just what the officers want them to do and justifies additional physical alternatives should the subjects continue to resist.

- **Stabilizing Commands.** When the subjects begin to comply, the officers should continue to communicate with them to expedite handcuffing by commanding them to "Get on your stomach! Hands out to your sides! Palms up! Don't move!" At this time the subjects should be handcuffed using the officers' department handcuffing techniques. Failure to follow these commands may justify additional physical force to get the subjects stabilized in order to accomplish handcuffing.

- **Monitorings.** After the subjects are handcuffed and under control, the officers should check to see if the subjects are injured by visually inspecting the subjects and asking, "Are you sick or injured?" If they are injured, it is better to find out early, especially if the subjects complain later about the officers' failure to provide "due care" to prisoners.

- **Debriefing.** Finally, the officers should debrief the subjects by telling them to "Calm down." "Just take it easy." "It's all over," or "Just relax" in an attempt to calm the subjects down so that further physical force will not be necessary.

Answer the following three questions to determine whether this type of training and tactics are important:
1.) Would well trained, reasonable officers respond in this manner?
2.) Compared to other possible responses, how would witnesses respond to these officers' verbalization skills coupled with physical alternatives?
3.) If these actions were captured on video tape, could this video tape be used to show that the officers acted reasonably?

Officers who responded in this manner would have tried everything possible to avoid and minimize the use of force through the proper use of verbalization skills. Remember that officers who use this combination of verbalization skills coupled with physical alternatives usually have to resort to the use of physical force less often. When they do use force, they are more effective, as well as being in a better position to justify their use of force. This dual training should be done each time officers practice defensive tactics' techniques. If officers train this way, not only will they verbalize during defensive tactics' situations, but they will breathe properly, because one has to breathe in order to be able to talk.

Officers who have practiced appropriate verbal commands will have gone a long way towards not responding to high stress situations with inappropriate verbal commands. These officers have programmed their minds to use appropriate verbal commands and not sound like a take-off from a Clint Eastwood movie. There are numerous cases where, what the officers said — not what they did — was the deciding factor in a finding that excessive force was used.

Officers who have developed a firm grasp of the first premise that refers to the relationship of verbalization skills and physical alternatives are ready to move on to the second premise. This premise states, "The purpose of all defensive tactics training is to establish control." Establishing control is the officers' primary goal in any situation.

Many officers believe that the sole purpose of defensive tactics' training is survival in the physical sense. Although physical survival is initially the most important element of officer survival, once officers have physically survived the incident, legal survival becomes paramount. For that reason, officers should not attempt to explain their actions in "grunt speak;" the "down and dirty" way officers sometimes talk to each other in locker rooms. For example, if officers were required to "direct subjects to the ground" during a confrontation, this should not be described as "slam dunking."

Officers must develop a "court speak" for communicating with supervisors and other criminal justice professionals, and for writing reports and testifying in court. The concept of "establishing control" must include "court speak," because the officers' force response needs to be based on maximizing physical survival while minimizing legal risks. Officers must be able to accomplish both goals. They have to survive incidents physically, but they must also factor in "legal risks" that may lead to criminal charges, civil lawsuits, and disciplinary actions.

To understand how to balance these two seemingly contradictory concepts of physical and legal survival, officers have to realize that control is not a 50/50 proposition. Officers don't want to have a fair fight, because officers can lose a fair fight, and a plaintiff's attorney can distort this explanation of the officers' actions. Instead, officers should use "court speak" to explain that they must maintain the position of advantage. In other words, officers must always stay at least one step ahead of resisting or assaultive subjects in order to "establish control."

Proper police action balances safety and efficiency. Officers have to be able to control situations, but not at needless risk to the officers or with "unreasonable" risk to the subjects. Officers must use the "minimum level of force" necessary to control the situation.

In order to do this, officers are always permitted to disengage or escalate in order to take proper police action. This means that officers may avoid contact or disengage from a situation until additional officers can be brought to the scene to control the situation safely and efficiently. On the other hand, officers may engage the subjects and escalate to whatever level of force is reasonable and necessary to control the threat. Sometimes it is appropriate to disengage while at other times escalation is the correct response. The subjects are really the ones who dictate the officers' actions.

In justifying the officers' use of force, the officers have to go beyond the fact situation to the perceptions they had at the time. These perceptions are based on their departmental assignments, special knowledge, formal training, existing departmental policies and procedures, and personal and departmental "past practice."

When officers understand the two premises outlined in "An Introduction to Defensive Tactics," they are ready to begin defensive tactics' training. The officers now understand the importance of verbalization skills to their safety and efficiency, and how the concept of "establishing control" contributes to overall officer survival. The officers have a better grasp of how and when to apply the defensive tactics' techniques they were taught. Even more important, the officers know how to defend any force response when they are "forced" to use force.

About the Author

Lt. Gary T. Klugiewicz is one of the best known defensive tactics' instructors in the United States today. Gary is employed as a lieutenant with the Milwaukee County Sheriff's Dept. where he currently serves as a Field Operations Supervisor. He was one of the primary instructors for Calibre Press Street Survival® Seminars. He was also a contributor to the officer survival classic, **The Tactical Edge: Surviving High Risk Patrol** *and a technical adviser for the highly acclaimed and award winning video,* **Surviving Edged Weapons.** *Gary is probably best known for the development of the Active Countermeasures System of unarmed blocking and striking techniques. Most recently, he has been featured on the Law Enforcement Television Network (LETN) on the "Drug Crackdown" series with training designed for undercover and tactical officers.*

Jim Lindell

    Mr. Lindell is nationally known as the developer of the Kansas City/Jim Lindell Handgun Retention System, the Kansas City/Jim Lindell Lateral Vascular Neck Restraint System and the Kansas City/Jim Lindell Knife Defense System. The Handgun Retention System was the first program of its kind designed specifically to protect officers from being disarmed, and has saved countless lives. The Lateral Vascular Neck Restraint System is the only method of neck restaint that has been medically researched and determined to be the safest for both officers and subjects. The Knife Defense System was developed to combat edged weapon attacks on police officers. The system fills a void in most police curricula.
    Mr. Lindell is a third degree black belt in judo and a certified teacher in the state of Missouri. He conducts national seminars for law enforcement trainers on a regular basis. He is Physical Training Supervisor of the Regional Police Academy in Kansas City, Missouri and the President of the National Law Enforcement Training Center.

Chapter 25

Handgun Retention System

by Jim Lindell

You know that as police officers you can never afford to lose a physical confrontation with a subject . . . not even once!

Sounds unreasonable, doesn't it? Everyone wins a few and loses a few in everything they do, but everyone is not an armed police officer. However, you are going to be one, and if your gun is ever taken away from you because you are physically beaten by a subject, or you fail to defend your gun successfully for any reason, it just might be the first and last time it ever happens to you.

Officer Disarmings

Fact: Law enforcement officers carry guns.
Fact: Incidents of assaults against law enforcement officers have increased tremendously in recent years.
Fact: More officers are being killed with their own guns than ever before.

In view of the onslaught against officers' lives, the law enforcement community cannot take a defensive position and simply hope that future assault statistics will be lower. What is required without delay is a coordinated offensive by all law enforcement agencies to provide more and better methods of protection for their officers.

The incidence of officers being disarmed and killed with their own weapons is not a statistical phenomenon that becomes dated as years go by. It is a timeless tragedy that is repeated annually and only varies by who will be next, circumstances, and statistics.[1]

Distance From Victim Officer to Subject During Incident

An important factor with respect to conditions present at the time of the incident is the distance between the victim officer and the subject. Most significantly, 21 or 52.5% of the killings occurred when the distance between the officer and the subject was 0-5 feet, compared with 25% of the officers assaulted.

However, when only looking at the 93 officers shot in the assault incidents, the findings show that 42% of the officers were within 0-5 feet of the subject when assaulted.

In 21 killing incidents, officers were shot at a distance of 0-5 feet. This number represents eight officers (including 6 shot with their own weapons) who were killed following a physical struggle with the subject.

Method By Which Subject Obtained Victim Officer's Firearm

39 Assaults   6 Killings

83% Lost during physical confrontation
17% Pulled or lost from holster
0%   Given up by officer

The method by which the subject was able to obtain the officer's firearm varies. The majority of officers killed and assaulted with their own firearms or another officer's firearm lost it during a physical confrontation. The two other means by which officers lost their firearms to the subject were: the subject pulled it from the holster without a struggle; and the firearm was voluntarily given up by the officer. It should be noted that none of the officers killed voluntarily gave their firearm to the subject.

In five of the six killing cases, the subject was able to obtain either the victim officer's firearm or another officer's firearm and use it against the officer. In the sixth case, the subject, under the influence of PCP, was able to rip the officer's shotgun and locking mount from the patrol vehicle and use the shotgun on the officer. Of those officers assaulted, but not killed, 7% were assaulted with their own firearm or another officer's firearm.

When comparing the physical condition of the victim officer with those officers that lost their firearm to the subject, it was found that in the killing cases, three officers were reported as being above average and three average. In the assault incidents, out of a total 38 reported incidents, 8 (21%) were above average, 29 (76%) were average, and 1 (3%) was reported as being below average in physical fitness.[2]

In an attempt to meet and overcome this growing threat, the Kansas City, Missouri, Police Department and the author developed the Handgun Retention System, which offers a totally new approach to the problem of officer disarmings.

Within an 18-month period starting in January 1975, nine officers of the Kansas City Police Department were disarmed, with one incident resulting in the slaying of an officer with his own gun. In the remaining eight incidents, one officer was shot in the leg as the attacker tried to remove the officer's gun from its holster; another was brutally beaten with his own weapon and left unconscious by his attacker, who subsequently robbed and killed a taxi driver with the officer's gun.

One officer had his own weapon taken from him twice. "I was trying to disarm an intoxicated 'mental' in a narrow hallway," he related. "There were a lot of people around and it was hard to maneuver. She grabbed my flashlight, and as I wrestled it away from her, she removed my gun from its (unsnapped) holster." Fortunately, in that instance, another officer knocked the gun from her hand. The second disarming incident occurred when the same officer, responding to an officer assistance call, walked into a bar during a wild melee. "As I entered the bar I saw a vice officer in a tussle with a male subject," he said. "I encircled the subject with my arms from the front and pushed him onto the bar. We both fell to the floor and as we rolled over and over he must have taken my weapon, because as we fell I reached for my gun, still thinking it was in my holster. The next thing I knew he hit me alongside the head with it . . . just then a shot rang out. Luckily, it was wide of the mark, but I hope I never have to come any closer."

In reviewing occurrences of officers being disarmed, one thing becomes clear — no two instances are ever exactly the same. Therefore, any training program designed to guard against officers being disarmed must concentrate on common denominators rather than on any specific attempt that has already occurred. The Administrative Analysis Division of the Kansas City Police Department conducted interviews with officers who had been disarmed and determined a number of factors were instrumental in the officers' failures to retain their weapons. The most notable were:

- The holster was left unsnapped or was snapped improperly on calls.

- There was a lack of support or assistance due to a failure to comply with one-man car procedures.

- The officer was subject to an assault that incapacitated him immediately and gave him no opportunity to resist.

- The officer failed to react in a specific manner under the circumstances to prevent his gun from being taken.

- There was no training program of weapon retention against a variety of attack situations aimed at disarming the officer.

As a result of the numerous disarming attacks and using data from the surveys, the Physical Training Department of the Regional Center for Criminal Justice was directed in January 1976, to study and formulate improved methods of weapon retention. There were apparently no existing techniques to effectively counter disarming attempts; research showed the only information available advised officers of techniques to regain a weapon **after** it had been taken from them.

The process began with an intensive search in various law enforcement journals and manuals for previous studies in the area. When it was determined virtually nothing had been written, further research was done by soliciting reports from the FBI and various police departments on incidents in which officers had been disarmed. It was discovered that officers had often unknowingly encouraged attacks on themselves by having their holsters unsnapped or snapped incorrectly, not being fully alert to the suddenness and surprise of attacks, or by reacting improperly when they realized their weapon was being grabbed.

A picture began to emerge that showed three general situations faced by the officers:
1.) The weapon had been removed from the holster.
2.) The attacker had grabbed the barrel of the officer's gun.
3.) The attacker had grabbed the officer's wrist that held the gun, and attempted to wrench the weapon from the officer's grasp.

The Handgun Retention System was developed as a result of trial and error experimentation with various defensive and offensive techniques, including wristlocks (jujitsu) and blocks (karate). These techniques were employed to overcome the various kinds of attacks generally used when disarming police officers. A study of nerves, leverage, and body mechanics also contributed several effective release techniques to the system. However, certain criteria had to be met before a technique could be considered for inclusion in the system.

The first criterion was that the kind of attack to be defended against had actually occurred or could conceivably occur with some degree of frequency. The second was that all retention, release, and defense techniques were required to have an extremely high degree of probability of success when properly applied. The third was that when attacked, the officer must be able to effect a release in 1 to 2 seconds.

The Handgun Retention System training manual outlines basic techniques designed to be effective in any situation or combination of situations.

Dominant Hand and Weak Hand Grabs

When the attacker grabs the holstered or drawn gun with **both** hands, the hand that grabs **first**, or has the tightest grip on the gun is called the **dominant** hand. Maximum force and leverage can be generated against the **dominant** hand because it remains in a fixed position on the gun until the release is applied. When the **dominant** hand grip is broken, the other hand (**weak** hand) also simultaneously loses its grip, because of the resultant sympathetic nerve reaction.

The reason a strong hand (**dominant**) and **weak** hand grab are present in every **two**-hand gun assault situation is that the gun butt or frame is too small for both attacking hands to get a strong grip on it.

With practice officers will be able to feel the difference in **dominant** and **weak** hand gripping power. If they attempt to apply a release against the wrong hand (**weak** hand), they must quickly shift their grip to the other hand (**dominant**) and apply an appropriate release.

If the attacker has drawn the officer's gun, one hand will be holding the gun butt (**dominant** hand). To counter this attack the officers will grab the entire gun barrel with the near hand as they simultaneously reach for and grab the same (**dominant**) hand with their **far** hand to apply the correct release technique. This action allows the officers to exert superior force and leverage at all times because both the officers' hands are

dominant hands during each handgun defense while the attacker is always limited to **one dominant** gripping hand.

The Three-Step System of Handgun Defense

Most of us are inclined to do things in the simplest way possible, because it takes less mental and physical effort if we reduce a task to basic steps and apply them in order. This is a good idea when applied to defensive tactics training, because generally, the more basic a given technique, the easier and more effective it is for officers to apply.

To simplify the Handgun Retention System a three-step integrated action sequence was devised so that regardless of the kind of attacks, the officers' initial response is always appropriate to the situation and provides the best opportunity to safely defend their guns and themselves.

Before you begin to practice the techniques, the three principal objectives of the Handgun Retention System should be understood and applied in the proper order as each technique is practiced. They are as follows:

> **STEP ONE — Secure the gun**
> Since the attackers are concentrating on grabbing the gun from your holster or hand, the first thing you must do to counter the attack is to secure the gun in the holster with one hand, as you prepare to use the other hand or arm to complete a release. In the event the gun in your hand is grabbed, you will check the attempt to disarm with your free hand, and then complete the release. So in every instance, secure the gun first and then prepare to apply the release technique.

> **STEP TWO — Position**
> As the gun is secured, it now becomes necessary to move maximum leverage and physical stress against the attackers. This ensures that a release is accomplished, and at the same time, provides body movement that has the effect of protecting you against additional assault as you apply the release. The various foot, leg, and body movements then serve two purposes as each technique is applied. They both position and protect you as you move to apply the release technique.

> **STEP THREE — Release**
> By the time you prepare to apply the release technique, approximately one second has elapsed and the attackers are already at a considerable disadvantage, because they have been checked in their attempts to gain control of the gun, and also have been restricted from any continued assaults on you.
> At this point, as you apply the release with the appropri-

ate technique, you will simply be applying more leverage and physical stress against the attackers than they have the ability to withstand, and the release is assured.

Holstered Gun Security Grips

As noted in Step One of the Three-Step System of handgun defense, it is **imperative** to secure the gun in the holster during an assault on it to prevent it from being drawn or discharged in the holster during the attack.

Two methods of gripping the holstered gun have been formulated to accomplish this goal. The officer's **right** hand grip is referred to as the Rear Gun Hand Grip and the **left** hand grip is called the Front Cross Grip. The proper application of these grips will make it impossible for the attacker to pull the gun from the holster or cause it to discharge in the holster, should the trigger be pulled during an assault.

When the officer's **holstered** gun is grabbed and the officer uses the proper grip to keep it in the holster, the gun remains in a relatively fixed position on the hip which allows for control to be maintained and allows for sufficient force to be developed against the attacker's **hand**(s) or **arm**(s) by the officer's **hands**, **arms**, and **body** to apply a release technique. The holster, because of its tight fit to the gun, also helps contain and prevent the gun from being drawn out, so long as the gun is being held down with a proper grip and the holster does not tear out in back.

If your holster design prevents or limits any of these gripping actions, modify your grip to achieve the same results which is to prevent the gun from being fired in the holster or drawn out of the holster by an attacker.

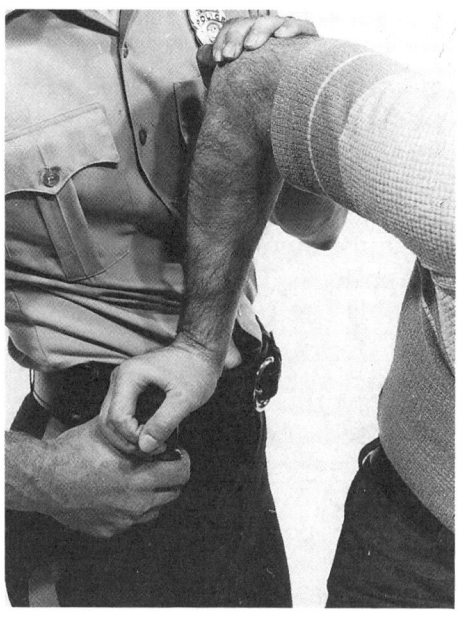

Rear Gun Hand Grip: Bring your RIGHT hand up behind your holstered gun so your RIGHT thumb is between the gun and the holster. Your RIGHT index finger now wraps around and on top of the hammer so your palm covers the entire trigger guard, and the two bottom fingers grasp the top front of the holster. Now push down hard on the gun to prevent it from being drawn or fired in the holster.

Handgun Retention System

The majority of officers who took part in formulating these techniques were completely unprepared to cope with two major areas of weapon protection and defense: How to maneuver to meet someone at their rear, and how to regain a gun taken from their holster.

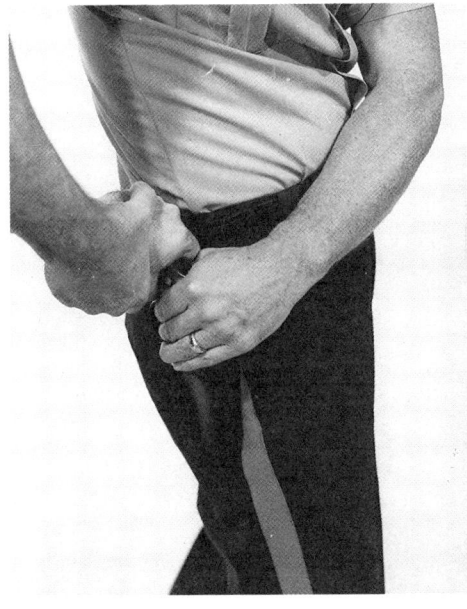

Front Cross Grip: Reach across your waist with your LEFT hand, palm down, and place the palm down on the hammer with your LEFT thumb between the gun and the holster. Simultaneously insert the index finger into the trigger guard behind the trigger, and the middle finger into the trigger guard in front of the trigger. Now push down hard on the gun to prevent it from being drawn or fired in the holster.

It is probably safe to say that most law enforcement officers have never given much thought as to how they might turn to the rear to best protect themselves and their weapons from attack. Because they are armed, officers should move in a manner that offers them protection and allows them to withdraw their weapon side quickly.

Lower Forearm Strike: You learn to turn properly to defend your weapon against assault from the rear and to block an attempt to remove your weapon from its holster.

There are four ways to turn to the rear:
1.) Cross step to the right with the left leg.
2.) Cross step to the left with the right leg.
3.) Pivot to the left on the right foot and swing the left leg to the left rear.
4.) Pivot to the right on the left foot and swing the right leg to the right rear.

Forearm Leverage Release: You are taught to use your arm as a lever to affect a release against a two-hand grab of your weapon or your wrist.

Disarming With Wristlock Release: You are taught how to effect a handgrip release by the use of properly applied wristlocks.

Handgun Retention System

If officers carry their weapons on the right side, only the last tactic offers a maximum degree of safety and an opportunity to defend their weapons with specific, effective techniques.

Retention Against A Palm Down Gun Grab: You are shown the proper method to apply pressure against nerves in the attacker's hand which will affect a release against a one or two-hand grab of the weapon barrel.

This change in position allows officers to turn their weapon side into and then away from the attackers, allowing no opportunity for the attackers to continue contact once their arms have been knocked aside by the officers' forearms. If the attackers have a tight grip on the holstered weapon, the officers can proceed to turn into a wristlock release.

Any of the other procedures provide the attackers an opportunity to move with the officers as they turn, making it difficult or impossible to move their weapon side away from the attackers, especially if the attackers already have a grip on their holstered gun. The preferred method should be used as a matter of course by officers to ensure maximum weapon security, even at those times when no apparent threat is present.

When officers were asked to try to disarm associates holding training guns in their hands, it was learned that an average of four out of five either pulled on the gun, or twisted it from side to side in an attempt to remove it from the hand.

This high ratio of ineffective attempts indicated that a large percentage of veteran officers had either never learned disarming methods, or had forgotten the methods that were taught to them as rookies.

In order for officers to regain their handguns or to disarm someone holding a gun at close quarters, it is imperative that the gun first be directed out of the line with their bodies as it is grasped.

Although not always possible, it is desirable in a disarming situation to take hold of the gun barrel first with either hand in a palm up position, because if the hand reaching for the gun misses due to movement, another attempt can be made without hesitation. Also, by seizing the barrel in a palm up position, maximum pressure is exerted upward and toward the subject's gun hand, causing tremendous pressure against the subject's thumb and forefinger.

If the forefinger is in the trigger guard, the subject must release the grip on the gun or suffer a fractured finger; if not, the gun will be forced out of the hand anyway, because of superior leverage exerted by the officers. A final reason for the officers to grasp the barrel of the gun first is to prevent the subject from taking hold of it, thereby having the position to exert more leverage and control over the gun than the officers.

In order to effect this release, the officers must secure the gun hand to prevent the subject from moving it as the release technique is performed. This is best accomplished if the officers place their thumbs on the back of the subject's gun hand and wrap their fingers into the palm of the hand as they push the gun barrel toward the subject's thumb and forefinger. If maximum force is applied, the subject will release the gun immediately.

This particular release is well known to many police instructors and is generally considered to be one of the surest and most effective disarming methods that officers have at their disposal. Law enforcement officers should become proficient in its use on the chance that they may have to recover their own gun from an attacker or disarm someone holding a gun in their hand.

The real difference between the weapon retention techniques and self-defense tactics routinely taught to police officers is that the former is weapon defense oriented rather than personal defense oriented. If the techniques are learned thoroughly and applied properly, personal defense is a natural consequence of the procedure.

The Handgun Retention techniques, now routinely taught at the police academy, were first introduced to police officers during training for the 1976 Republican National Convention. Acceptance of the techniques by the officers was almost universal, indicating a high probability of street use. Those who have undergone the program feel that it is one of the most practical in-service training programs they have ever received.

There have been a number of attempts to disarm officers since the Handgun Retention System was introduced. None have been successful to date against officers who have had the training; however, two officers who had not received the training were disarmed in the 12 months since the program was introduced.

It may be that the reduction of successful disarming attempts against trained officers is not necessarily limited to their ability to effectively apply these defensive techniques. However, it is as likely to be related to the officers' heightened awareness of the potential danger of being disarmed in various situations and the regular avoidance of dangerous practices as a result of the handgun retention training program.

Whatever the reason or combination of reasons, the goal of reducing disarming assaults against Kansas City Police Department officers is being attained to date by taking the offensive through progressive development and more advanced training methods.

In essence, the Handgun Retention System offers officers a definite

Handgun Retention System

course of action, increased awareness, and possibly ways to save their lives.

Now that a positive resolution to officer disarmings has been developed, it is hoped that full advantage is taken of it by all law enforcement agencies in order to ensure all officers greater safety during the performance of their duties.

The Handgun Retention System emerged from trial and error experimentation with various defensive and offensive techniques, including wristlocks, blocks, and throws. Since the original system was developed, improvements have been suggested by continuing research, practical training applications, and actual weapon defense situations experienced by officers in the field. The result was the publication of an updated version of the system late in 1980. The revised system of Handgun Retention is proving to be even more effective in training and application than the original system.[1]

The Kansas City Experience

The reports of disarmings among officers of the Kansas City, Missouri, Police Department who were trained in Handgun Retention virtually stopped for a period of 52 months. However, during the first year several officers who had not yet received the training were disarmed with no serious consequences.

There were a number of reported incidents where assaulted officers utilized the instructed techniques to retain their weapons. These officers reported using the Handgun Retention techniques far more often than any other method of defense to retain their weapons.

The notable reduction in disarming incidents among trained officers may not always have been due to direct application of techniques. Rather, it might have been the result of the officers' being more aware of the potential for being disarmed and therefore regularly avoiding dangerous practices. In either event, well-trained officers have proven to be better prepared to protect themselves and their weapons at all times.

The most frequently used holstered gun defense technique was the Lower Forearm Strike against an attempt to grab the gun from the side or rear. About half the reported handgun defense incidents involved the quick forearm strike and turn into and then away from the attacker in one simultaneous action. A number of officers also reported using the Disarming With Wristlock Release to remove the attacker's hands from the gun butt. One officer reported that a mentally disturbed person grabbed his drawn gun and he used a Retention Against A Palm Down Gun Grab to retain it. Also frequently reported was the use of the Handgun Disarming Method to remove guns and other weapons from subjects' hands.

In one instance a reserve police officer who had not yet undergone Handgun Retention training reported that he had received a copy of the training text and periodically practiced the techniques with his wife in their livingroom. The officer was working in uniform at an art gallery when he was assaulted and disarmed. The officer said that as he struggled with the attacker and had the gun ripped from his holster, the pictures from the Handgun Disarming Method flashed through his mind in sequence. He followed the procedure and disarmed the subject and regained his gun immediately. This of course is the kind of response that is ideally hoped for by all trainers and is directly related to the reason trainers recommend that officers practice instructed techniques on their own time to reinforce comprehension and reflex actions.

In contrast to the use of Handgun Retention techniques to retain their sidearms a smaller number of officers reported using a variety of other methods to protect their handguns from assault. These methods included fists, feet, elbows, batons, and hand radios. These kinds of personal defense tactics have worked and should continue to be used by officers whenever applicable. There should be no reservation in officers' minds about what they should or can do to protect their handguns from being taken.

The major reason that the Handgun Retention System has replaced personal defensive tactics as the most frequently reported way of defending officers' handguns is simply that in many instances they are the most practical, easy to apply, and effective handgun defense tactics available to assaulted officers. Without exception, those officers who defended their guns with Handgun Retention techniques reported that their defensive actions were spontaneous, appropriate, and effective.[3]

Conclusion

The Handgun Retention System was introduced in 1976 in response to an alarming number of officer disarmings and resultant deaths. Since that time thousands of law enforcement trainers have become certified instructors of the system and have taught the techniques to officers in their own agencies. The effectiveness of the Handgun Retention System is evident from hundreds of reports that certified trainers have sent to the National Law Enforcement Training Center (NLETC), the only recognized body that certifies instructors in the Handgun Retention System. Almost without exception, these reports tell how officers trained in the Handgun Retention System techniques successfully defended their handguns, or how they were able to disarm attackers who were holding weapons.

Furthermore, a number of officers have said that if they had been trained in the Handgun Retention System techniques, they would not have been disarmed and shot with their own weapons. Thankfully, these officers lived to tell their story and can stress to us the need for handgun retention training. Many others cannot.

The reports from trained officers illustrate how specific tactics, coupled with certified training can protect officers from the ever-present danger of being disarmed. In contrast, the continuing reports of officers being disarmed and wounded or killed with their own handguns dramatize the consequences of failing to provide this much needed training.

The evidence is there for all to see. Untrained officers are vulnerable and unprepared to deal successfully with attempts to disarm them.

Despite the gains that have been made in this area, and the many lives that have been saved since 1976, officers continue to be disarmed, shot, and often killed with their own guns. It has become increasingly evident from these disarmings that the entire law enforcement community must offer training in handgun retention.

Many farsighted agencies have begun teaching the Handgun Retention System as an integral part of, or an extension of their firearms' training. It is now time for the rest of the law enforcement community to recognize that the Handgun Retention System is a self-evident, proven means of protecting an agency's most valuable resource, police officers, from being disarmed and shot with their own guns. The use of this system has already provided hundreds of examples that officers can be trained to avoid serious injury or death by their trained response to an attempt to disarm them.

The National Law Enforcement Training Center (NLETC), a non-profit, educational training corporation with headquarters in Kansas City, Missouri, is the only national certifying body for trainer certification courses in the Handgun/Long Gun Retention and Disarming System, the Lateral Vascular Neck Restraint System, and the Knife Defense System. The center was formed to meet the increasing demand for training in these systems — a demand which no single law enforcement agency can meet in this time of limited manpower and tighter budgets. The NLETC is dedicated to insuring that all officers are trained and know how to defend their handguns against attack. We now ask the entire law enforcement community to join in this worthy goal to help save the lives of our police officers.

Bibliography

[1] FBI Law Enforcement Bulletin. 1978. (March).
[2] California Peace Officers Killed in the Line of Duty Study. 1980-1986.
[3] FBI Law Enforcement Bulletin. 1981. (September).

"Coach" Bob Lindsey

Mr. Lindsey is the Director of Security with the Jefferson Parish President's Office in Louisiana. He is also on the Board of Directors of the American Society of Law Enforcement Trainers (ASLET). Bob is a graduate of Loyola University and the FBI National Academy. He has been affiliated with law enforcement since 1964 and is the proud recipient of the 1990 Law Enforcement Trainer of the Year Award.

Chapter 26

Space, Time, and Distance

by "Coach" Bob Lindsey

Today's law enforcement officers have many responsibilities that relate to *Space, Time, and Distance.* These responsibilities may relate to the time of day they need to report for court duty, or for their tour of duty; how far away from a location they are when a call comes into headquarters, or how much space they need in order to park the squad car without scratching or denting the fenders. However, none of these are as important as the space immediately surrounding the officers, their distance away from assailants, or the time it takes for them to draw their baton to execute a blocking, striking, or control technique.

Officers need to understand the relationship that *Space, Time, and Distance* play in survival on the streets in the performance of their duties. Officers who do not understand how to protect themselves with the proper usage of *Space, Time, and Distance* may be doomed to injury, failure, or even death as the result of attacks. They need to understand simple and basic patterns of movement and other common sense self-defense skills that allow them to control the space and distance around them.

Officers' survival depends on knowledge, skill, and sometimes even chance. Their knowledge of laws, rules, and regulations serves to protect them in court. Proper tactics for building entry, vehicle pursuit, psychomotor skills, arrest and control, and firearms' skills protect them on the street. However, fundamental self-defense skills are paramount to self preservation when high risk and high stress close quarter confrontations are encountered.

Officers cannot expect chance or luck to open the doors for the proper execution of these skills. It is the officers' predetermined plans and intent to control their immediate environment that allows the proper tactics to be used to a successful conclusion of assailant control and officer safety. The three most vital areas the officers have to control to ensure a high probability of survival success are *Space, Time, and Distance,* and they are described below:

> **SPACE:** Defined as the area between officers and anyone else (not just an assailant). This area encompasses 360 degrees completely around the officers; the front, the back, and the

strong and reaction sides. Obviously, the more space between officers and potential assailants (or anyone else), the more room the officers have to maneuver, and this is of the utmost importance. Officers **must control this space**, because it is the their **circle of life or death**. This space also surrounds the assailants. Moving into their space with intent while using proper tactics should be done in a manner that works to the officers' advantage.

▸ **TIME:** The period that officers have to react to stimulus and cues from anyone. Time allows for the evaluation of existing situations. Should officers not allow for the proper use of time, the officers' actions could be "no action," and they could very easily be injured. The officers' lack of action or inappropriate action may also be scrutinized by a defense attorney or jury at a later time. Reaction time can be measured in seconds, or in fractions of a second.

▸ **DISTANCE:** How far officers are from anyone at any given time in any given circumstance. For example, as officers approach a possible high risk situation, distance can play a large role in the reduction of stress. The longer it takes for an encounter to reach a conclusion, the greater the chances the officers will be prepared mentally and tactically for an attack. However, if assailants close the Reactionary Gap and the officers are not prepared, they may not have enough time to recover from the initial startled response and take proper defensive action.

The greater the distance from the assailants, the better the officers' perspectives are of the overall situation. Distance can give the officers time to seek cover or to disengage from the encounter and to re-establish a more appropriate tactical response. Simply stated, distance buys the officers valuable life saving time so that space can be better controlled.

The golden rule is that *Space, Time, and Distance* must be controlled by the officers. To the degree that the officers control space, time, and distance, the officers improve their chances of winning. To the extent that the officers give up control of space, time, and distance, they give up control of the situation in direct proportion.

Officers must have it utmost in mind that the space and distance between themselves and anyone else are what buys them time. This is epitomized in the concept of the Reactionary Gap which is the space and distance between officers and anyone else. This distance should be approximately seven feet and maintained 360 degrees around the officers when possible.

Even an innocent bystander can, at any time, become a potential

Space, Time, and Distance

assailant. Therefore, officers must be cognizant of the fact that an assailant can close the Reactionary Gap of seven feet in less than one second. At 21 feet, an assailant can close the Reactionary Gap in less than 2 seconds. This may not be enough time for officers to escalate to the appropriate use-of-force level. There may not be enough time to draw their holstered firearm and stop the attack.

Many officers argue that they cannot work at this distance, but if at all possible, officers should get no closer than seven feet from an assailant. Officers need this time in order to respond.

This space and distance alone do not guarantee protection. When officers create this space and distance between themselves and the assailant, they may find themselves standing directly in front of the assailant. The officers are now only one step away from contact, and either the officers initiate contact, or the assailant makes contact.

When officers create the Reactionary Gap, the most vital thing they can have is a strategy that has been rehearsed and visualized, and that can be implemented instantly. The officers must plan what they will do WHEN something happens, and not IF something happens. If they do not have a plan of action and the Reactionary Gap is closed, by either the officers or the assailant, they will have to formulate one at a critical moment. This time of formulating a strategy is very costly to the officers because in all probability they have lost control of the space surrounding them.

The officers have created space and distance by creating, maintaining, and controlling the Reactionary Gap, and they have a plan built on when something happens, rather than if something happens. The officers must remember that they are standing directly in front of an assailant who has an arsenal of weapons that can be used against them without notice. The assailant's arsenal consists of two hands, two forearms, two elbows, two feet, two knees, and a head that can be used to attack the officers. The assailant can also easily reach across the seven feet of space and distance and grab an officer's gun.

The officers should now perform the Seven Principles of Officer Survival which are based on sound judgment and the proper use of space, time, and distance. These principles place the officers in a position of defense with the ability to engage the assailant, to take control, or to disengage and re-establish the Reactionary Gap. The Seven Principles of Officer Survival are as follows:

1.) **Turn the gun away.** Step to the rear with the strong foot while rotating the hips which moves the holstered guns further away from the assailants and out of their view. If the assailants try to disarm the officers, they are not pulling the guns forward, but at an angle which diminishes their pulling ability.

2.) **Cover the gun with the biceps, elbow, and forearm.** The officers should wear their holstered guns on their belts so that when they drop their arms, biceps, elbows, and forearms, they cover their holstered guns. This simple action increases the amount of time it takes for the assailants to grasp the holstered guns and gives the officers time to perform proper weapon retention tactics.

Stepping to the rear with the strong foot while rotating the hips moves the weapon away from the assailant.

3.) **Hands up to chest level, but not on the chest.** The officers should keep their hands up to chest level with their hands either bladed toward the assailants, or with their palms facing the assailants. This gives the officers the advantage of time by reducing the distance their arms and hands have to travel in order to effect a block or perform a self-defense technique. The officers should not turn their hands toward their own bodies which would allow potential assailants to overpower the officers easier. Note: The holstered guns are still covered by the biceps, elbows, and forearms when the officers' hands are up to chest level.

4.) **The officers' eyes should be on the assailants' hands, and particularly, their palms.** The assailants could very quickly produce weapons. As soon as the officers see a weapon, they should yell, "Gun" or "Knife." This auditory cue reduces the

Space, Time, and Distance

amount of time it takes for the officers to react to the threat of lethal force and prevents the officers from holding their breath.

The officer blocks the punch and clearly stops the attack. Standing in front of the assailant, however, allows him to follow-up with a subsequent attack.

5.) **The officers should be on balance mentally and physically,** and have a plan. They should strive to remain on balance throughout the encounter.

6.) **The officers should be mentally prepared;** relaxed, but alert.

7.) **The officers should establish, maintain, and control the Reactionary Gap of 7 feet.**

The officers have now enhanced *Space, Time, and Distance* to their advantage. They are in control of the space and distance giving themselves more time to react.

The officers are still directly in front of the assailants; the attack/kill zone. They should exit the attack/kill zone as soon as possible. The officers' movement should be bilateral; they should move to their strong or reaction side. Movement towards the outside of the assailants lessens the opportunities for the assailants to hurt the officers. The practice of exiting the attack/kill zone should be part of the officers' plan.

The attack is blocked. The officer rotated his hips causing the assailant to move further away. The officer is now out of the attack/kill zone.

It is of special interest to note that officers may exit the attack/kill zone by moving themselves or by moving the assailants. In either case, the officers are safer, because they are not directly in front of the assailants.

Officers are encouraged to give **loud, verbal commands** to the assailants which mentally imbalances the assailants. Verbal commands should be **loud, repeated**, and **simple**. Some examples of verbal commands are "No; Stop; Down; and Back."

Officers should strive to continually imbalance assailants physically. They should also continually endeavor to remain physically and mentally on balance themselves. A good technique for officers is to keep the assailants' heads over their knees.

Officers must be in **control** of themselves and their assailants. An excellent method of establishing and maintaining **control** is the use of *Space, Time, and Distance* as a vital part of their plans in the performance of their duties.

Chapter 27

Patrol Response to Hazardous Materials Incidents

by William A. May, Jr.

At 0230 hours, you and a traffic accident, investigation unit are dispatched to check the report of a personal injury accident on a stretch of interstate highway infamous for fatal accidents. Arriving first, you find an over turned 18-wheel, semi-tanker leaking a foul smelling substance from a gaping hole in the rear section. The unknown substance has already pooled on the highway, and is starting to run downhill into a stream that feeds the lake which supplies your town's water. While you survey the scene and formulate a plan, cars are continuing to drive through the liquid and trail it down the highway. Curious bystanders have crowded around the scene, and some are actually standing in the unknown substance. Unfortunately, the driver is dead.

Does the above scene sound familiar? It should, because patrol officers respond to the above type of scenario hundreds of times each year. However, our response to and the handling of this type of situation has changed dramatically. In days past, we would concern ourselves only with the investigation of the accident, while letting the local fire department handle the spill and the EMS treat the victims. Events have changed, and today an accident involving hazardous materials presents not only a danger to the public, but a danger to officers as well. Hazardous materials incidents are officer survival problems too!

Hazardous materials do not shoot at us, they do not resist arrest, and they don't take hostages. Nonetheless, they rightfully deserve their name — silent killers. If you have a high school chemistry lab, a truck terminal, a railroad yard, a drug store, or even a discount department store on your beat, then you stand a good chance of being the first on the scene of a hazardous materials incident. When that happens, your actions in the first few minutes may well determine the outcome of that incident, in addition to who lives and dies (you and your partner included).

Before you can formulate a plan for your response to a hazardous materials incident, it is important to know just what is a "hazardous" material. The U.S. Department of Transportation has defined a hazardous material as . . . "a substance or material, in any quantity or form, which poses an unreasonable risk to the health and safety of people and property, when transported in commerce." Many common everyday substances, which we use and often take for granted, fall into this category.

Hazardous materials are classified according to:

- **Chemical properties.** Chemical properties relate to health, flammability, and reactivity.

- **Physical properties.** Physical properties relate to whether the material is a solid, liquid, or gas.

As a patrol officer or patrol supervisor, it is extremely important that you be familiar with the nine hazardous materials classifications. The following is the classification of hazardous materials as set forth by the United Nations:

United Nations System		
Hazard Class #	**Placard Colors**	**Description**
1	Orange; black lettering	Explosives
2	White; black lettering	Gases — compressed, liquefied, or dissolved under pressure
3	Red; white lettering	Flammable liquids
4	Red & White stripes; black lettering	Flammable solids — substances likely to combust spontaneously; substances which, on contact with water, emit flammable gases
5	Yellow; black lettering	Oxidizing substances; organic peroxides
6	White; black lettering	Poisons (toxic) and infectious substances
7	White or white & Yellow; black lettering	Radioactive substances
8	Black & White; black & white lettering	Corrosives
9	Black & White stripes;	Miscellaneous dangerous substances

Patrol Response to Hazardous Materials Incidents

Hazardous Materials Warning Placards

Additionally, it is important for you as a patrol officer or a supervisor to be familiar with the colors and symbols used on placards. "Why?" If you stop a semi-tractor for a traffic violation or spot a truck leaking its contents on the roadway, you may have a hazardous materials incident on your hands and not even realize it! You should have some idea of what the truck is carrying before you make the stop. For that reason, every patrol car should have a copy of the "Emergency Response Guidebook" (information on this booklet is available from the U.S. Department of Transportation, Research and Special Programs Administration, Office of Hazardous Materials Transportation [DHM-51], Washington, DC 20590-0001). This booklet is your best source of information as a first responder to a hazardous materials incident. Use this guide to determine the materials involved. If you don't know what materials you are dealing with, it may well be the last traffic stop you make or the last accident you investigate.

When stopping a vehicle or investigating an accident or incident, remember that the placard must be displayed on all four sides of the vehicle. However, these placards are often torn off or mangled in an accident and may not be present or readable. If the driver is injured or dead, and you are not sure what the substance might be, check the shipping papers. These papers should either be in the driver's door or within the driver's reach in the cab. If there are no placards, or no one at the scene to assist you, and you strongly suspect that you have a hazardous materials incident (always assume the worst — assume that the materials involved are hazardous until proven otherwise), then there are four general ways to identify a hazardous material. These methods are:

1.) shipping containers
2.) shipping papers
3.) placards
4.) markings

If you still cannot determine the material involved, have the dispatcher contact the trucking company or railroad, etc. Give the truck number — not the license plate number — or rail car number if appropriate. The company or manufacturer should have a Material Safety Data Sheet (M.S.D.S.). Everyone who handles a hazardous material must have a M.S.D.S. for that material. It is a sheet packed with valuable information, ranging from the name(s) used for this substance to first-aid treatments for exposure or contamination.

Responding to a hazardous materials incident does not have to be a complicated process if you remember a few basic rules. These rules are listed below:

Hazardous Materials Incident Checklist — First On The Scene Checklist

- **Respond Upwind and Upgrade.** Give the dispatcher the exact location and request assistance. Do not concern yourself with attempting to save the material or substance, or the container; they can always be replaced. Keep dispatchers informed of all actions taken so that they can inform other responding agencies. Advise appropriate response routes for these units.

- **Isolate the Area and Remove or Keep All Non-Essential Personnel Out.** Eject everyone not directly involved with the incident until the on-scene commander, usually the highest ranking fire official, arrives. Remember, the goal is to remove the threat to the public. If personnel are not directly involved in the mitigation of the incident, they have no business at the scene.

- **Avoid Contact With Liquids, Fumes, or Vapor Clouds.** Remember, just because a substance has no smell or color, it doesn't mean it is harmless. Do not dip your finger into a substance to conduct a taste or smell test; that may work on television, but it does not work well in real life. Additionally, do not stand in the substance. You can track a liquid back to your patrol car, then back to the station or to your home, contaminating each of the places where you stepped.

- **Eliminate Ignition Sources.** Remember, flares for traffic control, your cruiser's running car engine, and smoking materials are ignition sources. Many of these hazardous materials are highly flammable. Watch for open flame!

- **Rescue the Injured Only If Prudent.** Do not compound the problem by attempting a rescue for which you are not trained or ill-equipped. You may have to delay first-aid or rescue in order to save the lives of others. Do not take a true emergency situation and escalate it into a catastrophe where you have to be rescued too!

- **Identify the Materials and Determine Conditions.** Determine if the incident involves a spill, leak, fire, solid material, gas, vapor, etc. If possible, determine if the cargo being transported is a single load (one material) or mixed load (several materials). Check for waybills, shipping papers, consists, or any other identification which may be of assistance. However, remember not to endanger yourself or others to get this information.

- **Initiate Evacuation of Persons Downwind.** Evacuations can pose a real problem. They can be very tricky (invalids, for example, can take two or three officers to move). The logistical problems can be a real nightmare. Where will they go? How long will they be there? Do they need to be fed? Is mutual aide from other departments or support agencies needed? As you can see, the situation may demand that a decision be made by the first arriving officers shortly after their arrival at the scene. Don't let these things scare you — do what needs to be done. Remember when dealing with hazardous materials it is better to err on the side of being too cautious than not being cautious enough.

- **Establish a Command Post.** Where? How about your unit? It is easily recognized and highly visible. Do responding units know where to report or will they drive right up to the spill and endanger themselves? You are in charge until the fire department or the primary agency arrives and takes over. If you are a state trooper or deputy sheriff, you may patrol a rural area where there is no fire department, or the local fire department lacks the necessary expertise to handle a situation like this. Subsequently, you may be at the scene and in charge for an extended period of time until someone like the State Fire Marshal can respond and take charge of the scene.

Hazardous materials incidents can be divided into three basic categories:
1.) fixed facility
2.) transportation incidents
3.) point of use incidents

As you can see, hazardous materials are indeed stored, used, or transported through your jurisdiction, probably with great frequency. Many times they are transported or used with very little thought or care, and that's where you, as a police officer, come into play. How does this effect you as a first responder? Let's take a closer look at what we call "environmental pathways." That's how you become contaminated from a hazardous materials incident. The four primary pathways are:
1.) soil
2.) air
3.) water
4.) food

A police officer on the scene of a hazardous materials incident can become contaminated by direct contact, such as touching or tasting the product, or by indirect contamination, such as from run-off water during fire-fighting, by the actions of clean-up personnel, by the movements of response personnel, or from the soil beneath contaminated areas. Not only can you become contaminated by your own actions, but by the inappropriate actions of others at the emergency scene. A mistake by a co-worker can be extremely dangerous for you.

"All of this is fine," you say, "but I don't plan on being that close." Just remember that the operative word is "plan." As police officers, we know too well that things usually don't go as "planned." In reality, you don't have to be that close to a hazardous materials incident to become contaminated. This is especially true of powders and dusts, whose minute particles become airborne after an explosion, or solids that can be transported by run-off water from fire-fighting activities.

Think back about how often you have directed traffic at a fire scene, not even knowing or realizing what was burning, and stood in the run-off water from fire-fighting activities. Perhaps you were contaminated and did not even know it! That's why it's so important to think before you smoke or eat after being at one of these incidents. Hazardous materials

Patrol Response to Hazardous Materials Incidents

are introduced into our bodies in three ways:

1.) absorbed
2.) inhaled
3.) ingested

Watch what goes into your mouth! If you think that you have become contaminated, check with the fire department or other agency handling the incident, or go to the hospital immediately. DON'T DELAY. Seek professional medical assistance at once!

Also remember that when you respond to the scene of a hazardous materials incident, and you're the first-on-the-scene, your actions may set the tone for the entire incident. Do you have a plan? Have you practiced that plan? Do you have a worksheet so that you can assign tasks and positions? This is especially important if you are a first-line street supervisor or acting in that capacity.

A hazardous materials incident requires the expertise of many people, both from within the government, and from outside private contractors. No one person or agency has the necessary experience or expertise to handle a problem of this magnitude alone. Subsequently, it is important to know what additional agencies or companies in your jurisdiction can lend a hand when a hazardous materials incident strikes. Some examples of support agencies are:

- U.S. Coast Guard
- local water company
- local sewer utility
- EMS
- public works department
- local or state Disaster & Emergency Services (the old Civil Defense)

The list is almost endless. It is also important to equip your patrol unit with a basic hazardous materials incident response kit. These can be made with little effort or cost involved. This kit should include (but need not be limited to) the following articles:

- binoculars
- self-contained breathing apparatus
- D.O.T. Emergency Response Guidebook
- list of support agencies
- list of contact persons for companies on your beat that use, store, or manufacture hazardous materials
- flares, traffic cones, signs, etc. for stopping or re-routing traffic
- first-aid kit with bottled water or saline
- worksheets for haz-mat incidents

- ☐ telephone numbers for CHEMTREC (the Chemical Transportation Emergency Center, the 24-hour emergency number for all chemical emergencies is 1-800-424-9300)
- ☐ miscellaneous equipment that you determine is needed, drawing from past experiences or from the unique nature of your beat.

In dealing with hazardous materials, you will learn a whole new vocabulary from the support agencies you deal with at each scene. Like law enforcement, they too have their own terms. These are terms and phrases that you should know:

Hazardous Materials Incident Terms and Phrases

Absorption — process of being transferred into the blood stream.
Acute — occurring over a short period of time (usually a few hours or less).
Adsorption — process of adhering to a surface.
Asphyxiant — any gas which produces damage by replacing oxygen in the atmosphere.
Carcinogenicity — ability to foster, produce, or initiate a malignancy.
Ceiling — concentration of a chemical or substance in the atmosphere that should not be exceeded (usually expressed in parts per million or parts per billion).
Chronic — occurring over an extended period of time, usually days, weeks, or even years.
Contamination — depositing a toxic or hazardous substance in a place where it is not wanted or desired.
Decontamination — the removal or neutralization of a toxic or hazardous substance from a designated place or spot.
Dose — the quantity of a substance to which you are exposed.
Dose Response — the relationship between the magnitude of a toxic response and the dose of the toxin producing it.
Exposure — the condition of being subjected to a toxic or hazardous material or substance.
LC50 — the atmospheric concentration which is expected to be fatal to half of the people exposed.
LD50 — the dose expected to be fatal to half of the people exposed.
Lacrimation — tearing produced by the eyes.
Local — contact within a limited area.
Mutagenicity — the ability to produce a change in genetic structure (mutant).
Odor Threshold — the lowest concentration or amount in the atmosphere that can be detected by the nose.
STEL — short term exposure limit; the maximum concentration to which one can be exposed for 15 minutes without suffering significant symptoms.
Synergism — the joint action of agents in which the effect is greater than that predicted by the additive effects of the individual substances.
Teratogenicity — ability to produce birth defects.
TLV — threshold limit value; highest concentration of a chemical in the air to which a person can be continuously exposed without adverse effects.

Obviously these terms are scary, and one soon starts to get the idea that this is indeed an officer survival problem. There is nothing "routine" about any radio call or assignment in law enforcement. Certainly there is nothing "routine" about any call to an incident involving hazardous materials. Hazardous materials incidents, like domestic trouble may be alike, but yet somewhat different each time you respond. It is impossible to set down hard and fast rules and guidelines to use for each situation. That's why you must draw upon your past training and experience to make decisions. Your response and approach to a hazardous materials incident is just as important as your approach to any felony-in-progress call.

About the Author

Captain William A. May, Jr. is with the Louisville Division of Fire, and is assigned as an Arson Squad Firearms' Instructor. Captain May is an experienced law enforcement trainer and has written numerous articles for many law enforcement magazines.

Dr. Murlene "Mac" McKinnon

Dr. McKinnon is CEO of MACNLOW Associates, a company specializing in criminal justice training. Her field is communications with a special emphasis on nonverbal behavior, management communications and team building, and problem solving. Mac does one-on-one executive development and has taught at the FBI Academy, the Canadian Police College, and numerous other academies and departments.

Chapter 28

Looking Glass Cops

by Dr. Murlene "Mac" McKinnon

It is no wonder, with some of the footage that police officers are treated to on national television, and phrases that often ring in their ears — such as, "Why don't you go catch some real criminals?" — that police officers frequently feel under siege. The truth is, although the Rodney King incident in 1991 was a setback to policing and some cop shows a continuing insult as they portray police as bumbling fools, the majority of Americans have a love affair with the police. Television builds on that affair with prime time shows such as 911, Top Cops, American Detective, and FBI, the Untold Stories. The noncriminal population wants to view police as heroes and helpers. Community policing, DARE, and school liaison programs enhance that image. The smart department today builds on that image by developing a total quality police force offering extraordinary customer service.

Lack of public support for police can make law enforcement an unpleasant and life threatening job. For this reason, officers must look at themselves to see what kind of persona they are presenting to the community. Is the image professional, honest, and ethical; one that makes the department proud, or is the officer a detriment to the department and an embarrassment to the profession? In a time of increasing civil liability for police departments, no agency can afford the latter. From agency heads to dispatchers, law enforcement personnel have a responsibility to themselves to be aware of the picture they present to citizens, and to recognize how that picture affects their community relations and public support.

This chapter describes the verbal, nonverbal, and vocal communication behaviors which demonstrate understanding, caring, and support for citizens, as well as those appropriate for regulating and controlling their behavior.

Three Messages

Messages in law enforcement encounters are generally sent simultaneously and communicated in three ways. They include: verbal - by words; vocal - by voice; and nonverbal - by eye contact, facial expression, gesture, proxemics (distance), appearance, and other facets of demeanor.

Whether an officer makes a traffic stop, handles a domestic dispute, testifies in court, or receives an award, the three delivery modes always operate. Only in telephone conversations does the nonverbal message not make itself apparent. The importance of each mode is illustrated in Figure 1 below:

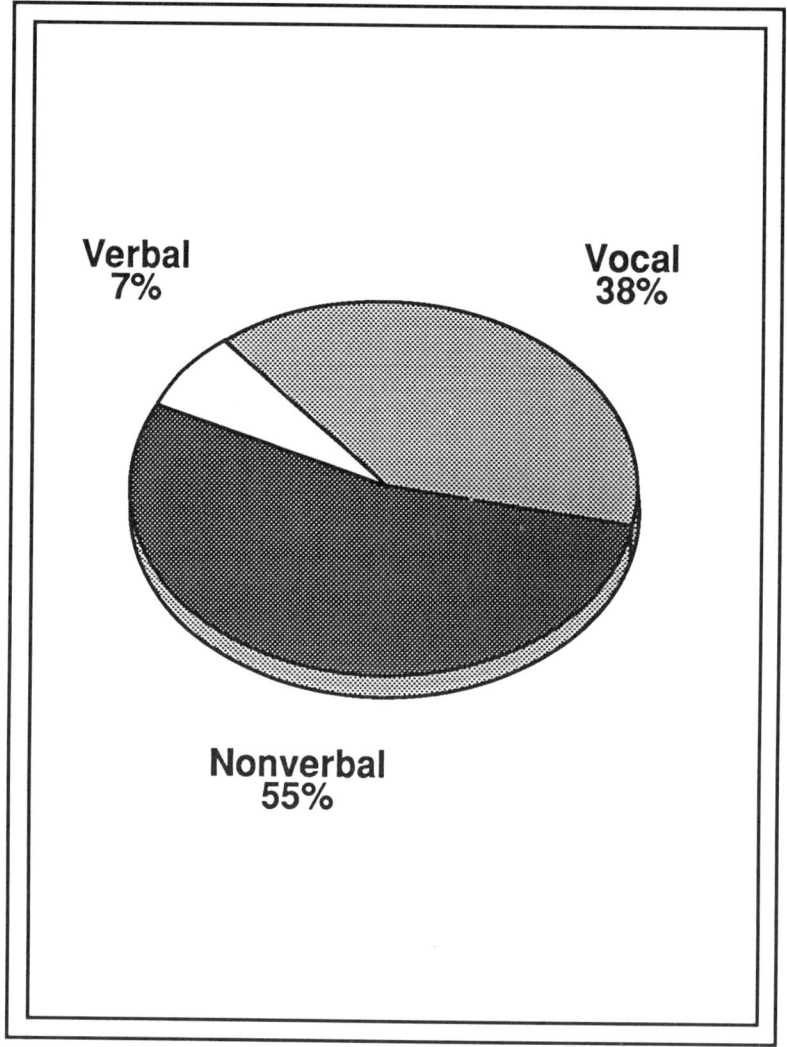

Based on SILENT PASSAGES, Albert Mehrabian, 1971

Figure I

Words that an officer chooses in interactions with a citizen set the tone for how the citizen responds, as well as for how the citizen views both the officer and the department. Officers who are attempting to maintain control may choose stronger, more strict sounding words (require; must), as in some traffic stops or when containing violence in a domestic dispute. They recognize when they do so that the likely response will be defensive and even hostile, but in many cases that is a necessary choice. Officers who give support and understanding in domestic disputes, serious automobile accidents, and even traffic stops choose softer, more flexible words (let's; agreeable; perhaps; likely) that often bring appreciative, or at least conciliatory responses.

Today experienced police officers recognize that human beings react negatively to stereotypical labels and extremes in language (wop, kike, nigger, broad), and they avoid using them. When such words are used to refer to an officer (broad, bastard, pig, motherfucker), the experienced officer also recognizes that the reaction is generally to the situation. If officers take the labels personally, it simply activates their emotions, clouds their judgment, and causes them to react without thinking. In a similar vein, if an officer does not allow a citizen to have the opportunity to explain, but instead prejudges the circumstances and interrupts the person in mid-explanation, the result can only be counter productive.

A uniformed officer, carrying a badge and a gun, possesses a natural authority. Most citizens are conditioned to respond to these symbols as clear indicators of legitimate power. However, when an officer chooses to project an attitude of superiority over, as opposed to equality with, everyday citizens, that officer has chosen to intimidate, and the guaranteed response is lack of understanding, dislike, mistrust, resentment, defensiveness, and hostility. The attitude of equality invites a positive response, mutual understanding, attitude adjustment on the citizen's part, empathy and ultimately acceptance. If the officer can gain compliance in this manner, it makes both the officer and the department look good.

Vocal behavior also escalates or de-escalates the tenor of an interaction. The major vocal components affecting outcome are volume (how loud or soft), pitch (how high or low), rate or tempo (how fast or slow), and pause and fluency. Confident voices tend to have high energy, a moderately fast rate, louder volume, fewer and shorter pauses, a more varied pitch, and greater fluency.[1] The officer's message, "I am in control. I am competent." If the voice becomes overly loud, the pitch higher, and the rate extremely fast, an officer may send a message of anger and irritation. To the average human being such a message is often intimidating or even condescending. By choosing to soften the volume a bit, keep the rate moderately fast, and use some pitch variation, the officer adds the message, "I am courteous. I am concerned." Apparent as common sense behavior in everyday situations is, this knowledge may be ignored when officers are caught up in a crisis. In some types of crisis this is expected, because the strong voice of command is imperative as a means of establishing compliance quickly. The important consideration is recognizing when the need is for control of the subject versus support. If verbal and vocal messages contradict each other, the recipient will respond to the vocal because it carries more weight (see Figure 1 on page 240).

Obviously the same rule applies in nonverbal communication because it makes up 55% of the message meaning. When other message components send contradictory information, people will believe the nonverbal. An additional problem exists, because most people also consider their personal nonverbal behavior to be unintentional, while that of others (particularly authority figures such as police) is viewed as intentional.[2] For this reason, police need a thorough understanding of how nonverbal messages which they consider to be harmless, unintentional, and non-threatening may be perceived very differently by the public, and indeed by a judge, a jury, or a citizen review board. These considerations make a knowledge of nonverbal behavior and the ability to monitor one's own nonverbal behavior highly desirable skills for an effective police officer.

Communication Blindspot

Achieving a working knowledge of nonverbal communication is not that difficult. Pertinent information will be provided in the remainder of this chapter. What remains a problem, however, is that much nonverbal behavior exists in the communication blindspot. Figure 2 on the following page shows the Johari Window, originally developed by psychologists Joseph Luft and Harry Ingham. It illustrates the four window panes of communication:

1.) **The Arena** — a public area of communication where information about an individual is known to both the self and others.
2.) **The Blindspot** — an area where others perceive idiosyncrasies, attitudes, and nonverbal behaviors which are not in the self's awareness. Feedback from others provides the self with knowledge in this area.
3.) **The Facade** — an area hidden from others because an individual chooses to mask it. Information in this area becomes known to others when the self chooses to disclose it.
4.) **The Unknown** — an area unknown to the self and others. This is revealed to an individual as the self practices the communication skills of feedback and disclosure.

As one might suspect, feedback which illuminates the self's blindspot may be difficult to come by if friends or working associates are reluctant to provide it. Nevertheless, if an officer wants to project the strongest professional credibility possible, it is in that officer's best interest to:
1.) seek feedback, and
2.) give that feedback some analytical thought, rather than reject it out of hand.

JOHARI WINDOW

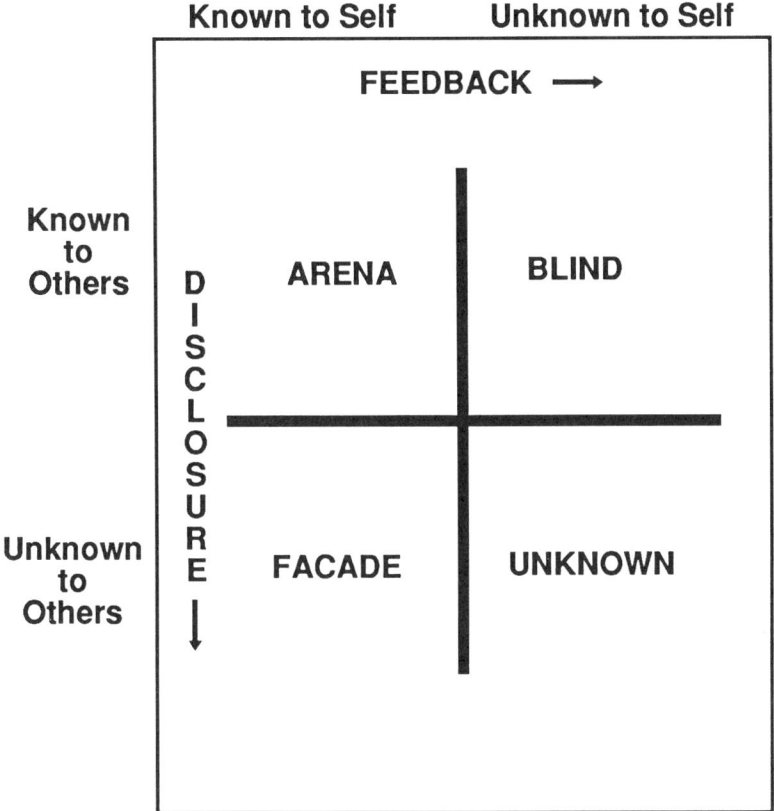

Joseph Luft, OF HUMAN INTERACTION, 1969

Figure 2

A highly motivated officer picks up feedback from working partners, supervisors, the public, and the courts. An officer may also choose to utilize one of the many self assessment instruments available (answered and scored by the self) to develop personal insights as to others' perceptions. These assessment tools clarify various personality traits which affect the way people choose to communicate and are therefore valuable as a starting point for awareness.

Another extremely effective feedback mode is video. If an officer has the opportunity to see his or her performance on video tape, say in a

DARE program, a response to the media, a team building exercise, or in some training event (such as role play), this also provides enlightening feedback. As difficult as some feedback may be to receive, it can only help officers who wish to develop their most competent, professional selves.[3]

Messages of Personal and Professional Credibility

Why are many police officers so highly effective and successful in almost all of their encounters with the public and others such dismal failures? Why do some officers never or rarely receive a complaint in twenty or twenty-five years of service and others get accused of rudeness, bias, harassment, intimidation, verbal abuse, and even insubordination?

A major answer is attitude. The underlying attitude that an officer carries into each interaction is betrayed in demeanor. If the attitude is superior, no matter how professional the officer may imagine him or herself to be, citizens pick up vocal and nonverbal cues from the officer's blindspot that irritate and anger them. While the officer selects entirely positive words for the conversation, a few vocal and nonverbal behaviors scream out a very different story. Thus, officers who take time to listen to people and who make a rule of treating them objectively and fairly are far less likely to elicit citizen complaints.[4]

Eye Contact

Eye contact operates as one of the first nonverbal behaviors perceived by the public. Officers choose direct, sustained, and frequent eye contact in order to create open lines of communication. Direct eye contact leads citizens to believe that the officer is interested and concerned. This is one of those immediacy behaviors that tends to build psychological closeness.[5] Sustained, frequent eye contact means that the officer sustains it long enough to make the connection, but breaks it frequently enough, by looking away occasionally, to avoid causing the person discomfort.

This, of course, presents a problem. While an officer can afford to look away when dealing with most citizens, looking away from some individuals constitutes endangerment to the officer. This is where the experienced officer is at an advantage, because he or she has frequently developed an instinct about people.

Sustained eye contact, without frequent breaks, is very dominant. Used to control the behavior of others, it is also frequently perceived as intimidating. When one adds reflective sunglasses on routine traffic stops, it is easy to understand a citizen's reactions. (When citizens cannot see into the officer's eyes they usually conclude that they are being stared at). Where an officer recognizes the need to provide a supportive or less controlling environment, it is recommended that the direct, sustained, and frequent rule be observed.

Facial Expression

Facial expression also affects the reaction of others. Selecting a less responsive, impassive expression when exerting control over citizens may seem like the natural thing to do. This expression will often suppress the response of less dominant and lower status individuals, but make others, who see themselves as of higher status or dominance, more argumentative. Thus, the more often a non-responsive expression is displayed, the less likely it is that effective communication will occur. The person who is actually dominant in an interaction has the option of using all of the nonverbal codes to make him or herself more dominant and powerful.[6] With criminals the officer's choice may be to exercise that option, but with ordinary citizens it amounts to overkill. The less the status difference, that is the more the officer decides to equalize the situation and down play his or her stronger status in the interaction, the more likely it is that positive, mutual communication will take place.

The most positive facial choices are expressions of interest and attentiveness. Utilizing such expressions, the officer transmits concern, a willingness to listen, and an attitude of understanding. These facial expressions, plus a smile when appropriate, encourage a successful interaction. Such choices also contribute to reducing the dominance of prolonged eye contact. Where the police officer wishes to sustain the eye contact without frequent breaks, the above behaviors generally mitigate a negative reaction. In addition, the pleasant facial expression makes a significant contribution to the citizen's perception of an officer as professional and credible.

The rule, then, is that increased facial expressiveness on the officer's part leads to stronger perceptions of potency and dominance, while at the same time sending messages of believability.

Proxemics

The quality of the interpersonal communication is also affected by the distance at which the officer chooses to conduct business. When an officer approaches a car and stands next to the door, often slightly behind the driver's shoulder, the advantages are safety and the ability to see the inside of the car. But this approach, in itself, violates the space of the driver. The driver sits. The officer stands. The driver cannot see the officer without turning and looking up (in a very inconvenient manner). The officer can see everything. The officer is generally quite close to the person, usually within two feet. The driver feels vulnerable, as is the intention, but probably does not recognize that the officer also feels vulnerable to the traffic at his or her back. Due to that traffic, the officer may move even closer.

It is at this point that the officer needs to be particularly aware of the response of the driver. From physical contact to one and a half feet equals the intimate zone.[7] Most Americans get irritated and hostile when someone, not an intimate, invades that space. One and one half to four feet is personal-casual space, and although this is usually space reserved for friends and close acquaintances, it is not quite as discomforting when an authority figure moves into this area.

Once again, the nature of police work demands a lot of controlling behavior, but if an officer escalates it into intimidation by adding an insulting attitude which infers that an ordinary citizen is a "scum bag," the citizen has a right to complain.

A domestic dispute is another area where officers can escalate a situation by pushing into the intimate zone — standing face to face with one of the disputants, punctuating his or her comments with a jabbing index finger, and talking in a loud and commanding manner. While this might occasionally be necessary, every person needs to be able to save face. If the police officer does not provide some way for that to occur, the result can easily turn into a situation requiring the use of force. Staying at the four foot range of the personal-casual zone, unless it is necessary to exert control, allows a disputant some vestige of comfort and pride, and a negative reaction is much less likely.

So, the rule is, give people their space, unless control is a major concern.

Gestures

Gestures are an important factor in one's ability to communicate with others. They are more diverse than most people imagine, with four types available to us for sending messages: illustrators, regulators, emblems, and adapters. Of these, the two most important to the law enforcement officer are illustrators and regulators.

Illustrators are gestures which accompany speech. When individuals converse, they often use illustrators to describe what they are talking about. Sometimes such gestures are of the kinetograph variety. That is, they represent different forms of bodily action, such as:
1.) spatial relationships among people or things (showing distances for example),
2.) rhythmic movements which demonstrate the timing of events (much like those of a music conductor), or
3.) deictic movements which show where objects are located (such as pointing).

Other times illustrators are used to:
1.) accent or emphasize words and phrases (batons),
2.) represent the cognitive processing of the talker, such as tapping the head when trying to remember a thought, or snapping the fingers when one finally remembers (ideographs), and
3.) refer to pictures of objects of the conversation, such as pear shaped, oblong, etc. (pictograph).

The importance of illustrators is that they appear to increase the credibility of the speaker by showing his or her concern, competence, and involvement with the issue. Such speakers also look more dynamic. Finally, the rule is that illustrators contribute to persons having more influence on others, being more persuasive, and possessing more credibility. Although the evidence is stronger for facial expressiveness being perceived in this manner,[8] the implication is that using them together would greatly enhance credibility.

When an officer seeks more control of a situation, regulator and perhaps some emblem gestures are called for. Regulator gestures initiate, terminate, and control the flow of conversation. For instance, holding one's hand, fingers extended upward and palm towards the person, signifies for them to stop talking or to stop whatever they are doing. Regulators can be separate from speech or accompanied by it. Emblems are gestures which can also be used with or without speech, but are so well recognized in one's own culture, that we know exactly what they mean without speech. The thumb out hitchhiking gesture and thumb to forefinger A-OK gesture are two examples. An officers who wishes to exert control in certain low tension situations, might try using these types of gestures first. They are a softer way of getting a message across and will not, generally speaking, escalate tenseness in a situation. This is not to suggest that the officer stop speaking altogether, but simply to emphasize that there are a number of ways to gain compliance and that in most cases, the less intimidating types should be tried first. The jabbing, pointing gesture, particularly when it is pushed in someone's face, ought to be avoided entirely. This is a demeaning signal and no one cares to be subjected to it.

Gestures are valuable tools for getting important messages across to people and probably could be utilized more than they are.

Conclusion

The police officer of the twenty-first century needs better communication skills than ever before. Failure to listen, unwillingness to receive the messages of the public, inability or unwillingness to show sensitivity to diverse populations, and lack of awareness concerning the messages sent out through daily police work and captured by the media, can only lead to increased polarization between the public and the police.

The tendency of the public is to back those who serve and protect them. It is only right, then, that police be aware of and work steadily to improve their knowledge of effective verbal, vocal, and nonverbal communication in an effort to achieve increased interpersonal understanding with the public. It is a result of the ability and the willingness to use these skills successfully, that the police officer's image and sensitivity to the public will improve. That improvement will lead to increased trust and safety for us all.

Special Thanks to Lieutenant Howard Powers, Instructor, and

Captain Gene Hoekwater, Commander of the Michigan State Police Training Academy.

Bibliography

[1] Burgoan, Judee K. 1989. *Nonverbal Communication.* New York: Harper and Row. 247-250.

[2] MacKay, D.M. 1972. "Formal Analysis of Communicative Processes," in *Nonverbal Communication*, R.A. Huide, ed. New York: Cambridge University Press. 24. See also Knapp, Mark. 1979. *Nonverbal Communication in Human Interaction.* New York: Holt Rinehart and Winston. 5-9: 11.

[3] Some training firms, such as MACNLOW, regularly use video replay as a means of demonstrating to officers how they appear while responding to media interviews, testifying during mock cross-examination, role playing various supervisory and management techniques and developing team work skills in management team exercises.

[4] Cheathem, T.R. and Erickson, K.V. 1984. *The Police Officer's Guide to Better Communication.* Glenview, IL: Scott, Foresman and Co. See p. 25 for additional comments on attitude.

[5] Immediacy refers to degree of psychological of physical closeness. Mehrabian, Albert. 1971. *Silent Messages.* Belmont, CA: Wadsworth. 1. See also Richmond, et.al., 1987. *Nonverbal Behavior in Interpersonal Relations.* Englewood Cliffs, NJ: Prentice-Hall. 185-204.

[6] Richmond, V.P., et.al., P. 236.

[7] Hall, Edward T. 1959. *The Silent Language.* New York: Doubleday, and Hall, Edward T. 1969. *The Hidden Dimension.* Garden City, NY: Anchor Books. Chapter 10.

[8] Burgoen, Judee K. 1990. "Nonverbal Behaviors, Persuasion and Credibility," *Human Communication Research.* (Fall) P. 160.

Chapter 29

Courtroom Demeanor and Testimony

by David W. McRoberts

Negative Feelings Toward Testimony

"The truth, the whole truth, and nothing but the truth, so help you God . . ." Facing the judge with their backs to the jury, officers hear these words and ask themselves why they feel as though they were on trial rather than the accused. Trial, hearing, and appearance, depending on the region of the country and the court system, are titles for court proceedings that reflect different reasons for giving testimony. The universal concern of most officers is not these titles however, but the reasons they experience negative feelings as they prepare to give testimony.

First and sometimes lasting impressions are made on the judge and jury, and as the officers prepare to testify, they can be overwhelmed by nervousness, fear, and the unsettling feelings of being examined. These feelings are real, though some officers will never admit, even to themselves, that they are bothered by them. They vary in intensity, depending on the personality and experience of the officers, and they can have devastating effects on the ability of the officers to testify credibly.

These negative feelings sit like steaming lava in the pit of the officers stomachs and thoughts of self consciousness, not being prepared, and anguish race through their minds. These thoughts, like ash from a volcano, eventually surface and affect officers' appearances, deliveries, and demeanors. Not a pleasant experience, but one that is played out thousands of times each day by officers taking the witness stand. The necessary testimony is transformed from a clearly understood requirement of the job into an experience that is often avoided like an infectious disease.

As the officers wait to deliver clear, honest, and credible testimonies, their personal torture takes shape in some very undesirable, visual displays for judge, jury, and others present to observe and criticize. Hands that provided direction on the street now quiver. Authoritative voices that delivered clear commands on the job now crack. Faces that put feelings into the uniformed command presence now turn damp with perspiration and red from distress. A court appearance can be so painful for some officers that adjustments are made in their activities in the field to avoid enforcement action that would create a greater chance of them being called as a witness.

No officer will escape these feelings completely, but as individuals, law enforcement officers would benefit from a closer look at the reasons these feelings exist. The reasons and their effects are many and complex; so complex that officers must examine their personal beliefs, attitudes, and job skills in an attempt to compensate for them.

No Sweat, No Problem, No Big Deal!

At the other extreme are officers who experience absolutely no negative feelings from testifying. Admittedly, experience in this area is helpful and the more the officers repeat this skill the better at it they become. However, an adjustment may be in order if the requirement to testify expands their egos or alters their demeanors. These officers need to reflect on who and what they are.

I Know What It Takes To Do My Job, You Don't!

The responsibilities of law enforcement officers are incredible. The decisions they are required to make in just one tour of duty, and the impacts these decisions have on the lives of people, rival the judgments of top executives in corporate America. One such responsibility is the accountability required of officers in a court of law, and weeks, months, or even years after the fact, accountability and clear recall can be unrealistic expectations.

Modern day police work is often compared to other professions as to the requirements and skills necessary to perform the job. There can be little argument that many Fortune 500 executives could take a lesson or two from police officers and their ability to cope in the reactionary world of police work.

Many seasoned officers feel that no real comparison can be made due to the unique nature of police work, and they may be right. However, these officers could take lessons from corporate America by learning what successful businesses committed to memory long ago. A thorough knowledge of all employment responsibilities is necessary in order to remain effective, competitive, and to survive.

For law enforcement officers this translates into high profile aggressive enforcement action in the field, and the ability to be an effective witness in court. Clear, accurate, and credible testimony as to the facts and circumstances concerning field activity are absolute necessities for all law enforcement officers. Make this statement to some officers and you may detect quiet contempt. "There's no comparison to what we do on the street and what goes on in some high rise office building," many will snap. "I know my job, and I know that testifying in court is the last thing I'm thinking about on the street. There's just not enough time."

Anyone with field experience can sympathize with them, but if

Courtroom Demeanor and Testimony

more officers operated as though every call would end up in court and require their testimony, the result may be fewer problems. Some of the best intentions by officers in the field have resulted in some very poor case presentations and court testimonies.

The bottom line is that complete police work must include acknowledgment that every case could result in a court appearance, and officers should conduct themselves accordingly. Very often the opposite seems to rule activity in the field; "Let's do this and hope we don't have to go to court." It is this approach that results in fear, not being prepared in the courtroom, and damages officers' testimony and effectiveness.

With the reality of hidden video cameras and tape recorders capturing anything and everything, officers should realize that their statements and actions could be heard and viewed by the public at any time. Also these scenes may be edited or enhanced to suit whoever is replaying the material.

Remember the steaming lava? Why fuel this destructive force when there are steps that can be taken to help diminish these feelings?

The Right Stuff

Any attempt to list what it takes to be an effective law enforcement witness creates disagreements within the ranks. The difference in officers' backgrounds and experience controls their beliefs on what it takes to be a good witness as well as a good officer. The following are qualities that seem important to officers who work in the field.

Integrity

Don't ever lie. This is often easier said than done in a profession where there is so much room for discretion and judgment. In our court system, the testimonies of officers are given more weight and credibility than those of other witnesses. What some officers seem to forget is that this credibility comes from just being officers, but it doesn't come free. For being granted immediate credibility in court, officers are held to a higher standard of behavior and shouldered with a greater burden of proof.

This trust is very easily shattered. Officers who choose to violate this standing, this trust, put themselves and the whole law enforcement community at risk. Officers who knowingly lie in a court of law have chosen to throw a boomerang at their careers. Boomerangs return to the spot from where they were thrown and there is no way of knowing when they will return. When they do, they approach swiftly and silently to do their damage; loss of career, credibility, trust, and self respect.

The constant fear of the lie being discovered have the officers looking over their shoulders, feeling unsettled and paranoid. What a feeling of confidence they must have while approaching the witness stand the next time. Why fuel the fires of self destruction? Save your credibility and self esteem. Don't ever lie!

Understanding

There is no single method of achieving greater confidence as law enforcement witnesses, but a basic understanding of what their function is in court and how they fit into the system is necessary.

The criminal court system in the United States is adversarial by design. So what's new? Unfortunately, many officers have never fully accepted or understood what the courtroom stand-off has to do with them. Caught in middle of the legal gymnastics displayed in the courtroom, officers often feel like objects whose only purpose is to recite things from memory.

Officers must learn to accept that by being adversaries, the prosecution and the defense will always be at odds, and the officers will always be on one side or the other in the courtroom. Law enforcement witnesses cannot straddle the fence. Any attempt to do so will result in positions, opinions, or commitments being extracted from them through questioning that at times can be brutal.

If this seems too simple to cause confusion consider the following: when officers who are usually called on to testify by the prosecution are called on by the defense, the issues and questioning changes. In non-criminal matters, such as civil damage cases, the clarity of the positions and issues become blurry. Testimony in these cases can often have personal and financial impact on those involved. This position may become awkward, and for good reason.

Now consider for a moment the requirement to testify for the defense. Officers become paired and pitted against other officers as to differences in observation, perspective, and even experience. Long term resentments have been generated between fellow law enforcement officers as a result of not being mentally prepared for the tactics used in such cases.

As roles change and adjustments made, officers are faced with some occurrences that appear so contradictory that no amount of understanding or explanation is sufficient. Attorneys can argue and shout viciously during a court appearance and at its conclusion, calm conversation, hand shaking, and even joking are observed. As quickly as it takes a judge to drop a gavel and conclude a formal proceeding, courtroom warriors can become colleagues.

Truly by design, officers are caught in the middle of what is described as either a contest, or a performance. If it is a contest they see themselves in, they are uniformed participants with a professional interest in the final outcome. As for the performance, officers are actors trying to convince the audience to agree with the finding of fault.

Consider how long ago our court system was developed and what influenced its structure. Think about what kinds of activities and physical structures are similar to those of a court of law today. What kind of building do these figures represent, and what kind of activity takes place inside?

Courtroom Demeanor and Testimony

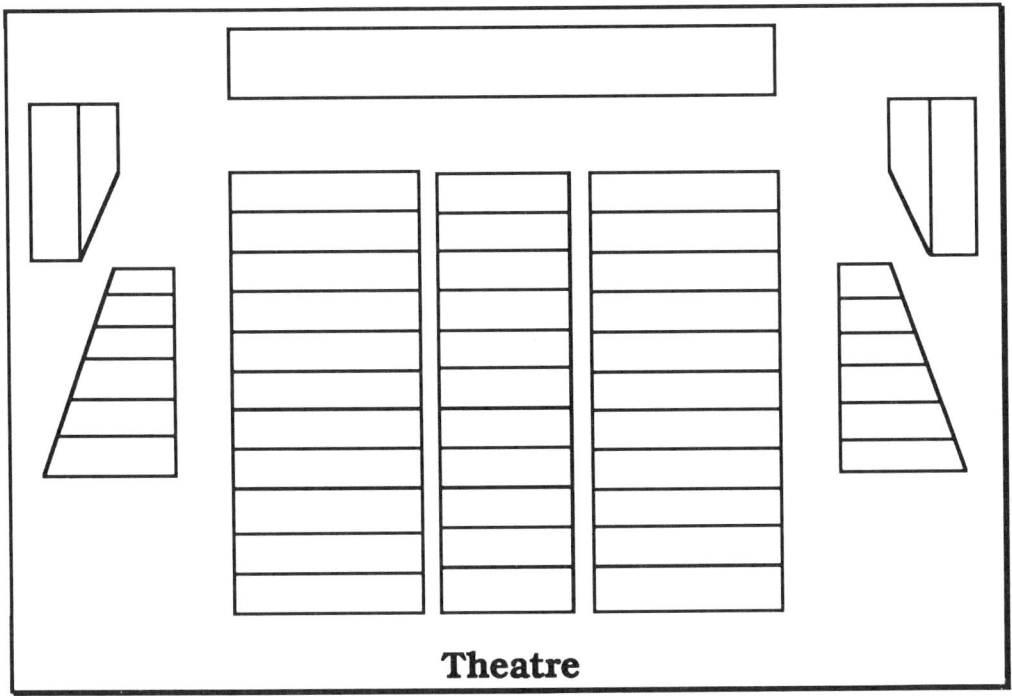

Theatre

Positioned from front to back and a separated area for performers. Often there are special seats closer to the stage for special or honored viewers. Silence is commanded until speaking is allowed or requested.

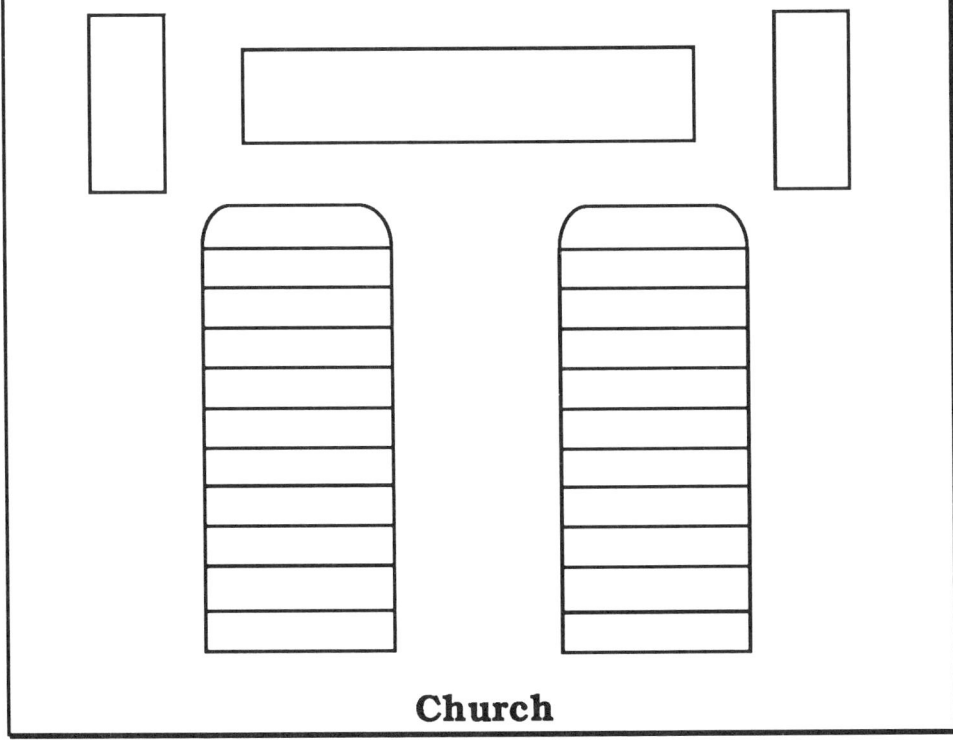

Church

Positioned from front to back and a separated area for clergy and providers. Often there are special seats closer to the altar area for the choir, elders, guests, or other special people. Activity controlled by a chosen representative of a supreme being. Observable effect is awe and reverence for viewers. The focus is on good over bad. Silence is requested and accepted until speaking is allowed or directed.

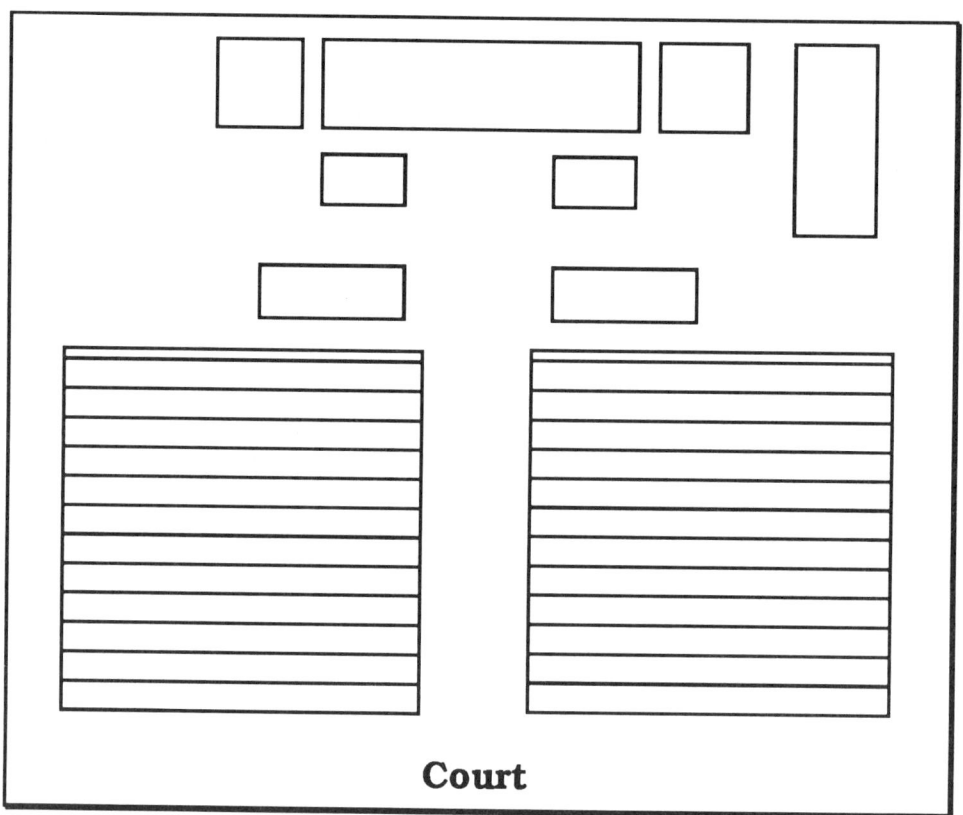

Positioned from front to rear and a separated area for participants. Special seating is closer to the exhibition for jury and attorneys. Proceeding is controlled and directed by a supreme person who sits in judgment and has absolute control of activity in the room. Observable effects are power, authority, justice, and truth with the focus on good over bad. Silence is demanded unless permission or requirements allow speaking.

For each of these, consider that the requirement for presentation is very similar. Entrance is almost always from the back or side to the front. The final position is in front of the gathering of people. Silence is required as a matter of practice and acceptance. When silence is broken by the spoken word, the focus is on the one person speaking. That per-

Courtroom Demeanor and Testimony

son is on display and must speak out loud.

Now consider what is anchored in fact, but rarely acknowledged; for each situation or circumstance, there is a certain degree of fear. This becomes an important issue for police officers if they remember that the number one fear for people in our culture is speaking before a group. The job description, the uniform, and the weaponry are of little significance. To speak before a group or public gathering has always caused panic in actors, clergy, citizens, witnesses, and officers. Considering our culture, education, and conditioning, this fear is not likely to disappear. For most people, even death is often mentioned lower on the list of fears than speaking before a group.

There is no simple solution, but officers can begin to adjust their reactions by accepting that their nervousness is normal and manageable. As with other activities, practice will improve performance. Speaking in front of a group is no different; perfect practice makes perfect performances.

Preparedness

Officers must be as prepared as possible for their courtroom testimonies, and the basics are usually covered prior to taking the stand. Dates, times, locations, and other facts are reviewed for accuracy. Often, time permitting, an exact rehearsal of testimony will occur between officers and attorneys. Some officers do themselves discredit by either not reading the reports concerning the case prior to testifying, or by pretending they didn't when asked on the stand. Officers' reports combined with knowledge of what other reports contain remains the best method of avoiding simple errors which chip away at the image desired of officers in court.

"How far" and "How long?" These can be questions from Hell unless qualified by an estimate only, or by having actually measured or timed them in the field. Officers making the mistake of not indicating something is an estimate only, may find themselves in embarrassing situations. In an effort to show the fallibility of officers, attorneys may request several visual measurements of everything, from the distances between objects in the courtroom, to ceiling height. Officers may attempt these while remaining seated on the witness stand; the obvious probability of error is clear. As the attorneys make accurate listing with the aid of a tape measure or clock, officers' professional images can suffer. Stay out of the time and distance trap.

Appearance

The personal appearances of officers are really two separate issues.

First is the condition and appropriateness of clothing worn, and the second is the hygiene and grooming of the officers. If either is lacking, their total image is damaged.

For officers required to testify in uniform, the rules are the same. Clean and pressed clothing over clean and groomed officers commands the respect necessary to be effective on the stand. This should remain constant in the field as well, but there are thousands of duty requirements that soil and damage the best uniform presence.

It is doubtful whether officers earn sufficient pay to afford the latest in the continual changes in high fashion clothing, but what is of greater significance is that they represent mainstream society. This image calls for conservative dress. Any drastic deviation from this by high fashion or dramatic apparel interferes with the reason officers are present in court in the first place.

Officers have always been the visible form of government. A review of the majority of government officials should reveal the main stream appearance. The pastel suit, baggy slacks, sleeveless shirt, and canvas shoes with no socks only detract from the officer's professional image.

The requirements of testimony almost never allow an officer's personality to be displayed. Judge and jury along with other citizens present only see WHAT an officer is and not WHO an officer is. However, to appear as a mutant or slug only serves to diminish an officer's credibility and effectiveness.

Clean hands and nails, groomed hair, and a general well kept appearance are essential for the total package necessary to the professional image of a law enforcement witness. Finally, as an officer walks past the jury, if what lingers in the air is the odor of a locker room after a full contact athletic contest, expect a technical foul to be assessed on the officer's performance.

Demeanor

The slow swagger, stroll, or strut can be the beginning of an officer's presence in the courtroom. Then again, an officer's approach may be a purposeful stride that displays no tentativeness or hesitation. For some a purposeful stride is normal, but for others a conscious effort is required for the desired results.

Critics may suggest that this is too much like a put on, but unfortunately some officers need to practice a little self esteem projection. All officers could use a refresher on feeling good about who they are, what they are, and what they are doing. This is a most difficult job to do well, and those who measure up to the test should wear it well. Head up, back straight, and an attentive acknowledgment of the surroundings is all part of the total package.

For those who let their projected attitude slip, even for a moment, into arrogance, indifference, or contempt will wear them like neon signs. Effectiveness will be destroyed by the presence of these attitudes that are disturbing to most, and despised by many. To be recognized as the good the officers represent, they must look the part, act the part, and live the part.

Delivery

"Da, dis, dem, you know, well ah, ya, na, cause." Sound familiar? This list of non-words and phrases guarantee officers poor marks in court, and the best testimony can be distorted by not speaking well enough to be understood. Officers are not expected to sound like network television anchors, but simple word use and pronunciation can do wonders for credibility.

Inner city groups, gangs, and juvenile culture groups all have a speciality language that can rub off onto officers' deliveries. To use appropriate words, preparation and effort are needed. Anything less may give the impression that the officers are part of whatever group they sound like, and this is undesirable in a law enforcement witness.

Speak clearly, loudly enough to be heard, and concentrate on a smooth delivery. Under stress, officers often submit to speaking too quickly. This rapid fire testimony combined with voices that tend to rise from the pressure can leave officers sounding animated. A Woody Wood Pecker delivery won't do much for an officer's confidence or effectiveness.

Too quick deliveries lead officers into another deadly trap on the stand; answering too quickly and an inability to limit their response. Two of the best suggestions for officers giving testimony are; answer only what is asked, and after being asked a question, wait just a moment longer before answering.

For reasons of nervousness or inexperience, some officers just can't shut up when they are questioned and continue to speak after they have given an appropriate answer. This overflow of information is often ill timed or a repetition of information already given. Either way, the longer the officers speak unnecessarily, the greater the chance the attorneys will ask additional questions based on the extra information.

This is not to suggest that yes and no are the only answers that should be offered, but sticking to the facts in the order they are requested or presented can eliminate the need for extensive explanations. However, look to the judge for the time and opportunity if the need exists for additional clarification. It's unlikely that a sincere request for such latitude would ever be denied a law enforcement officer.

Even with the best delivery, disciplined officers need to take an extra moment after they have heard the question to understand it fully, and only then to give their answer.

The Package of Effectiveness

The best of the best is how law enforcement officers are referred to by the public and media; that is unless there exists reasons for this image to be diminished. Unfortunately, there need not be any final determination of wrong doing to cast a shadow on officers or departments. Often, accusations are all that is needed for suspicion and doubt to be generated.

Testifying in court as a law enforcement witness is by no means a method of eliminating the public's uncertainty, but it is an opportunity to display the positive profile all officers strive to assume. This exposure reaches more of the public in a shorter period of time than most officers realize, and the more significant the case the better, and the more media coverage the better.

A well-packaged, law enforcement professional giving credible testimony in court is representative of what the public sees as quality police protection. While ability in court does not mean that an officer or an agency is effective, it is certainly a means of measuring preparedness. It is after all, these two components of the job that are criticized most often.

The public has been, and will continue to be, critical of government and its actions. As officers move through their careers, they can lose sight of the fact that they are the most visible form of government in action. They are all reflections of one another; good and bad.

A good performance as a law enforcement witness, will have positive and compounding effects. It will ensure that the criminal justice system and the government's enforcement are functioning properly. It will also project a strong character of the officers, their agencies, and the communities they serve. The complete package of effectiveness is the variable that is the most desired, most difficult to achieve, and the hardest to maintain. Officers and agencies that succeed in this area will have an advantage in the realization of their collective mission.

About the Author

Lieutenant David W. McRoberts is a patrol shift commander for the Kenosha County Sheriff's Department in Wisconsin. With 15 years experience as a law enforcement officer, he has held the ranks of patrolman, sergeant, and lieutenant. In addition to regular duties, he is the Entry Team Leader for the Tactical Response Team for the Sheriff's Department. His involvement with the speciality unit requires him to coordinate approach and apprehensions of many violent and sometimes barricaded persons including drug offenders.

Since 1985, Lieutenant McRoberts has been a State Certified Law Enforcement Instructor for the Wisconsin Department of Justice, Division of Training and Standards. He is a national trainer and has trained thousands of law enforcement officers and protective service personnel. As a trainer and presenter, he is a featured speaker at many professional conferences and workshops.

Lieutenant McRoberts is the author of many written contributions to various law enforcement publications and periodicals nationwide. He is a Charter Member of the American Society of Law Enforcement Trainers (ASLET), the largest training organization for law enforcement personnel in the United States.

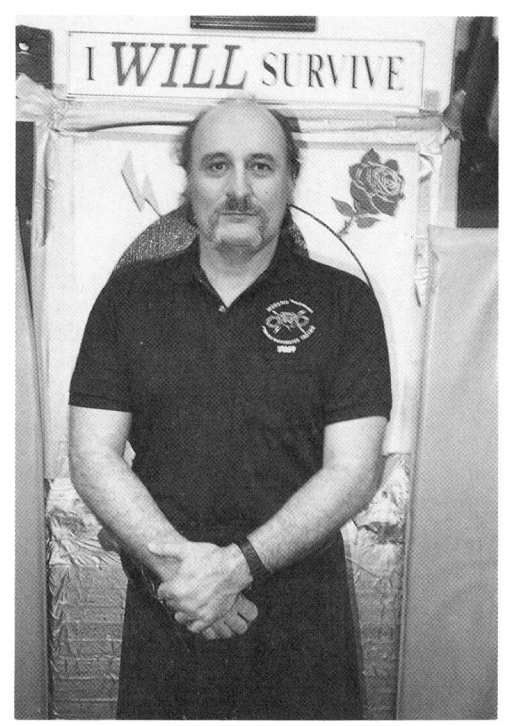

Phil Messina

Mr. Messina is a retired New York City Police Sergeant who was highly decorated in both uniform and plainclothes assignments. He has been featured numerous times in magazines, newspapers, and on television before and since his retirement. He is internationally recognized as a martial artist and a police survival instructor.

Mr. Messina was one of the first western instructors invited by the Chinese government to demonstrate his training methods for mainland Chinese television and newspapers. He was also the first American to demonstrate Multiple Assailant Combat Training at the Shaolin Wu Shu Training Center in mainland China.

Chapter 30

Multiple Assailants: A Test of Mind, Body, and Spirit

by Phil Messina

Mind

The first rule is simple. If you don't believe you can win against multiple assailants, you can't. That's right! The first step in defeating multiple assailants is believing you can. Think about all those times you've watched four or five fellow officers trying unsuccessfully to control one perp. Remember how clumsy they looked; how they constantly seemed to get in each other's way? The plain fact is that **more** is not necessarily better. Only **better** is better, and often even that theory doesn't hold up.

A great warrior was once asked the following question: What would you do if one day you ran across three warriors equal to you in all respects except one. The first is stronger than you are, the second faster than you are, and the third more durable than you are. If you had to fight each of them, which would you choose to fight first? Without hesitation the great warrior answered, "I would simply fight all three at once." When asked why, he responded, "Because I have practiced fighting against the wolf pack, but I doubt they have practiced fighting as the wolf pack." When you think about it, you find it really does make sense. Therefore for the rest of this chapter we will refer to multiple assailants as the **wolf pack.**

In order to mentally prepare yourself for multiple assailant confrontations, you must first understand some basic concepts. You don't have to like them or even agree with them, but you must understand them.

Although it seems logical that a multiple assailant confrontation is a deadly force situation, in reality it largely depends on the jurisdiction you are in. Although an officer in El Paso might get a medal for drawing and firing on three unarmed assailants, an officer in New York City would probably get indicted for it. Therefore it is essential for officers to come to terms with what level of force they are willing to use against assailants.

You must also come to terms with the fact that if you lose such a confrontation you will most likely be seriously injured or killed. It is essential that you realize that if you lose a multiple assailant confrontation, your gun is their gun. You must know what your justification is and mentally prepare yourself to explain that justification in a court of law.

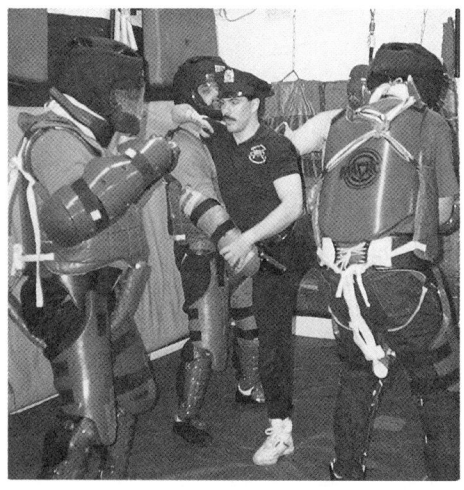

Officer counterattacks as he protects his firearm.

As police officers we have taken an oath to protect the citizens of our community. Whenever we lose a confrontation we not only endanger ourselves, but we endanger the very citizens we are sworn to protect. In other words, the citizens who pay our salary are paying us to win, not to lose. Sounds corny doesn't it? But it is the very thing that juries want to hear and it's exactly what we should be telling them. Once you understand **why** you should win, you are ready to understand **how** you can win.

Officer prepares for full-contact, confrontational simulations.

Multiple Assailants

It is hard to believe that although more than forty percent of assaults on officers involve multiple assailants, less than one percent of the defensive tactics' training we receive is directed towards multiple assailant confrontations. This is especially distressful when we realize that many of the training concepts we apply to single assailant confrontations are actually detrimental against multiple assailants. In many cases we are trained to lose against multiple assailants. Some examples of this are as follows:

- **Reactionary Gap.** We are constantly being reminded to "maintain a four to six-foot Reactionary Gap" and many of the techniques we are taught are designed around this gap. Yet the human body is designed to move almost four times as fast forward as it does backward. This makes it not only impractical to maintain this gap in single assailant confrontations, but virtually impossible in multiple assailant confrontations.

- **Step-Drag.** The step-drag or shuffle step is designed to provide good balance and to allow officers to keep their firearms further away from a single assailant. However, better balance is only provided from a frontal assault and creates poorer balance from all other directions. In multiple assailant confrontations there will seldom be more than one assailant in front of the officer while the other assailants seek other angles of attack. Therefore mobility becomes essential and balance must be maintained through **fluid motion** rather than ridged stability. In fact, keeping the firearm back actually makes it easier to grab for all assailants **except** the one directly in front of the officer.

The officer executes follow-through on one assailant, but his firearm is susceptible to the second assailant.

The easiest way to correct this problem is by moving officers' holsters approximately four inches forward and tilting them twenty to thirty degrees (depending on the holster type), muzzles forward. Extensive tests conducted by Modern Warrior Defensive Tactics Institute have shown that while this position not only enhances officers' access to their firearms, it also increases their ability to maintain control of their weapons by three fold against a single assailant and by ten fold against multiple assailants.

This is the most applicable holster position for multiple assailant confrontations.

There are other negative points to using the step-drag in multiple assailant confrontations. During the entire process of a step-drag the officers' torsos (and therefore firearms) only move an average of twenty-two inches and only half of that distance is achieved with each leg motion. Taking a normal step forward carries the torso an average of forty-five inches with a single leg motion, thereby carrying the officers' torsos four times the distance with each leg motion. The advantage of this increased motion is the use of less energy which is critical during multiple assailant confrontations and positioning within the **wolf pack** is an essential ingredient to achieving victory.

The step-drag also tends to turn officers into one-sided fighters and one-sided fighters are easy to predict. Taking full steps tends to encourage officers to practice all techniques from both sides and in all directions, thus making them less predictable and more adaptable. How many times have we heard trainers tell us not to cock our hand before throwing a strike because it telegraphs the strike? Well then, doesn't the step-drag telegraph our direction? Doesn't the first leg tell our assailant where the second leg is going? Doesn't this also make our first leg vulnerable to attack while the second leg is in motion? The answer to all these questions is yes. Like it or not the step-drag tells our assailants exactly where we're going before we go there. This may explain why the weak leg injury is the second most common arrest related injury to police officers (the strong hand is the most common).

Multiple Assailants

▸ **Follow-Through.** Follow-through is always good, right? Wrong! The fact is many officers lose their firearms during follow-through, especially during baton techniques. Follow-through enables us to hit harder and also keeps our strong arm further away from our holster for longer periods of time. It therefore allows easier access to our firearm and this is especially dangerous in multiple assailant confrontations. Just as more is not always better, harder is not always better either. In fact short, compact, and penetrating motions work much better against multiple assailants than wide, sweeping motions do.

The officer draws the PR-24™ with his strong hand and the firearm with his weak hand.

▸ **Targeting.** Since most of our training deals with single assailants, most of our practice is done on low level of force targets. Although pain compliance, pressure points, and fluid shock are perfectly valid against single assailants, they leave officers extremely vulnerable during multiple assailant confrontations. During that one half second it takes for one assailant to comply to pain or react to a fluid shock technique the rest of the **wolf pack** will be eating you alive. As much as we trainers hate to say it, the plain fact is to survive a multiple assailant confrontation, you must cause physical damage.

You simply cannot risk your life on pain or nerve reaction. You must visualize yourself counter striking to vital targets. Non-muscular targets are best, and each target you strike must effect your assailant in a physiologically and psychologically disabling manner. In other words, "make every strike count."

The officer uses a double elbow lock on two assailants as he kicks the knee of the third assailant.

Visualize your assailants as robots that you must physically take apart until they either cease their attack, or there is only one left.

As the officer falls, he counterattacks, striking the legs and hips of his assailants.

At Modern Warrior Defensive Tactics Institute where multiple assailant training is a way of life, students are taught to think constantly "Vision, Wind, and Limbs" during multiple assailant confrontations. This type of "Goal Oriented Training" has been proven repeatedly by officers in actual street confrontations. Yet, these officers maintain an outstanding record in "Use of Force" litigation and their agency has never been subjected to a training lawsuit of any kind. Part of the reason is that these officers are not only taught how to defend themselves in the street, but in the courtroom as well. Mental training and preparation are the first elements officers must achieve when training for multiple assailant confrontations.

Body

Training the body is another important element in multiple assailant training. Contrary to popular belief, officers don't have to be per-

Multiple Assailants

fect physical specimens to defeat multiple assailants. As a matter of fact, training the senses is probably more important than training the muscles. Two of the biggest enemies officers confront when under stress are tunnel vision and auditory exclusion. However, what few people realize is that these phenomena need not occur, and are relatively simple to train out of officers.

Many trainers believe that officers cannot do more than one thing at a time. The fact is that officers are not **trained** to do more than one thing at a time. If the first time they have to do at least two things simultaneously is in a highly stressful street situation, it's only natural for involuntary discharges and other disasters to occur. Experiments at Modern Warrior have shown that with proper training, officers can excel at doing several things at one time, and they can do so under extraordinary stress.

While groundfighting against two armed assailants, the officer uses his feet, baton, and firearm at the same time.

However, if this type of training is unavailable there are several things that officers can do themselves to condition their bodies to do several things at one time. An example of this follows: Set up three striking bags in a triangle with each bag no more than eight feet away from the other bags. These can be either commercial heavy bags, stuffed duffel bags, or small canvas bags filled with dried peas. Make sure each bag is a different size and weight and that one bag is hung high enough so you can duck under it. Next, turn on a radio (to a talk show) or a loud fan and begin striking and kicking the bags at a comfortable pace as you walk through and around the triangle. Try to avoid being struck by the swinging bags by moving, ducking, and redirecting as you strike, kick, and block.

The officer practices the three-bag exercise.

When you start to get good at this add the following elements:

- Recite a poem or sing a song while you are working out.

- Have a training partner walk around the room and ask you questions which you must answer while working out.

- Have a partner walk around the room and count by twos. Each time your partner calls an odd number point at your partner without stopping your workout.

- Have a partner walk around with rolled up newspaper while you try to keep the bags between the two of you. Each time your partner has a clear shot the newspaper will be thrown at you, which you will block or avoid while continuing to work out.

Other exercises should include falling, rolling, recovering, and groundfighting, all of which are essential in multiple assailant confrontations. Also when practicing firearm retention and grappling techniques, do so blindfolded. Your body and your instincts will make a transition which even you will find hard to believe after just a few weeks of doing these exercises.

Now under stress your vision will expand outward rather than inward and your sense of hearing and touch will increase drastically rather than disappear. You will find yourself acutely aware of everything going on around you. You will have the ability to strike, kick, and block things without having to look at them.

Multiple Assailants

The officer practices retaining her firearm while blindfolded.

This is a tremendous asset when confronting a **wolf pack**, because usually they will be looking at your eyes to determine who you are about to counterattack. By the same token, you should not look into the eyes of your assailants. Although many martial arts masters will tell you, "Look into the eyes, because the eyes are the windows to the soul," the plain truth is that it's not their souls that will hurt you. It's their hands, feet, elbows, knees, or some other part of their bodies that will injure you. With this thought in mind, your job is to take care of their bodies and let their priests, pastors, rabbis, monks, or shamans worry about their souls.

The best place for you to look is just below shoulder level of average assailants and spread your vision. The shoulders of assailants will indicate weight shift. Their weight shift indicates which way they intend to go or what type of attack they will launch, whether it be punches, kicks, grabs, throws, or tackles. Police officers tend to be very observant people and with a little training they can read body language better than most.

In summary, while training your body, you can also train your awareness and doing them both at the same time has been proven to be the best method. By keeping the conscious mind busy, the subconscious mind absorbs at a much faster rate. The human body is an incredibly adaptable tool and with proper training you would be amazed at what it can do.

Officer shoulder locks one assailant with his strong hand and draws the firearm with his weak hand.

Spirit

Spirit is the last of the three essential qualities needed to win multiple assailant confrontations. It may be the most important quality, although it is placed last in the chapter.

Many believe that spirit cannot be trained into people, but once again, observations made at Modern Warrior and other progressive training facilities prove otherwise. It appears that once students develop a certain level of self esteem and confidence, the warrior spirit becomes a by product of their training. One notable advantage to "Goal Oriented Training" is that once students learn how to achieve goals they soon begin to go beyond their normal capabilities.

It is vital, however, that students do not confuse ego with confidence. Ego is believing that you are in some way superior to other people. Confidence is knowing that you can rise to the occasion and defeat people and situations that might ordinarily defeat you. In other words, people with big egos usually only win confrontations they are supposed to win while people with warrior spirits win confrontations they are not supposed to win.

Multiple Assailants

Therefore, humility is an important element necessary to maintaining the warrior spirit. Humility helps people face their fears and view them as advantages rather than disadvantages. To put it simply, do not try to conquer fear, befriend it. Fear is the one thing you can always count on in a battle.

There are also other ways you can develop the warrior spirit. The easiest way is to challenge yourself constantly as you work out. For example:

- When you do your three-bag exercise, place plastic (Kordite) bags all over the floor to make the ground slippery.

- Wear a weight vest while you work out.

- Hold up dumbbells until your arms are exhausted before you start your routine.

- Soak your clothes and yourself before working out.

- Tie one hand behind you or onto your belt.

- Put a small stone in one shoe to simulate a foot or leg injury.

- Wear safety goggles smeared with petroleum jelly to blur your vision, wear an eye patch, or even a blindfold sometimes.

- Hang signs, such as "I Will Survive" and "Rise To The Occasion" in the training area to help reinforce the "warrior spirit."

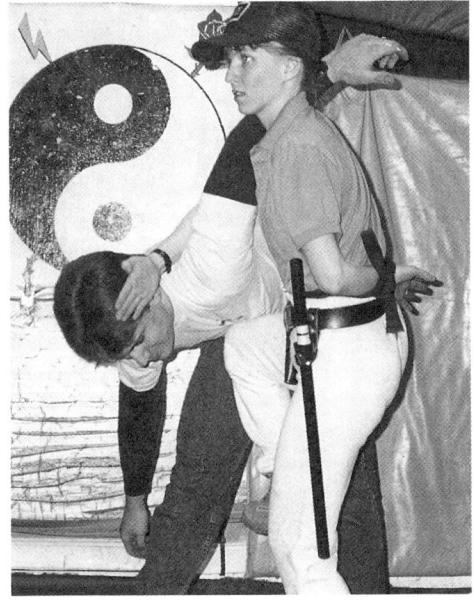

The officer practices a close-in confrontation with a simulated arm injury.

By forcing yourself to go beyond normal limitations, you will create a training environment that accounts for the unexpected. If you train under these conditions and your assailants do not, you will have a distinct edge in any confrontation. In police work, the **unexpected** isn't the exception to the rule, but rather it is the rule itself. If you accept this as a way of life and train for it, you will not only survive, but you will win the battles you're not supposed to win.

In every good police officer there is a warrior. It is important that we constantly remind ourselves of that warrior's presence. Good officers are willing to do things that most people are either afraid or unwilling to do. Although that doesn't make them better than others, it does make them a bit special, and special people with special training can do extraordinary things.

Once the Mind, Body, and Spirit have come together in the training arena they can come together in the street as well. When you are ready, you will know you are ready and so will those who attempt to assault you. When you look at potential assailants and your mind starts to tell you that they are better than you are, the warrior within will look right through them. "Maybe yesterday and maybe tomorrow, but not today, not now," the warrior will say. And when that **wolf pack** looks into your eyes they will see something also. For when the confrontation begins, though your heart may be saying, "I'm scared," and your voice is saying, "Get down! Don't resist," your eyes will be saying, "Who's next!"

Chapter 31

Methodology vs. Madness: Self-Directed Firearms' Training

by John Morrison

A Day on the Range

Under a sweltering August Sun in San Diego while swimming in the sticky subtropical humidity, a ragged line of officers forms on the 25-yard line of the police pistol range. This is the last afternoon session of their four-day semiauto qualification course. The course, designed and taught by range master and lead instructor, Sergeant Don Knoll, is tons of fun. It is also an absolutely demanding mile-a-minute and flash-or-failure test conducted in a steaming pressure cooker. An objective of the course is for officers to meet new and higher standards for converting from revolvers to semiauto, nine millimeters. Another of Sgt. Knoll's objectives is clear from the onset; if the officers or weapons are to fail, they must fail here on the course, not in the street where failure is final.

The twenty-odd officers released from regular duties while undergoing the course, come from all seven area commands of investigative units, with rank structure from rookie to senior captain represented. Neither rank nor age has any privilege on the firing line. All must run, shoot, and reload to the same high standards. Most are dressed in shorts or light trousers and T-shirts or tropical short sleeves. All are aching and sore to varying degrees, nursing scraped elbows, slide-slashed hands, asphalt-burned knees.

A few complaints are registered about the physical demands of the course; the running, use of cover, crawling, twisting into contorted positions in and around police cars, behind trash cans, phone poles, and even simulated curb berms. Sgt. Knoll smiles politely and explains, "Gunfights are demanding, death is worse," then blows his whistle and the class resumes.

A middle-aged detective steps up to his place in line, tucking his handcuffs in his belt. He pulls on a fingertip-length jacket and thrusts his hands into the front pockets, apparently checking the contents. A young patrolman dressed like most in a T-shirt and shorts, can't hold it any longer and has to ask him, "Why the jacket? It's hotter than hell out here and you've been wearing it for three days. And shouldn't you get rid of that stuff in the pockets? It just gets in your way. Man, I even leave my cuffs in the car."

The detective, continuing his methodical check of belt gear and accessories, calmly explains, "I wear a suit when I'm working and the coat is about the same length and weight of this one. The gear on my belt is the same that I carry on duty, in exactly the same place. The things in my pockets are the things I carry all the time. They effect the way my coat hangs and swings, and the way I draw, fire, and reload. That's the only thing wrong with this course. You ought to be shooting in uniform with all your gear on. And," he adds tapping the kid on the chest, "with your issue vest on too."

Later that day, this detective was pitted against a much younger, swifter, SWAT officer in one of the timed competitive phases of the course. Before the shooting began, the detective told his young companion, "Watch. I'm pretty sure I'll beat this guy. He may have youth and speed, but he hasn't done a lot of competition shooting. Every time somebody gets close to him, his concentration breaks. He looks over to see if they're gaining on him, and he drops shots. When I shoot, all I'm gonna see are the silhouettes and my front sight blade. Watch him."

The one-on-one shoot involved two officers running through a series of obstacles to a given firing point, "sweeping" a bank of silhouettes, reloading, and sweeping them again. Elapsed time and accuracy were both figured in the scoring. The SWAT officer beat the detective to the firing line by fifteen yards, and had engaged three silhouettes before the detective fired a shot. True to prediction though, as soon as the detective started hammering through the targets, the SWAT officer's concentration broke. He twice glanced over at the gaining detective, dropping two rounds out of center and one completely off a target. The detective locked on and fired like a gun turret, sweeping calmly and evenly, reloading with his eyes fixed on the next target, and walked away the winner.

As the group filed away from the firing line, a handful of individual off-duty officers began arriving, fresh targets in one hand and rendered-safe weapons in the other. The San Diego Police Department has a policy of allowing officers to practice free with at least fifty rounds per month on their own time. Most don't take advantage of it. Individual coaching is also available; but again, most don't avail themselves of it. The patrol lieutenant approaching the line was typical.

"Hey, Lieutenant," an officer greeted him. "Going to make a little smoke? Anything special?"

"Nah," the lieutenant replied. "Just gonna pop some caps, put some lead downrange." Over the next forty minutes, he stood flat-footed with a two-handed hold, victimized a single unmoving target and reloaded straight from a white plastic tub of loose rounds. That is exactly what he did; popped some caps, put some lead downrange, and that's all he accomplished.

In one day on the range, both ends of the training spectrum were clearly evident. At one extreme, a full time, concentrated practicum of shooting skills developed, based on real-life gun fighting scenarios. The practicum followed and achieved articulated goals and behavioral objectives, which were closely observed and monitored, and incorporated the elements of competition, recreation (fun), and pass-fail risk. On the other extreme was the lone and undirected effort, and absent was any of the elements by which the definition of discipline means training.

Whether officers work for a large, well-funded and progressive department or the smallest, least solvent agency, the conflict in law enforcement firearms' training tends to be the same. Officially sponsored training concentrates on the basics; it provides a foundation of knowledge and ability, and then launches the officers on their course with little more in-flight support (refueling) than a perfunctory re-qualification.

Before taking issue with this definition, ask yourself, "How many agencies demand higher scores and greater skills as officers gain rank or seniority?" Perfunctory it is, then. Most agencies, due to the considerable costs of firearms' training, particularly in higher skills' development, require no more than basic recruit academy, qualification scores throughout an officer's long career.

On the other side of the conflict, officers, like other skilled trades' workers, must enhance and increase their proficiency levels, building continuously and consistently on the basic training foundation. This task is theirs, not their department's. Success or failure — life or death — depends upon their efforts, not the organizations.

When the majority of officers engage in off-duty shooting at a range, they're not really engaging in self-directed training, they are simply "popping caps," putting rounds downrange. There is value even in this; the sheer familiarization of feel and function of the weapon, limb and body balance, rapid focus change, sight-picture routine, and even the noise and odor of burning gunpowder, but the value is limited.

Beyond an eleventh-hour decision to "work on my weak hand shooting a little" or "practice a couple of speed-reloads" there is little goal setting going on, and even less development of skill-building discipline. Sadly, for most officers, it isn't even that much fun.

Essential Elements of Firearms' Training

To be effective, individual firearms' training has to include certain essential elements:

> **Direction and Documentation.** Firearms' training must address specific skills and abilities based on an objective personal assessment of shooting related strengths and weaknesses. Officers' shooting strengths should not be overlooked in favor of weaknesses, because even strengths must be polished and perfected and continually assessed.
>
> Each aspect of shooting skills — reloading, one-hand and two-hand shooting, positions, barricade and obstacle shooting, night firing, and more — should be evaluated, articulated qualitatively by the shooter, recorded, and progress-charted. It is amazing how many officers create and main-

tain meticulous tables documenting their progress and achievements in weight training or martial arts, yet it never occurs to them to devote the same attentiveness in charting their firearms' skills.

- **Realism.** All self-directed firearms' training must be based on real-world conditions; a prime example being the detective who wore a suit-simulating jacket and belt gear during autopistol training. The relative degrees of freedom or restraint posed by on-duty clothing and equipment must be duplicated in training. The fastest and surest moves made under athletic clothed conditions do not necessarily translate — and are often precluded — in real world garb and gear.

  Patrol officers should all keep a "graveyard" set of uniforms for this purpose and for investigators those old suits with the fraying cuffs have another life to live. Specially treated glasses and goggles made for simulating low light conditions are available now from several sources.

  There are a growing number of officers competing in different schools of practical shooting who compete only in their actual issue gear with issue weapons; the best form of training. Knowing they are giving up significant advantage to their less restrained peers is a point of honor. The whole purpose of practical shooting is to save your life. To a great degree, the issue becomes whether the officers want to win matches, or win gunfights.

- **Observation and Monitoring.** Even the best world-class shooters benefit from critical observation. That's why so many of them go to the lengths of having themselves video taped as they run through their motions. An observer cued to watch closely for inefficient moves and unconscious mistakes, and downright deadly oversights can add immeasurably to the real training worth of any shooting session. Each observation should be discussed, replicated in slow motion, and analyzed by both the shooter and the observer. Changes in technique or correction of faulty moves should be worked through slowly and methodically at first, then developed for smoothness and speed.

  Typically, the shooter and observer will trade positions throughout the session for more reasons than just to take breathers. This way, both have the opportunity to observe each other's moves and techniques during initial warm-up periods when they are both fresh. Speed rather than smoothness is emphasized initially and during each staged later part of a multi-phased shooting session greater speed comes into play. Very often, the worst shooting habits only come out when the transition from slow-motion to fast-urgent takes place.

▶ **Competition.** Untold numbers of competitive police shooters have over the years verified with their lives the fact that frequent and practical competition significantly enhanced their ability to win street gunfights. As a set of neuromuscular reflexes, the physiological pathways created by continual repetition give well-trained officers the same sort of effect as a train running on a well laid track. The application of energy and the assessment of terrain and situation can be given more attention when direction and movement control are not an issue.

Competition also reinforces concentration skills, as in the case of the competition-honed detective who out-shot the SWAT officer largely through his ability to shut out non-critical input and devote full attention to crucially important factors. In that instance, due to competitive experience, the detective simply wasn't distracted by his competitor, the houting and cheering of other officers, the jet passing overhead, or anything except "front sight squeeze — front sight squeeze."

On a purely psychological plane also, competitive experience pays enormous dividends. Officers who shoot regularly and well in a competitive environment cannot help developing a higher degree of calm confidence which non-competitors lack. For police officers, it also develops a critically necessary sense of reasoned restraint. The better officers manage lethal force, the less likely they are to use it rashly or unnecessarily, or to be prompted by a sudden anxiety-laden, fight-or-flight reaction.

▶ **Recreation and Risk.** The two may sound opposed, but for most officers, risk and recreation can be easily intertwined. Recreation — having fun — should be a major component of any shooting program. If it isn't fun to do, if it isn't something looked forward to for pure enjoyment, it won't last long. No matter how much the participants consider it necessary to their careers or for their survival it will ultimately become just another task to be done and increasingly avoided.

Part of the camaraderie enjoyed in shooting with and against other officers can and should revolve around the recreation factor, and each taking a turn to come up with new challenges.

Risk, in a competitive shooting sense, is a product of winning or losing. Although loss of a dollar bet is nothing compared to the loss of one's life, officers who are competitive by instinct and winners by nature will give as good a performance on three-dollar wins as they would for $1,000.

On the other hand, most well-motivated officers will avoid the tag of "low shooter" or "loser" with the same fervor they would avoid leprosy; good cops are just made that way.

Preventing the Failure of Shooting Programs

The best self-directed firearms' training programs will involve several officers, with at least three and a maximum of four shooting at the same session. The more officers involved, the greater variety in competition; the more skilled the officers will become as coaches, observers, inter-unit, and inter-agency pride is developed. Three officers allows for a designated shooter, an observer or timer, and a range safety officer. With a fourth, the next officer "up" can be loading and preparing for the next course of fire. More than four officers creates too much lag time between turns in shooting, which drags down the "fun factor." Nobody likes waiting in line.

One of the common causes of failure of multi-officer shooting programs is inherent in law enforcement; different shifts and days off, court appearances, etc. If the program is interesting, fun, and challenging, the officers involved will put at least as much effort into recruiting new "members" as doctors do into organizing a foursome for golf on Thursday; in other words, considerable.

In the assessment and analysis stage, as well as in considering each new course of fire, officers should study past shooting incidents and ask themselves questions such as: How many occurred at night? What were the ranges involved? What percentage involved multiple officers? How many involved multiple subjects? In how many situations did the officers use cover, or should they have used it and didn't? Barricades or obstacles present? How many cases found the officers with items in their hand's, baton, citation book, notepad, flashlight, etc., which had to be dropped or thrown before drawing their weapon? On average, how many rounds were expended or reloads completed? Were the officers involved coming from holstered positions, or were their weapons already at the ready?

These are only a few of the questions whose answers can help set priorities in self-directed training programs. This research also has the added advantage, if taken from local or regional situations, of lending real world, known-locale immediacy and credibility to the officers' efforts. A further benefit of such research is that it sharpens officers' skills in tactical analysis, another area gravely overlooked in most agency-sponsored programs.

Stages of fire can be as varying and creative as the officers' imaginations and range rules allow. In many cases, range masters who are staunchly opposed to "self-monitored" shooting will not only drop their opposition, but will assist officers who demonstrate that they are methodical, determined, and safety-oriented. This is where the use of a third officer as a range safety officer can pay big dividends.

The variety of simulated-hallway shooting scenarios and shooting through trash cans and walls to hit the targets on the other side also lends itself to fulfilling the needed fun factor. Balloons, bowling pins, flash-reactive targets, steel "popper plates," and jugs of water can all add to the participants' interest levels. Officers tend to enjoy things that fall, explode, make noise, or flash, but then, most shooters do.

Competing for point and time scores should always be present in the final phases of fire, and it's not that difficult to factor time against points. Both are accomplished for example, when seven or nine bowling pins are set up and officers, on signal, try to sweep left to right while competing officers sweep right to left. The winner, obviously, is the first one to "clean" the sweep and then put down the center "odd" pin. Any manner of change can be thrown in, for instance, by adding a midstream mandatory reload. In such events, the signal to fire or "shoot stimulus" can also be something other than an aural signal. In most gunfight situations, it is a visual rather than an aural stimulus that prompts an officer to pull the trigger.

After such a program is well established every competing officer, regardless of ability levels, should also have a chance to be a winner. Better and faster shooters should be handicapped against the less experienced, especially in "action" events. Those handicapped should take pride in their status, and the less accomplished competitors get to share the thrill of winning.

Another important element of any sound, self-directed program is the exercise of shooting restraint, and is another good reason why all stages should be individually documented by participating officers. More than one officer involved in a "clean" shooting has gone through hell in civil court a year or so later. They try, in that calm and sanctified atmosphere, to prove that no, that shot couldn't have been "rushed" or accidental, and yes, their training included assessment of "friendliness" among the targets, or other situations where restraint and precision were emphasized. It's relatively easy to stage events where the officer must first hold fire and move, perhaps two or more times, to avoid danger to a friendly before taking a shot on target.

Imagine the frustration of some shyster shark in a thousand-dollar, three-piece suit trying to make an officer look like a poorly trained, rash, accident prone duffer, when that officer slips out two inches of documentation showing every round fired in three years of extraordinarily specific, self-initiated training? There is nothing officers can do to better prevent the loss of their jobs, homes, savings, cars, and the garnisheeing of their paychecks into the 22nd century.

When the shooting session is over — it's not over. Then it is time for officers to step down, clean guns, make notes, and let the Adrenaline ebb before leaving the range. Nothing cements the validity of this type of training, or the camaraderie it engenders, more than getting together afterward for a meal, or even a relaxed cup of coffee. If the family can participate, it's even better. What's more important, what better excuse for an occasion, than having completed another pleasant, enjoyable, goal-oriented exercise that actually helps an officer stay alive?

The choice is up to the individual officers; the responsibility extends to partners, squads, and divisions. The one true path in self-directed firearms' training is methodology — anything else, eventually and ultimately, is madness.

About the Author

Mr. John Morrison is a Detective Lieutenant and 24-year veteran of the San Diego Police Department. He is widely known for his work as an officer safety trainer and innovator. He writes a number of columns for various police publications and co-wrote **Contact & Cover: Two-Officer Suspect Control** *with Steve Albrecht and published by Charles C. Thomas.*

Chapter 32

Use of Force

by Mildred K. O'Linn

Why Officers Use Excessive Force

The use of force by law enforcement personnel is a matter of critical concern both to the members of the general public and the members of the law enforcement community. In the 1990's the use of force by law enforcement became one of the hottest topics in America's headlines. As a result of the "Rodney King incident" in Los Angeles the use of force by law enforcement agencies from coast to coast was the topic of conversation. The number of committees and commissions formed, panel discussions held, and policy and training reviews conducted as a result of that one incident will most likely never be tallied.

One of the inquiries addressed after the King incident was why officers use excessive force. The consensus of a study of "Use of Unauthorized Force by Law Enforcement Personnel," conducted by major city chiefs and the F.B.I. in late 1991, was that there are six major reasons why law enforcement officers use more force than is necessary and include:

1.) Poor training in how to avoid confrontations or how to prevent confrontations from escalating.
2.) Poor training in defensive tactics and having too few force options between words and firearms.
3.) Personnel involved are psychologically unfit for duty — either when hired or because of drug or alcohol use.
4.) Peer pressure involving a "them vs. us" mentality.
5.) Extreme cowardice compensated for by over-reacting and trying to prove themselves.
6.) Racism, sexism, cultural ignorance, and a "holier-than-thou" attitude.

The results of these and other similar group-type efforts have been the most significant overhaul of law enforcement in this century. Use of force policies, supervision, field training officer programs, and defensive tactics' training are just a few of the areas of concern which are being subjected to scrutiny.

As expected, the number of civil suits and criminal actions brought against law enforcement personnel has increased since the televising of the King incident in early 1991. As a consequence of such adverse publicity there has been a negative impact on the public's confidence in officers. Police defense attorneys on the west coast have noted with dismay the immediate and negative impact the King incident has had in the civil courts. Long term damage was done to the jury pool which is, not surprisingly, comprised of television viewers who may have thought that officers wore a big red "S" on their chests. Now they are not sure what to think. Police no longer get the benefit of the doubt as they did previously when it was their word against the plaintiff. Jury awards to plaintiffs have increased substantially and there appears to be a whole flock of attorneys considering the lucrative aspects of suing law enforcement.

Responsibility of Government Entities

In vesting officers with the authority to use force to protect the public, a balancing of all human interests is required. Officers must have an understanding of, and a true appreciation for, the limitation on their authority, particularly with respect to overcoming resistance. Each agency provides guidance to the individuals selected to enforce the law through the policies, procedures, customs, and practices of the agency. By its decision in *Monell v. Department of Social Services* in 1979,[1] the United States Supreme Court held that municipalities could be sued for civil rights violations if they maintained an unconstitutional custom, policy, or practice that caused constitutional deprivation. Subsequent cases have wrestled further with what evidence is required to prove the existence of a custom, policy, or practice. The Supreme Court has held that a failure to train constitutes a municipal policy for purposes of *Monell* liability if the failure to train reflects a deliberate indifference to the constitutional rights of individuals.

Monell established the guidelines for imposing liability on governmental entities for the actions of officers in the field. The requirement of proof of an unconstitutional policy may be met by either proving the existence of an express and explicit pronouncement of such policy by an agency, or by showing that this "custom, policy, or procedure" caused an officer to violate the plaintiff's constitutional rights. In short, the importance of a written policy may become negligible given an agency's custom and practice. Thus, an agency's "policy" is comprised of the position instructors have taken on the use of force; the philosophy of the field training officers which is passed on to their trainees; the feedback, discipline, and guidance provided by supervisors; and the agency's response to citizen complaints regarding the use of force which either approves or disapproves the force used with regard to a specific set of facts.

Evaluating Officers' Use of Force Decisions

It is estimated that officers encounter resistance and must use force in about 3% of all contacts. The National Lawyer's Guild estimated a few years ago that 20,000 to 30,000 claims of excessive force were filed against law enforcement each year. Balance this against the fact that according to the Department of Justice, approximately 17% of the nation's law enforcement personnel are assaulted annually. From the smallest agency to the largest, peace officers are called upon to make decisions that witnesses, jurors, lawyers, and judges will debate the propriety of with infinite more time than the officers had to make the decisions in the field. With these concerns in mind, we will examine the standards set forth by the United States Supreme Court for evaluating officers' use of force decisions.

The Supreme Court since 1985, has given us two landmark decisions which provide guidance for street officers regarding the parameters for use of deadly and less-than-lethal force. A clear understanding of *Tennessee v. Garner*[2] and *Graham v. Connor*[3] is essential for officers in preparing to make such decisions in the field.

In *Tennessee v. Garner*, the Supreme Court dealt in general with the issue of when the use of deadly force is justifiable, and specifically addressed the when such force may be used to prevent the escape of an apparently unarmed felony subject. In this case, Memphis Police Officers responded to a prowler call. Upon arrival they were told by a neighbor that the sound of breaking glass had been heard and that someone was breaking into the house next door. One of the officers went around the house, heard a door slam, and saw someone run across the back yard. The fleeing subject stopped at a six-foot high, chain-link fence at the edge of the yard. The officer, aided by a flashlight, was able to see the subject's hands and face. He saw no signs of a weapon and was reasonably sure that the subject was unarmed. The officer ordered the subject to halt, but the subject attempted to climb over the fence. To prevent the subject's escape the officer shot him, resulting in the subject's death. Ten dollars in a purse taken from the house were found on the subject's body. Both a Tennessee statute and the Memphis Police Department's policy authorized the use of deadly force to prevent escape. The statute provided:

> *If, after notice of the intention to arrest the defendant, he either flees or forcibly resists, the officer may use all the necessary means to effect the arrest.*

The department policy was slightly more restrictive, but still allowed the use of deadly force in cases of burglary. On appeal, the United States Supreme Court stated that, "There could be no question that the use of deadly force is a seizure subject to the reasonableness requirement of the Fourth Amendment."

When Is the Use of Deadly Force Justifiable?

In evaluating the use of deadly force the Court has suggested that we need to balance the nature and quality of the intrusion on the individual's Fourth Amendment interests against the importance of the governmental interests alleged to justify the intrusion. In other words, the type of force used and the manner and means used to effect an arrest will be balanced against the type of offense committed or the facts and circumstances surrounding the need to search and seize the individual in question. Reasonableness depends not only on when a seizure is made, but how it is carried out.

The Court went on to discuss the use of deadly force to prevent the escape of felony suspects. The Court held:

> *The use of deadly force to prevent the escape of all felony suspects, whatever the circumstances, is constitutionally unreasonable. It is not better that all felony subjects die than that they escape. Where the subject poses no immediate threat to the officer and no threat to others, the harm resulting from failing to apprehend him does not justify the use of deadly force to do so.*

From the language of the Court it is clear that deadly force may only be used to:

- Prevent death or serious physical injury to an officer or another.

- Prevent escape when the officer reasonably believes
  - the subject has used deadly force in the commission of a felony, and
  - if the subject is reasonably thought to be intent on endangering human life unless arrested without delay, and has the means to do so.

Additionally, the Court noted that when using deadly force officers should not reasonably nor unnecessarily endanger themselves or the public in the application of deadly force and whenever possible, the officers should use verbal commands of authority to avoid using deadly force.

In May 1989, the Supreme Court in the case of *Graham v. Connor* officially recognized excessive force claims as violations of the Fourth Amendment right against unreasonable search and seizures. In this case the plaintiff, *Graham*, a diabetic, requested that a friend drive him to a convenience store to purchase some juice to counteract the onset of an insulin reaction. When they arrived at the store *Graham* decided to go to a friend's home instead because of the number of people in line at the

Use of Force

store. *Graham's* hasty exit from the store drew the suspicions of Officer Connor, who stopped the vehicle. While Connor was attempting to determine what had occurred at the store, backup officers arrived and handcuffed *Graham.* During the encounter *Graham* sustained a broken foot, cuts on his wrists, a bruised forehead, an injured shoulder, and claims to have developed a bad ringing in his ears. *Graham* filed an excessive force claim under 42 U.S.C. #1983.

The district court granted a directed verdict for defendant Officer Connor after applying the standard established in *Johnson v. Glick*,[4] which up until this point was a frequently cited district court case on this issue. *Johnson* provided a four-part test to determine if an excessive force claim existed. The four-part test included:

1.) The need for the application of the force.
2.) The relationship between the need and the amount of the force which was used.
3.) The extent of the injury inflicted.
4.) Whether the force was applied in a good faith effort to maintain or restore discipline or maliciously and sadistically for the very purpose of causing harm.

The Court of Appeal affirmed and the case was subsequently reviewed by the Supreme Court. In reviewing the *Graham* case, the Supreme Court made it perfectly clear that the *Johnson* four-part test was an inappropriate standard for evaluating an officer's use of force during an arrest. The Supreme Court decision in *Graham* as it applies to the evaluation of use of force decisions may be summarized as follows:

- Excessive force claims under Section 1983 are not governed by a single generic standard.

- Excessive force claims arising during the course of an arrest, investigative stop, or other "seizure" fall under the Fourth Amendment, and must be judged by the reasonableness standard.

- A "reasonableness" determination is based on whether the officers' actions are "objectively reasonable" in light of the facts and circumstances confronting them, without regard to their underlying intent or motivation. Reasonableness is judged from the perspective of a reasonable officer on the scene at the time of the incident. Allowance should be made for split-second decisions about the force that is necessary in a particular situation.

- *Johnson v. Glick* is incompatible with a proper Fourth Amendment analysis. The "malicious and sadistic" inquiry is rejected as a means of describing conduct that is objectively unreasonable. While an individual officer's motivation may be of central importance in deciding use of force issues in a convicted prisoner context under the English Amendment (cruel and unusual punishment), it is incompatible with a Fourth Amendment analysis.

The Need to Document Use of Force Incidents

Graham v. Connor thus instructs us that an officer's good intentions will not make an unreasonable use of force constitutional, nor will an officer's bad intentions make a constitutional violation out of an otherwise reasonable use of force. This case points out that it is critical for officers to articulate the facts and circumstances which precipitated the use of force. An officer must use force which is reasonable given the facts and circumstances known to the officer at the time the decision was made. Such decisions do not occur in a vacuum — a number of factors come into play and should be articulated in the incident report.

Some of the factors which may effect the "reasonableness" of the level of force used include:

- Officer's age
- Officer's size
- Relative strength of the officer
- Skill level of the officer
- Number of officers versus the number of subjects

Additionally, there may be factors which require an officer to rapidly accelerate through the use of force options available. For example, if an officer has special knowledge about a particular subject, such as a tendency to assault officers or a propensity to be armed, the officer will be justified in using a greater amount of force to achieve control. Likewise if the officer is injured or exhausted it may be proper for the officer to escalate rapidly to a higher level of force. Proximity to the officer's firearm and the amount of time available to formulate a response also impact heavily on the reasonableness of the force used by the officer.

Documentation of what transpired is in some ways more important than what actually occurred. Reports should accurately and thoroughly reflect the nature of the confrontation and the dynamics involved in the officer's decision-making process. One method of describing the contents of a report, and consequently to encourage thoroughness and completeness, is to suggest that officers think about their reports like the drafting of a movie script — with all the nuances that would be necessary to tell the entire story. This issue might not be so critical if all the judgments and decisions about the reasonableness of the officer's actions were going to be made in the immediate future. However, the nature of our judicial system is such that the officer may be subject to questioning regarding the decision many years after the actual incident happens. Written support for an officer's actions will be very helpful in the event of subsequent litigation.

Conclusion

Inevitably, law enforcement personnel are involved on a daily basis in numerous and varied encounters with the public. They are called upon regularly to choose between a wide range of options available to them in their contacts with individuals, and when warranted to do so, in effecting the arrest of those persons involved in unlawful acts.

Officers will continue to be called upon daily to make acute use of force decisions in the field and, even at its lowest level, the use of force is a serious responsibility. Those decisions, which are more often than not made in split seconds, will be reviewed not only by the officer's peers, supervisors, and administrators, but will be repeatedly reviewed by individuals with no true understanding of what it takes to do the job.

Like it or not, the use of force must be deemed to have been reasonable not only by the officers and the members of their peer group, but also by the members of the public who comprise such groups as: the citizen's police review board, the city council, the courts, the media, the jury, and even neighbors and family. All of these individuals and entities will have millions of more seconds to decide what the officer should have done than in fact the officer had at the time the decision was made and action was taken.

Clearly the bottom line in the use of force arena is the reasonableness of the action taken by the officer. The officer's actions will be evaluated in light of the department's policy and the applicable laws. In large part the officer's ability to articulate effectively the nature of the encounter and the dynamics which effected the decision will decide whether a use of force, which the officer believes to have been righteous, is deemed reasonable by those sitting in judgment of those actions.

Bibliography

[1] 436 U.S. 658, 56 L. Ed. 2d 611, 98 S. Ct. 2018 (1978).

[2] 471 U.S. 1, 85 L. Ed. 2d 1, 105 S. Ct. 1694 (1985).

[3] 490 U.S. 386, 104 L. Ed. 2d 443, 109 S. Ct. 1865 (1989).

[4] 481 F. 2d 1028 (CA2), cert. denied, 414 U.S. 1033 (1973).

About the Author

Ms. Mildred K. O'Linn is an attorney with the law firm of Franscell, Stickland, Roberts & Lawrence in Pasadena, CA. She was previously the Technical and Legal Adviser for the Law Enforcement Television Network (LETN) in Dallas, TX. Prior to that she was with the Kent State University Police Department for eight years. Ms. O'Linn moved from patrol officer to manager of the police academy, and finally as Administrative Assistant to the Director of Police. She has an extensive defensive tactics' instructor background and is an International PR-24™ Instructor.

Chapter 33

Management of Aggressive Behavior

by Roland Ouellette

If subjects communicate 90% through non-verbal communications, then the understanding of non-verbal communications is a must for officers who want to survive on the street.

The frequency of assaults on officers continues to rise at an alarming rate. Officers are being killed and disabled for life. The officers' odds of coming out of encounters are greatly increased by understanding body language signals. Understanding the three areas of non-verbal communications can stack the odds in the officers' favor. They are space, eye contact, and gestures.

Space

Personal space is an area around us which others are generally not expected to intrude upon (see chart on page 290). The four zones around us are oval in shape and consist of the intimate, personal, social, and public zones. The intimate and personal zones cause the most problems for officers. Generally, officers have a habit of entering these two zones which greatly increases subjects' anxiety. Within a three to four foot area, officers also lose their ability to react to an attack.

As a general rule, officers should maintain a minimum of four feet between subjects and themselves. If subjects enter the officers' space or if the officers have to enter subjects' personal space, the officers' hands should go up in front of them in a non-aggressive manner to reduce the reaction time against an attack. A large percentage of officers who are disarmed, stabbed, or injured with personal weapons (fist, feet, knees, etc.) often do not understand the concept of space. Therefore, when approaching subjects officers should:

- Allow enough space to control subjects, but not to violate their personal space (4 to 6 feet). Officers should approach from the 1 position or from a 45 degree angle to the subjects (refer to chart on page 290).

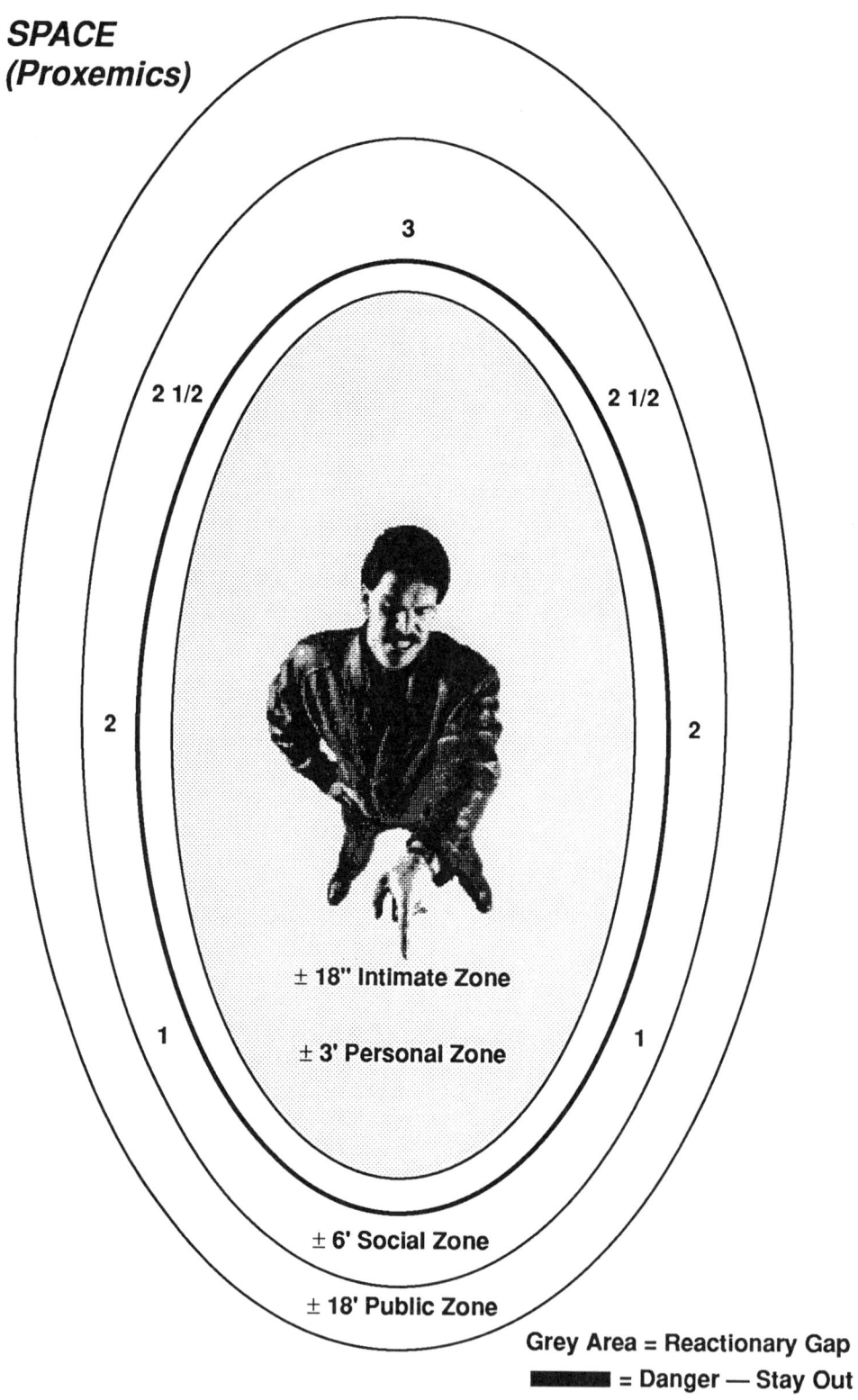

Management of Aggressive Behavior

- **Approach to subjects' weak side.** Some ways of identifying the weak side include:
  - Nine out of ten people are right handed.
  - People gesture with their strong hand.
  - A watch is generally worn on the weak side.
  - A belt end generally points to the weak side.

- Use the supportive or defensive stance which lessens the subject's anxiety, reduces attack possibilities, and puts the officers on proper balance. Their bodies should be at a 45 degree angle relative to the subjects. Their weak foot should be forward and strong foot to the rear. Their feet should be shoulder width apart or wider. Their heads should be directly over their hips and their weight equal on both feet with knees slightly bent. The safest distance is a minimum of 4 to 6 feet from the subject, depending on the stage of conflict. Whenever officers enter within a 6-foot range of the subjects, both hands should be at waist level or above.

Eye Contact

- **Proper use of eye contact is an important non-verbal communications' skill.** If officers properly use eye contact, it can convey concern, support, confidence, and authority. Observing eye movement while communicating with subjects can give important signals, such as:
  - Whether subjects are submissive, angry, or deranged.
  - Whether subjects are looking for an escape route or weapon.
  - If an attack is imminent.
  - Where subjects will strike the officers.

- **Length of eye contact varies among ethnic groups.** Also in our society, **not** making eye contact gives the impression of insecurity, shyness, or deception. On an average, the following ethnic groups maintain eye contact:
  - Caucasians, 45% of the time.
  - Blacks, 30% of the time.
  - Hispanics, 25% of the time.
  - Orientals, 18% of the time.

- **Constant eye contact by officers as they speak** can be interpreted by subjects as an attempt to dominate. It can also be seen as an aggressive act which usually raises the subject's anxiety. Reducing eye contact diminishes the power role, increases the helper role, and helps to lessen subjects' anxiety.

- ☐ **When officers are taller** than the subjects and the officers maintain constant eye contact while speaking, this may be interpreted as an attempt at dominance.
- ☐ **When officers are shorter** than the subjects and the officers maintain constant eye contact while speaking, this may be perceived as a sign of over confidence or a challenge.
- ☐ **When subjects are speaking to the officers,** direct eye contact, along with a slightly bowed head or small nod of the head, decreases officers' power roles and shows support.
- ☐ **To show support,** officers should maintain eye contact while subjects speak. The officers should shift their eyes to the chin or neck area of the subjects occasionally while the subjects speak. This shift can be as short as a 40th of a second to reduce dominance.

- ▣ **When attack is imminent** and the officers are using positive and extending commands (i.e., "STOP! DROP THE CHAIR! DO IT NOW!"), direct eye contact should be used. Direct eye contact along with other body language signals and defensive tools can be used to sufficiently intimidate the subjects to submit without a fight.

- ▣ **Mirrored or dark glasses** change both officers' and subjects' appearances, act as a constant intense stare, and is generally perceived as **aggressive**. Mirrored or dark glasses hide the whites of the eyes which usually provide a constant source of information during conversation. These types of glasses take away the ability to see signals such as, darting eyes, jerking eyes, glazed stares, empty stares, look-through stares, target glances, etc. Officers or subjects can only guess what is taking place behind the glasses. Also, different types of glasses have different effects. Heavy, upper rimmed glasses tend to make the wearer look more fierce and domineering, whereas heavy rimmed glasses tend to make the wearers look as though they have a permanent aggressive gaze.

Officers have been trained to watch the hands of subjects, because hands kill. However, officers may want to reconsider this. What else can eyes tell officers? A LOT! Subjects' eyes are the opening to their minds and tell officers what the subjects' hands will do before the hands do them. After assessing the hands for hidden weapons, the officers' primary vision should be on the eyes. The secondary vision should be on the hands. 87% of information relayed to the brain comes via the eyes, 9% via the ears, and 4% via the other senses.

Management of Aggressive Behavior

Consider this, eyes are 1000 times more effective than their ears in sweeping information. For example, the eyes are efficient up to 1 mile and see light rays at frequencies of 10 million, billion cycles per second. Ears are efficient up to 100 feet and can hear frequencies of 50 to 15,000 cycles per minute. Therefore, the eyes can tell officers much needed information about subjects:

- **Subjects' pupil size.** The pupils will dilate or contract as subjects' attitudes change from positive to negative or vise versa. When subjects become excited the pupils can dilate up to 4 times their normal size. When subjects become angry the pupils contract. Contractions of the pupils are also known as "snake eyes" or "beady eyes."

- **Subjects' eyes alternate between officers' eyes, chest, and hands.** The subjects are sizing the officers up. The officers should maintain proper distance and establish good defensive positions.

- **Subjects' eyes jerk.** This may indicate that the subjects are hallucinating, communicating with God or Satan or a non-existent friend, or feel they are being spied upon by an imagined person. The officers should create space and establish good defensive positions.

- **Subjects' eyes dart.** Subjects' eyes dart from side to side or up and down and indicates agitation. This is common when subjects feel cornered by officers. The officers should create space and establish good defensive positions.

- **Subjects' look around.** This may be a sign that the officers have cornered the subjects or they are looking for an escape route or weapon. The officers should create space and establish good defensive positions.

- **Subjects' eyes are glazed, empty, or "looking through the officers."** This may indicate one of several conditions; drugs, alcohol, deranged, medical problems, or etc. There exists a higher potential for aggressiveness since they may be inflamed with little or no provocation. The officers should create space and establish good defensive positions.

- **Subjects use target glances.** Most subjects will look at their target before they attack; subjects look at an officer's gun before grabbing it, looks at the officer's chin before punching it, looks at the officer's groin before kicking it, or looks at the officer's throat before cutting it. This knowledge gives officers a tremendous advantage. There is usually a pause of at least four tenths of a second between the glance and the actual attack. This pause provides officers with sufficient time to exit the attack zone or to create space.

- **Subjects break direct eye contact.** Subjects who are trying to intimidate officers by yelling, screaming, pointing their fingers, or using direct eye contact, will often break eye contact just before they progress to the next stage - physical attack. The subjects depersonalize officers by looking down or away and then proceed to look at their target just before attacking.

- **Subjects' eyes widen with the whites showing.** This is a basic response of surprise or fear as when officers snap open the expandable PR-24™, and is usually followed by signs of submission.

- **Subjects' eyes glisten.** The surfaces of their eyes are slightly overloaded with secretion from the tear glands caused by aroused emotion, anguish, or distress and stops just short of crying. Distressed subjects may also constantly blink which may be a desperate attempt to bail out the eyes before crying. This is usually not a danger signal to officers.

As a general rule, officers should occasionally break eye contact when they speak to subjects to decrease the power role and reduce anxiety, and maintain eye contact when the subjects speak.

Gestures

In addition to understanding space and eye contact as non-verbal communications' skills, officers continue to communicate through their gestures and posture. If they say one thing, but send out a signal that differs, the non-verbal signal will probably prevail.

Again, if subjects say, "I give up," the appropriate body signals have to match. If there is a discrepancy between verbal and non-verbal messages, believe the non-verbal messages. These are much harder to fake. Officers cannot rely on one signal. They must look at several signals or a cluster of signals along with rate, tone, and volume of speech.

Listed below are some basic gesture and posture signals that officers should recognize and understand:

- **Head:** back — aggression; bowed — support; straight — assertiveness.

- **Face:** muscle tension, twitching, jerking, teeth clenched — anxiety or aggression.

Management of Aggressive Behavior

- **Change in skin color:** white — rage; red — anger; pale — fear.

- **Lips:** pushed forward bearing the teeth — anger; tight lipped — possible attack.

- **Breathing:** rate increases and deepens — aggression.

- **Shoulders:** back — aggression; forward — support; straight — assertiveness.

- **Arms:** crossed in the thinker (Jack Benny) position — support; crossed with fists closed, gripping upper arms — aggression.

- **Palms:**
  - [ ] above the waist, palms out — non-aggressive.
  - [ ] above the waist, palms in — possibly aggressive.
  - [ ] above the waist, bladed — aggressive.
  - [ ] below the waist, palms in — non-aggressive.
  - [ ] below the waist, palms out and elbows away from the body — non-aggressive.
  - [ ] below the waist, palms out and elbows close to the body — possibly aggressive.

- **Hands:**
  - [ ] opening and closing (pumping) — anxiety or aggression.
  - [ ] on hips — assertiveness.
  - [ ] folded in front of groin — non-aggressive.
  - [ ] the hand set — aggressive.
  - [ ] the boxer stance — aggressive.
  - [ ] the martial arts' hands — aggressive.
  - [ ] closed fists, white knuckles — aggressive.
  - [ ] close to the body, palms to the rear (open or closed) — possibly aggressive.
  - [ ] one hand open, one hand closed — possible weapon.
  - [ ] hidden behind back, one or both hands — possible weapon.

- **Elbows:** close to body — tense; away from body — relaxed.

- **Index finger:** pointing trigger finger, finger across the throat, middle finger up — aggressive; index finger and middle finger, peace sign — non-aggressive.

- **Legs or Stance:**
  - [ ] weight equal on both feet — non-aggressive.

- raising up and down on balls of feet — aggressive.
- rocking toes to heels — aggressive.
- front knee bent, rear knee locked — aggressive.
- shifts toward officers — possibly aggressive.
- shifts away from officers — possible threat, looking to escape, looking for a weapon, a signal.
- shifts 10% of weight to the front and 90% to the rear or 30% to the front and 70% to the rear — martial arts' stance.

▄▆▶ **Standing and sitting:**
- officers stand, subjects sit — more aggressive.
- officers stand, subjects stand — less aggressive.
- officers sit, subjects sit — least aggressive.
- officers sit, proper distance, body bladed, subjects sit — supportive.

▄▆▶ **Body:**
- expanding the body — aggressive.
- contracting the body — non-aggressive.

Recognizing Threats

Generally, aggressors who are aroused to fight do not go into an all out attack, because they fear injury to themselves. Aggression from the sympathetic nervous system drives them on, but fear from the parasympathetic nervous system holds them back. The aggressors begin by threatening to attack which is ritualized combat. If there is sufficient intimidation, their opponents back off, and the aggressors win without injury to themselves. When threats and counter threats fail to settle a dispute, an intense state of inner conflict arises and physical action takes place.

The following are external changes that take place when the aggressor goes from ritualized combat, when the attack is not probable, but possible, to the attack being imminent:

▄▆▶ Face turns from red to white.

▄▆▶ Lips push forward to tighten over the teeth.

▄▆▶ Eyebrows go from frowning to drooping over the eyes.

▄▆▶ Heads go from tilted back to a down position to protect the neck.

- Eye contact goes from direct stare to breaking eye contact, and then to looking at the target of attack.

- Breathing goes from quick to rapid, and then deepens.

- Shoulders go from squared toward the officer to bladed.

- Hands go from opening and closing to closed fists.

- Verbalization goes from belligerent, yelling, and cursing to no verbalization at all.

- If the aggressor is beyond the reach of the officer the final gesture will be to lower the body in order to push off for a dynamic attack.

About the Author

Mr. Roland Ouellette is the President and founder of R.E.B. Security Training, Inc. He is nationally known as one of the leading trainers of law enforcement and security. Since 1983, he has been providing his training and consulting services to numerous law enforcement agencies, correctional agencies, corporations, hospitals, military agencies, universities, and colleges.

Mr. Ouellette retired from the Connecticut State Police as a lieutenant and served in the Army Security Agency. He was also a correctional officer for the Connecticut Department of Corrections and has conducted security and law enforcement courses at a Connecticut college.

Roland Ouellette is well known for the development of the "Management of Aggressive Behavior Course" which is based on his expertise as well as the input of hundreds of officers and trainers, including numerous medical personnel. He is also the author of the book, **Management of Aggressive Behavior.**

Tracy Robinson and Douglas Chu

Sergeant Robinson and Detective Chu are currently members of the New York City Police Department. They are both Senior Instructors at Modern Warrior Defensive Tactics Institute and were among the first students to earn their black belts under the teachings of Phil Messina. Both hold numerous training certificates and teach defensive tactics' and martial arts' programs.

In 1988, while on training tour with Modern Warrior in Hong Kong and Mainland China, Sergeant Robinson and Detective Chu were invited to demonstrate their fighting skills on Chinese National Television.

Chapter 34

Tactical Groundfighting

by Tracy Robinson and Douglas Chu

A fear of being thrown, knocked, or tackled to the ground is in the back of every law enforcement officer's mind. It is not an unreasonable fear for it happens quite often. However, the most common misconception that law enforcement officers have about being on the ground is that they are defenseless. This type of negative thinking can be detrimental to officers in life or death confrontations. The fact of the matter is that, with a survival attitude and proper training, officers can effectively defend themselves while on the ground and turn a potentially lethal situation in their favor.

Let's consider a hypothetical scenario which can have either a positive or a negative outcome. An officer gets a call stating that there is a violent man in a parking lot. He arrives at the job, exits his vehicle, and attempts to engage the subject in a conversation. The subject rushes the officer, knocks him to the ground, and then backs off.

The officer chases the subject by using a crab-walk type movement. He can feel the Adrenaline pumping through his veins and can hear his heart pounding in his chest. He is tiring rapidly, his bulletproof vest is restricting his chest cavity from expanding, and his breathing is coming in short gasps. He tries to move in toward the subject, but the subject stays just out of the officer's range by jumping back as he laughs and taunts the officer.

The officer is nearing exhaustion. He can't get to his equipment on his duty belt, because it fell behind him and he can't reach it. The subject quickly circles around to the officer's head, kicks him in the face, and stomps on the officer's elbow joint, breaking it. The officer is stunned and his arm is useless to him.

The subject then rips the officer's firearm out of the holster and kills him with his own weapon. If you think this sounds far fetched, consider this: Over 50% of New York City Police Officers shot in 1991, were shot with their own firearm.

The mistakes this officer made could easily be made by any officer who lacks Groundfighting knowledge. With a few simple changes, this scenario could turn out quite differently.

An officer gets a call stating that there is a violent man in a parking lot. He arrives at the job, exits his vehicle, and attempts to engage the subject in a conversation. The subject rushes the officer, knocks him to the ground, and then backs off.

The officer immediately makes himself into a small target. He pulls his knees into his chest, crosses his ankles, and puts his hands in a defensive blocking position. He keeps adjusting his position by using his feet to pivot on the small of his back as the subject jumps from side to side, laughing and taunting the officer.

The officer feels the Adrenaline pumping through his veins and concentrates on controlling his breathing as he waits for the subject to move within range. Suddenly the subject pulls a knife and circles around to the officer's head. The officer draws his baton, strikes the subject's leg, and spins around with his feet pointing toward the subject. The subject steps into range and the officer thrusts a kick at his leg and breaks it. As the subject crumples to the ground the knife falls from his hand. The officer radios for backup. The subject is stunned and the officer moves in and safely handcuffs him. With a few key changes, the officer was able to defend himself successfully against a violent assailant.

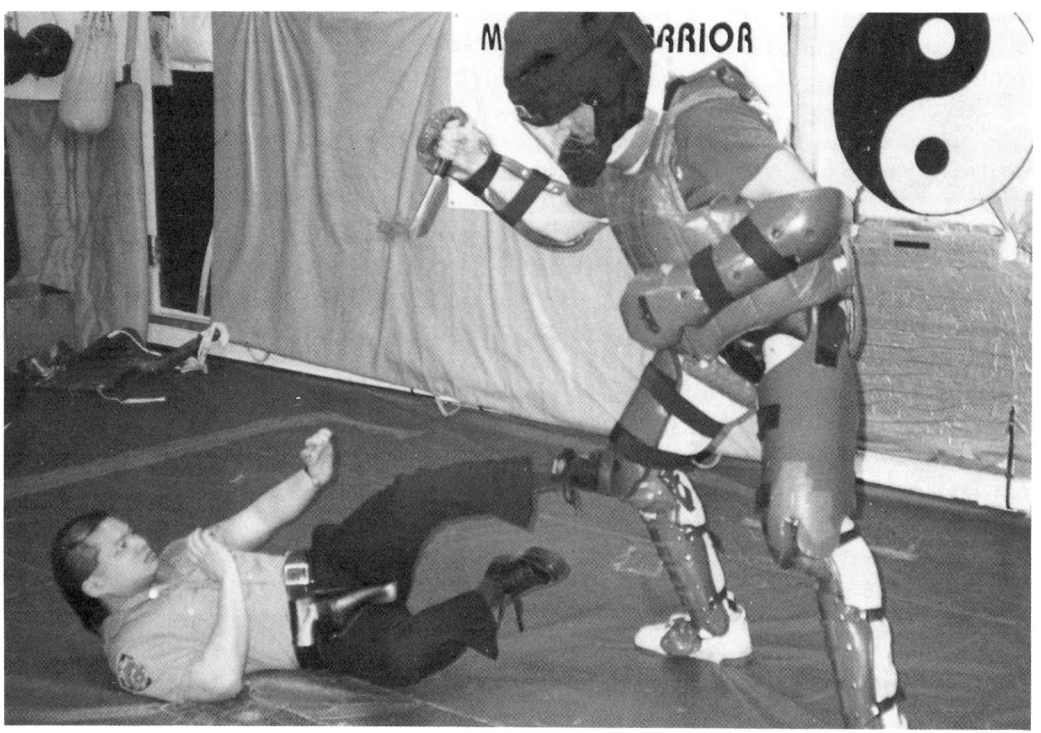

The officer attacks the leg of the knife wielding assailant.

Officers of the 1990's have to be prepared to defend themselves from the ground and correct the belief that if they get knocked to the ground it is the beginning of their end. To survive an attack from the ground is simply a matter of breaking some bad habits. Practicing simple training exercises replace misconceptions with the knowledge of valid

Tactical Groundfighting

techniques which rely on solid principles.

The first step in learning how to ground fight is to overcome the fear of falling to the ground. Sometimes officers are taken by surprise and knocked down before they know what hit them. At other times, the situation could be avoided by officers if they were aware of their surrounding environment. Many times officers encounter adverse conditions, such as uneven pavement and slippery surfaces, or situations which are bad for balance, such as working on ships or standing on staircases. These could be contributing factors to them falling to the ground. Awareness of potential danger and making defensive positioning a priority could be instrumental in preventing serious injury to officers.

In the training environment these conditions can be anticipated. The training exercises practiced at Modern Warrior are designed to prepare officers to adjust to changes in the environment they may encounter on the street.

A beginning exercise to get officers accustomed to falling is for them to start by kneeling and falling on their forearms with their fingers extended and their head turned to either side. When they feel comfortable with this exercise, the same exercise can be done from the standing position, but they must be certain to land on their forearms' first. Finally, this exercise advances to the officers closing their eyes. The instructor starts by pushing them with a hand from behind and advances to striking them with a poker which is a rolled up newspaper covered in duct tape. These exercises help officers overcome the fear of falling and to develop good instinctive reactions when they are taken by surprise.

Another exercise officers should work on is falling to the rear. The officers start by squatting, kicking one leg out, and falling to the rear. They must be sure to keep their chin tucked to their chest and their spine curved. They should then advance to the standing position with their eyes closed and the taped poker exercise. It is important that they do not let their legs kick up on the fall which exposes their spine to the assailant. The officers build a great deal of confidence when they realize that they are able to execute these simple falls without injury.

The officers demonstrate a few basic Groundfighting firing positions.

Once on the ground, the most practical, economical, and versatile position for the officers to be in is the basic Groundfighting position; officers on their backs with knees pulled in toward the chest, ankles crossed in front of the groin, hands up ready to block, and chin tucked to the chest. This position is similar to the fetal position and enable officers maximum defensive ability to protect their vital organs and permits them easy access to equipment on their duty belt. This is an excellent neutral position in which the officers don't have to worry about balance and allows them to use their hands and feet defensively and offensively.

This is the basic Groundfighting position.

The following is a series of exercises for blocking that also develop awareness of the environment. It is common for officers to focus their attention on one person or object and to be taken by surprise by multiple assailants while under stress. These exercises force officers to take in the entire environment while under stress and to create a reverse funnel with their vision. This is extremely beneficial in developing instinctive reactions to unexpected events.

- The instructor throws punches and kicks at officers in the Groundfighting position. This gives the officers good blocking practice.

- The instructor throws objects, such as pokers or throw-darts, at the officers in the Groundfighting position.

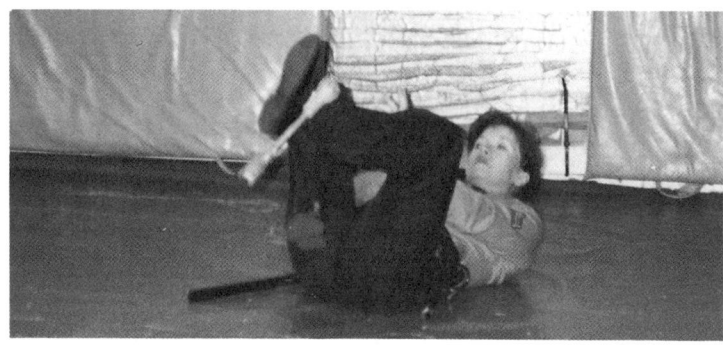

The officer blocks throw-darts with the legs.

Tactical Groundfighting

A throw-dart is PVC pipe with a padded golf ball on either end and is entirely covered with tape. The officers practice blocking with their feet.

- The officers face the instructor on their hands and knees. The instructor hurls throw-darts at the officers. The object is to evade the throw-darts by moving only the necessary parts of the body. The officers should practice economy of movement and moving the limbs independently of each other.

- The officers are in the hands and knees position. They must now concentrate on keeping their vision constantly on the instructor as they roll laterally to either side to evade the throw-darts. If they tuck their chins to their chests they will lose sight of the instructor. It requires negative discipline to roll this way, but it can be accomplished with a little practice.

- The officers lay prone on their stomachs with a simulated firearm in their hands. The instructor hurls throw-darts at the officers. The officers concentrate on keeping the simulated firearm pointed at the instructor as they roll laterally to avoid the throw-darts. As they complete the roll, the officers must keep their body slightly tilted to one side. This keeps their vital organs off the ground which is a good defensive position.

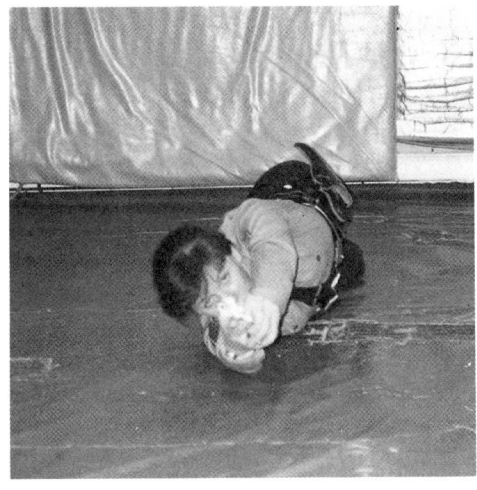

The officer practices the prone firing position.

After practicing these blocking exercises, the officers should get back up on their feet with little effort. However, they should get up from the ground when it is defensively advantageous, and not necessarily at the first opportunity.

There is an easy and safe way for officers to practice getting up from the ground without giving up their defensive advantage. First, the officers should sit on the ground with one leg straight and the other leg tucked beneath the buttocks. They should rock their weight onto the knee which is tucked and then stand up. By getting up from the ground this way, officers have both hands free enabling them to block, strike, call for assistance on the radio, or draw their baton or firearm.

The Modern Warrior Tactical Groundfighting System includes several types of rolls which are used to cover distance, recover weapons, and to take cover. The following real life incident is a good example of how training, a positive mind-set, and awareness of the environment can save officers' lives.

A New York City police officer was performing a routine car stop. As the officer approached the vehicle, the subject exited his vehicle. He spun toward the officer with an UZI sub-machine gun in his hand. The officer did a dive roll back to his radio car as the subject fired approximately 30 rounds over the officer's head. The officer took cover behind the door of the radio car. The subject ran from his car to a driveway of a private home. The officer called for backup and pursued the subject into the backyard. The officer heard the voice of his instructor yelling in his head, "Expand your vision; span out!" As the officer made it to the end of the driveway, his peripheral vision caught the subject hiding off to the side. Before the subject could turn his head, the officer punched his firearm out to the side, and fired two rounds which fatally wounded the subject.

This particular officer was trained at Modern Warrior and hated to practice rolls during training sessions. As it turned out, the exercise that he disliked the most was the beneficial one in saving his life! Under stress, he did what he was trained to do.

The following are training exercises which will condition officers, both physically and psychologically, to accomplish various goals.

- Officers begin from the squat position to practice both forward and backward rolls. They should make sure to tuck their chin to the chest to avoid a neck injury and advance to the standing position. When the officers feel confident, they can practice this exercise with their eyes closed.

- The instructor trips the officers as they walk slowly with their eyes closed. They practice going into a forward or backward roll. The goal of this exercise is to train the officers to roll instinctively rather than struggle to regain their balance.

- The instructor stands behind the officers who have their eyes closed, and throws a simulated knife onto the mat. The officers open their eyes, take two steps, and do a dive roll to recover the knife. This exercise is designed to train officers

Tactical Groundfighting

to quickly recover a weapon before the assailant has a chance to get it.

- An object, such as a box or a heavy bag, is placed on the mat. The officers practice diving over the object and onto their stomachs. They flatten their body into a prone position, using the object as cover, and draw their simulated firearms and point them in the direction of the assailant.

The officer practices using low cover.

Officers should also practice preserving their energy. They begin in the Tactical Groundfighting position with the instructor at their feet. The instructor tries to get around to their heads. The officers use one leg to turn in a circular movement while the other leg stays bent in toward the chest with the foot protecting the groin. They can switch feet to turn as long as the feet continue to point toward the instructor.

In a one on one confrontation, this is the safest position for the officers to be in. The officers maintain this circular pattern of movement as the instructor picks up the pace and changes direction. After a few minutes of this, the instructor is very winded, but the officers have not even expended enough energy to be out of breath.

If this were a perfect world, officers could always keep their feet pointing at the assailant and their head away. But for the times when the assailant does get to the officers' heads, the officers should practice the following exercises to get their feet pointing toward the assailant again:

- The instructor stands at the officers' heads. The officers push off the instructor's leg, pick their shoulders up, and spin on the small of their backs. They can either drop their shoulders or elbows or use their feet on the instructor's leg to stop the spin.

- The officers should have objects, such as simulated batons, radios, or firearms in their hands and use the objects to push off with. In the street, the push could actually be a strike. This exercise will get officers used to accomplishing the same goal with their hands full.

In life or death confrontations, officers must rely on techniques that have a lasting physical effect on assailants, and not just those that cause pain. Officers have many offensive options from the ground. Vital targets which effect vision, wind, or limbs are most effective in controlling assailants. If the officers are faced with multiple assailants, which happens quite frequently, then their primary goal is to protect their firearm while they deliver vital blows to the assailants. These may include strikes, kicks, and throws.

- Officers in the Groundfighting position should practice protecting their firearm by keeping it positioned in front of the hip, almost in the groin area. As the instructor grabs for the firearm, the officers block, redirect, and then strike.

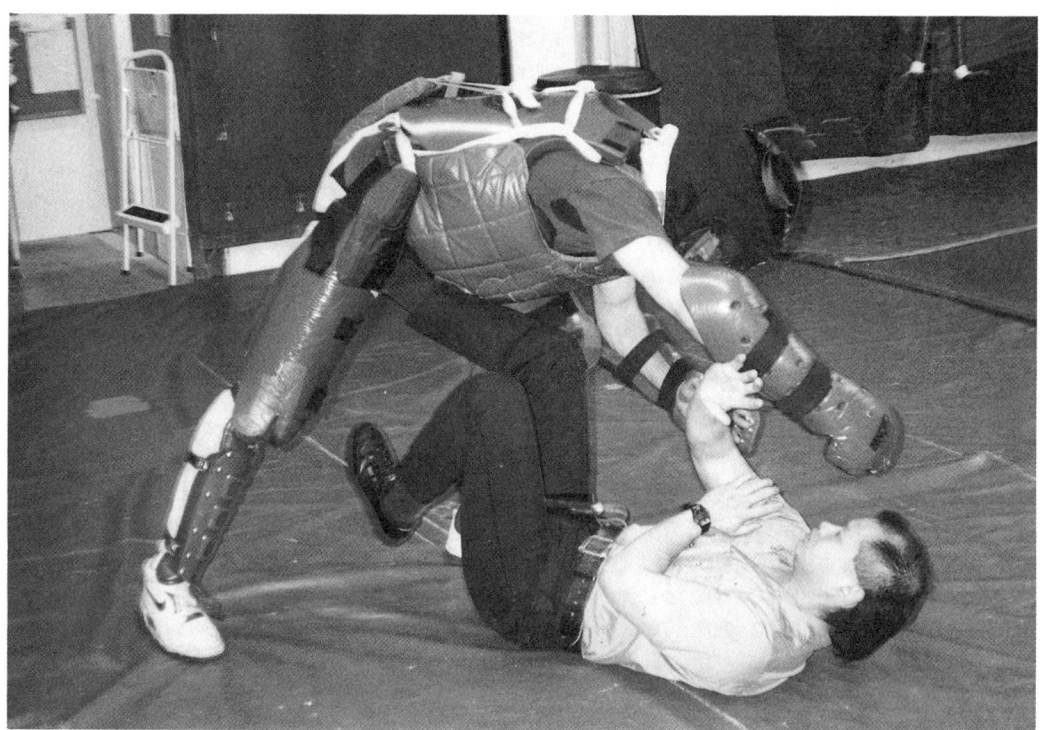

The officer blocks punches, protects the firearm, and redirects the attack.

- The officers are in the Groundfighting position. The instructor holds a pad and moves around the officers at different

Tactical Groundfighting

angles. The officers should practice kicking the pad from all directions.

🔹 The officers should practice throwing the instructor from various angles while in the Groundfighting position. A trip throw which is simple to do can break an assailant's leg. A trip throw requires the creation of a fulcrum and the addition of momentum to make it work. Officers can make up their own trip throws by using different parts of their body.

Training aids help officers practice baton techniques at full power and at various angles of attack.

Confrontational simulations are an excellent learning experience for officers. By videotaping each round, the instructor can review the tape and point out mistakes as well as the things the officers did well.

Instructors protect themselves from injury by wearing full protective equipment. If at any time during the confrontations a piece of equipment is lost or comes loose the monitoring instructors will call a break.

🔹 In the first round, the officers are in the Groundfighting position. During this exercise padded instructors try to get the officers' firearms. The officers must protect their firearm and deliver vital blows to the assailant before the attack will end.

- In the second round, the same exercise occurs, except distractions, such as loud radios, sirens, flashing lights, and people screaming will happen simultaneously.

- In the last round, the officers will defend themselves against multiple assailants. This exercise will not end until the officers successfully deliver vital blows to each of the assailants.

The experience of the confrontational simulations gives officers' confidence in their ability to survive which is crucial in life and death confrontations. A positive mind-set and the will to survive carry officers through attacks even when they are seriously injured. They have learned to complete their goals during training, to continue fighting even when they make a mistake, and to adjust to the environment.

The fear of being down on the ground is a very real one. However, through realistic training, officers learn that they can function through the fear, focus on their goals of effecting the assailant's vision, wind, and limbs and defend themselves from serious harm.

This survival attitude combined with good defensive instincts and offensive targets can keep the officers alive. Always remember, "Your survival begins and ends with you."

Chapter 35

Practicing for the Street

by Guy A. Rossi

The midnight tour has just begun. As you load your briefcase into your portable office, you hear the alert tone on the car radio. "All cars and stations prepare to copy felony wanted subject. Wanted for the attempted murder of a Jefferson County Sheriff's Deputy is one Karl Schmidt. Schmidt is a white male, six-foot-two, two hundred pounds. He has neatly trimmed blond hair, blue eyes, and was last seen wearing a blue denim jacket with German Army SS Gestapo collar brass on it and blue jeans. Schmidt was stopped by a Jefferson County Deputy for a traffic violation and was able to gain control of the deputy's sidearm and shoot him. The weapon was recovered at the scene. The deputy is currently undergoing surgery. Schmidt fled in a gray Ford Taurus last seen southbound on Route 15."

Since Jefferson County is two counties to the West, you decide to grab that second cup of coffee before setting up radar on the interstate. Your radio sparks back to life as an officer in an adjoining beat car indicates that he is following a gray Ford Taurus. A chase ensues and the car is stopped. You are the second officer on the scene of this high risk stop. The subject fails to follow the contact officer's verbal commands, exits his car, and runs toward an abandoned warehouse. The coffee and doughnut you consumed fifteen minutes earlier feel like lead at the base of your throat as you pursue him on foot. He peers over his shoulder and in that moment you are certain it is Schmidt. He continues to run. Cursing the department's restrictive shooting policy under your breath, you follow. He stops, turns, and instantly you react to your firearms' training by drawing your new Glock .40 caliber pistol.

"Police, don't move!" you command as you scan his hands for weapons. Schmidt bends at the waist and charges you with the all the enthusiasm of an NFL defensive linebacker.

I can't shoot him you say to yourself as the scene switches to slow motion and you feebly attempt to re-holster your pistol. Your mind begins to poll its short and long term memory banks for that dusty videotape on a shelf somewhere entitled, "Defensive Tactics." It's forth and goal . . . you suddenly realize that you are alone . . . no coach to call the play.

Sound familiar? Officers who mentally prepare for encounters call my fictional scenario a crisis rehearsal; those who don't call it a police officer's nightmare.

Too few police departments throughout the country provide the training hours necessary in the areas of conflict management and defensive tactics to inspire confidence. Many departments spend less than half as much time instructing defensive tactics as they do instructing firearms' training. Learning to apply an arm lock is as much of a skill as learning how to shoot a firearm and just as important. Both skills can be learned easily after repetitive training.

Learning concepts associated with evaluating threats that may require force options are far more complex. In essence, a trainee may be able to perform a technique flawlessly, but may not have the slightest idea of when to apply it. Being able to "read" a situation requires experience. Even the best laid plans fail. Repetitive physical as well as mental practice is required to enhance performance under stress and helps to establish an experience base in evaluating factors that determine the escalation or de-escalation of force.

The old adage, "Colt made all men equal," was applicable in the Old West when the bad guys ate beef and drank whiskey for stamina. However today's criminals may use mind altering drugs that can transform the most timid into ruthless, super-powerful, violent offenders. Many such offenders will sell their souls in a heartbeat for another fix, and those who dare to stand in their way are simply "expendable."

So how do you develop the physical and mental conditioning required to respond adequately to a variety of threats? The first step is **Commitment**. Learn to accept your present assignment as a positive challenge. You can only give one hundred percent of your attention to something you truly enjoy doing. In order to succeed you **must** be willing to invest your time in order to achieve confidence in a particular skill. The will to survive must become paramount!

Law enforcement officers must be mentally and physically prepared to deal with confrontational situations.

Practicing for the Street

The second step is **Mental Focus**. Your subconscious mind races to find a file on a particular subject in your short term memory in high stress situations. The more your brain has been exercised to accept a certain stimulus the less likely the action will require lag time. If there is no file in your short term memory, the long term memory will be called upon to intervene. Hopefully, there will be an alternate plan in the long term memory. For example, while driving down a street the driver in front of you suddenly slams on the brakes. Fearing an accident your subconscious brain commands your foot to apply the brakes. The reason this reaction is automatic is that it was ingrained in your short term and long term memories by daily driving habits. In order to apply this theory to defensive tactics', firearms', and officer survival training you must commit yourself to training your mind and body to react instinctively under stress.

The third step is **Repetitive Physical Practice**. In order to maintain a skill in your long term memory you will have to have performed at least three thousand repetitions of it. You simply cannot short cut this process by mental rehearsal alone. **Physical practice must be performed on a regular basis.**

While researching the topic of visualization training during confrontational situations I studied a book entitled, *Mental Toughness Training for Sports — Achieving Athletic Excellence* by James E. Loehr, Ed.D. Since few studies have been done in the area of winning confrontations in the police field, I decided to research the next similar occupation — professional athletes. Dr. Loehr states in his book, "Visualization is not magic and does not take the place of hard, physical practice. There is no substitute for physical practice, but physical practice wins only half the battle; thinking in positive pictures wins the other half."[1] Therefore, training your mind and body to react as one synchronized unit under stress will lessen lag time and will program specific action-reaction file tapes in both your short term and long term memories.

The formula for retaining officer survival skills lies in the commitment to a regimented program of physically practicing specific psychomotor skills and visualizing reactions under stressful conditions. By practicing under simulated conditions, whether real or imaginary, muscle memory based upon stimulus response is developed. Therefore it is important to consciously avoid negative thoughts or the positive reinforcement of poor technique applications while in the simulated training environment.

Some of the more generic techniques that you can practice daily are:

> **Verbalization.** Practicing simple commands, such as, "You're under arrest! Don't resist arrest! Hands out at your sides! Drop the knife! Don't move!" force you to breathe and clearly define exactly what you want the subject to do. Such warnings are key factors in determining whether the subject will be compliant or resistive. They also serve to alert potential witnesses of the officer's sole intent . . . control.

- **Movement.** When the Adrenaline starts pumping, movement may be initially perceived as awkward. In a high stress situation the ability to move out of harm's way becomes critical. Practice side stepping movements toward cover or around stationary objects. As you walk in on a situation think, *What cover options are available to me?* Placing something between you and an aggressive subject will buy you time.

- **Deflection.** When you find yourself in an intimate range encounter (four feet or less) any aggressive act on the part of the subject must be deflected **first** prior to disengagement. In essence, action by the subject is quicker than reaction by you. For example, you are interviewing a subject on the street. You notice as you converse that the back of the subject's hand is positioned so that the fingers are bent. The subject becomes aware that you have noticed that the hand is concealing something and lunges toward you. You recognize the threat as an edged weapon, but by the time you disengage, choose the appropriate weapon, and react to it you've already been cut several times. Therefore program your mind to develop "If — then thinking." In other words, if the subject does something you will respond with an appropriate, trained response.

    Once again, whenever you are in an intimate range encounter where the subject moves to assault you, you must first deflect that movement prior to moving away from it. Remember, it is much quicker for someone to move forward than it is for you to move back. Deflect and move laterally thereby forcing the subject to take the time to change the plan of attack.

- **Weapon Retention.** Approximately fifteen percent of all law enforcement fatalities are committed with the officer's own sidearm. The ability to maintain control of your sidearm should always be your first concern. Moreover, whenever you walk into any encounter there is always at least one firearm — yours! Regardless of what weapon retention program you were instructed in, weapon retention simply means that one of your hands is used to maintain the subject's hand on your holstered sidearm while the other hand effects the release of the subject's hand.

    You can easily reinforce your holstered, weapon retention grip as you drive your patrol car one handed. Simply reach with the opposite hand and assume a Front Cross Grip or a Rear Hand Gun Grip on your sidearm. Driving is the most common example of multi-tasking that most people perform. Therefore you can program your conscious mind to do one thing (drive) and your subconscious to do another (weapon retention grip). This will also assist your mind in accepting the many additional factors that encompass any encounter.

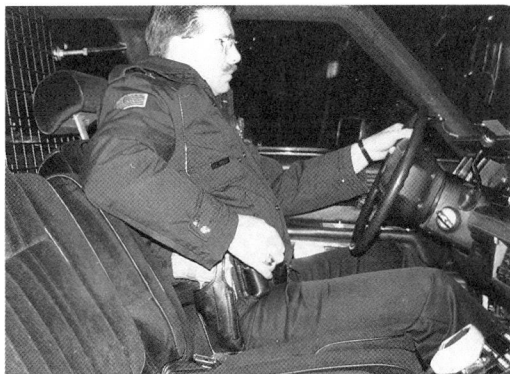
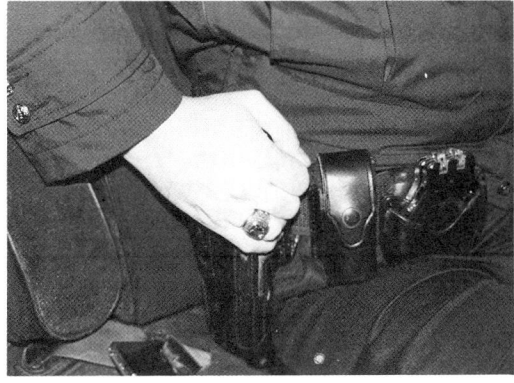

The officer reinforces weapon retention grips while driving one handed.

Accessing Weapons. Under stressful conditions one of the most difficult tasks to perform is to evaluate the need for supplemental weapons (batons, firearms, etc.) and then to simultaneously access them. Drawing these weapons under simulated confrontational simulations will ingrain in your subconscious the pre-emptors that should spark reaction. **It is extremely important that non-functional or inert weapons be used.** Condition your mind so that when necessary the appropriate defensive weapon "magically" appears in your hand as if you "wished" it there. Most law officers who have been involved in confrontational incidents will tell you that they never saw their sights. Therefore the ability to point-shoot or "index" your weapon for use is critical to neutralizing a threat.

More important, practice a consistent indexing of your weapons against a simulated opponent, such as a silhouette target. This is true of non-lethal weapons as well. For example, if you're spraying an oleo resin aerosol, practice drawing and spraying an inert unit in the face of a silhouette taped to an object at different levels and angles. You can also practice drawing your baton in an on-guard stance and side stepping the silhouette while aiming at non-lethal areas.

The officer practices with a safe, inert weapon. This will sharpen reaction under stress.

▶ **Tactic of the Week.** Keep an updated list of the techniques instructed by your department in your locker. While in the locker room prior to starting your shift, practice one technique in the air against an imaginary opponent. The last thing learned is always the first thing remembered. After a few weeks you will be amazed at your increased confidence in choosing appropriate non-lethal options in confrontational encounters.

The officer practices countermeasures (forearm strikes) prior to beginning his tour of duty.

Practicing for the Street

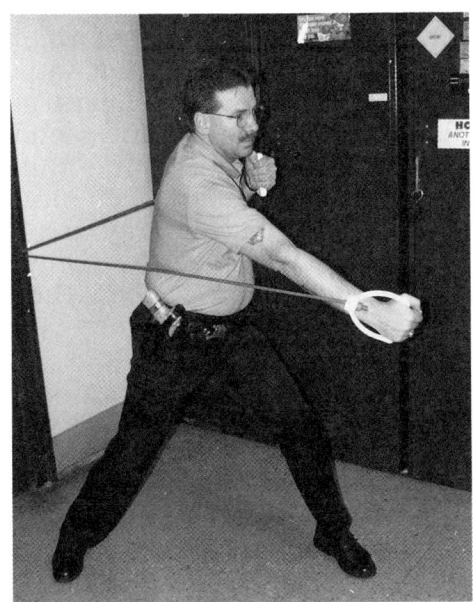

The officer warms up and builds strength for vertical jabs and punches with the aid of a Lifeline® gym.

▶ **Police Periodicals.** Stay current with police periodicals. There are many to choose from with varying points of view; for example, *Police* for broad based reporting of topics relative to law enforcement. *The Police Marksman*, a tactical and officer survival training magazine, *Law Enforcement Technology*, a broad based magazine dealing with technological advancements in products and procedures, and *Law and Order* and *Police Chief*, administrative magazines exploring current legal and procedural standards of law enforcement throughout the world. In addition, law enforcement officers should continually read published updates on legalities that effect search and seizure, and penal and constitutional law. Officer survival means winning on the street and in the courtroom. Poor judgment used today could affect you and your family for many years to come.

Communication Skills. Carefully pre-plan your radio transmissions. As you respond to calls in progress, imagine what you would transmit if on arrival the call turned into the worst case scenario. Think about informing the dispatcher of multiple subjects or setting up perimeters to avert avenues of escape. It's better to have a plan than to "wing it" under stress.

Gray Areas. In confrontational situations, officers must be alert to quick as well as slow, clandestine hand movements. It is extremely difficult to predict how much latitude to give a subject when conducting a field interview. Much of our work in this area is not either black or white, but gray. Obviously, if a law enforcement officer has probable cause to arrest, the subject would be handcuffed and secured in a squad car prior to further questioning. Remember, officers get killed most often during the first few moments of interaction with a subject. Nearly all of the situations involve the initial approach or resistance upon arrest. Therefore, you must learn to operate safely as well as legally in this gray area if you are to be effective. Ask yourself *Do I have the right to stop and frisk this person?* If the answer is *No*, then there will always be another day. If the answer is *Yes*, keep your eyes on the subject, challenge furtive movements, seek appropriate backup, and whatever you do keep your gun hand free.

Affirmations. Begin each tour with affirming to yourself, *No matter what happens today, I will survive.* There are many affirmations that can be used to elicit strength when the odds are against you, or simply to achieve certain goals. Survival means to train the **mind** and the **body** to survive. Just as you can't just think yourself out of every situation, you can't fight yourself out of every one either. In a high stress situation your emotions will want to drive your mind to remote control and with practice comes awareness, confidence, and knowledge. Your goal is to rehearse so that every thought and action made will be precise and deliberate.

No one holds a score card that shows the many times that officers, justified in using higher levels of force, took risks and used lesser force options or simply "talked the subjects out of it." As a professional police officer you will be held accountable for your actions. Therefore, when you practice do not flood your mind with too many alternatives within the same force level. Not every tactic will work for you, but keep an open mind to change and practice the tactics that remain simple and effective for you.

Special Thanks to Officer Dennis Jurasz of the North Tonawanda Police Department and Connie Dees, Editor of The Police Marksman.

Portions of this chapter have been reprinted courtesy of The Police Marksman *Magazine.*

Bibliography

[1] Loehr, James E. 1982. *Mental Toughness Training for Sports — Achieving Athletic Excellence.* Massachusetts: The Stephen Greene Press. P. 110.

About the Author

Sergeant Guy A. Rossi is with the Rochester, New York, Police Department. He is the National Public Relations Director for the prestigious American Society of Law Enforcement Trainers (ASLET) as well as a member of the International Association of Law Enforcement Firearms Instructors (IALEFI).

He is an International Instructor in the Monadnock PR-24™ and Straight Baton, and an Instructor-Trainer for the National Law Enforcement Training Center, Pressure Point Control Tactics System, and Active Countermeasures.

Sergeant Rossi is a Technical Editor for **The Police Marksman** *and writes for several law enforcement magazines. He is also currently instructing seminars throughout the country on officer survival and defensive tactics.*

Ed Sanow

Mr. Sanow is a Corporal with the Benton County, Indiana, Sheriff's Department. His instructor duties include firearms and chemical agents. He also serves as the countersniper rifleman on the special response team. Sanow has written over 300 articles on ammunition and stopping power in police and popular periodicals. He was the first of the police gun writers to make extensive use of ordinance gelatin in evaluating bullet performance.

Mr. Sanow is the coauthor with Sergeant Evan Marshall of the book, Handgun Stopping Power, The Definitive Study. This book details the results from 6800 actual gunfights and explains how to use the street results with gelatin to predict future performance.

Chapter 36

Ammo Evaluation Basics

by Ed Sanow

It is widely known that the Federal Bureau of Investigation conducts ammunition testing and evaluation. The Bureau publishes and widely distributes these ammo results and their recommendations based on these tests. However, many other federal agencies, like the U.S. Secret Service, the U.S. Border Patrol, and the U.S. Marshal's Service also conduct ammo tests. The results from these in-house tests are available only on special request. These more confidential studies are still as valid as the more publicized ones.

In all cases, the agency sets up the testing based on its own assumptions. These assumptions are based on perception at the time, and on the recent events that may have led to the testing. The tests may be set up to duplicate the average gunfight scenario, or they may be set up to duplicate any of a number of worse case scenarios. Realistically, personal bias by the test administrator and bias based on the overall goal of the agency enter into both the test design and especially the **interpretation** of the raw results.

Basically, each agency tests and evaluates ammo as **they** see fit, for **their** scenarios, in response to **their** police management or police function. Since the assumptions going into the testing are different for various agencies, the final recommendations are different even though the raw results are all identical. This should not surprise anyone.

The ammo choice made by each agency is neither right nor wrong. It is what they wanted based on their assumptions. However, **it is wrong** for a state, county, or city police department to outright adopt any of these ammo recommendations on face value. These departments must know every aspect of the other agency's testing including all assumptions, test procedures, arbitrary minimums or maximums, and the final decision methodology.

The classic example of blindly accepting some other department's work comes from a midwestern sheriff's department. The sheriff of the large department flatly stated he did not trust "jello testing" and further stated when it came to ammo selection he was not going to "reinvent the wheel." Instead he was going to "rely totally" on the FBI report. This man, responsible for the safety of numerous deputies and thousands of civilians, was totally unaware that the Bureau's testing was done exclusively in "jello."

Defense of Ammo Selection

The point to all of this is each police department must be able to defend its own ammo selection process in court. Specifically, there must be a "process." Simply buying what the state uses, or what the county uses, or what the Bureau uses is not defensible. You are not them. Your scenario is different. Your policies and procedures are different. Your rules of engagement may be different. The firearms' training in your department may be different.

Most officers do not need to be told that "differences" exist between city, county, state, and Federal police departments; neither do most lawyers need to be told this. The point is each agency must decide for itself how to evaluate ammunition. They must tailor the ammo to **their** patrol scenarios just as the Federal agencies have done for their job tasks.

More and more agencies are using ordnance gelatin to evaluate bullet performance. This is the test medium used by most major police agencies and all major ammo manufacturers. Even agencies who do not use gelatin, can obtain the raw bullet results from the manufacturers or a larger department.

A great deal of the raw results are now being published, including in the ammo maker's police catalogs. Published results include:

- Recovered bullet diameter.

- Percentage fragmentation.

- Total penetration depth.

- Size of the permanent (crush) cavity.

- Size of the temporary (stretch) cavity.

What is **not** widely known, is how to interpret these raw results. The Bureau has published its assumptions and ways to interpret them. However, other Federal agencies who have adopted ammo **very different** from the Bureau have kept a much lower profile. This is regrettable. Some Federal agencies, like the Border Patrol and Marshal's Service, have test methods and assumptions that point to police service ammo which turns out to have the **best** street record in actual gunfights.

Ammo Evaluation Basics

The following assumptions differ from those presented by the Bureau. This is the other side of the story; a way to view penetration in a different light, a position on bullet fragmentation that is different from most agency's preconceptions, and an encouragement to include the temporary cavity in the overall bullet effectiveness evaluation. These are the assumptions that result in Border Patrol-type gunfight results.

Results of Available 9 mm Ammo Tested

Agency	Selected	% of Time Effective
FBI	147 grain hollowpoint	72 %
U.S. Marshal's Service	124 grain +P+ hollowpoint	81%
U.S. Border Patrol	115 grain +P+ hollowpoint	89%

* Different assumptions produce different conclusions.

Penetration

"Adequate penetration" was the ammo hot phrase of the late 80's. And now after a half dozen years on the street we have found adequate penetration for the worst case scenarios really means excessive penetration in most scenarios.

In the early 70's, the National Institute of Justice funded a study through the Law Enforcement Assistance Administration (LEAA). This resulted in the famous or infamous Relative Incapacitation Index (RII). This was the first widely published use of ordnance gelatin. It was also the first time most people ever heard of a temporary stretch cavity.

The RII was based on frontal shots to the torso. This fact was clearly stated but not emphasized. As a result, the RII was only concerned with penetration 8.7 inches deep in 20 percent gelatin. This is still correct for the frontal shots typical of home defense, civilian concealed carry, and police backup scenarios.

On the street, the loads with an RII between 10 and 30 performed fairly well. Based on an analysis of 6800 actual and documented police shootings, the RII predicts reality with a .67 correlation coefficient. Theories with a coefficient closer to 1.00 give better predictions of reality than those closer to zero.

Some of the high RII loads however gave inconsistent results. They were either great or awful. The Southwestern Institute of Forensic Sciences (SIFS) in Dallas was the first to identify why.

The SIFS shot a bunch of gelatin with their local police loads and recorded how the loads worked. They then compared those results to their limited number of actual shootings. They found the high RII loads that gave inconsistent street performance also produced the least penetration in gelatin.

The SIFS wisely did **not** set a minimum penetration distance. Instead, they required that a load **exit** a 5 1/2 inch block of 20 percent gelatin. The load had to dump 200 ft.-lbs. of energy, minimum. It also had to exit with at least 10 percent of its impact energy but **no more than** 25 percent.

This early 80's research resulted in excellent street performance. The SIFS followed the scientific method by changing their theories and test procedures based on the realities from the street. The result was an impressive .81 correlation with reality.

On April 11, 1986 American law enforcement experienced the failure of a single bullet to penetrate deeply enough. Expert opinion was gathered by the Bureau from medical examiners, college professors, and military surgeons. This group of experts seized on the hush-hush 9 mm 147 grain subsonic load developed for the U.S. Navy SEAL Team Six. This load produced extremely deep penetration because it rarely expanded. Even vocal enthusiasts of the Olin Super Match or Type L agree that the expansion is at best .58 caliber.

The FBI developed tests that required the police bullet to penetrate a **minimum** of 12 inches of ordnance gelatin. Some experts said 10 to 12 inches. Other experts said 20 inches would be better. The bullet also had to meet that minimum in metal, wood, plaster, and especially glass. Cops ended up with bullets labelled "deep penetrators."

Little did anyone know at the time that these loads would exit 65 to 75 percent of the time on torso shots in police scenarios. Little did anyone know that the 9 mm 147 grain hollowpoint would **over penetrate** on a solid torso shot to **kill** a Los Angeles storekeeper. Or that it would **over penetrate** on an extremity shot to **kill** a University of Tucson police officer.

An excellent example of sticking to the theory of deep penetration in spite of reality is the Bureau's Firearms' Training Unit evaluation of the Cor-Bon 9 mm 115 grain +P JHP. This ammo uses a Sierra power-jacket hollowpoint driven 1325 fps. This load performs **exactly** like the Winchester 115 grain +P+ JHP used by the Illinois State Police. And **exactly** like the Federal 115 grain +P+ JHP used by the U.S. Border Patrol. And **exactly** like the Remington 115 grain +P JHP used by the Los Angeles Police.

These agencies and others have chalked up 163 police action shootings with the 1260 to 1325 fps 9 mm 115 grain hollowpoint. Of these fully-documented, officer-involved shootings, 89 percent were one shot stops. The Cor-Bon version, however, like the Winchester version,

Ammo Evaluation Basics

does not meet the Bureau's minimum penetration depth in gelatin. With a depth of just 8.95 inches, the FBI gave the Cor-Bon load a Wound Value of "zero."

From 163 shootings, this kind of ammo works 89 percent of the time with just one torso shot. The FBI test methodology represents it to work zero percent of the time. This appears to be a failure to use the scientific method which would force the test method to agree with reality. The assumption that 12 inches must be the minimum acceptable penetration distance in calibrated ordnance gelatin is the source of the concern.

From the forensic folks, we know that:

- the average thickness of the human torso is 9.4 inches,

- the major blood vessels in the torso are located within 6.0 inches from the front,

- from angled and cross torso shots, the heart and major vessels can be 7.9 inches deep, and

- bullets penetrate **deeper** when they hit clothes of any kind before hitting tissue.

All this tells us the minimum should be changed from 12 inches to 10 inches or maybe 9 inches of ten percent gelatin.

From actual street results we know the 12 inch minimum is not necessary for excellent results. LAPD .38 Special +P duty ammo; Cook County, IL, Sheriff's .44 Special second gun ammo; and Illinois State Police 9 mm +P+ duty ammo all fail to meet the 12 inch minimum. Except each still works very well on the street.

We compared the depth of penetration in gelatin to the number of one shot torso stops for the ammo in 1800 police shootings. After 7.9 inches, as the depth of penetration increased, the stopping power **decreased.** Everyone knows a hollowpoint which penetrates 12 inches of gelatin works better than hardball which penetrates 24 inches in gelatin.

The best police loads penetrate just 13.0 inches. The good performing police loads go in an average of 15.3 inches. The poor police loads pound in to 23.9 inches deep on the average.

We need to re-think the whole issue of adequate penetration with maximum effectiveness and controlled penetration in mind. Penetration in gelatin in excess of 16 inches results in the bullet exiting a torso 70 percent of the time based on 499 police-action shootings. The acceptable depth of penetration in lightly clothed gelatin should be changed from 12 inches minimum and 18 inches maximum to 10 inches minimum and 14 inches maximum.

We did not have large numbers of fully documented police shootings available when the 12 inch minimum was arbitrarily set five years ago. We do now.

Fragmentation and Expansion

Bullet fragmentation after expansion is even more widely misunderstood and misinterpreted than bullet penetration depth. Bullet fragmentation after expansion is a sign the ammo will work under the widest range of scenarios. Police ammo that violently expands and then fragments in gelatin **at least reliably expands** in the various densities of living tissue.

We compared the recovered bullet diameter in gelatin to the number of one shot torso shots for the same ammo in 1800 officer-involved shootings. In general, bullets with large recovered diameters had more stopping power than bullets with small recovered diameters. This should not surprise anyone.

The 9 mm hardball recovered at .36 inch works about 62 percent of the time. The 9 mm Nyclad hollowpoint expands to .68 caliber and has a 81 percent one shot record. Big bore .45 Auto ball which measures .45 inch when recovered works about 64 percent of the time. The .45 Auto Hydra Shock opens to .76 caliber and has a 90 percent record.

However, the problems of accurately predicting stopping power go way beyond such a simplistic bigger-is-better analysis since:

- bullets that fragment have a **better** street record than their recovered diameter would indicate;

- bullets that expand in gelatin, even to sometimes twice their caliber, don't always expand on the street. However, bullets that fragment in gelatin do nearly always expand in **tissue;**

- sometimes a bullet will spin off a fragment of lead that will hit vital tissue missed by the main core. This of course greatly increases stopping power.

Consider the recovered diameters of the 9 mm 115 grain +P+ JHP, the .357 Magnum 125 grain JHP and the .45 Auto 185 grain +P JHP. Each load expands and fragments back to just about caliber diameter. The loss of the plump mushroom on the 9 mm +P+ and .357 Magnum results in .40 to .50 inch diameter slugs. This is instead of .68 to .70 caliber of the slower loads. The .45 Auto is recovered from gelatin measuring

Ammo Evaluation Basics

just .50 to .55 caliber instead of the common .80 caliber.

Yet each of these loads has an extremely good stopping power record. In fact, the fragmenting 9 mm +P+ and .357 Magnum loads produce the **most** documented stopping power in their caliber. The fragmenting .45 Auto +P is third over all .45 Auto loads.

We compared loads that fragment to leave a smaller recovered diameter to the exact same bullet that goes slower but retains a plump mushroom. According to 458 officer-involved shootings, the loads that fragment when tested in gelatin actually have a 11 percent better street record than loads that do not fragment. That increase in stopping power is extremely significant if for no other reason than it is an **increase** and not a decrease as some would think.

The real shock comes when examining bullets recovered at autopsy. Bullets that normally expand to twice their caliber in gelatin sometimes do not expand at all in tissue. The CCI .45 Auto 200 grain JHP "flying ash can" is an example. The 200 grain Speer hollowpoint expands to between .78 and .90 inch in ten percent gelatin. **No** other handgun load expands to these kinds of diameters, period. LAPD SWAT was the first major agency to make wide use of this load. In spite of enormous recovered diameters in gelatin, this load would sometimes fail to expand at all when used by SWAT officers. The perps still went down due to surgical shot placement but the bullet did not expand.

Now, think about bullets like the 9 mm 147 grain JHP that barely expand to .58 caliber in gelatin. If bullets that easily expand in gelatin frequently do not expand in tissue, the hard to expand bullets will obviously never expand in tissue.

Ten percent gelatin was designed and developed to duplicate the amount of penetration, expansion, and fragmentation in living muscle. Depending on the impact velocity and the design of the bullet, it does just that. However, people are obviously not all muscle. An upper torso shot involves an inch or two of skin, muscle, and fat and then air-filled lungs the rest of the way. It takes an extremely fragment prone bullet to even expand in this combination of tissue.

Heavy and winter clothes enter into the problem also. Two very different .40 S&W loads were tested in bare gelatin and then in heavily clothed gelatin. Both were high speed, lightweight hollowpoints. The 155 grain was specifically designed by the manufacturer to suppress expansion and to absolutely avoid fragmentation. The 150 grain was a conventional JHP.

The conventional JHP hit the bare gelatin, expanded and fragmented for a recovered diameter of .55 inch. The permanent and temporary wound cavities gave an estimated stopping power of 83 percent. This is based on formulas from the book, *Handgun Stopping Power, The Definitive Study*. The deep penetrator 155 grain bullet expanded to .68 inch and gave an 87 percent reading. The better load in this first scenario was the 155 grain hollowpoint deep penetrator with a larger recovered diameter.

Heavy clothes turned the tables on the deep penetrator load. This time the 155 grain JHP only expanded to .51 inch for a 71 percent rating. The 150 grain JHP load that previously fragmented in gelatin was now recovered at .65 inch after clothes and gelatin. Its stopping power rating remained almost unchanged at 82 percent. **A bullet that expands and fragments in gelatin will at least expand under adverse scenarios.**

This logic holds true even for the 9 mm 147 grain hollowpoints which are the worst bullets of our time. One of the 147 grain bullets has been criticized for fragmenting in gelatin. In 57 shootings it has a stopping power record of 72 percent one shot torso shots. Another 147 grain load never fragments in gelatin. Based on 106 shootings, its record is 69 percent. Fragmentation in gelatin is a good thing.

Fragmentation inside the torso is **also** a good thing. Occasionally a hollowpoint will spin off a 5 to 10 grain piece of lead that will exit the main bullet path. This is as opposed to leaving pieces of lead harmlessly in the wake of the bullet. Secondary missiles like that can travel through 4 to 6 inches of tissue by themselves.

These fragments can do two things. First, they can put holes in vital tissue that was missed by the bullet. Some experts make a big deal out of one shape of bullet pushing a major vessel aside while another bullet puts a cut in it. And that is a big deal. But it is even a bigger deal if the bullet core puts a hole in one vessel while one of its frags puts a hole in another. Fragmentation from handgun ammo that causes secondary injury **has** been documented by medical examiners.

Second, fragments can put holes in tissues that sets them up for damage from the temporary stretch cavity that instantly follows. The frags perforate and the stretch tears. This can in fact dislodge sections of tissue. This too has been documented. It is rare for hollowpoints to cause this kind of damage but extremely common for exotic frangible bullets that totally fragment to cause this wounding.

As more police departments follow the FBI lead and do their own testing in gelatin, we need to change our thinking about what fragmentation and recovered bullet diameters really mean.

- Bullets that barely expand in gelatin will **not** expand on the street.

- Bullets that easily expand in gelatin to large recovered diameters will **probably** expand a little on the street.

- Bullets that violently expand and then fragment **will** at least expand on the street.

Bullet fragmentation is a sign that the bullet will be its most effective even under the worst scenarios.

Stretch and Crush Cavities

The most controversial aspect of evaluating bullet performance in gelatin involves the stretch cavity left in the wake of the passing bullet. For the record, the size and shape of the temporary stretch cavity formed in ordnance gelatin gives us valid and meaningful information about stopping power. We do not know exactly why handgun bullets with larger stretch cavities work better than bullets with smaller stretch cavities, all else equal. We do not know the exact effect the stretch or stress cavity has on the central nervous system. The medical community is not in total agreement on the incapacitation mechanism known as neural shock.

We **do** know, however, that bullets with large stretch cavities put people out of police gunfights faster than bullets with small stretch cavities. And that is a fact based on over 6900 actual police action shootings. Some of those were caught on live video so we can see in real time exactly how and why some people fall to gunfire.

What is the temporary stretch cavity? As the bullet enters a fluid-filled object like tissue, it violently pushes the tissue it hits out of its way. Once struck and propelled outward, the inertia of that tissue keeps it stretching to a larger diameter away from the bullet's path.

A .65 inch diameter expanded bullet will actually only touch or crush, for example, a .65 inch diameter path of tissues. However, that bullet will force elastic tissue to stretch many times that diameter depending on the density and elasticity of the tissue. Also depending on the tissue and the energy exerted on it by the bullet the tissue can stretch to the point where it will tear open and be physically damaged.

The volume of trauma exerted on tissue in the wake of a passing bullet is called the temporary cavity. This cavity stretches outward and collapses, then outward again, and collapses again for a number of cycles in under a second. This violent disruption or blunt trauma to vital organs has some effect on the brain and consciousness even if the vital organs are not actually damaged.

People fall to gunfire when they have lost enough blood to deprive the brain of oxygen, when support bones have been struck, and when the central nervous system has been hit. Some people fall to gunfire as an acquired psychological response. However, some people fall to gunfire when none of the above happens. When highly motivated people fall to the ground in under two seconds with their vascular, skeletal, and nervous systems intact, the reason for collapse is the effect of the temporary stretch cavity.

Live video footage shows the classic, knee-buckle collapse that points to the brain shutting down all the systems. The person may or may not lose consciousness. But they are out of the gunfight for the time being, regardless. Police officers who have been hit, and have collapsed but remain conscious then later recall they just could not get their hands and legs to respond, yet their extremities were not injured. We may not fully understand it but some handgun loads cause a large temporary cavity that can instantly incapacitate.

We compared the size of the temporary stretch cavity in gelatin to the number of one shot torso shots for the same ammo used in 1800 police-action shootings. This included hollowpoints, softpoints, and hardball ammo from the 900 fps .380 Auto and .38 Special to the 1400 fps .357 Magnum and back to the 700 fps .44 Special and 900 fps .45 Auto. The result was bullets that produced larger stretch cavities, produced more stopping power. This was true for **all** velocity ranges, **all** calibers, and **all** bullet designs. Remember, this was for handgun ammo only, and not rifle loads.

The size of the **crush** cavity is a good indication of stopping power but only below 1300 fps in handgun ammo. However, the size of the **stretch** cavity is an accurate prediction of stopping power at all handgun velocities from 700 fps to 1450 fps.

The size of the stretch cavity at all velocity levels has a .80 correlation with actual street results. The size of the crush cavity at all velocity levels has a .58 correlation with actual street results. The crush cavity jumps to a .87 correlation when the ammo has a velocity less than 1300 fps.

This means we should consider **both** the crush cavity and the stretch cavity when we test ammo performance. It is statistically wrong according to street results to ignore the volume of the stretch cavity. It is also wrong to depend entirely on the stretch cavity to predict stopping power. Street results tell us we should equally consider **both** types of wounding.

The stretch cavity in gelatin shows us a totally unique aspect of wounding. In addition to the calculated volume, it is extremely helpful to know:

- the maximum diameter of the stretch,

- how deep that maximum occurred, and

- over what range most of the stretch occurred.

By sectioning the gelatin block along the bullet path we can see this so-called wound profile.

The profile that is circular, or basketball-shaped, indicates a rapid energy dump. Ammo with this kind of wound profile is **not** suitable for police or civilian use according to thousands of actual shootings. This kind of ammo carries with it out the back of the torso energy that should have been transferred to vital organs. Examples of this are the lead semiwadcutter, roundnose lead, full metal jacket ammo, and some heavy hollowpoints.

Following the scientific method, the best theory of stopping power is the one that accounts for **all** the available data and has the least number

Ammo Evaluation Basics

of exceptions. The best way to evaluate bullet performance is to fully and realistically consider total penetration, recovered diameter and bullet fragmentation, the size of the crush cavity, and the size, shape, and volume of the stretch cavity. Officer survival is too important to ignore any aspect of wounding.

Arthur N. Sapp

Lieutenant Sapp has been a member of the law enforcement community since 1972. After working with the El Paso County District Attorney's Office as an investigator and researcher, he became a clerk with the FBI, General Investigation Division, in Washington, DC. He was then accepted on the Colorado Springs Police Department where he now serves as lieutenant.

Since becoming a member of the force on April 1, 1975, Lt. Sapp has served in various assignments. These assignments have included the Special Anti-Crime Squad, Tactical Enforcement Unit, Metropolitan Specialized Criminal Apprehension Team, Police Training Academy Instructor, and K-9 handler assigned to narcotics.

Lt. Sapp holds a B.A. in Criminal Justice and has written two training manuals and one training video that are currently on the market. As an international police trainer he has traveled and instructed various police, government, and civilian development and rape prevention techniques. He was selected to be profiled in the book, Tribute — A Day On The Beat With America's Finest. He was also the recipient of the Albert J. Grazioli Award for outstanding contribution to criminal justice training and education, and the 1992 Outstanding Citizens Award.

Chapter 37

Tactical Conditioning for Law Enforcement: The Triad of Strength

by Arthur N. Sapp

The triad of strength represents the never ending cycle of spiritual, physical, and mental conditioning that you must strive for if you are to become a survivor. Some people survive by luck while others survive by design. There are no guarantees in life and that is why even the most prepared individual can lose a confrontation. Sometimes the loss is emotional, sometimes it's physical, and sometimes it's terminal. The only shame in losing comes when you don't know how to win! The failure to increase knowledge, develop skills, and enhance ability has been the downfall of many law enforcement professionals. This failure can be summed up in one word: complacency.

Sometimes it takes a conscious effort to get rid of complacency, but more often than not, it is pure unadulterated fear that drives us to change. If you think that's a lie just ask the officer who suffered a massive heart attack, only to be given a second chance after receiving major surgery. Or the officer who only by the grace of God and the arrival of backup survived a life and death physical encounter with someone 20 years his junior and twice his strength. Those who do change are more than willing to describe for you the preparations they're doing now in order to more effectively survive or stave off their next encounter. So what does being fit mean?

Fitness is the ability to perform at your maximum level when called upon to do so. The ability to assimilate information, process it, and act upon it requires the mental processes be void of any "fatty deposits." You must be able to instantly turn that processed information into a physical response. The inability to react effectively, swiftly, forcefully, and efficiently to a given stimulus can have disastrous results on the street. You must never forget that before you can effectively survive on the street you must train for survival and you must be fit to train.

The triad of strength is within each of us but only you can unleash it. The triad includes fitness, training, and survival. An overview of fitness and training concepts will be addressed in this chapter. Like so many things in life physical conditioning doesn't come easily. In the beginning you'll find it easy to talk yourself out of working out, especially that first morning when you wake up and see that it's a cold, rainy, miserable day outside while your bed feels warm, comfortable, and oooooooh so good. When this happens don't let yourself fall victim to the six most famous words ever uttered by man or woman, "I will start working out tomorrow." Motivation is the key here; do what has to be done and take that first step.

Developing a Program

A fitness program doesn't have to be complicated, time consuming, or expensive. There are many fine police or fitness trainers, instructors, and coaches that will help you in designing an excellent fitness program to meet your needs. However, one of the first things you need to do is assess your own needs by asking yourself five basic questions and listing your answers. Why do you need to write them down? Because writing it down makes it real, makes it concrete and not just something you plan to do "really soon."

- **What do you want to accomplish?** Any program you come up with should have a goal in mind. Once you have agreed to the condition (with yourself), lock your sights on the objective and don't let anyone stand in your way. Remember to set realistic goals and have various levels of success that can be realized throughout your training. Always keep in mind that it's not about competing with others and trying to live up to their expectations; it's about competing with yourself and living up to your own expectations. If you are honest with yourself, you know what limitations you might have to overcome.

- **What are your physical requirements?** Take a look at what you do or are required to do on the job. Most law enforcement jobs will involve some form of running, jumping, climbing, pushing, squatting, carrying, wrestling, boxing, shooting, or handcuffing ability.

- **What is your time availability?** Decide on what time of day and how many days a week you want to train. Some officer's schedules are very hectic and may require several short training sessions rather than one long one. Your body will adapt to the schedule you set for it but it is best to try and maintain consistent training times. Look at your schedule and see whether morning, noon, or evening will work best for you.

Tactical Conditioning for Law Enforcement

- **What are your physical limitations?** If you're new to this game it never hurts to get an assessment or physical exam. Discuss your plans and limitations with a knowledgeable health care professional. If you suffer from physical restrictions, don't let that become a crutch. Learn to improvise by taking a more imaginative path toward your ultimate goal.

- **What training do you need?** Specificity of training is going to be one of the most important parts of developing any program for yourself. Look at your physical requirements and design a program to meet those needs. The "On the Job Training" part of this chapter will go into more detail.

On the Job Training

Most officers, along with some of the more successful criminals take great pride in keeping themselves in shape. This is accomplished with a training regimen designed to keep their bodies and minds physically and mentally strong. Both groups know what is at stake if they cannot perform at peak efficiency when it's time to "go to work." And training doesn't always have to occur in a gym.

Television Training

If you don't have time and you are sitting down relaxing and watching television, that's O.K. Sit there and relax until the commercial comes on. Commercials can range in length from 15 to 30 seconds on average. So before the commercial comes on decide what exercise you are going to do and whether you will do the total repetitions every single commercial or every commercial break. Examples of exercises that can be accomplished during the break include, but by no means are limited to:

- **Pushups** — regular, fist, finger, narrow, wide, incline, decline, and hand stand.

- **Sit-ups** — regular or crunch.

- **Jumping jacks** — regular or 4 count.

- **Leg lifts** — 6" to 8" off the floor and hold, flutter, crisscross, vertical rise to 90 degrees and lower back down to 6" from the ground, or tuck knees to chest and extend back out.

▭ **Side-to-side bends.**

▭ **Step-up and downs** — onto a step stool, low platform, or chair.

During an average thirty-minute, television show there will be between seven and eight commercials or two to three commercial breaks. If you decide you are going to do 10 pushups every single commercial, you can accomplish approximately 70 to 80 pushups. If you decide to do 25 each commercial break you can accomplish approximately 50 to 75. When regular programming resumes, you relax until the next set of commercials. You decide how many repetitions you want to do based on your fitness level. Just think how fit you could be if you were watching a miniseries. The possibilities are limitless.

Officer exercises during commercial breaks and relaxes when the television program resumes.

Work Related Training

The next time you are working your district or beat, look around and you will be surprised at the number of training opportunities just waiting for you. First, think about what exercises you want to do and how

Tactical Conditioning for Law Enforcement

these exercises might relate to work requirements. As an example, what two exercises do you accomplish when you climb up onto a roof? You do a pull up and a dip. Here are three examples of specificity of training:

Specificity of Training

Work Related Task	Part Exercised	Environment
1. Squatting down behind cover.	Thighs (lower body).	Free standing or one leg squats using door knob, fence, or dumpster for balance. Walking stairs instead of taking the elevator.
2. Pulling yourself up onto a roof, into an attic, or over a fence.	Arms, lats, and grip (upper body).	Pull ups using an attached roof, ladder, or fire escape. Use the bottom rung only or climb up the first four (as long as you're there the roof might just as well be checked).
3. Pushing a subject away from you.	Pectorals and triceps (upper body).	Standing pushups using an entrance way, wall, or fence.

The officer exercises by doing pull ups on an attached roof ladder.

The officer practices standing pushups using an available fence.

Some cities have fitness courses set up for runners or walkers; take advantage of these. Also, don't forget that parks and playgrounds have a lot to offer; e.g., monkey bars, balance beams, jungle gyms, and chin-up bars.

The officer takes advantage of a jungle gym and balance beam at a local playground to exercise.

You don't have to do 20 or 30 repetitions of your selected exercise; take "smaller bites." Think in terms of your repetitions being cumulative throughout the day, rather than needing to accomplish them all at one time (this also keeps your uniform from getting really sweaty). Pick an exercise and repeat it throughout your shift 2 or 3 times, more if possible, and you will be surprised at the results at the end of the month.

When you think about it, officers will be using a "weight" while doing some of these exercises; their body weight. The weight will range from minimum (door pushups) to medium (squats) to maximum (pull-ups). Don't forget one important point. The average officer weighs 15 to 20 pounds heavier once in full uniform when you take into consideration the weight of the vest, gun, ammunition, leather, shoes, and if you're wearing a coat or not.

Sedentary Training

Don't let working in an office or attending a seminar stop you from exercising. Even some exercise is better than none. Break up the day, get the blood "moving" again by doing quickie exercises throughout the day. Plan on doing some type of exercise when the class is given a break when you attend a seminar.

Example: If the facility has a chin-up bar available, then at the beginning of each break you do 10 pull-ups. Additionally, you add 10 pull-ups before and after lunch, and at the end of the day. When class is over you will have accomplished 100 pull-ups based on a 0800-1700 training day with hourly breaks. If it is a week long seminar you can achieve 500 by week's end. You pick the number: 5, 10, 15, or 20, and the exercise: pull-ups, pushups, sit-ups, or side-to-side bends.

If you're in an office, use a chair. For example, sit on the edge, grasp the seat bottom for support, and lean back. Then do straight leg lifts, knee to chest crunches, flutters, or use the chair to step-up and down on. Caution! Make sure the chair doesn't have wheels, as this could prove to be harmful to you but entertaining to your "friends." Your day can be broken up on the hour, as described above, or whatever schedule you choose. The point being, you will be getting some exercise, will have plenty of rest between sets, and don't need special clothing or equipment. All you need to have is desire.

If you face restrictions on time, equipment, and physical limitations, yet have a longing to be or stay fit, then you must be willing to adapt to the situation. Improvise by using available resources, and overcome the physical and mental obstacles that often prevent you from obtaining your goals in life. Set realistic goals that can be accomplished; don't set yourself up to fail!

Ultimately, proper fitness and training will lead to an enhanced survival attitude, because you have overcome many obstacles to get to where you are today. You must always train and be prepared for that inevitable day when you, as a guardian, will be called upon to defend those who believe in, trust, and need you.

Anthony J. Scotti

Mr. Scotti is the President of the Scotti School of Defensive Driving. He holds a B.S. in Engineering from Northeastern University. A nationally recognized authority on both safe driving and terrorism, he has recently written two books for Prentice Hall Publishing, Emergency Driving for Police Officers and Executive Safety and International Terrorism.

Since 1974, Mr. Scotti has trained governments, corporations, law enforcement agencies, and military organizations in defensive and offensive driving. He has been the subject of numerous interviews in the national media, and has been a speaker at terrorism conferences around the world. He has also been a guest speaker for many organizations including the American Management Association, the International Chiefs of Police, and the American Society of Industrial Security.

Mr. Scotti has published articles in Security Management Magazine, Assets Protection, Security Industry Product News, TVI Journal, and UNISAF Publications Ltd., and his training programs have been taught to more than 80% of the top 100 of the Fortune 500.

Chapter 38

The Technicalities of Speed

by Anthony J. Scotti

Speed

One of the major problems police officers face is when, for whatever reason, they have to drive fast. The problem starts with the definition of fast; fast depends on the environment and the department's policy. This chapter will discuss the technical aspects of driving fast and the problems it can create. From a technical standpoint the problem with speed is the device used to measure speed — the speedometer. It is not the accuracy of the speedometer that creates the problem, it is how speed is measured. Speedometers measure speed in terms of miles per hour (mph). However, in the event of an emergency the driver will not have an hour to make decisions. Decisions must be made in seconds. The driver does not have a mile to maneuver the vehicle. There is only a couple of feet between success and failure.

Table 1: Conversion from Miles Per Hour to Feet Per Second.

Speed	Distance
20 mph	29.4 ft./secs.
30 mph	44.1 ft./secs.
40 mph	58.8 ft./secs.
50 mph	78.5 ft./secs.
60 mph	88.2 ft./secs.
70 mph	102.9 ft./secs.

A new frame of reference needs to be established when discussing and measuring speed. Speed needs to be discussed in terms of feet per second (fps) not miles per hour (mph). A vehicle traveling 40 miles per hour is moving at the rate of 58.8 feet per second. To convert miles per hour to feet per second, multiply the miles per hour by 1.47. The 1.47 is derived from dividing how many feet there are in a mile (5280 feet) by 3600, which are how many seconds there are in an hour.

Case Study One

While driving in an urban environment, traffic comes to an abrupt stop 125 feet in front of the officer's car. The officer is traveling 40 mph which means the vehicle is closing in on the stopped traffic at the rate of 58.8 fps. If the brakes can be applied in three quarters of a second, the officer uses 44 feet reaching for the brake pedal (.75 x 58.8). At the point of applying the brakes, the officer is 81 feet from the stopped traffic, still doing 40 mph (58.8 fps). Can the officer stop in time? Traffic is 81 feet in front of the car. The car is moving 58.8 feet per second. The vehicle would need to stop in 1.4 seconds from 40 mph (81 feet/58.8 feet per second).

At this point, avoiding a collision would depend more on luck than skill. The problem here is speed, and paying attention to the driving task. Diverting attention away from driving for three seconds at 40 mph in an urban environment can create a disaster. At 60 mph looking away for three seconds will carry the vehicle 264 feet.

Table 2: How Far a Car Will Travel at Various Speeds.

	One Sec.	Two Secs.	Three Secs.
20 mph	29.4 ft.	58.8 ft.	88.2 ft.
30 mph	44.1 ft.	88.2 ft.	132.3 ft.
40 mph	58.8 ft.	117.6 ft.	176.4 ft.
50 mph	73.5 ft.	147.0 ft.	220.5 ft.
60 mph	88.2 ft.	176.4 ft.	264.6 ft.
70 mph	1022.9 ft.	205.8 ft.	308.7 ft.

Following Distances

Police officers must maintain a safe distance between their vehicle

The Technicalities of Speed

and the vehicle in front of them. A rear end collision reflects badly on both the officer and the department.

Case Study Two

A motorist is driving at 30 mph and a police cruiser is following the motorist at the same speed, some 60 feet behind. Both cars approach an intersection and the light changes yellow. The motorist hits the brakes. The officer in the cruiser is not paying much attention and allows a full second to pass before reacting to the situation. Once the motorist applies the brakes it will require about 55 feet to stop the 30 mph car. So now a stopped car is 115 feet in front of the cruiser (60 feet + 55 feet). If the cruiser is doing 30 mph, it is moving at the rate of 44 ft./sec. Assuming a normal reaction time of .75 seconds, and adding the fact that the officer's attention was diverted for one second, means the officer will not get a foot to the brake pedal before having traveled 77 feet.

If the front of the motorist's car is 115 feet from the cruiser's starting point, and the motorist's car is 15 feet long, then its rear end is 100 feet away from the cruiser's front end. Since it's going to take 77 feet before the officer gets a foot to the brake, the police car will be 23 feet behind the stopped car when the brakes are applied. Everyone involved is in for a whole lot of hurting.

The problem? The cruiser was following too closely, and the driver's attention was diverted for one second.

To prevent the above, use the "Two Second Rule." Pick a fixed object on the road, and when the car ahead of you drives past the object count two seconds. When the two seconds are up, you should pass the object. If you get to the fixed object before the time is up, you are following too close.

Peripheral Vision

Speed also affects the driver's visibility. The faster a car is driven, the less the driver can see. Speed has a dramatic effect on peripheral vision. An average person with good peripheral vision can see about 180 degrees from side to side when the vehicle is stationary. Traveling at 40 mph, a driver's peripheral vision is cut to 120 degrees; at 50 mph, peripheral vision is reduced to 90 degrees; at 60 mph, down to 60 degrees; and at 80 mph, peripheral vision amounts to a mere 30 degrees.

Many times officers will say, "I just didn't see the other car." Due to this loss of peripheral vision they're often correct; they really didn't see the other car. This loss of peripheral awareness explains why drivers can cruise right through intersections, narrowly missing cars they never even saw.

Case Study Three

An officer is in pursuit, traveling 50 mph as the vehicle enters an intersection. The intersection provides unlimited visibility. Traveling 50 mph converted to feet per second is roughly 75 ft./sec. Coming the other way in the intersection is another car also traveling 50 mph (75 ft./sec.). Using some simple arithmetic and some plain geometry we find that although there is unlimited visibility neither car will see the other until they are both 200 feet from the intersection.

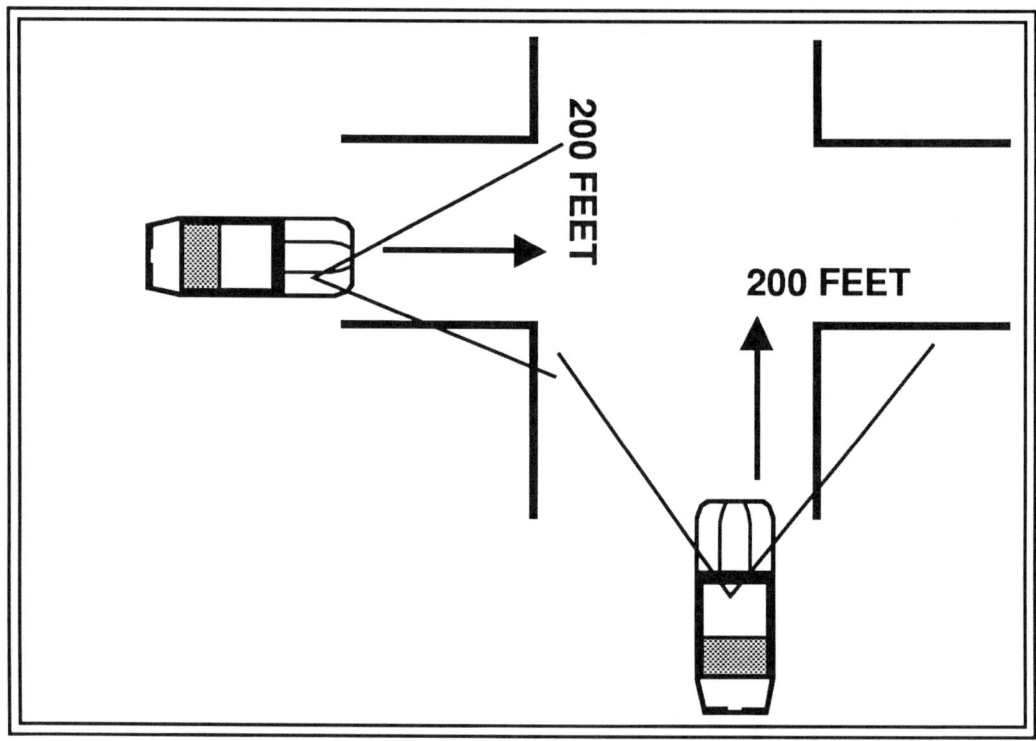

Figure 1: We have two cars driving towards the same spot on the road 200 feet away at the rate of 75 ft./sec. and they just saw each other.

What do we have? Simple arithmetic tells us that these cars have 2.7 seconds to stop (200 ft./75 ft./sec.). It will take .7 seconds for them to reach the brake pedal. When they get their foot to the brake pedal they now have approximately 150 feet to stop, traveling at the rate of 75

The Technicalities of Speed

feet per second. This is a borderline problem. Why? Add another .8 seconds for indecision on the part of both drivers and we have a delay of 1.5 seconds before brake application. They are now about 88 feet from the intersection traveling 75 feet per second. Do they have a problem? They're both in for a great deal of hurt.

To prevent an accident, the officer needs to see the accident developing. The way to spot conflicting traffic is to scan every intersection, every opening of every side street, before proceeding into it. At high speeds, this is going to mean a lot of eye movement, but at high speeds, virtually every other part of the nervous system is working at maximum speeds; why shouldn't the eyes pitch in and help?

Stopping

The higher the car's speed, the more distance required to stop. That's a given. No special braking techniques can change it. It's the law of physics. A lot of space and time can be spent writing and explaining the equation for Kinetic Energy, but to simplify the matter, if the speed is doubled, the stopping distance increases by a factor of four.

Table 3: How Long Does it Take to Stop a Car?

MPH	Dry (ft.)	Wet (ft.)	Snow (ft.)	Ice (ft.)
20	25	70	105	160
30	55	110	170	275
40	105	170	275	
50	188	250	410	
60	300	350		
70	455			

These basic principles hold true for everyone. There are no exceptions, no special cases. No matter how good the driver is it takes four times as much distance to stop a car going 60 mph compared to one that's traveling at 30 mph. The driver has no control over this. What officers need to do is to understand this.

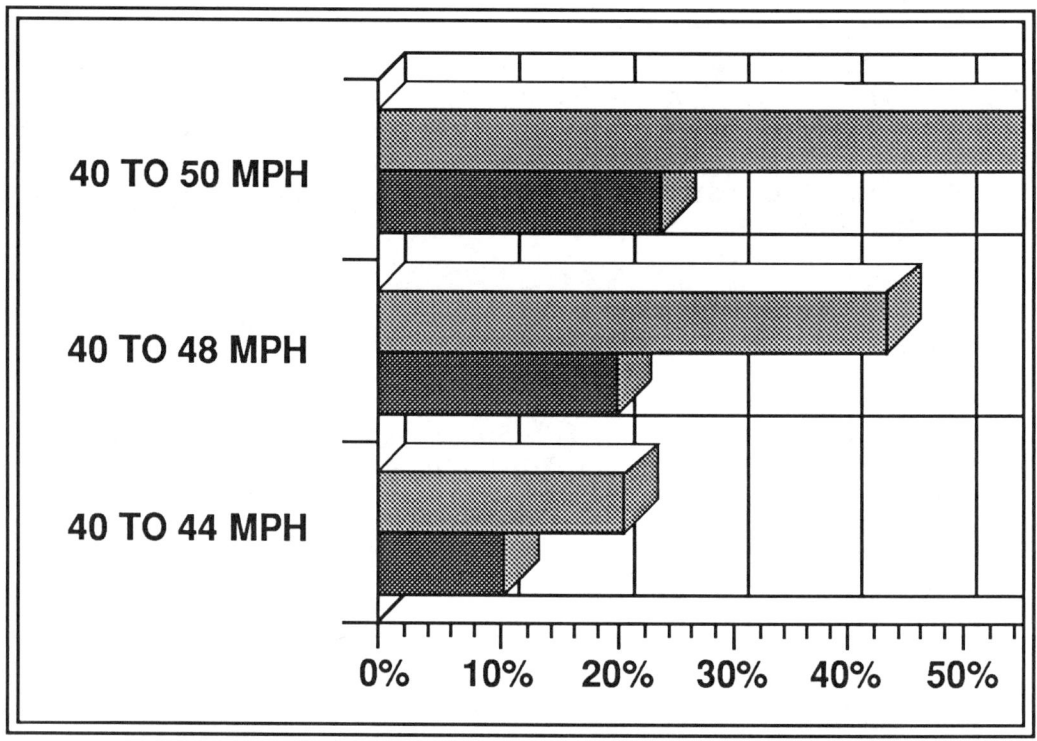

Figure 2: A graphic example of speed and stopping distance.

- If the speed is increased from 40 to 44 mph, speed has increased by 10% but stopping distance has increased by 20%.

- If the speed is increased from 40 to 48 mph, speed has increased by 20% but stopping distance has increased by 40%.

- If the speed is increased from 40 to 50 mph, speed has increased by 25% but stopping distance has increased by 50%.

It must be understood that drivers cannot arbitrarily increase their speed; it's literally deadly. A note to driver trainers: If, during training, speed is not accurately measured as the student drives into a braking exercise, the instructors are guessing at the most important skill that can be taught in a driver training program — the ability of the student to stop the car.

The Technicalities of Speed

Sirens

Most drivers don't hear the siren in time to react to it. A test conducted for the U.S. Department of Transportation investigating the effectiveness of sirens indicated the severe limitations of those devices. Under ideal traffic test conditions, the maximum distance the siren was audible was 440 feet but when all the test subject's scores were compared and compiled, the average distance came to just 125 feet.

Table 4: Warning Time When Sirens Are in Use.

SPEED	TIME AT 440 FT.	TIME AT 125 FT.
70 mph	3.25 secs.	0.9 sec.
60 mph	5.00 secs.	1.4 secs.
50 mph	6.00 secs.	1.6 secs.
40 mph	7.00 secs.	2.0 secs.

In the worst case scenario, drivers won't have much time to react to the siren. At 50 mph, perhaps six seconds is enough time to react, but two seconds certainly isn't. When on an emergency call, an officer should assume that no one can hear the siren and proceed on that assumption. The officer should also assume that if they can hear the siren they have no idea from which direction it's coming.

At speeds of above 50 mph in the worse case scenario, the officer does not have much time to react. To make matters worse, add the peripheral vision problem. An officer is coming up to an intersection at 50 mph. At that speed the officer will not see a car coming from the side until it is 200 feet from the intersection. Also, that car will not be able to hear the siren.

Driving fast has it's own set of problems. There is no question that there are situations that come up that demand an officer exceed what would be called "safe speeds." If involved in an accident at a high speed every decision made that day, from the time the officer woke up until the time of the accident, will be examined by "experts." This examination, including the definition of safe speed, will be performed three or four years after the event. Everyone will have an opinion on what the officer "should have done."

When the decision is made to drive fast by officers, they should keep in mind the following:

- ▰▶ It will take a considerably longer time to stop the car the faster it's driven. No matter how quickly the driver can react, the faster the vehicle is driven the more distance it takes to get to the brake pedal.

- ▰▶ When driving fast, the ability to see has decreased. The faster cars are driven the more officers need to move their eyes.

Mirrors

A police car is driving down the road and suddenly another car moving in the same direction as the police car drives into the police car's lane. The officer wonders why anyone would try to cut off a police car. The driver obviously did not see the police car in the mirrors, or simply did not look before turning the steering wheel. Many times the latter is blamed for the problem, but in reality most of the time the driver looked but simply did not see the police car. The mirrors were not adjusted properly. This is a common problem with most drivers. However, all drivers have one to three mirrors on their vehicle; it's the law.

The most important issue is that all vehicles should have three mirrors. There is no excuse for having cars with only two mirrors (a rear and left side mirror). Most drivers don't understand the importance of a right side mirror. Having no right side mirror assumes no one will ever pass the vehicle on the right, or that they will never have to move to the right. It is important to have all three mirrors functional. Most police cars have three mirrors as standard equipment. Also, it is important that all mirrors be adjustable from the driver's position.

How important are mirrors? Without them the only way to know what's behind or along side cars is to turn and look. No problem. It only takes a second or two to look. It may not seem like much but at 50 mph cars are traveling at the rate of 75 feet per second. If the drivers look over their shoulders for two seconds they would cover 150 feet without the knowledge of what's going on in front of them. At 65 mph, they would cover almost 200 feet. An officer cannot afford to turn and look while driving on a highway, nor in slow city driving. Attention must be focused on what's in front of the car. Consider that at 40 mph it would take average drivers 44 feet to get their foot from the gas pedal to the brake pedal.

Start with the right side mirror. Adjust it so it gives a clear view of traffic on your right (Zone 1). It must be adjusted so you can see the vehicle or part of the vehicle on the right. Therefore, as the vehicle leaves vision in Zone 2 (rear view mirror) it must appear in Zone 1, the right

The Technicalities of Speed

side mirror. As it leaves Zones 1 and 2 it must appear in your peripheral vision.

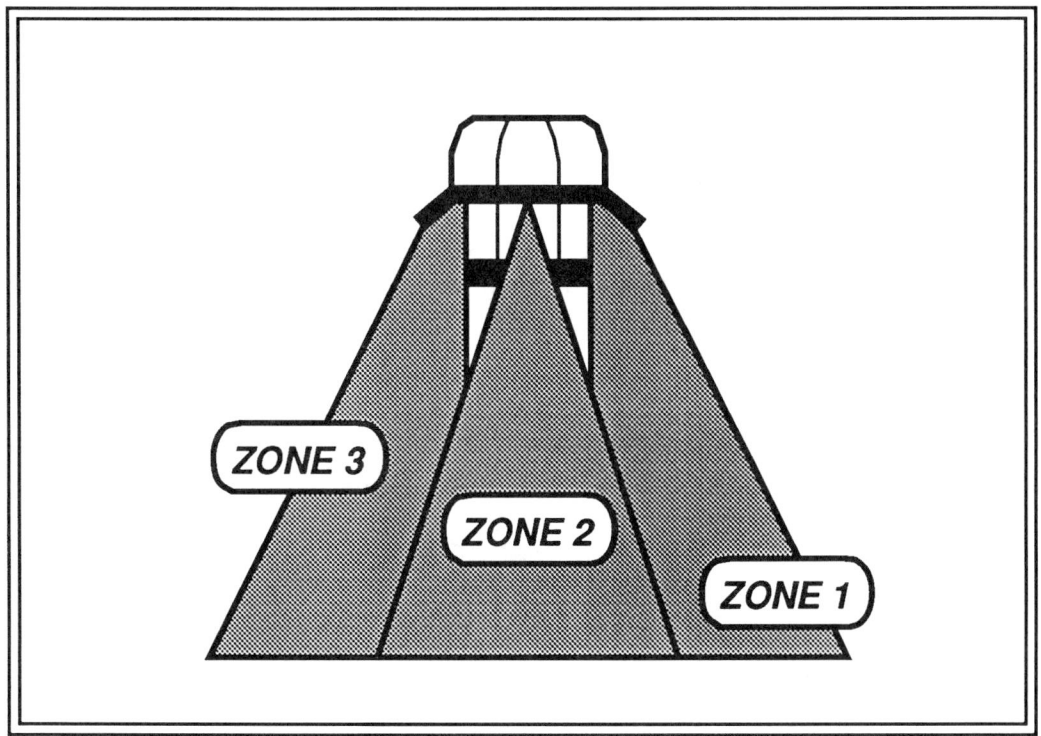

Figure 3: A look at how your mirrors should be adjusted.

Now adjust the center mirror (rear view mirror) on your vehicle (Zone 2). The center mirror will cover everything directly behind you but it also covers the blind spot on your right that your right mirror failed to pick up. It must also cover part of the left side of the vehicle where you will also have a blind spot on the left mirror. The rear view mirror must be adjusted so that as a vehicle disappears from its view it will appear in one of the side mirrors (Zone 1 or Zone 3).

Now adjust the left mirror. Adjust it so you can see a vehicle coming up on your left side and keep it in view until your peripheral vision picks it up. Why is it so important to know if a car is coming up behind you? When you have to make an evasive action, you need to know what's behind you and what may inhibit a move to either left or right. Therefore, when the vehicle leaves the rear view mirror, Zone 2, it must appear in the left side mirror, Zone 3. When it leaves the left side mirror it must appear in the driver's peripheral vision.

All drivers should be cognizant of what is in their mirrors every few seconds; traffic changes — so do your escape routes.

Well-adjusted mirrors will give you up-to-date information every few seconds. Properly adjusted mirrors could give you the emergency time you need to avoid an accident.

Night Driving

The accident rate at night is **three times higher** than it is during the day. The biggest problem with night driving is, "When it is dark out you can't see." Most drivers, however, do not slow down when driving at night. The end result is that they tend to drive **faster than they can see**.

Most of the light available for our use at night comes from our car's headlights. If the vehicle is moving 40 mph, it is traveling approximately 60 ft./sec. If the vehicle's headlights emit a 200-foot beam, the driver has a little more than 3 seconds of vision. That's not good.

Table 5: Feet of Vision with Seconds to Stop

With 100 feet of vision:

MPH	Seconds to Stop
10 mph	6.7 secs.
20 mph	3.3 secs.
30 mph	2.2 secs.
40 mph	1.2 secs.

With 200 feet of vision:

MPH	Seconds to Stop
10 mph	13.3 secs.
20 mph	5.7 secs.
30 mph	4.4 secs.
40 mph	3.3 secs.
50 mph	2.7 secs.
60 mph	2.2 secs.

Keep the headlights clean. As much as half of a headlight's total output can be absorbed by dirt on the light's surface. Keeping headlights

The Technicalities of Speed

clean is especially important in winter when they're frequently covered with road dirt and salt.

Likewise, a clean windshield is vital for driving, whether day or night. Make sure windshield washers work, that windshield wiper blades are clean and not old and worn out, and that the windshield wiper fluid container is kept filled. Keeping the inside of the windshield clean is equally important. If people in the car smoke or if you drive with someone who does, the inside of the windshield needs to be cleaned every other day.

Here are some rules to help minimize the hazards of night driving:

- Adjust your speed to the range of your headlights. When clean and working properly, high beam headlights illuminate the road for about 330 feet ahead and low beams for a much shorter distance.

- Keep your eyes moving. Don't fall for the temptation of focusing on the middle of the lighted area in front of you.

- Keep windshield and headlight lenses clean.

- Avoid steady driving at the hour of your usual bedtime. A person's alertness level decreases around the time they routinely retire for the night. If you must drive past your usual bedtime, stop every hour or so and walk around. Stretch your legs. Get some air. Wash your face with cold water.

Larry Smith

    Mr. Smith is an independent law enforcement training specialist. He served 34 years with the San Diego, California, Police Department as a lieutenant and police academy instructor. Now retired, he is a Smith & Wesson Certified Chemical Agent Instructor, a PR-24™ Baton International Instructor, and a practitioner of Aikido.

    Mr. Smith has written many articles on police training and his experience as a field commander during the demonstrations and riots of the 50's has given him an insight into the use of chemical agents for crowd control.

Chapter 39

Compliance Holds

by Larry Smith

Beyond the Need to Control

The fear that prevents some people from relinquishing control is the fear of being dominated. Some people unconsciously hold the belief that a person who dominates is the winner and that a person who is dominated is the loser. When this kind of polarization occurs, there will be conflict because no one wants to feel like a loser in an exchange with someone else. It may be helpful for us to expand our point of view beyond a win or lose mentality. We must understand that as law enforcement officers we have no choice but to control situations.

It is important to keep in mind that conflict has a positive aspect; it helps us to grow. Each conflict has the potential to be a valuable lesson in human dynamics. With each interaction . . . even unpleasant or frustrating ones . . . we have a chance to look inside ourselves and ask, *What issues did I bring into this confrontation? How did I get involved in this incident?* These questions are asked, not to blame ourselves or the subject, but to help us understand the dynamics and to work toward a resolution of the issues.

To understand we must consider all the factors beyond the act of controlling the conduct of others. We must empathize so we can get compliance with the least amount of effort. Controlling conflict begins with the mere presence of law enforcement officers and can often be resolved without the use of force. Then again, verbalizing may not lead to compliance and other alternatives have to be explored.

When to Use Compliance Holds

Law enforcement officers must learn compliance holds in order to handle situations that go beyond verbal control. Although compliance holds do not work on everyone, they provide an avenue for the escalation of force. Compliance holds are not easily learned because many officers do not have a good knowledge of the theory of how they work. If they fail to grasp the theory, they will be unable to master the holds.

Compliance holds not only require the manipulation of fingers, joints, and nerves, but the use of the whole body. Inner strength is necessary for the application of the holds and concentration also plays a key role in the effectiveness of the applications.

A factor, often not considered, is our sense of the subject's pending action. Knowing when to move before the subject moves, increases our chances of success. Did you ever notice how experienced police officers seem to have subjects under control even before they make a hostile move toward the officers? Usually, the officers have had the same experience before and are only reacting to past encounters.

Most law enforcement officers had very little if any training in physical control before being hired by their agencies. Many even after training still have difficulty placing their hands on subjects who need to be controlled or arrested. Positioning, awareness, and goals are all components of successful compliance holds.

As we progress further into the theory of compliance holds, we must understand about setting goals. Even before applying a hold, we must have something that we wish to accomplish and this goal must include good verbal skills.

Each time we get involved in an incident we have an audience. Using good verbal skills to give directions helps to insulate the officers from possible civil action when using a compliance hold. A compliance hold becomes the basis for giving directions. Once the subject complies, the pressure on the hold must be reduced. This principle is also used in training animals. Every time the animal obeys, food is the reward. Releasing the pressure of the hold is the subject's reward for compliance.

It is important that police officers never use a compliance hold as punishment. The purpose of these holds is to get the subjects to comply without the officers having to escalate to a higher level of force. Sometimes officers continue to apply a hold even though it is not working. When this happens, officers must disengage and attempt another hold or escalate to a higher level of force to get compliance.

The Application of Compliance Holds

Compliance holds may be applied to four major parts of the body. The bending or twisting of the wrist seems to be the most commonly used hold; putting pressure on the joints in their normal bending direction or against their natural bends follows as second choice. Nerve motor points are used more often since the development of organized training and standardization. Finger bending is less successful due to their flexibility and they break easily under severe pressure.

The wrist, even on well-developed weight lifters, is one of the weakest parts of the body. The best compliance hold is to move the wrist in a circular motion in the same direction it normally bends. The wrist can be bent in the opposite direction to achieve the same effect. Twisting the wrist and fingers simultaneously is a good combination to position subjects to stand on their toes.

Other joints, like elbows and knees, can be manipulated in different positions to get compliance. Defensive tactics' instructors consis-

Compliance Holds

tently teach bar-arm take downs which use pressure on the elbow to bend the arm in the opposite direction from which it normally bends.

The infra-orbital nerve, the hypoglossal nerve, and the common peroneal nerve are a few of the motor nerves that can be used to control subjects. Touch pressure and strikes are methods of disabling the motor points.

Bending the fingers in the opposite direction produces instant compliance, but there is a high risk of injury. The best way to use finger control is as a distraction technique to gain an advantage. Pressure on the fingers usually breaks a subject's grip long enough to slip into a wrist compliance hold.

Psychological Factors

The physiological make-up of a subject is a factor to consider when using compliance holds. We find that a subject who is in good health and physically fit is not always a good subject for a compliance hold. They usually have a higher tolerance for pain. The basic body structure and flexibility of a subject may also have a direct relationship on resistance to compliance holds.

Psychological factors may be the most unpredictable element in compliance holds. The mind can trigger emotional responses that can affect how a subject will react. We find that anger and hostility creates an unpredictable response to compliance holds. Mental illness, without a doubt, is where we usually see the highest resistance to any attempt to gain compliance.

The psychologically passive and aggressive are two types of personalities that are resistant to compliance holds. Caution should be used with any attempts to control these subjects and usually a higher level of force is necessary.

Subjects who are goal oriented and refuse to show pain outwardly is another group that is difficult to handle with compliance holds. One major problem is that they usually get fractures of the arms or wrists when officers apply too much pressure. The longer they resist, the more pressure the officers are required to apply.

To law enforcement officers the real problem subjects are drug and alcohol abusers, since drugs or alcohol affects their pain response. Most deaths in use of force cases can be attributed to this class of subject.

An aspect that influences compliance holds is the size of the officer and the subject. Training that results in the improper application of holds may also influence the results of compliance holds. The officer must apply pressure at the right point and in the right direction with maximum effort.

Finally, officers' attitudes toward survival may be a direct relationship toward the outcome. Officers have been known to freeze in motion when involved in a high stress situation. Others have panicked and lost control of the incident through the lack of self-confidence. Worse yet, some officers have just given up. Verbalization skill, proper technique, a survival attitude, and the ability to recognize when to escalate or de-escalate make a good combination for controlling a subject's behavior and getting compliance.

Simple Compliance Holds

The following are five simple compliance holds that can be used against subjects. They can be used to extract passive or hostile subjects from automobiles, buses, and theaters, or to remove demonstrators from buildings and sidewalks. These holds, however, are less likely to be effective if the subject is aggressive and escalation to a higher level of force may be necessary. The most difficult part of a compliance hold is getting close enough to the subject to set the hold, but never jeopardize your safety to accomplish your goal.

- **Reverse Wrist Lock:** To apply a *Reverse Wrist Lock*, start at the escort position. Place your elbow tightly in the middle of your stomach. Grab the subjects' hands with your outside hand, palm down. Bend their wrists in the same direction they normally bend with their fingers pointing to the rear as their arms are placed behind their backs. Your outside hand grabs the subjects' hands while stabilizing their elbows with your inside hand. The palm cups the back of the subjects' hands. Apply pressure to the back of the subjects' hands and using a pushing motion with your stomach, apply additional pressure to their wrists.

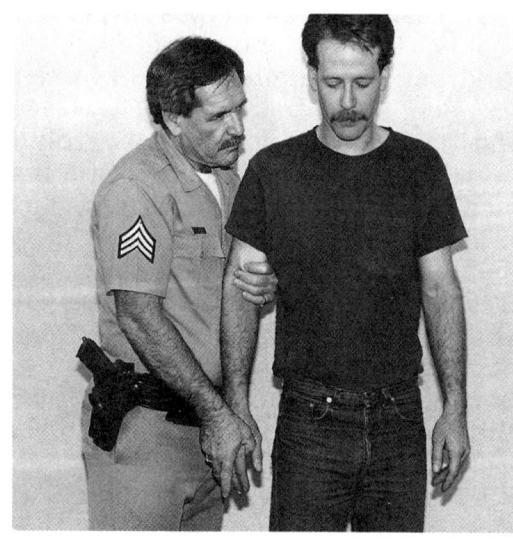

This is a simple hold to apply.

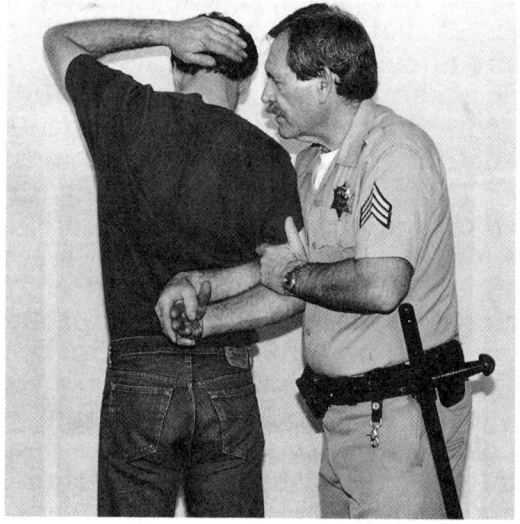

The next step is handcuffing.

- **Wrist Twist:** The *Wrist Twist* is an excellent control technique. It can be used to deliver instant pain to even the biggest subjects. Once control is maintained, the hand can

Compliance Holds

be brought behind the subjects' backs to apply handcuffs from a *Reverse Wrist Lock*. The *Wrist Twist* is an excellent hold to extract subjects from chairs or vehicles.

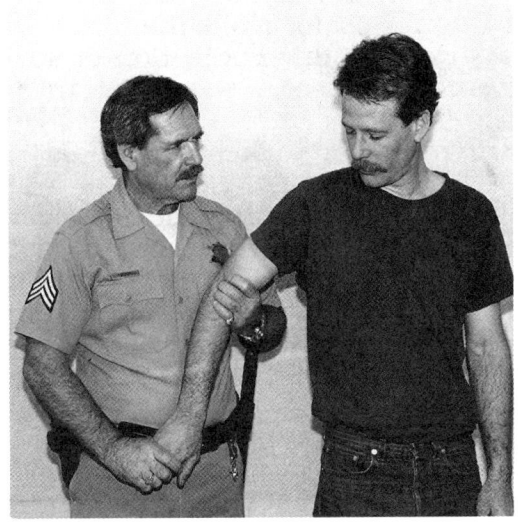

Grab the subject's fingers with your outside hand so he cannot curl his finger tips.

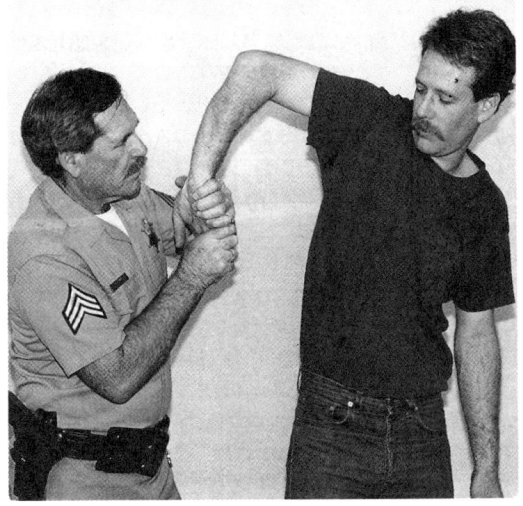

Elevate the subject's elbow to a 90° angle by using a counterclockwise twisting motion.

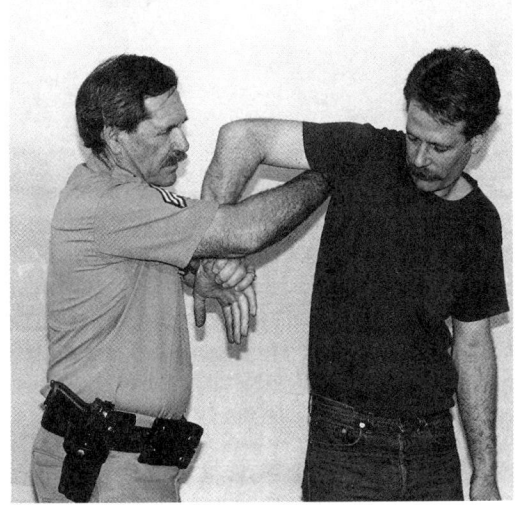

Release your outside hand from the subject's fingers and place it against his back.

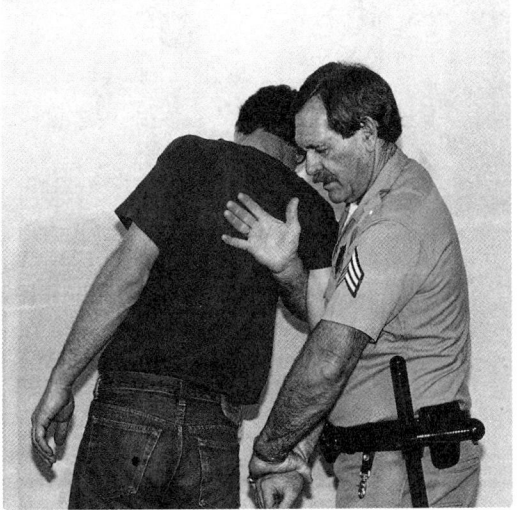

To maintain control continuously twist the subject's wrist in a counterclockwise motion.

The theory of application is an important ingredient of applying successful holds. Pressure must be applied in a lateral rotating fashion with an upward spiraling movement using your entire body, similar to a baseball swing. The positioning of subjects' elbows and wrists are at 90 degree angles. Both of your hands twist their fingers and upper parts of their hands toward their body. Your hand around their fingers must be below their finger tips to avoid them curling their fingers to relieve pressure. The first indication of success is when subjects rise onto their toes. It is important to apply pressure, then release it when compliance is reached, but still maintain constant pressure to keep the hold in place.

Once control is established, turn toward the subjects. Place your hand that held their fingers underneath their arms to keep the subjects from turning. Drop their arms to the middle of your stomach while still maintaining a twisting motion on their wrists. Next, reverse their wrists and bend them in the same direction they normally bend and place their arms behind their backs. It is time for you to change your hands and grab the back of the subjects' hands with pressure. Meanwhile your elbow must be placed in the middle of your stomach for a backup and to hold their arms ridged. From this position the handcuffs can be applied.

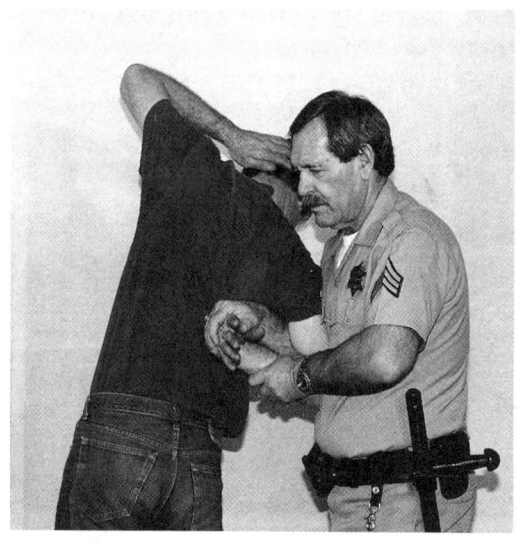

The subject's wrist is reversed and brought up behind his back into a Reverse Wrist Lock. His free hand is placed behind his head to prepare for handcuffing. The subject can now be easily moved to another location by walking him backwards while using pressure on his wrist.

The *Wrist Twist* can be applied from a variety of positions with equal ease. Understanding the theory and mechanics is the basis of being successful. Also when to move to the next level of force is just as important as learning the hold. The most important facet of compliance holds is getting subjects into a position where they can be restrained with handcuffs.

◐ **Goose Neck Come-A-Long:** The most common complaince hold is the *Goose Neck.* It is easy to learn and retain. Apply

Compliance Holds

the hold from the escort position by bending subjects' elbows and bringing the backs of their hands toward their shoulders. The wrists are bent forward in the same direction they normally bend. Apply pressure by placing your outside hand on the back of the subjects' hands. By placing their elbows in the middle of your stomach, you stop any downward motion of their arms. Applying pressure to the back of their hands and by reinforcing their elbows with your stomach, pain increases at their wrists. Your hand, close to the subjects' body, stabilizes any movement of their arms trying to escape the hold.

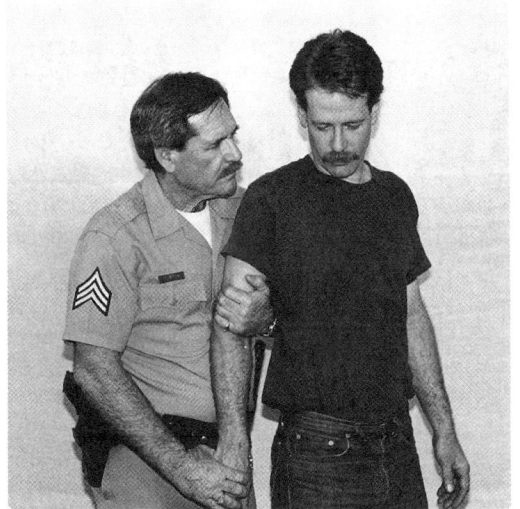

One of the most common holds.

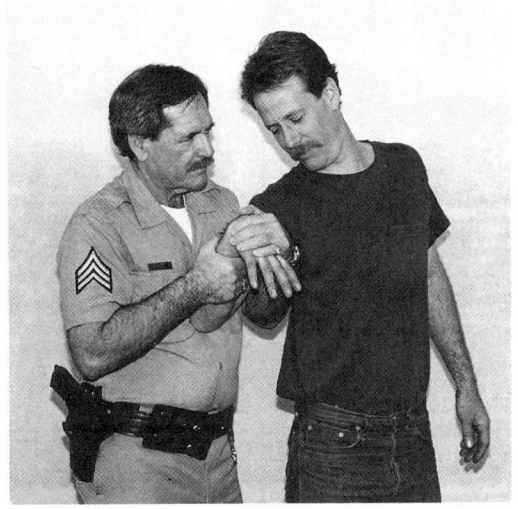

Pressure is applied to the wrist.

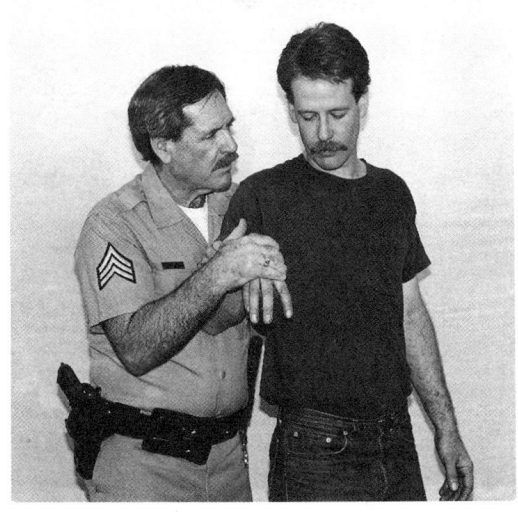

Officer switches hand positions.

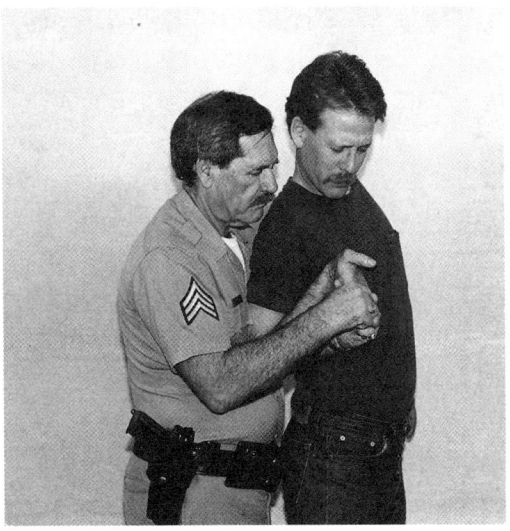

Pressure is applied to fingers.

Horn Come-A-Long Hold: The *Horn Come-A-Long Hold* is another type of compliance hold that uses the twisting and bending of the wrists. It is generally applied from the escort position. With a few modifications, it can be adapted to other positions too.

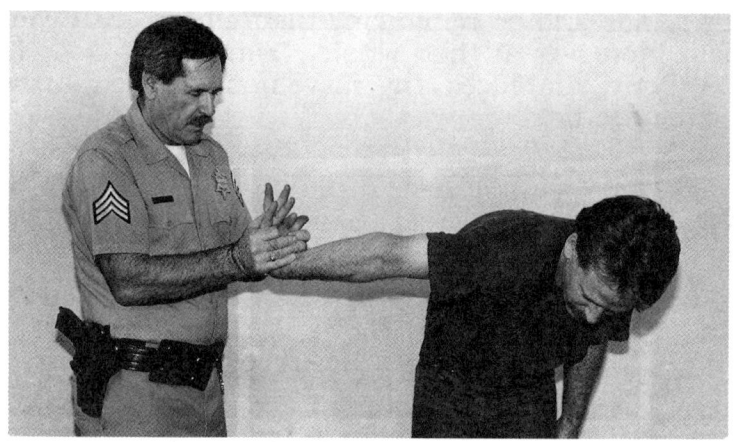

The subject's arm is brought back perpendicular to his body. His wrist is bent at a right angle using both of your hands. His arm must be kept straight to keep him in position.

Bring the arms back perpendicular from the subjects' body, making sure they keep their heads down. Apply pressure down their arms by bending their wrists to a right angle. Grab their thumbs with your inside hand and slide your outside hand just past their elbows. Pressure must be kept constant at their wrists to make it work. Rotate subjects' fingers clockwise and forward as their arms pass under their arm pits. With their elbows locked in your lower abdomen and pressure at their wrists, begin twisting their wrists to the outside to increase pain. A *Reverse Wrist Lock* can be applied from this position to finish the hold.

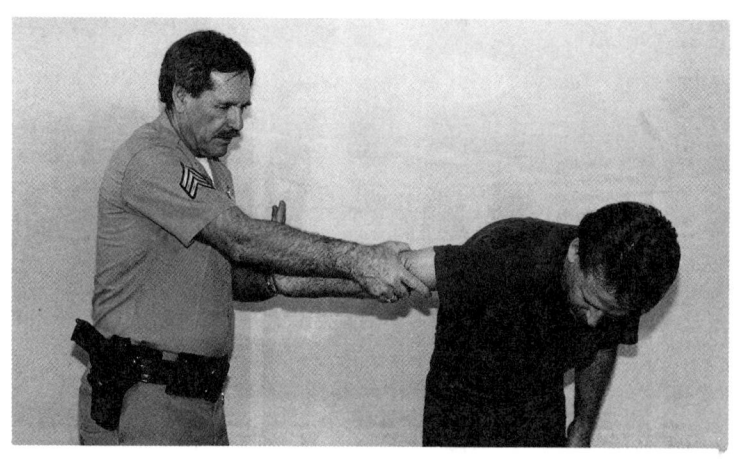

With your inside hand grab the thumb of the subject. Slide your outside hand just past his elbow and keep pressure on his wrist.

Compliance Holds

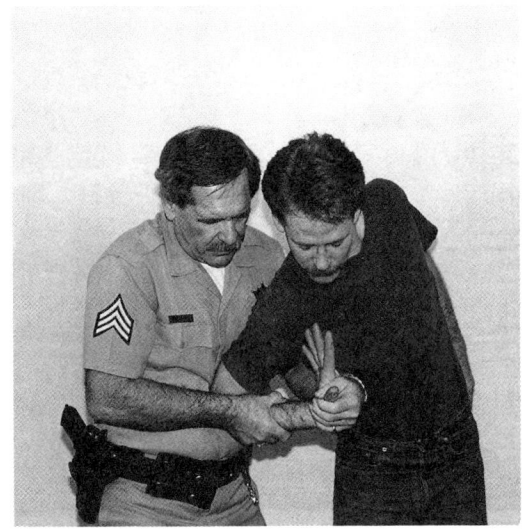

Rotate the fingers clockwise under the subject's arm pit and bring his elbow to your lower abdomen. Apply additional pressure by twisting the wrist outward in a clockwise direction.

- **"Z" Arm Control Hold**: The most painful compliance hold is the *"Z" Arm Control Hold*. Grab subjects' arms at the elbows with your inside hand. Bring their arms straight out perpendicular to their body, palms up. With your opposite hand, grab the back of the subjects' hands. As you drop their arms to their sides, keep their elbows bent at a right angle. Next, with your hand around the back of the subjects' hands, push their hands upward so their wrists are bent and their fingers extend at a right angle. Apply pressure as you turn the fingers toward the center of the subjects' body. Their elbows and wrists must be bent at right angles.

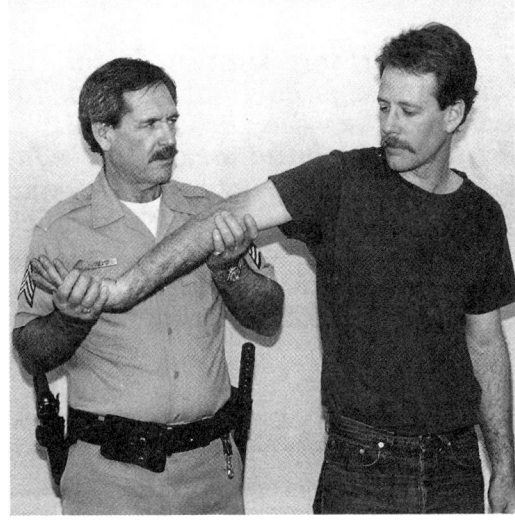

Raise subject's arm perpendicular to his body, palm up.

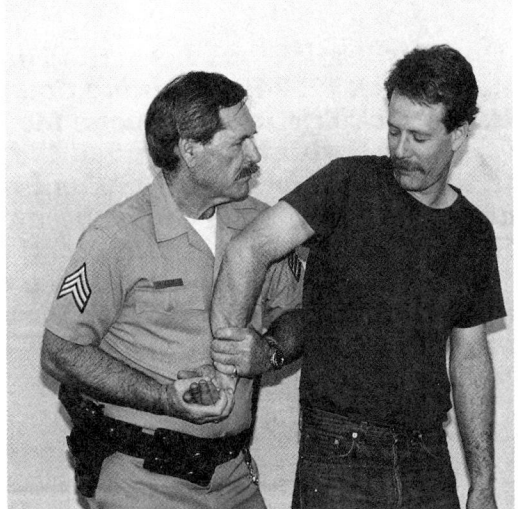

Drop subject's arm toward his waist with his elbow bent.

Terry E. Smith

Mr. Smith has been the Director of Training Standards for the Monadnock PR-24™ Training Council, Inc. and Systems Coordinator for Monadnock Lifetime Products, Inc. since 1988.

Mr. Smith has attended the International Monadnock PR-24™ Instructor Seminar since 1980 and has been a staff instructor at the seminar since 1981. In 1986, he became one of the first fourteen Monadnock PR-24™ International Instructors.

Previously, Mr. Smith was a deputy sheriff with the Marion County, Indiana, Sheriff's Department for ten years. He has been in law enforcement for seventeen years.

Chapter 40

The Impact Weapon: The Need for Greater Understanding and Function

by Terry E. Smith

Introduction

It is important that officers, trainers, supervisors, administrators, and the public view the term "impact weapon" beyond its conventional function as a **strike only** implement. A better term to describe this police use of force option might be "Assisted Empty-Hand Tool." By using this new phraseology, the police baton immediately expands both in meaning and function. Today a triad of baton self-defense capabilities can be instituted that include blocking, subject control, and striking techniques rather than depending on its striking potential alone.

Blocking, subject control, and striking skills (or perhaps better stated as counterstriking techniques) are all vital elements in any officer survival plan whether it involves empty-hand or assisted empty-hand tool training. By providing these three dynamic and sensible alternatives, police officers have an increased probability of managing a confrontation at a much lower level on the use of force continuum. With these alternatives they don't have to rely on one or more striking techniques or a firearm to do the job.

However, there must be balance between blocking, subject-control, and counterstriking skills. One part of this triad cannot dominate another; each part should be easily integrated with the others. This will offer officers a higher degree of universality relative to creating a conflict resolution strategy; something they desperately need.

As a result of much media attention, there has been a steady increase in public concern over how police select and implement empty-hand tactics and assisted empty-hand tools. The public is also concerned how officers integrate such information and equipment into their daily conflict resolution strategy. Therefore police officers, trainers, supervisors, and administrators must be much more responsive to public sensibilities in the future than they have been in the past.

The introduction to the text entitled, *Weaponless Defense: A Law Enforcement Guide to Non-Violent Control* by Mr. Jack Hibbard and Mr. Bryan A. Fried, states the following:

> "No self-defense method is foolproof, nor can any one method take into account all the possible variables that may be present in a dangerous situation. The success or failure of any task is ultimately dependent on the caliber of the man who handles it; the more well equipped the man, the better are his chances."[1]

Mr. Joseph Truncale, a twenty-seven year police veteran of the Glenview, Illinois, Police Department, an accomplished police trainer, and author of the Monadnock Straight Baton Training Manual, states, "If officers don't have options to deal with problems on the street, they cannot perform adequately or in the most appropriate manner possible. Options make the difference between a professional and a non-professional police response." Such statements dramatize the importance of having alternatives whether it be between officers' hands, their batons, or their firearms.

Within each use of force option there must be other available selections because of what Mr. Hibbard, Mr. Fried, and Mr. Truncale stated above. If "Plan A" doesn't work and there is no "Plan B," officers are going to get hurt and maybe even killed. The issue of expanding the meaning and function of the police impact weapon demands a switch from the traditional **strike only** mind-set to one which is more contemporary. It must be representative of the real needs of officers today . . . a philosophy of **protect** and **restrain**.

Building a Bridge Between Empty-Hand Skills and Assisted Empty-Hand Skills

By virtue of holding police batons, officers are not granted magical powers that command respect from would-be attackers, nor does holding batons bestow on them the power of wizards. Would-be attackers' fury cannot be wished away by passing a magic wand in front of them. Where does success come from then? Success comes from informed users; a point that many officers and trainers overlook. This can be a catastrophic error. A police baton (assisted empty-hand tool) is only an extension of an officer's body and nothing more.

Only through proper, documented training can officers become informed on how to correctly use this use of force option or how to maintain their newly acquired survival competence. Proper training by experienced and qualified police trainers is vital in both creating and maintaining officer's survival spirit when it counts the most — in combat. How training is documented is just as important as teaching officers the mechanics of officer survival. This is especially true when it becomes necessary for officers to support their actions in a department review process or in a courtroom.

Officers are quick to point out that they are too busy to practice, the technique hurts when applied to them, or it takes too much time to learn to do a particular subject-control technique. The more we hear such statements the more some believe them. In fact, even some contemporary training programs themselves reinforce these types of statements. Social psychologists have identified this phenomenon which they call *mere exposure*.[2] Politicians use this tactic a great deal with much success (if the campaign chest has enough money) and is often referred to as *name recognition*, but that's another story.

The truth is that there is time to learn and practice if both are done correctly. Mr. Arthur Sapp, a lieutenant with the Colorado Springs, Colorado, Police Department and whose career was profiled in *Tribute: A Day on the Beat with America's Finest*, devised a unique learning enhancement he calls "The One Minute Drill." Plainly stated, an officer performs all thirty-seven techniques of the Monadnock PR-24™ Basic Course in one minute or less. This is first done under the watchful eyes of an instructor or student coach. Mr. Sapp currently holds the Monadnock PR-24™ Training Council's record at approximately twenty-five seconds. Mr. Sapp is quick to point out that officers no longer have an excuse for not practicing because they have at least one minute a day to dedicate to their personal safety.

Mental Preparation

Mental rehearsal, mental imaging, or visualization techniques are alternative training methods that officers can practice to enhance their current and long-term performance of learned self-defense skills.[3] Through such exercises of the mind, officers can successfully rehearse a particular self-defense skill that they might use in a confrontation under a variety of hypothetical conditions. By instructing officers how to see their technique working within the province of their mind is a vital ingredient in that skill succeeding under the reality of combat. The use of visualization techniques are well founded in sports' psychology and its relevance can often be seen in the actual performance of athletes in major sporting events. By combining physical and mental practice techniques, law enforcement officers can better learn how to win.

The process of training officers is both complex and costly. It involves teaching them how to identify a threat in terms of kind and degree and then asking them to plan a response to the threat in a millisecond. Officers' responses have to be reasonable, necessary, humane, and certainly within their agency's use of force policy. Officers must also develop a working understanding of the law, interpersonal communication techniques, availability of community human resources, as well as a hundred other things, in order to make the right decision. What great demands society places on these men and women whom we simply call police officers!

The Proper Training Foundation

Officers should receive training on how to properly perform self-defense skills such as blocking, subject control, and counterstriking. The task of training is generally accomplished at a state or local police academy under the supervision of an experienced and capable staff. Today, many people who enter the law enforcement profession through these academy gates have little or no "life experiences" beyond the classroom. Many have never raised a fist in anger or defense, nor have they found the limits of their body, mind, and spirit. Mr. Lon Anderson, the man responsible for the Monadnock PR-24™ Police Baton and the PR-24™ Basic Course (circa 1970-71), put it another way. He said, "We now have too many baby-faced trainers training baby-faced recruits!"

Without a proper foundation a house cannot long stand. Therefore, certain adjustments must be made within the educational process itself. A top-to-bottom re-examination at the academy level as well as at the department training unit level should be considered. One such adjustment for consideration revolves around the concept of commonality in self-defense training. Under this concept, officers are taught to recognize and apply self defensive principles. It is like glue which bonds two things together. Only here the glue is a self-defense principle that bonds empty-hand skills to assisted empty-hand tool skills.

Blocking the Threat

A self-defense principle called blocking has certain requirements that must occur if a block is to be successful. First, officers must recognize the need to stop a threat coming at them. Once a threat has been identified a plan of action must be quickly set in motion. In an empty-

The Impact Weapon

hand block officers' forearms are the most likely blocking surface and are quickly placed in front of the threat in order to stop it.

This is the most important detail relating to any blocking skill . . . stopping the threat. This principle of putting a barrier between a threat and an officer's face or body equally applies when it comes to using an assisted empty-hand tool, such as a Monadnock Straight Baton (rigid or expandable) or a Monadnock PR-24™ Baton (rigid or expandable). Some officers, police trainers, and police training organizations believe that blocking with a police baton in such a manner is unnecessary because the same goal can be accomplished by using a striking-type block instead.

We will use the sport of baseball as an analogy to better illustrate the difference between these two blocking styles. The baseball represents an impending threat in this analogy. Let us assume that a baseball is a wild, independent object once it leaves the pitcher's hand. It is also moving toward home plate with great speed. The batter standing at home plate with bat in hand will try to hit this comet. As the ball nears the plate, the bat will be swung by the batter in an attempt to hit the baseball, perhaps for a home run. The swing of the bat by the batter represents the second wild and independent object in this analogy. The pitcher's goal is to have the batter not hit the baseball. The pitcher uses a wide range of pitches to accomplish this goal, successfully defending the batter's attempt to hit the baseball.

The same goal may be in the mind of a would-be attacker planning to punch an officer's lights out. A quick review of baseball statistics easily shows how difficult hitting a ball really is. Just hitting a ball is hard enough without adding the pressure of hitting it for a home run for the team. However, if a batter is given the option to use a bunt the success rate increases. True, the baseball doesn't go as far with a bunt as it might with a swing of the bat, but a bunting motion has a greater likelihood of making contact with the baseball. The statistics bear this out.

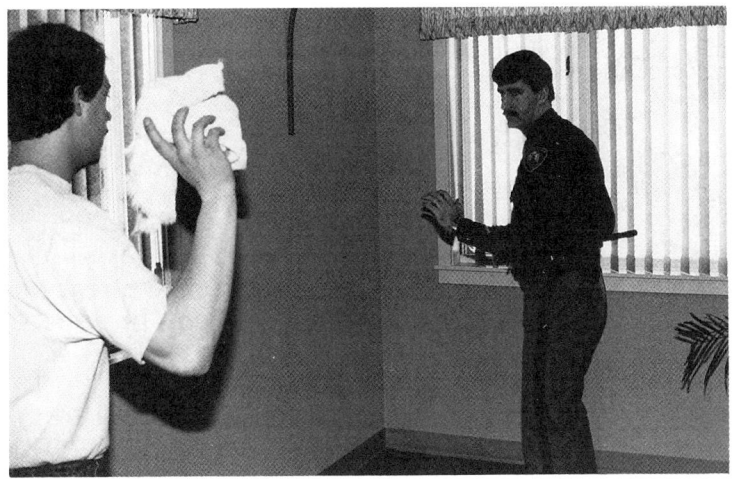

The officer stands 5-6 feet from the other officer who holds a knotted towel. The officer will try to stop the towel from hitting him in the chest using a striking-type block. In this example, the officer will be using a Forward Spin.

The point is this; when two wild and independent objects moving at different rates of speed try to meet, they seldom do. However, when one of the wild and independent objects can be held steady and moved to meet the second wild object, like in a bunt, the success rate for making contact significantly increases.

Officers trying to stop a punch with a baton using a striking-type block are far less likely to succeed than when using a steady (barrier) blocking method . . . just like bunting a baseball. A simple experiment can easily confirm this observable phenomenon: It will require two officers.

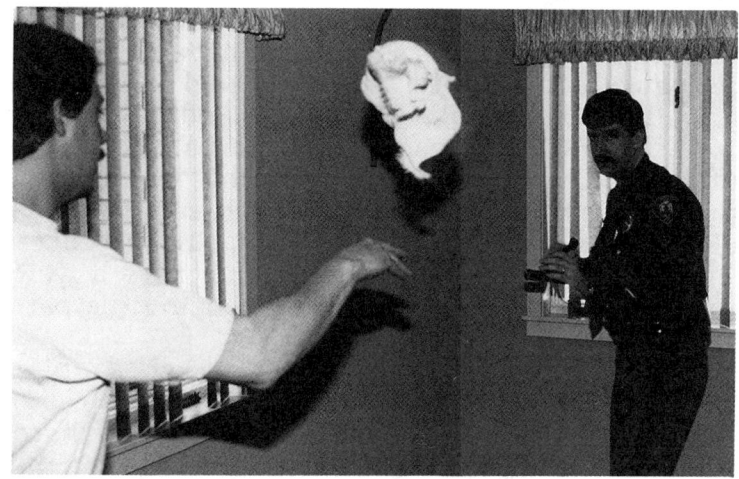

The officer throws the towel at full speed toward the officer. The officer begins to react to the threat.

The towel hits the officer's chest before the Forward Spin can be used to stop the knotted towel.

One officer stands five to six feet from the other with a towel in his or her hand. The towel represents the threat in this experiment. The towel will be thrown at full speed by the officer toward the officer holding

The Impact Weapon

a police baton. The officer will first try to stop the towel from hitting him or her using a striking-type block with the baton. Only one trial is allowed, just like on the street. What happened?

Now repeat the same process but this time the officer with the ba-on will use a steady-type blocking motion to stop the threat . . . just like bunting a baseball. What happened?

The experiment is repeated but this time the officer will be using a steady, barrier-type block called a Basic Position Strong Side Block to try to stop the towel. Again, the officer is 5-6 feet from the officer throwing the knotted towel.

As the towel nears the officer, he begins to raise the Monadnock PR-24™ Baton into the Strong Side Blocking Position.

If the towel was stopped using a striking-type block with the baton the officer should be commended and consider a career in the major leagues. However, if the towel got through the striking-type block, it proves the necessity of having another option. Just as a batter needs the option of a bunt, officers need a steady, barrier-type baton block to stop a threat, such as a punch to the face. When a **block** doesn't stop a punch on the street, unconsciousness follows. This is the reality of working the street.

The Strong Side Block is in position to stop the knotted towel from hitting the officer in the chest. The steady, barrier-type blocking method of the Strong Side Block worked, just like bunting a baseball.

The officer is beginning to control the subject using an empty-hand armlock. The officer's forearm is is placed between the subject's upper arm and body to begin the empty-hand armlock.

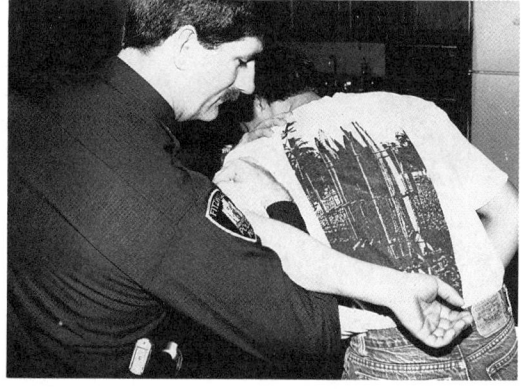

The officer steps behind the subject to better control him and to complete the empty-hand armlock. Notice that the officer's upper arm stops the subject's forearm from moving.

Teaching by basic principles works. In another example, an armlock which is a standard empty-hand control technique will be used. After a tactical advantage has been gained, an officer can quickly insert his or her forearm between the body and upper arm of the subject. Then by

The Impact Weapon

applying enough pressure to cause the subject's arm to bend naturally at the elbow, the officer moves behind the subject. This provides the officer with a better position for controlling the subject. The officer's upper arm is used to stop the subject's forearm from moving, thus completing an armlock by gaining control over the subject's whole arm. The officer's other hand is free to further support the armlock or to provide better steadiness when the subject is escorted from the arrest location.

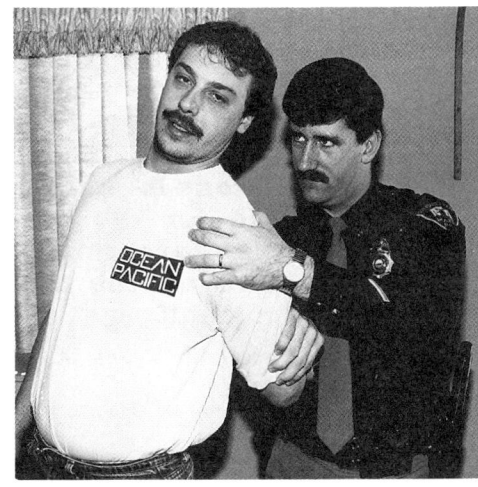

The officer now has the subject under control using an empty-hand armlock. The officer's free hand (on subject's shoulder) is used to provide additional stability in escorting the subject from the arrest location.

Officers can use an assisted empty-hand tool, such as a Monadnock Straight or PR-24™ Baton, to accomplish exactly the same thing. However, certain substitutions between the officer's arm and baton have to be made. How does this work? On the tactical insertion between a subject's body and upper arm the long portion of a Monadnock Straight Baton or the long extended portion of the Monadnock PR-24™ Baton assumes the role of the officer's forearm. When the baton is in position, the officer's free hand grabs the top of the baton. Once in position the baton is used to bend and move the subject's arm behind the back. The officer's lower hand (the hand first placed on the baton and closest to the subject's mid-line) takes over the role of the officer's upper arm in an armlock. The subject's forearm, as well as the whole arm, is now controlled by the assisted empty-hand tool and the process of moving the subject's arm behind the back is much the same. However, the short handle of the Monadnock PR-24™ Baton does most of the control work rather than the officer's hand or wrist.

What has been described here is the formula for an armlock whether it is done by empty-hand means or through the use of an assisted empty-hand tool, such as a Monadnock Straight or PR-24™ Baton. The principle is the same.

Some officers, trainers, and even a few police training organizations argue that using an assisted empty-hand tool — Monadnock Straight or PR-24™ Baton — in such a subject control manner requires too much

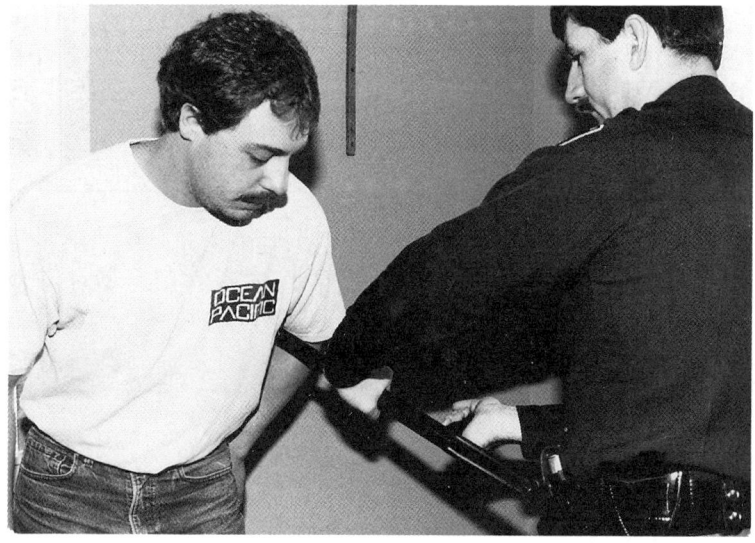

The officer begins to control the subject using the PR-24™. The long extended portion is substituted for the officer's forearm as shown on the bottom left of page 368.

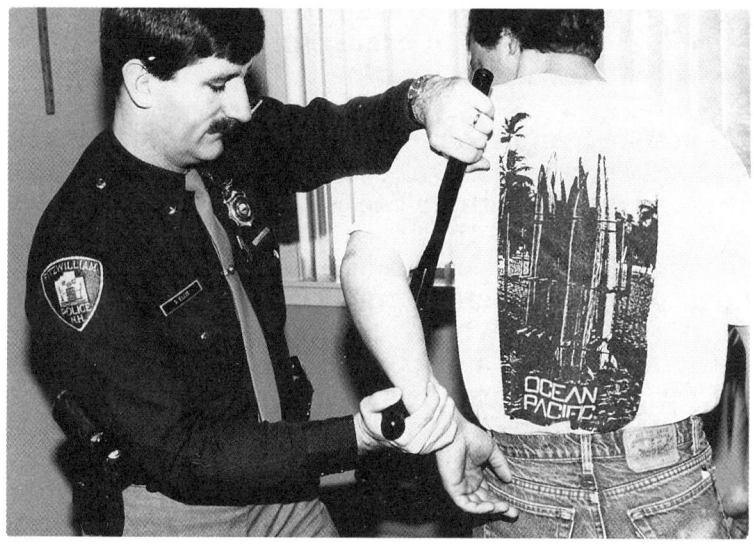

The short handle of the PR-24™ is substituted for the officer's upper arm as shown on the bottom right of page 368.

work to make it a viable option during a moment of high need. Such arguments lack understanding of the commonality between an armlock done by hand and by a police tool. Moreover, in the case of the Monadnock PR-24™ Police Baton, twenty years of independently corroborated data has been compiled by major law enforcement agencies in the United States. This data proves that officers can and **do** apply subject-control techniques with the PR-24™ Baton when under stress.[4]

The Impact Weapon

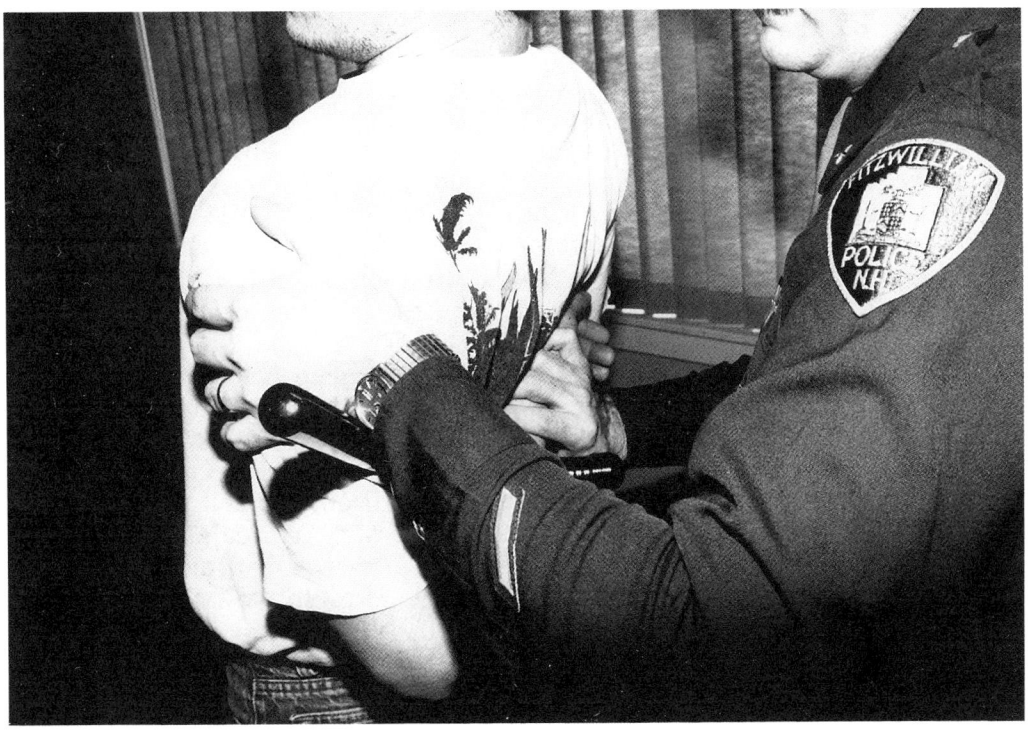

The officer is completing the PR-24™ Basic Course control technique called the Strong Side Armlock or Running Armlock. The subject can be easily escorted from the area using this empty-hand armlock technique.

To bar such a significant option as using a police baton for subject-control because of ignorance, mere exposure, or disapproval based on a personal basis rather than on facts is dangerous, not only to police officers but to those they are sworn to protect. The incident in Los Angeles in 1991 involving Rodney King clearly demonstrates the fallacy of training officers only how to strike with a police baton.

There is a more valuable training lesson to be learned from this incident. What is the lesson? It is exemplified by the Monadnock PR-24™ Police Baton training program called the Basic Course. This unique training program provides officers with skills, or better stated, options, which they need to **protect** themselves from hostility. It also gives them the means to reasonably and humanely **restrain** a hostile subject. **Protect** and **restrain** is a baton training approach for teaching self-defense skills to police officers for the field and in court. This baton training approach is built around blocking, subject control, and counterstriking skills rather than on the baton's striking potential alone. This is the lesson to be learned.

Summary

The implementation of a police impact weapon must move beyond the generally accepted assumption held by officers, trainers, and administrators as being used only as a **striking** implement. Otherwise, as a profession, we will be damned to repeat the errors of our past; a past full of images of police officers hitting unarmed civilians in the head with batons. How did this happen? Was it due to lack of concern? Was it a lack of not knowing anything else? Was it just a lack of understanding or indifference? Whatever its cause or causes, it must change, not it will change. Change has already begun.

A new and broader understanding relating to the role of the police impact weapon within the use of force continuum is gaining momentum among officers, trainers, and police administrators. Just as a pitcher needs a wide range of pitches to strike out the most accomplished batters, so officers need options which **protect** them from harm as well as provide them with the ability to **restrain**. As Mr. Truncale said, "Options make the difference between a professional and a non-professional police response." Commonality in training between empty-hand skills and assisted empty-hand tool skills makes such options easier to learn, to do, and to remember when it becomes necessary for officers to **protect** and **restrain**.

Bibliography

[1] Hibbard, Jack, and Fried, Bryan A. Fried. 1980. *Weaponless Defense: A Law Enforcement Guide to Non-Violent Control.* Springfield, IL: Charles C. Thomas. P. vi.

This is a well-rounded self-defense text. It represents one of the earliest examples where nerve centers and pressure points were advocated as a means of control for law enforcement personnel. (Chapter 2, pp. 9-13).

[2] Christensen, Larry B. 1977-91. *Experimental Methodology.* Needham Heights: Allyn and Bacon. P. 6.

[3] Loehr, James E. 1982. *Mental Toughness Training for Sports.* Lexington, MA: The Stephen Greene Press.

[4] The following references represent only a small sample of the

available independent, field research data that has been done by Monadnock on the effectiveness of both the design of the PR-24™ Baton and its **protect** and **restrain** training philosophy over the conventional straight baton and the traditional training program for it.

Sheriff's Department, Training Bureau. 1974. *An Evaluation of the Monadnock PR-24™ Baton.* Los Angeles County, CA. (October): P. 5.

> "A surprising number of evaluating deputies indicated that they had utilized the special baton (Monadnock PR-24™ Baton) come-along holds in restraining and arresting intoxicated persons. Because the holds instructed were not as instinctive as the defensive and offensive maneuvers, the instructors believed initially that they would be used less extensively. However, this did not hold true."

Rochester, New York, Police Department, Research and Evaluation Section. 1977. *Evaluation of the Monadnock PR-24™ Baton.* P. 7.

> "One hundred percent of the evaluators stated that blocking techniques utilizing the PR-24™ provided them greater protection than a conventional baton could. In terms of armlocks and come-a-long techniques, ninety-six percent of the evaluators indicated these techniques are more easily executed, with far greater leverage and defensive capabilities, with the PR-24™ than with a conventional baton."

Waterloo, Iowa, Police Department. 1983. *Evaluation of the Monadnock PR-24™ Police Baton.* P. 4.

> "The results of the above use with the PR-24S™ Batons incurred no injuries and did not generate citizen complaints of physical abuse or excessive force. As was documented, all use of the PR-24S™ Baton centered around control techniques and not striking techniques."

Letter from Mr. James W. Lindell, Supervisor, Physical Training, Kansas City, Missouri, Police Department, December 11, 1991.

> "Kansas City officers are still reporting an eighty percent use of the PR-24™ for control purposes and only twenty percent impact use. It's use for subject control provides options they did not have available to them in the past and appears to make officers

more confident in subject confrontations. The psychological effect of the PR-24™ on subjects is frequently reported and often makes using it unnecessary."

Chapter 41

Special Purpose Police Firearms

by David J. Spaulding

The year was 1966. What started out as a pleasant day in the City of Austin, Texas ended in horror as a young, emotionally disturbed man by the name of Charles Whitman climbed to the top of a 230 foot tower and began a killing spree that was to change the course of American law enforcement forever. What has become known as "The Texas Tower Incident" occurred in the tranquil setting on the campus of the University of Texas at Austin.

The people on the campus that day were totally unprepared for the carnage that was about to unfold. Even responding police were unsure of how to react to the crisis. Police officers and private citizens alike began to arrive with personally owned hunting rifles and started shooting, without any fire discipline, in the direction of the tower. Whitman was finally stopped by two brave Austin Police Officers who slowly climbed to the top of the tower and killed Whitman with handgun and shotgun fire.

This incident was followed several years later by a sniper who stationed himself on top of a Howard Johnson's Hotel in New Orleans. This subject also killed a number of people before he was neutralized by police gun fire. But once again, the police response was haphazard and thrown together as the situation unfolded. Police administrators across the country realized very quickly that they needed to have special teams of police officers who could respond to these unusual situations. The Special Weapons and Tactics (SWAT) concept was born. The Los Angeles Police Department was the first to organize a paramilitary response to this new breed of criminal. Many other departments quickly followed suit.

It was quite obvious to these tactical pioneers that these special teams would need special weapons. The standard police revolver and shotgun were not suitable for the desired function. The police SWAT weapon needed to be light and easy to use. It had to be either full or at least semiautomatic and quick to reload. The natural progression was to look at military weapons.

In the early years, many agencies adopted the Colt M-16 rifle. Since a large number of police officers during that period were Vietnam veterans, the M-16 was too long for close quarter fighting and the full metal jacket ammo had far too much penetration for law enforcement applications.

Fortunately, the search continued and today we have a wide selection of special purpose police weapons. There is no doubt a weapon exists that will meet the needs of your special purpose team, and this doesn't mean only the SWAT team. Today's war on drugs has reached the most violent level in history. Gun play between competing drug dealers and drug dealers and police is a daily occurrence. The weapon of choice for these armed criminals is the assault rifle and submachine gun. Patrol and narcotics' officers must at least meet, if not surpass, this very real threat.

The following is a look at a select number of special police firearms that are currently available to American law enforcement. It would be impossible to look at everything that is available, but all of the weapons discussed have been proven to be very reliable and effective. However, as in anything else it is up to the officer or department to decide what best fits their needs.

Long Distance Rifles

What has also been called the "sniper" rifle, should be standard equipment in any agency, large or small. A long distance rifle and an officer trained in its use may very well be what is needed to stop a tragic incident like those described at the beginning of this chapter. The large majority of police departments in this country do not have tactical teams. Often times the closest team cannot respond as rapidly as needed. Small agencies must be prepared to handle these situations. Having a good long distance rifle in the department's inventory, and an officer or two who can use it, may save a life in the future.

The long distance rifle does not have to be expensive. There are a number of sporting models that can fill the void if needed. However, if the department is going to purchase a good rifle, it would definitely be to their benefit to look at the models that are designed for that function.

Remington 700P

This gun has been around for almost 30 years and was one of the first rifles ever to be used for police countersniper duties. The 700P is a bolt-action model that comes in either .308 or .223 caliber. For the purpose of countersniper duties, the .308 is recommended because of its

Special Purpose Police Firearms

greater weight and ability to resist deflection.

Remington has built the 700P for law enforcement. The gun has a 24" heavy barrel with a parkerized finish for a professional look. It is also equipped with a black Kevlar stock which is more rigid, does not absorb moisture, and is totally unaffected by temperature. This is quite important when just a fraction of an inch can mean the difference between hitting a hostage taker or a hostage. The stock is an ambidextrous high cheek stock so that it may be used by either right or left handed shooters. With match grade ammo, such as the Federal 168 grain boat-tail hollowpoint, the gun is capable of shooting one inch groups or less at 100 yards consistently! With many custom guns costing over $1,500 the Remington is a terrific buy at about one half that price.

The Remington 700 .308 bolt-action rifle with camo stock and scope.

Heckler & Koch 91

Ten years ago, the American law enforcement officers would not have recognized the name Heckler & Koch. Now it is almost as common as the word SWAT. H & K offers some of the best weapon systems currently available and their model 91 rifle is a good example.

The H & K 91 is the semiauto version of the popular G-3 assault rifle. The G-3 offers a select fire mode which has a fire rate of 600 rounds per minute, and is available for government sales only. The 91 was not designed for countersniper work, but it has been proven to work out quite well for this use at a greatly reduced price over the PSG1, which was designed for this serious need. Most agencies just can't afford a PSG1, which is a semiauto rifle in a class by itself.

The H & K 91 is 41 inches in length and can be purchased with either a retractable or full synthetic stock. For countersniper duties, it is recommended that the full stock be used. The 91 uses a box magazine that will hold 20 rounds of .308 ammunition and comes standard with a black phosphate finish that looks quite professional. The standard sight arrangement is a ring post front with a Diopter (similar to a "ghost ring") rear. However, if the 91 is going to be used for countersniper duties, a quality scope is highly recommended. The 91 weighs around 10 pounds which is not unreasonable, especially for a gun that will be rested when fired. The draw back to the 91 is its price, which is in the area of several thousand dollars. However, if you are looking for a semiautomatic rifle capable of sniper grade accuracy, the H & K 91 just might fill the need.

There is an on-going controversy over whether the police countersniper should use a bolt-action or semiauto weapon. The bolt-action rifle is thought to have greater accuracy for the pin-point shooting that is needed in this delicate work. The semiauto has a quicker follow up shot for those times when the first shot misses its mark. This decision is up to the agency making the purchase. However experience has shown that with match grade ammo, the H & K 91 is capable of firing 1 inch groups at 100 yards when using quality optics. Hopefully a second shot will not be needed, but if it is, it is hoped that either a second bolt-action rifle is on target or semiautomatic capability available.

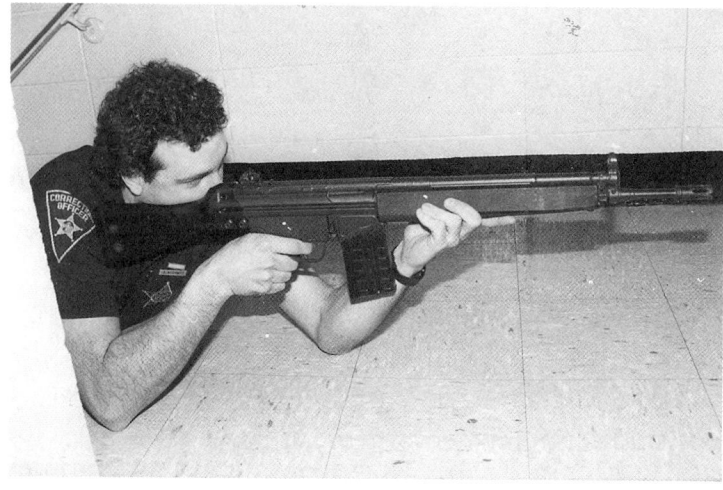

The Heckler & Koch 91 .308 semiautomatic rifle.

Assault Rifles

The term "assault rifle" has received a great deal of negative press of late. The term comes from the military for a rifle that is also known as a "battle rifle." They bridge the gap between sniper rifles and light machine guns and smaller close battle weapons, such as submachine guns and pistols. The assault rifle is designed to be issued to the infantry sol-

Special Purpose Police Firearms

dier. It is a weapon that is light enough to be carried for long periods, easy to operate and care for, capable of semiauto or full automatic fire, and shoots a cartridge capable of good accuracy at battle field distances. It was meant to be a military weapon.

Currently the term "assault rifle" has been used to mean semiautomatic weapons that resemble their military counterparts but are designed to be sold on the civilian market. These civilian versions fill a need in the law enforcement market. The police administrators or officers should not turn their backs on these very useful weapons because of current media coverage relating to them.

The assault rifle for law enforcement makes an excellent perimeter weapon in police SWAT operations as well as a good choice for rural or desert patrol beats. These rifles can fire groups that will easily stay on a human size target out to 800 yards without optical sights! Remember, these are not countersniper rifles. They are offensive weapons that can be used at distances far beyond the capabilities of the police handgun or shotgun.

Colt M-16 and AR-15

The original M-16 was not thought of fondly by many veterans of the Vietnam conflict. Numerous stories of jamming and fouling in the wet jungle led to a congressional inquiry of the weapon. The current weapon, the M-16 A2, no longer displays the previous problems. This weapon is now sought by many of the world's armies and has become the standard by which many battle rifles are judged. The AR-15 possesses many of the same qualities as the M-16 except for the full auto capability and the short barrel versions. This rifle is currently called the "Sniper Rifle" by Colt.

The M-16 is a gas operated weapon that fires from a closed bolt for greater accuracy. The barrel, bolt, recoil buffer, and stock are assembled in a straight line for greater reliability and recoil control. The M-16 fires the .223 cartridge which many feel is not appropriate for law enforcement due to its extreme penetration with full metal jacket ammunition. Recent tests in ballistic gelatin have questioned whether this is a real concern. However, there are a number of different .223 hollowpoint cartridges available that will address the over penetration concern.

The sight system currently available uses a rear sight that has a dual aperture that allows for ranges out to 800 meters. With the standard 20-inch barrel, the M-16 is 39.6 inches long and weighs 7.5 pounds without a loaded magazine. The magazine capacity is 30 rounds and weighs one pound when fully loaded.

Probably the most handy version of the M-16 is the "Commando" model which has become popular with military special operations' teams. This weapon has a collapsible stock and an 11.5 inch barrel which makes for a very compact rifle. Any police tactical team who wants a submachine gun size weapon that fires a rifle cartridge should evaluate the Commando" model.

The Colt AR-15 with a collapsible stock is the civilian version of the full auto "Commando" model.

Steyr AUG

The Steyr Armee Universal Gewehr (Army Universal Rifle) is truly one of the most innovative weapons currently available. It is a .223 caliber weapon that uses what is commonly referred to as the "bullpup" design. What this means is that the weapon's receiver is housed in the butt stock which results in a shorter overall weapon.

Like the Colt, the AUG comes in several different versions, the most popular being the AUG-SA and AUG-P. The SA model is a semiauto version that was originally directed at the civilian market. The SA has a green one piece synthetic stock which incorporates the grip, butt, storage compartment, trigger guard, trigger, safety selector, and magazine well. The barrel group, the receiver group, and bolt group are separate assemblies that fit neatly into the stock. This allows for rapid parts replacement in a crisis situation. The AUG is one of the simplest weapons' systems available.

What is really unusual about the AUG is the liberal use if synthetic materials throughout the weapon's working parts. The majority of the hammer assembly is made of space age synthetics. Tests have shown that this hammer assembly will withstand 50,000 firings without breakage. The magazine is also made of the same synthetics and has been proven to be tough enough to have a vehicle drive over it without it breaking. The AUG-SA has a 20-inch barrel for an overall length of 31 inches. It weighs 9.3 pounds fully loaded with a 30-round magazine.

The AUG-P is the police model. It is very similar to the SA model but uses a black stock and a 16-inch barrel. It also incorporates a hammer group that is capable of being set on 3 shot bursts or full auto fire.

Special Purpose Police Firearms

This makes for a rifle caliber, full auto weapon that is roughly the same size as an H & K MP-5 submachine gun. As with the Colt "Commando," these small size, rifle caliber weapons could prove to be very handy in tactical situations where the distances of encounter are unknown. Military special operations teams are using these short battle rifles more and more in place of the submachine gun unless they are sure that the possible altercation distances are going to be short. After all, the short barrel battle rifle can be used at short distances, whereas the submachine gun is designed to be used at close quarter distances.

The real advantage of the AUG is the integral 1 x 5 power scope that is standard on all models of the AUG. The reticle of this sight is nothing more than a circle which will encompass a human body at 200 yards. Knowing this will allow the shooter to estimate distances at a glance. This feature will not be needed in most law enforcement applications, but it is possible, especially in rural areas.

Submachine Guns

The submachine gun can be defined as a full auto weapon that fires a pistol caliber cartridge. Guns of this type date back to the turn of the century but did not really come into their own until General John T. Thompson invented his classic .45 caliber submachine gun in the 1920's. The Thompson served our armed forces well during WW II, Korea, and into Vietnam before being replaced by more modern weapons. The Thompson is probably most famous for its use by mobsters of the 20's and 30's, something that greatly discouraged its inventor.

It seems that the "Roaring 20's" have once again returned to our society as criminal gunplay is once again common place. Criminals arming themselves with powerful weapons have created a great interest in the submachine gun by law enforcement.

UZI

The UZI is one of the most famous guns ever produced. Its use in many Hollywood productions has made it recognizable by most of the American populace. The UZI comes in three sizes, a standard version, a medium sized model called the Mini-UZI, and a pistol size model called the Micro-UZI.

The UZI is currently produced by Israel Military Industries to the same basic specifications as the original UZI models that were designed for the Israeli Special Forces. While the two smaller guns would be good choices for some special details, such as dignitary protection, the standard size UZI would be the best choice for use by American law enforcement. The smaller versions are more difficult to shoot and unless they are to be concealed, offer no real advantage over the larger standard model.

The UZI SMG can be obtained in three calibers; 9 mm, .45 ACP, and the new .41 Action Express. The .41 is not a common caliber for police use and for the most part, should be ignored for the more common 9 mm and .45 calibers.

The biggest criticism of the UZI is that it fires from an open bolt. This means that on the first round fired the bolt slams home before the firing pin engages the primer. Tests have shown that this feature does affect accuracy. However, on a weapon that is designed to be used for close quarter confrontations, the accuracy loss is minimal. The UZI has been proven to be a rugged and reliable weapon while maintaining a relatively low cost. It is a good choice for any police department.

The UZI 9 mm submachine gun.

Beretta PM12S

The PM12S is probably one of the most underrated guns available to American law enforcement. This fine Beretta SMG is blowback operated and, like the UZI, fires from an open bolt. The PM12S has a folding metal stock that collapses against the receiver which makes for a nice compact weapon, being only 16 1/2 inches in length. The Beretta only weighs 7 pounds and is quite easy to shoot.

The PM12S has very adequate sights as well as a very useful grip safety that is located just below the trigger guard. This safety is easy to use and renders the gun useless if it were to be dropped. The magazine capacity is 32 rounds and its cyclic rate of 550 rpm makes it very easy to fire 2 and 3 shot bursts by just controlling the trigger.

Special Purpose Police Firearms

One of the most useful features of the Beretta PM12S is the front, full hand grip. This front grip allows the shooter to pull down on the front of the gun to help control recoil. This makes for a very fast responding weapon when rapid fire in a crisis situation is needed. The Beretta PM12S costs significantly less than many of the similar SMG's currently available. It is recommended that any agency in the market for a quality submachine gun look at the Beretta PM12S.

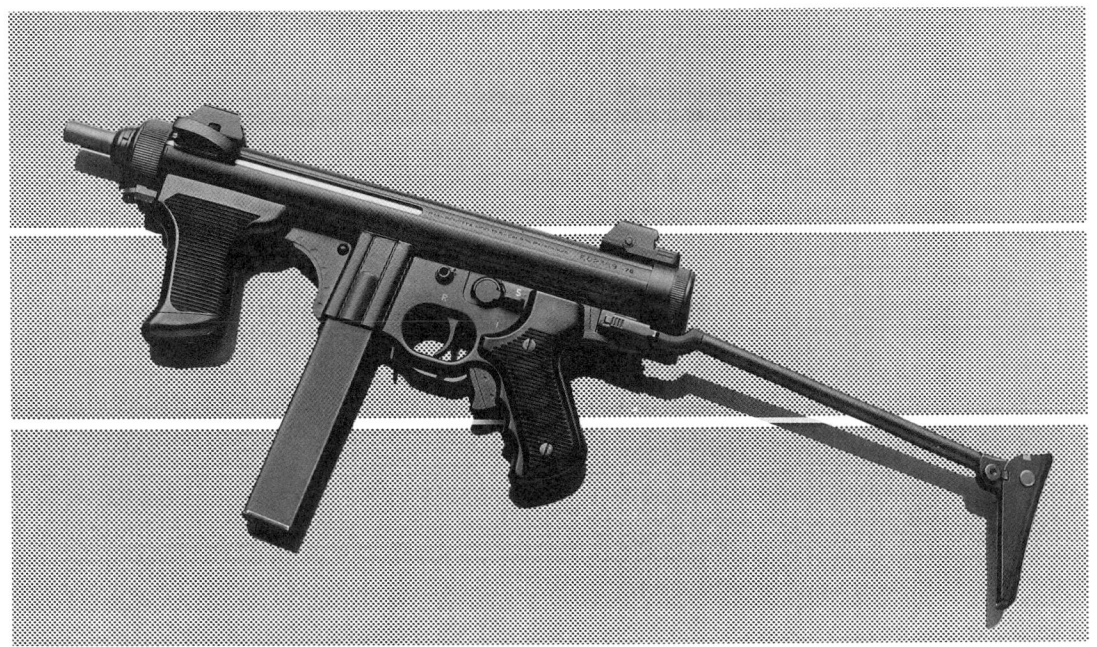

The Beretta PM12S caliber 9 mm submachine gun.

Heckler & Koch MP-5

There is no doubt about it, this is the submachine gun by which all others are judged. It has become known as the "fourth generation" of SMG's due to its firing from a closed bolt. The MP-5 is capable of accurate semiauto fire out to 100 yards, which is truly amazing since its intended purpose is close confrontations.

The MP-5 employs the same delayed roller-locked bolt system that was made famous by their G-3 Automatic Rifle. This aids a great deal in the area of recoil control, especially during burst and full auto fire. The MP-5 comes in several different versions including a semiauto only carbine, a briefcase size model, and a version which has an integral suppresser. The most popular model is probably the MP-5 A3 which has a retractable stock for close quarter situations but can be pulled out and shoulder fired like the full stock version.

The MP-5 has a cyclic rate of 800 rpm which is quite fast. The front sight is a circle enclosed post that can be ordered with a tritium insert which works very well in low light. The rear sight is the "ghost ring" like Diopter sight. With the stock extended, the MP-5 A3 is 26 3/4 inches long and only 16.5 inches long when closed. The MP-5 is quite expensive, but most of the users I've talked to feel that the gun is worth the price.

The Heckler & Koch MP-5 9 mm submachine gun.

All of the previously discussed weapons are capable of filling the demanding needs of law enforcement. It is advisable for any agency that is considering the purchase of any special weapon to contact the manufacturer and test them to see if they meet the perceived need. If the company is not willing to supply test samples of their product, it is probably not the weapon your agency wants or needs.

About the Author

Sergeant David J. Spaulding is a fifteen- year veteran of the Montgomery County Sheriff's Office in Dayton, Ohio. He is currently as-

Special Purpose Police Firearms

signed to firearms and tactics in the Training Unit. He has also been a member of the M.C.S.O. Emergency Services Unit (SWAT) since its inception in 1980 and has been its training coordinator since 1984. He is a member of ASLET, IALEFI, NTOA, and past president of the Ohio Tactical Officers Association.

Sergeant Spaulding is a certified instructor with pistols, revolvers, shotguns, select fire weapons, and scoped rifles. He is also certified to instruct in the area of defensive tactics, expandable batons, chemical agents, and the use of distraction devices. He has written articles for several magazines including, **Combat Handguns, Guns and Weapons for Law Enforcement, S.W.A.T., Police, Pocket Pistols, Special Weapons,** *and for several regional publications. He holds a B.A. in Psychology and an M.A. in Criminal Justice.*

Brian J. Stover

Sergeant Stover is a 20 year veteran police officer. Currently he is a sergeant with the Los Angeles County Sheriff's Department. He previously worked as a police officer in Illinois with city, county, and university police agencies. Sergeant Stover is a Charter Member of the American Society of Law Enforcement Trainers, a member of the National Advisory Board for The Police Marksman and Police magazines. He is also a certified member of Police Self Defense Instructors International, the National Tactical Officer's Association, and the International Association of Law Enforcement Firearms Instructors. He is a PR-24™ Instructor and an Advanced Instructor with the National Law Enforcement Training Center.

Chapter 42

Advice From the Pros: Frisking and Searching Methods

by Brian J. Stover

Frisking vs. Searching

Although the terms "frisking" and "searching" are sometimes used interchangeably, the two are actually separate procedures and used at different times. A "frisk" is used when officers can articulate that they have a reasonable suspicion that subjects they're contacting may be armed. The officers may then perform a frisk or limited search for weapons. In some areas the frisk is also referred to as a "pat-down search."

During a frisk officers are permitted to reasonably search subjects to determine if they are armed.[1] If during that search they discover a weapon or certain other types of contraband, they may arrest the subject and the evidence could be admissible in court. In some jurisdictions, this search is permitted by statute. In Illinois, "When a peace officer has stopped a person for temporary questioning . . . and reasonably suspects that he or she or another is in danger of attack, he or she may search the person for weapons."[2]

During a frisk subjects are not handcuffed and officers do not have as much control over them as during a "search."

A "search" is conducted after subjects are in custody or arrested. This type of search is much more thorough than a frisk and the subjects being searched should be restrained by the use of handcuffs. By the time officers make the decision to search subjects, in most cases, they have already determined that there is sufficient grounds to arrest the subjects. Therefore, there is now sufficient justification to handcuff the subjects for better control.

A search should be conducted as soon as subjects are under control. Over the years this procedure has often been referred to as "Arrest and Control." Unfortunately, officers have died trying to arrest and control subjects. Before officers make a physical arrest, they should control the subjects. By trying to arrest subjects who are not controlled, officers run the very real risk of being injured or killed.

Unlike a frisk, in a search officers are not just searching for weapons but for other types of contraband such as narcotics. While a frisk may turn up this type of contraband, the goal of a frisk is to determine if the subjects are armed. A search is much more thorough and should be conducted at the scene of the arrest, before the subject is transported, and again when the subject arrives at the jail facility. Every time subjects are placed in another officer's custody, moved to another location, or left unattended, they should be searched again.

Frisking: The Approach

As you approach subjects you intend to contact, begin looking for the obvious signs that they may be armed. Bulges under their clothing are the most obvious, but there are other signs. The way subjects move may indicate that they are attempting to hide weapons. Subjects may try to keep a portion of their body out of view, or they may walk stiff legged due to a weapon being hidden on their legs or ankles. Don't be in a rush to make contact. By watching the subjects you may not only spot signs that they are armed, but you may prevent an attack.

Whenever possible, subjects should be approached from the rear. By doing so, they are forced to turn towards you in order to attack. By forcing subjects to turn to attack, you will have the extra reaction time to counter the attack. As with any contact, safety is first and foremost. You should not ask for identification before you conduct the frisk. By asking for identification first, subjects are invited to reach into their pockets or to remove their hands from view. This may give them the perfect opportunity to reach for a concealed weapon. Instead of being presented with their ID, you could be on the receiving end of a bullet.

Before starting the search, subjects should be informed that they will be searched for your safety. By explaining what is about to occur you can often avoid an unexpected negative reaction from them. Many officers have been successful in making the contact uneventful by asking the subject, "You don't mind if I search you for guns, knives, atomic bombs, or a Cruise Missile, do you?" This technique can reduce tension, especially with innocent subjects and helps you obtain permission to search. The permission can further bolster your case in court should contraband be found.

Frisking: The Procedure

First of all, forget the "wall" or "prop" search. This technique is not only outdated but dangerous. Inmates have practiced defeating this search more than any other technique. Many of them have more experi-

Frisking and Searching Methods 389

ence getting out of this technique than some officers have in performing it. The only place for the wall search is on TV. This does not mean that you should forget about the wall or other stationary object. By having subjects face a wall or other stationary object, one escape avenue is eliminated.

Frisking Method #1

Direct the subjects to be frisked to face away from you (if they are not already doing so). Then instruct the subjects to move their hands away from their body and spread their fingers. Tell the subjects to rotate their hands so that you can see their palms. As the subjects are doing this, order them to spread their legs and point their toes outward. After they comply and you can see that their hands are free of contraband, direct them to bring their hands behind their back with the backs of their hands together. Have them spread their fingers and instruct them not make any other moves.

Now approach cautiously from the rear. Slide your weak hand between the subjects' ring and middle fingers, and grasp their ring and little finger tightly. As you do this grasp their shoulder on your strong side and pull them backwards until they are off balance. Now begin frisking in a systematic manner, starting with the upper body on your strong side and work from the front center to the back, then down.

Once you are satisfied that you have properly frisked the one side, re-grip their fingers with your strong hand, and repeat the frisking procedure for the other side of the body, making sure that the frisk overlaps the center front and rear areas to avoid missing anything in this crucial spot.

Should you encounter resistance when conducting the frisk, you can squeeze and torque the fingers sharply, while ordering the subjects to stop resisting. If the resistance continues or is violent, you may have to resort to stunning techniques or push them away to create distance.

If no resistance is encountered and you determine that you wish to handcuff the subjects, their hands are in a perfect position to be cuffed. Grasp your handcuffs in a pistol grip, holding onto the cuffs with your fingers around the chain or hinge portion. With the handcuffs loaded (so that the single bar is held closed by only one tooth of the ratchet), place the single bar of the handcuffs against the top of the subjects' wrist, and push down firmly. The bar should spin around the wrist and lock. Repeat for the other wrist while maintaining a grip on their fingers. After both cuffs are on, you can adjust the handcuffs as needed and then double lock them.

Frisking Method #2

Frisking method #2 is similar to the first method except that you instruct the subjects to be frisked to place their hands behind their backs with palms together. This method is often easier for some subjects to understand, especially those that have a diminished capacity.

Frisking Method #3

This method was developed by Sam Faulkner of the Ohio Peace Officers Training Academy and is named "The Faulkner Frisk." This method is another variation of the above techniques. Direct the subjects to place their palms together and to interlace their fingers. As in the other methods, the subjects should be directed to spread their legs to assist in keeping them off balance. Now tell the subjects to keep their fingers interlaced as they place the backs of their hands against their backs. When they comply, instruct them to keep their fingers interlaced and move their hands away from their backs and toward you.

Approach safely and grasp the subjects' interlaced fingers by reaching over the top between their backs and their hands. This is accomplished using your weak hand. As you reach around the subjects' hands, your grip must almost encircle their interlocked hands. You should be able to see their fingernails showing to the rear with your thumb over their thumbs.

After achieving the proper grip, roll the subjects' palms down and then back towards the small of their backs, removing the slack from their arms. This will also serve to tilt them back off balance. While maintaining the grip, lean them into your shoulder. Now the frisk may be conducted.

As in the other methods, you can handcuff the subjects from this position if you deem it necessary. As you grip your handcuffs (cuffs loaded and held in the middle) in your strong hand, move the subjects' arms slightly to your strong side to make room for cuffing. The bottom cuff is pushed onto the subjects' wrists on your strong side. After the one hand is cuffed, control that hand with the cuffs while you relax your grip on the other hand enough to allow their hands to separate.

You can still maintain control of the other hand by torqueing it counterclockwise. Now push the loaded handcuff onto the other hand.

This method may not work well when there is a great discrepancy between the officer's size and the subject being frisked. Officers who are small in stature or grip should not use this technique if they cannot get their hands around the subjects' hands. Also if the subjects are obese or very muscular, this technique may not work due to their lack of flexibility.

Frisking Method #4

Unlike the previous methods, this method does not involve the subjects placing their hands behind their backs. For this method you will again have the subjects face away from you and direct them to hold their arms out away from their body. Direct the subjects to spread their legs as you approach from behind. With your strong hand, grasp their upper

Frisking and Searching Methods

arms which are on the same side as your strong side. As you slide your hand down their arms increase your grip, and finally grasp their wrists tightly.

Pull down slightly on their wrists, taking out the slack before starting the frisk. With your weak hand begin frisking them on the same side as the arm being held. You do not switch hands to search the other side, but rather reach around the subjects while maintaining a strong grip on the original wrists.

Handcuffing from this method may require that you use a "Goose-Neck Grip" or a method similar to the Marsh Speedcuffing Technique.[3]

Safety Measures

When frisking subjects, you should conduct the frisk quickly but safely. A crushing motion on the subjects' clothing rather than a rubbing motion can help prevent injury to yourself. Often subjects the police encounter are drug users, outlaw bikers, the mentally unstable, or just plain bizarre. These subjects may have needles, razor blades, broken glass, or other sharp objects that can injure you during the frisk. You should avoid reaching into subjects' pockets or other areas that you cannot see without first checking from the outside. A needle stick from an AIDS infected junkie is not worth the risk.

One method of avoiding being stuck or cut is to use a mini-baton, Kubotan®, or mini-flashlight. By rubbing the flashlight or baton over the subjects, you can detect objects in and under the clothing that may constitute a weapon, while avoiding the risk of injury.

Another safety measure is the use of gloves. Contrary to popular belief, leather gloves do not protect you from disease. Leather gloves are porous and can transmit a virus through the material. Also when removing the gloves you often have to touch the gloves with your bare hands, thereby negating any protection. Latex examination gloves are excellent and inexpensive but they do not protect you from sharp objects.

The best method uses both techniques. You should first put on leather gloves, then place the latex examination gloves over the leather gloves. The latex gloves will help prevent the transmission of disease while the leather gloves help protect against injury. By placing the latex gloves over the leather gloves rather than under, the latex prevents the absorption of liquids by the leather. You can also remove the latex gloves by pulling them off inside out, tying them in a knot, and disposing of them.

Should you come into contact with blood or other bodily fluids, you should clean up and disinfect as soon as possible. While this is often impractical in most field situations it can be accomplished. Often K-9 officers have a disinfectant foam they use after their dog has bitten a subject. Any K-9 officer will be glad to provide you with a source to obtain the disinfectant. The local hospital emergency room may be able to provide or recommend a disinfectant that can be used. Another excellent and available product is Pro Care® by Sani-Fresh. This is an Isopropyl Alcohol gel that is easy to use, does not need water, and is inexpensive. It is easily carried in a plastic bottle that is small enough to fit in a jacket pocket.[4]

Searching Techniques

Unlike a frisk a search is conducted after a subject is controlled by handcuffs. The search will be much more thorough and entails a detailed check for not only weapons, but contraband. The search should be conducted as soon as the subjects are taken into custody. The longer you delay in your search the more likely the subjects are to avail themselves of weapons or to dispose of contraband.

Searching: The Approach

The approach to a search will be determined by the circumstances. The search may evolve out of a frisk situation. During the frisk you may have discovered a weapon or contraband, giving you cause to make an arrest or giving you probable cause to search further. In such a case after the subjects are handcuffed you can begin your search.

The search may be the result of reasonable suspicion that the subjects were involved in a crime. An example would be the "High Risk Vehicle Stop." After you safely remove subjects from the vehicle, handcuff the subjects (using either a prone or kneeling handcuffing technique), and then proceed to search the subjects.

Any approach should be made safely. Approach with your gun side away from the subjects and your handgun holstered. Not only should the handgun be in the holster, but the retaining strap must be secured. Approaching subjects with a gun out or improperly secured is asking for trouble. Desperate subjects will quickly avail themselves of your weapon if given the opportunity. The same goes for the shotgun or rifle.

Searching: The Procedure

Whether the subjects are standing, kneeling, or prone, the procedure is generally the same. You should first search the area of the subjects' rear waistbands. Since the subjects have their cuffed hands in this area it should be your first concern. Next, you should search the remainder of the waist area.

After you are satisfied that the subjects do not have any weapons in the waistband area, you should begin searching the subjects from the top down. If the subjects are wearing hats, remove them from their reach and search them afterwards. Check the subjects' hair for possible hidden weapons or contraband. Next, you should check the collars of the subjects' coats, moving down along the arms and the body of the coats.

Frisking and Searching Methods

Check inside the coats, in pockets, and for anything secreted in the linings. Repeat the procedure on the other side of the body, making sure to overlap in the center on the front and back. After you are satisfied that the coats do not contain contraband or weapons, you can pull the coats back down over the subjects' arms to better control their movements during the remainder of the search.

The next area to be searched is the subjects' shirts. Begin again with the collars and work down the front and around to the back, making sure once again to overlap as each side is searched. Carefully check the arms and under the arms in the armpits. Both locations are popular spots for hiding weapons.

Move down to the lower torso and the legs. As you move to this area you should re-search the waist area to better guarantee the area is clear. Now search one leg at a time, making sure that you move from top to bottom, then repeating the search from bottom to top. After searching each leg, loosen the subjects' belts carefully. Make sure the belt buckles don't contain disguised weapons. After the belts are loose, unhook the pants and search the inside of the waistbands. Check the groin area carefully. Subjects are counting on you to have reservations about checking this area. You are a professional and no amount of "sexual" comments should deter you from searching.

Direct the subjects to kick off their shoes and search their feet. After securing the subjects in the patrol car or other safe location, closely examine the shoes and hats that were removed earlier. Now is the time to search any items that are found during the original search, such as wallets, cigarette packs, etc. Nothing should be overlooked. If it can be hidden, a criminal will do it and do it well. Subjects have even hidden contraband under their watches.

When the subjects are secure, face them and look in their mouths. Have them move their tongues around, show their front teeth, and order them to swallow hard and cough. This may dislodge any hidden contraband.

The subjects should be re-searched after transporting them to another location, transferring them to another vehicle, or any time they are out of your sight. If you take custody of subjects from another officer they should be searched again, even if the first officer assures you that the subjects have been thoroughly searched. Subjects can never be searched too often.

Special Circumstances

Females

Frisking or searching females need not be a problem if handled properly. Obviously, if possible a female officer should search a female subject. If a female officer is unavailable, male officers should search females with other male officers present. If the male officer is alone, he should, if possible, have a witness, such as a passer-by (preferably female) to observe the frisk or search. The male officer should record the witness's name, address, and phone, should the female attempt to make any accusations against the officer.

Male officers should use the blade of their hands when searching or frisking females. By running the blade of the hand over the females, the officers can detect weapons and still avoid accusations of misconduct. Another option is to use a mini-baton to check for weapons. Depending on the circumstances, the officers may pull the blouse, skirt, dress, etc., from the back so that it is tight against the female's body. This may reveal hidden weapons. Another technique involves unhooking the female's bra through her blouse. This may allow secreted contraband to fall freely.

In most cases, to avoid false accusations, male officers should conduct only a search for weapons, and put off a more thorough search for contraband until female officers are available. There is no prohibition from male officers searching a female. However, if the circumstances do not dictate the necessity for an immediate search, officers may well be advised to frisk now and search later.

Handicapped

You should not hesitate to frisk or search handicapped or disabled subjects. A subject's disability should not be a factor in determining if you should search. Handicaps or disabilities can be used by subjects to their advantage and to your disadvantage. The subjects may try to berate or intimidate you into not searching them. You may feel uncomfortable or even feel pity for the subjects. Either way, you should treat the situation as if they were not handicapped.

The disabled can be just as dangerous to you. In California a few years ago, a subject who had been paralyzed from the waist down in an earlier shoot-out with police, shot and killed two detectives who had come to his home to arrest him on an outstanding warrant.

You should thoroughly search wheelchairs to which subjects are confined. Artificial limbs, crutches, walkers, canes, etc., should all receive the same attention as any other items within reach of the subjects. You must not let any feeling of embarrassment deter you from conducting a thorough search.

Juveniles

Juveniles should be treated the same as adults. Although there are some liberals who feel that juveniles are incapable of violence and should be treated differently, common sense dictates that you conduct the same type of search, regardless of age.

Summary

Whatever the technique you use, you should think safety at all times. Your primary goal should be to go home at the end of your watch. There will always be subjects unhappy about being searched or frisked. It is much easier though to explain to the citizen the reason for the search or frisk than it is to explain to a widow and her children why her husband, their father, is not coming home.

Professional police officers will rarely have a founded citizen complaint for conducting a search or frisk. Unfounded complaints are unfortunately part of the hazards officers face daily. However, by conducting the search or frisk properly, explaining their actions to the person, and acting professionally at all times, officers can safely get through their shifts with the support and confidence of the citizens they serve.

Bibliography

[1] Terry v. Ohio, 392USI, 88 SCt 1868, 20LEd (2d) 889 (1968).

[2] Illinois Criminal Law & Procedure-CH 38, ¶108-1.01.

[3] Desmedt, John, and Marsh, Jim. 1983. *SPEEDCUFFING, The Police S.A.F.E.T.Y. System.*

[4] Sani-Fresh International, San Antonio, Texas 78218.

Neal E. Trautman

Mr. Trautman is National Director of the Law Enforcement Career Development Center. You may know Mr. Trautman as a founder of the Law Enforcement Television Network, the nation's largest provider of enforcement training. As the Network's Director of Training, he was responsible for all aspects of training provided to 120,000 officers daily.

He was founder and charter president of the nationally respected Florida Criminal Justice Trainer's Association. He served as editor of the Florida Police Training Officer's Association Newsletter for three years and has written numerous articles relating to law enforcement training and professionalism. He has authored the following textbooks: Law Enforcement Training, Law Enforcement In-Service Training Programs, Law Enforcement - The Making of a Profession, A Study of Law Enforcement, 50 Things Teens Can Do to Fight Drugs, and forthcoming, Standards for Security and Law Enforcement Agencies.

Chapter 43

Dealing With Attitude, Anger, Lust, and Greed

by Neal E. Trautman

Ethics is the Most Needed Training Area in Law Enforcement

We, as a profession, have always done an absolutely terrible job of preparing officers to make difficult ethical decisions "on the street." This is incredible considering virtually every substantiated case of police corruption or brutality resulted from an unethical decision on the part of those involved.

Why has it continued? Because we haven't known how to correct it. We took the easy way out and ignored it. The following explains how to ensure that your department is ethical.

As a trainer, you have a responsibility to do the right thing. Get involved and make a difference.

Honesty, Or Lack of It

Everyone agrees . . . honesty is a worthy principle. Every major religion preaches it. Schools teach it. Civil litigation enforces it. Businesses, governments, and individuals claim they practice it.

It's common knowledge that honesty is frequently ignored. Self-serving interests often win out over doing the right thing.

Few endeavors offer more temptations to be dishonest than law enforcement. Finding an "open door" to a business at 0315 hours may tempt some officers to steal. Others find it difficult to answer questions during a deposition honestly if the answer makes them look bad.

Why is it so difficult to be honest? In a profession that represents integrity, pride, and protection and service to mankind, why is there a problem with officers being dishonest? Unfortunately, it has become part of our culture. The "American Way" includes cheating on your taxes, lying to take the easy way out of an awkward situation, and as a child, you grew up amid role models who constantly set seemingly harmless examples of dishonesty.

Major corporations aren't exempt from dishonorable practices either. All too often, multi-million dollar judgments are leveled against corporations who have served themselves at the expense of innocent consumers. The major decisions of corporate America are made by individuals or groups of individuals. The question they deal with is very similar to the one facing an officer alone in a closed business: "Will I be honest when confronted with self-serving temptation?"

Unlike a corporate board of directors, police officers don't have the same status, salary, or prestige. All too often, their training or past experiences have not equipped them to face the emotional, financial, or psychological stress of a police career. The key is to apply internal strength to an effective, ethical, decision making process.

Frequently, as easy targets for the venting of frustration by the public, police officers have few avenues to follow when dealing with their frustration and stress.

Responsibilities

Cops are only human. They have the same desire for nice homes, new cars, and luxuries as others have. Yet, they have additional responsibilities, as well. The fact is, cops have to be different! No other occupation is provided such enormous authority and responsibility. The trust given to every cop is incredible. How can more trust be bestowed than to say, "When we **really** need help, we'll call on you."

It is possible to remain honest and to succeed in a world often riddled with dishonesty. The necessary attributes are a healthy self-esteem and to truly believe in yourself. Stealing and lying will give you a reward for the moment, but in the "long run," you'll be the loser. Corruptible cops may believe they have won some small measure of success, but in truth, their success is short lived.

Cops have professional responsibilities. Law enforcement can not be a profession unless its members have a strong sense of obligation to their responsibilities. Responsibilities extend far beyond the specific orders given by a supervisor . . . they are much larger in scope.

Responsibility to Your Community

To fulfill their duties, police officers must comply with a higher standard of self-imposed responsibility; a standard based on the understanding that because they are afforded much power and authority, they are held to greater responsibility. This responsibility also includes leadership.

The "bottom line" is that officers must accept responsibility to provide leadership within their community. They are perceived to be a natural role model. When someone has a problem, needs advice, or seeks assistance, police officers are frequently sought, even when off duty. You can't ignore this responsibility.

Responsibility of Law Enforcement

True professionals realize they owe a commitment to their profession . . . one that is sincere, dedicated, and loyal. Regardless of rank, assignment, or seniority, every American Cop is a member of an everlasting brotherhood . . . for all the right reasons.

Cops have a duty to promote professionalism. There is nothing corny or outdated about this. Few feelings are more satisfying than giving your best effort for a worthy cause. What could be more worthy than justice and the protection of the innocent?

Responsibility to Citizens

After several years on the street, it's easy to feel suspicious or cynical about almost everyone. You can lose sight of the fact that most people are decent individuals.

Officers usually deal with the worst of society. Unfortunately, when officers are with good people, it is often during these people's worst moments. Most professions have established terms that explain the relationship between the professional and their "client." Physician and patient, lawyer and client, and teacher and pupil are logical and easily understood. In each situation confidence and trust exist. A bond of respect is directed toward those who provide assistance and guidance.

There is no reason why trust, sincerity and confidence can't bond citizens and law enforcement. Every department has a responsibility to the community they serve. It's a responsibility we must meet, without exception.

Most citizens form an opinion of their police department based on one or two isolated contacts with an individual officer. Frequently an individual's respect or lack of respect for the police came from an incident years ago in some other community.

Responsibility extends beyond the protection of the innocent, or providing professional and respectful service. Controlling your emotions, when all those around you are not, is the mark of a true professional.

Attitude, Anger, Lust, and Greed

Think about a particular case when an officer went bad. Consider every police brutality or other form of substantiated corruption incident you know of. With very few exceptions, the direct cause of every case of intentional police misconduct has been either attitude, anger, lust, or greed.

It is important to give some thought to these aspects of your career. Officers face a seemingly endless number of awkward situations as the months and years pass by. This is no place for a weak character. Few are so weak that they give in to major thefts, drug dealing, or bribery, but one bad cop is one too many.

True, life isn't always fair. There will be difficulties in both your career and your personal life. Accepting disappointment as merely a temporary setback will allow you to be a much happier individual. No one has the right to use life's "bad breaks" as an excuse to be corrupt or to have an "attitude."

Disenchantment and a lack of comradeship is common within a department where people look to place blame, or become defensive when things go wrong. Any situation that "goes bad" has the potential to be a good learning experience.

Make the best of every difficult circumstance. Learn from it, correct whatever allowed it to happen, and go on to bigger and better achievements. Remember, if someone is pointing their finger at someone else, they're pointing three fingers at themselves.

Every agency faces far too many problems on the street to be bickering and spending time fighting among themselves. Developing and keeping a good public image takes a never-ending effort. We've all got to pull together and be a team. A single act of corruption can destroy the entire image of a department.

Making a commitment to be an ethical, conscientious police officer is obviously an important ingredient for maintaining the image of any department. There's no way anyone can control everything that's going to happen on the street, in your community, or in your department, but one thing you can control, is yourself.

- Don't spend time trying to blame or change others — make the most of yourself.

- Don't spend time regretting or living in the past — live for the future.

- Don't develop a habit of criticizing others — strive to become the best you can be.

- Don't be a burden by nagging or arguing — search out your own short comings and improve yourself.

- Don't sit in judgment of others — allow them to be human and control their own destinies.

Never feel as though pride, loyalty, and high ethical standards are corny or naive. Sincerity and professionalism will make a long line of cops who wore the badge many years ago to look down upon you with pride and endearment.

Ethical Decision Making for the Street Cop

Human Reaction Under Pressure

As any experienced police survival trainer will tell you, under pressure you will react the way you were trained. How true!

We came to realize this, from the perspective of firearms' training, the hard way. After training on the range during the day between 21 and 150 feet for decades, we came to understand that most officers die at night and at distances of less than 20 feet from the perpetrator. We now train more effectively.

The same thing is true about ethics. We, as a profession, have always done an absolutely terrible job of preparing officers to make high stress, ethical decisions. The last decade has seen officers participating in very realistic firearms' scenario training. There's no reason we can't develop the same type of training for ethics. Remember, under pressure you will react the way you were trained!

Four Reasons Why Officers May Act Unethically

Said another way, there are four primary reasons good cops do unethical things:

1.) they lie to themselves with excuses;
2.) momentary selfishness;
3.) bad decisions; and
4.) they're afraid of "paying the price" for doing the right thing.

What Doing the Right Thing Requires

It doesn't matter how difficult or stressful the situation, in order for your decision to be right, it must support ethical principles. You do this by:

☐ first, setting aside unethical choices; and

☐ then, "doing the right thing."

Doing the Right Thing Means Three Things

1.) Wanting to be ethical;
2.) acting on your good, ethical intentions; and
3.) being able to think rationally.

Rational Thinking for Ethical Decisions

There are four steps to take when making an ethical decision:

1.) clearly understand the issues;
2.) evaluate the facts;
3.) make the decision; and
4.) follow through.

The Ethics Follow-Through

After making your decision, it's important to "check yourself." Ensure that it was the right decision by asking yourself three simple questions:

1.) Is it legal?
2.) Is it fair to all concerned?
3.) How will it make me feel about myself?

When There Seems to be No Good Solution

Being "the devils advocate" for a moment, let's create the worst of all situations. What do you do if, after following the ethical decision making process, the circumstances are so horrible that there just doesn't seem to be any way out? What then?

First, the process really does work. What we're talking about is not how to make the decision. There isn't a better way to make an ethical decision than the one we just discussed.

What we're actually concerned with here is dealing with your emotions or "second guessing" yourself. If you feel you're in this type of situation, asking yourself three questions should resolve it.

1.) How will I feel about myself 20 years form now?
2.) Would those who love me be proud or ashamed?
3.) Am I following the Golden Rule?

How to Tell If You Did the Right Thing

Did you:

☐ Use discernment?

☐ Consider if what you did was appropriate?

- ☐ Use your imagination?
- ☐ Compare your commitments?
- ☐ Accept accountability?

Staying Positive in a Negative World

On Duty and Off Duty Ethics

People often have higher ethical standards for their personal life than for their professional life. This is usually because there is so much career pressure to "get the job done" at work.

Many officers give in to the pressure . . . doing things they know are ethically wrong. In essence, they sell out. To be ethical, you must refuse to yield to the stress of police work. Your character must be stronger than the stress, and the temptations.

Life in the Department

Most police officers face more stress from within their own agency, than they do from "working the street." While this is sad but true, it doesn't mean we can't change things.

Here are merely a few things we, as a profession, need to change, and how to go about changing them:

- **It is unusual to reward ethical acts.** Most agencies give awards and medals for bravery, but there are no medals for honesty. This is easily corrected and the benefits would be great.

- **Ethics are sometimes the subject of jokes.** Don't let people make fun of honesty, dedication, and being ethical. These are what hundreds of great cops have died for.

- **Negative views and attitudes often become a way of life in an organization.** It doesn't have to be like this. In fact, administrators and supervisors usually create the "atmosphere" which results in either good or bad attitudes. However, changing the "organizational climate" within an agency is complex and difficult, and probably requires a good consultant.

- **A good role model is the single greatest factor in determining the atmosphere, attitudes, and ethical views within any**

organization. Although it seems simple enough, most organizations have found that finding a good role model is a very difficult task. The reason? It all comes back to attitude, anger, lust, and greed. You see, to be a great role model, you have to rise above these temptations just like everyone else.

- **Few departments have policies and procedures that provide constant "checks and balances" to ensure ethical conduct. The National Institute of Law Enforcement Ethics** is working hard to provide such sample policies and procedures.

Concluding Guidelines that Work

- ☐ Don't pass the buck.

- ☐ Find the solution, not excuses.

- ☐ Look for the ethical way.

- ☐ View every difficult ethical decision as an opportunity to do the right thing, instead of a crisis.

- ☐ Don't give up. Few ethical dilemmas just go away. Use the process and make the right decision.

Life isn't always fair. The future will hold difficulties in both your career and your personal life. Accepting disappointment as merely a temporary setback will allow you to be a much happier person.

Every agency faces far too many problems on the street to be spending time bickering and fighting among themselves. Developing and maintaining a good public image takes a never ending effort.

Everyone needs to pull together. A single act of corruption can destroy the entire image of a department. Making a commitment to be an ethical, conscientious cop is an important ingredient for keeping the image of your department shining bright. There's no way anyone can control everything that is going to happen on the street, but the one thing you can control is yourself.

- **Don't spend time regretting or living in the past.** Live for the future.

- **Don't develop a habit of criticizing others.** Concentrate on becoming the best **you** can be.

- **Don't be a burden by nagging or arguing.** Search out your own short comings and improve them.

✏︎ **Don't sit in judgment of others.** Allow them to be human and to control their own destinies.

Once sincere ethics are ingrained throughout an agency, the entire organization develops a new tone. Togetherness and camaraderie suddenly become a real part of everyone's life.

It takes guts to make sure the badge doesn't become tarnished. If it is to shine, the courage to stand up for what's right must be strong within every cop. Each cop across the nation has a reputation to earn and maintain. All of us must do something about that!

Professional Image

Attorneys and physicians provide services that usually go unquestioned by their clientele. An assumption of professionalism exists before individuals ever walk into their offices. Police officers, on the other hand, don't enjoy the luxury of working in an atmosphere of assumed faith.

Professional image comes in accordance with the degree to which it is deserved. The following accomplishments create a professional law enforcement image.

- **Officers at all levels must exhibit professional attitudes and conduct.** A positive, professional attitude by individual officers is essential for society to accept them as professionals. Officers who are driven by high esteem, pride, and sound moral values, will have no problem in sustaining conduct consistent with the highest ideals of the profession.

- **Professionalism must be instilled and reinforced throughout officers' entire careers.** Law enforcement agencies often fail to establish sincere respect in their officers, for police tradition, purpose, and value. The police academy, in-service training, and daily reinforcement by immediate supervisors, are logical opportunities for ingraining and maintaining the values of loyalty, dedication, service to others, respect, and pride in their officers and their agencies.

- **A high educational level is a fundamental prerequisite for the recognition of professionalism.** Chiefs and Sheriffs should immediately move to impose a two or four-year college degree hiring requirement. Initially, the sacrifice will be great. Higher standards of employment will mean a smaller recruitment "pool" from which recruiting agencies have to choose. The sacrifice, however, will be a wise investment in the long haul, because educated officers are better prepared to perform their duties and their professional images are enhanced.

- **Training must be enhanced in order for professionalism to become a reality.** Historically, police training has been terribly neglected. The advent of innovative technology has resulted in marked improvements, however. Nationwide standardization of in-service training is nonexistent.

- **Standards of employment must be raised and adhered to for society to accept the police as professionals.** Maintaining high standards of employment is, of course, much easier said than done. Some administrators argue that this belief is naive and unrealistic, since our salaries and benefits are lower than other professions. The irony of such logic is that justification for improved salaries and benefits may only be substantiated when law enforcement earns these benefits, as demonstrated by raising standards of employment and education.

- **The law enforcement code of ethics must become meaningful.** While the code is already established, it doesn't play an important role in the daily lives of officers. They don't receive regular reinforcement on the importance of the code of ethical conduct. Both individual officers and agency leadership must take responsibility for changing this situation.

- **An increased emphasis on human resource development must take place.** The most valuable resource in any organization is its employees. The law enforcement profession neglects to appreciate fully or to develop the abilities of their police personnel.

- **Management style must undergo a significant change if the police are to keep pace with the efficiency of other organizations.** Currently, most departments have bureaucratic and paramilitary management and leadership. Overwhelming evidence indicates a participatory and people-oriented style of management yields much higher levels of quality performance and effectiveness.

- **Improved career development enhances professional image. It must play a more important role within law enforcement agencies.** Many departments don't have a formal career development function. As such, they are missing a tremendous opportunity for improvement.

- **Lateral entry is a way of life in the corporate world.** Successful businesses seek the best people, wherever they may be. Law enforcement exists in the dark ages when it comes to ensuring the most qualified and proficient individual is placed in a particular position. Many business organizations would go bankrupt if they operated this way.

- **Without strong and harmonious community relations, police departments won't be recognized as professional.** The significance of community support will be appreciated when agencies fully understand their role as community servant. It's certainly possible to be a public servant and a professional at the same time; examples are hospital physicians and the ministry.

- **The most beneficial utilization of manpower is critical to reaching maximum efficiency.** The future must include increased use of civilian community service officers, selecting the right person for every position, effective manpower allocation of all patrol officers, and less anti-productive bureaucracy.

- **Little standardization presently exists within law enforcement.** This must change for proficiency of services to occur. State and national organizations must take more of a lead in this regard.

- **The national accreditation process should be viewed as the vehicle to be used in establishing nationwide standardization and improvement.** Agencies that refuse to acknowledge the wisdom of accreditation will eventually be forced to become accredited by community pressure and civil liability.

- **How the police perceive their own role in society is critical to future change.** Currently, most officers envision their roles as that of "crime fighters." Actually, they are highly specialized public servants more than crime fighters.

- **Enhancing the organizational climate within police departments is necessary to achieving a high level of productivity.** When a pleasant working environment doesn't exist, employees usually have low levels of morale and pride. The absence of pride equals an absence of quality.

- **A professional association with all police officers across the nation as members does not exist.** Unlike many other countries, America has chosen not to regulate mandatory membership of a single, nationwide police association. Instead, a variety of specialized, voluntary associations promote their views of professionalism. Although generally consistent, they are limited by their specific scope and their membership.

Chapter 44

Handcuffing and Officer Survival

by Joseph J. Truncale

Handcuffing procedures are the most important skills officers can learn to survive on the street. Unfortunately, this is also the least practiced area of police defensive tactics. Few police agencies require retraining and review in the proper use of handcuffs. In fact, the vast majority of officers receive no additional training in handcuffing after they leave police recruit training academies.

According to Terry Smith, former Indianapolis Police Training Academy Instructor and current Director of Training for Monadnock Lifetime Products, "Next to report writing the most used skill of an arrest is handcuffing. Yet officers seldom receive enough training in this essential area."

Statistics in resisting arrest injuries have demonstrated a need for more intense handcuffing training. Sixty-seven percent of resists occurred **after the first handcuff** was applied, so it is obvious police officers are not receiving enough training in this significant officer survival area. There are many reasons cited for the lack of handcuffing training in law enforcement.

- Administrators who believe that once officers have been trained in handcuffing at the academy they don't need to be retrained.

- Officers who hold the mistaken view that retraining and review is not necessary in handcuffing.

- The fact that there is some degree of pain and discomfort inherent in learning and mastering handcuffing techniques.

- The lack of qualified handcuffing instructors available to teach survival handcuffing.

- The fact that there is no standardized handcuffing procedure.

- ☐ Officers are more oriented toward equipment than training.
- ☐ There is a lack of good handcuffing textbooks and videos on the market.

Types of Handcuffs Available to Officers

There are four types of handcuffs available to law enforcement today. All of these handcuff models have both positive and negative qualities.

▶ **Chain Link Models:** These handcuffs are the traditional metal handcuffs and are the most popular, but hinged handcuffs are becoming the choice of many modern police officers.

A positive aspect of using the chain link model is that they are easy to carry on the duty belt because they fold together. They can also be employed in most handcuffing systems and are easily adaptable to a multiple of situations.

A negative factor of using chain link handcuffs is that subjects may be able to pull the chain link cuffs apart. Subjects have also been known to slip their legs through their arms and bring them to the front where they successfully attacked the officers. Finally, if subjects pull away from the officers with one handcuff applied, the chain can act as a swinging weapon.

Officers are going to carry what they feel comfortable using. Although chain link handcuffs will probably continue to be used by officers (old habits die hard in police work), there are better handcuffs and systems being developed.

The four types of handcuffs from left to right are: Chain Link, Hinged, Quik-Kuf, and Double Disposable by Monadnock.

▶ **Hinged Models:** The hinged handcuff was the first new design in handcuffs to be developed. Street officers quickly saw their value and they are becoming more popular every day in law enforcement circles.

There are many positive aspects of these new handcuffs. The breaking point of standard chain link handcuffs is about 550 pounds. This is adequate for the majority of police incidents, but people on drugs and liquor which dulls pain, have been known to break the chain link handcuffs.

The hinged handcuff does not rotate making it difficult for subjects to maneuver once cuffed. Both cuffing sections face in the same direction making it easier to handcuff subjects. Also the diameter of the hinged handcuff is 25% larger which means they can be used on subjects with larger frames. When one hinged handcuff is applied, officers have more control of subjects making it more difficult for them to pull free and use the handcuff as a weapon.

These handcuffs also have some negative factors. Certain handcuffing systems cannot be employed with them and some officers have complained about the hinge pinching their hands when applying them. Also certain handcuffing techniques have to be adapted when using the hinged handcuffs.

Quik-Kuf Model: The most innovative new handcuff model on the market is called the Quik-Kuf. This handcuff goes a step further than the hinged handcuff. The Quik-Kuf is a standard handcuff with a special hardened, plastic grip device which makes it an excellent control tool. This unique handcuff has the potential to become very popular with street officers, but more field testing with major agencies is needed before the law enforcement community will appreciate and accept this handcuff.

There are many positive factors in Quik-Kufs which make them appealing to police officers.

☐ The grip portion allows even the smallest officers to easily control subjects once these handcuffs are applied.

☐ Even with only one handcuff on the subjects, officers can easily control them because of their innovative grip.

☐ Due to their design, even with only one cuffed wrist, if violent subjects are able to pull the cuff away from the officers, every time the subjects throw a punch the handcuff will hurt their wrists.

☐ With these handcuffs officers can either stack the subjects' arms behind their backs or handcuff their hands with their palms facing outward.

☐ When subjects are handcuffed there is no way they will be able to slip the cuffs around their legs and bring their arms to the front.

- Unlike some handcuffing systems, Quik-Kufs control subjects with pressure on top of the wrists on the radial and ulna nerves, not on the sides of the wrists.

- Handcuffing two subjects with one handcuff is more effective with Quik-Kuf.

Although handcuffing subjects with their hands in front of the body is not a procedure practiced by the vast majority of law enforcement agencies, there are some departments who still employ this method. If an agency is looking for the best type of handcuff to use with front handcuffing, then Quik-Kuf is the best.

There are a few negative factors with the Quik-Kuf.

- Certain handcuffing systems cannot be employed using this model.

- The handcuff case is designed to be carried in front of the handgun and the top cuff sticks out making it seem uncomfortable to carry. Officers who have been trained and carry Quik-Kufs say they are more comfortable than they appear.

At this time there are few field evaluations of this new handcuff. This is sure to change as more law enforcement agencies adopt Quik-Kuf.

The author is wearing the Quik-Kuf model handcuffs.

Handcuffing and Officer Survival

▶ **Disposable Handcuffs:** There are several companies who make a disposable handcuff and many police officers carry extra sets in their briefcases. They are made of plastic and have a limited use in law enforcement.

There are many positive aspects of disposable handcuffs. They can be easily carried and used on subjects with extra large wrists. They can be used in multiple arrest situations where there are not enough standard handcuffs available. Also they can be used to secure things as well as handcuffing subjects, and they are inexpensive.

As with any handcuff model, disposable handcuffs also have negative factors. Once they are placed on subjects, officers need a sharp cutting tool to remove them. They cannot be loosened and may cut off the blood supply to subjects' arms. Also if they are not secured tight enough subjects may be able to slip out of them.

Officers should carry a few sets of disposable handcuffs for emergency situations, but they should rely on their regular handcuffs in most arrest cases.

Basic Handcuffing and Safe Searching Procedures for Survival

- ☐ Keep a proper distance from subjects.

- ☐ Keep the subjects off balance at all times.

- ☐ Place handcuffs on subjects as quickly as possible.

- ☐ Always handcuff subjects before searching them.

- ☐ Always double lock the cuffs and document this fact.

- ☐ Search subjects for any weapons.

- ☐ If a weapon is found, do not place it on the ground.

- ☐ If one weapon is found, keep looking for other weapons.

- ☐ Even after handcuffing subjects, they should be placed in a position which will ensure as little movement as possible.

- ☐ Do not be lulled into a false sense of security because of a subject's dress or demeanor.

☐ Do not relax too soon. Keep the eyes moving. Be alert and aware of what is going on.

☐ Think about safety and survival.

Basic Handcuffing Procedures: Non-Resisting Subjects for Minor Violations

Keep your distance from the subjects and advise them to open their hands and turn around so their back is to you. Have them widen their legs and place their toes outward. Tell them to put their hands behind their backs, palms together and facing away from the body.

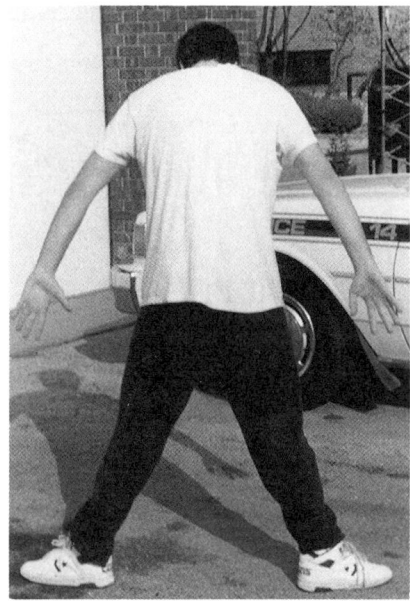

Subject stands with his palms open and his back to the officer.

Subject puts his hands behind his back with his thumbs up.

Carefully approach the subjects and as you grasp their hands immediately place the handcuffs on the wrists as quickly as possible. Make sure the handcuff holes are facing down.

There are variations to this method, such as using a Wrist Lock or

Handcuffing and Officer Survival 415

Thumb Lock to apply the handcuffs. These procedures can be applied with any model handcuff but they work best with hinge and Quik-Kuf handcuffs. Do not forget to **double lock the handcuffs**.

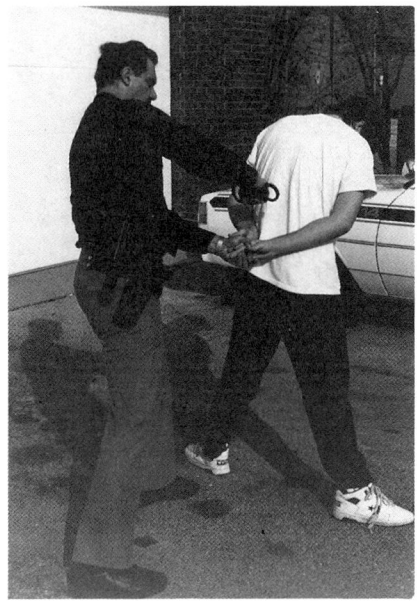

The officer approaches and grasps the subject's hands and prepares to cuff.

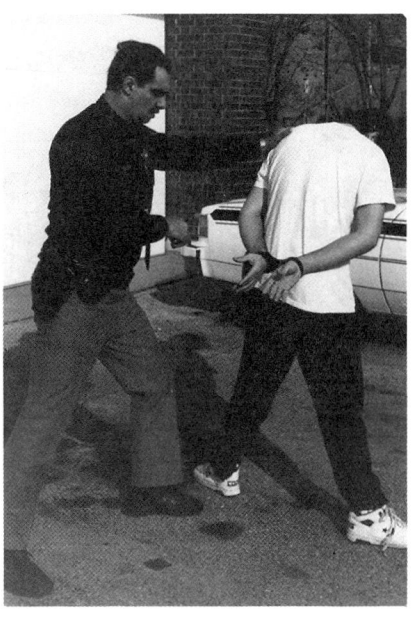

The subject's hands are handcuffed with thumbs out.

Basic Handcuffing Procedures: Cooperating Subjects for Misdemeanor or Felony

Standing: Order the subjects to widen their legs and to point their toes outward. Have them interlock their hands on top of their heads and to look away from you. Approach the subjects carefully with your handcuffs ready in your hand. Grasp the subject's hand and apply your top handcuff to the right wrist. Immediately pull that arm outward from the body and at the same time pull the free hand around in order to complete the handcuffing technique. The handcuffs are applied in a stacking position.

The subject's hands are on top of his head with fingers interlocked, legs spread, and toes pointing out.

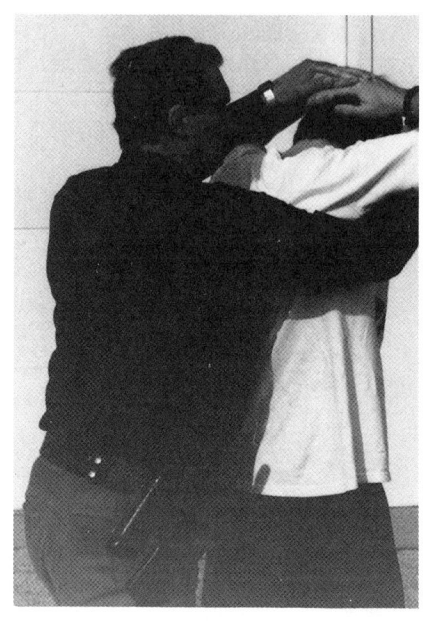

The officer approaches the subject, applies a handcuff, and grasps the subject's opposite hand.

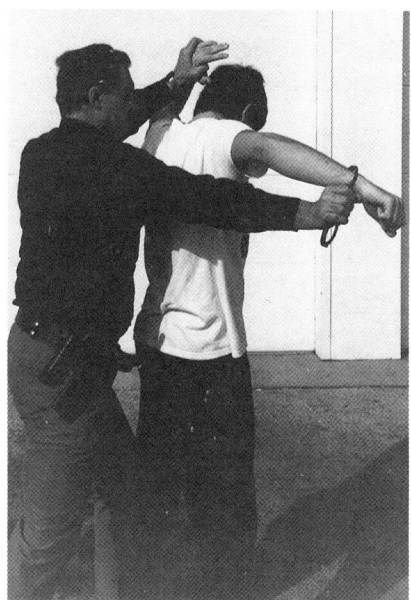

The officer immediately straightens the subject's cuffed arm to the side and controls the opposite hand.

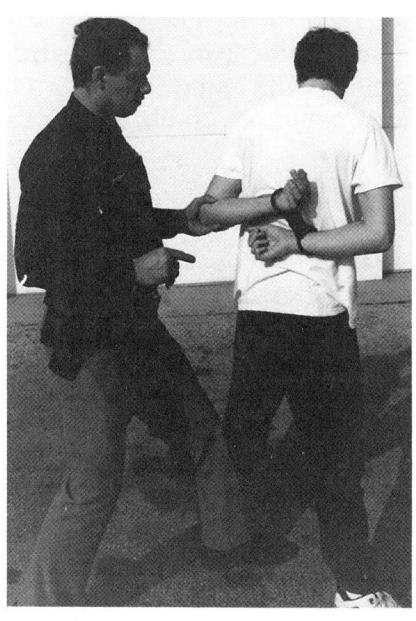

The officer completes the stacking handcuff method behind the subject's back.

Handcuffing and Officer Survival

- **Kneeling:** Order the subjects to place their hands on top of their heads and to interlock their fingers together. Have them kneel and cross their ankles.

    Carefully approach the subjects. Grasp their hands together and at the same time apply the top handcuff to the right wrist. Immediately pull the cuffed arm outward from the body and pull the free hand around to complete the handcuffing technique.

    For more control place your foot on the subjects' legs as you apply the handcuffs.

The officer brings the subject's right arm straight out and his free arm around.

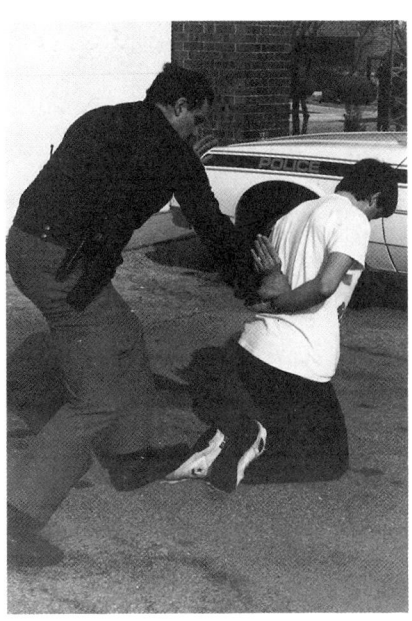

The officer completes the stacking handcuff method on the subject.

- **Ground:** Order the subjects to lie flat on the ground with their faces turned away from you. Instruct them to cross their ankles and spread their arms out with palms facing up.

    Approach the subjects carefully and grasp their arms in an Armbar. Place your knee in a 45 degree angle on their rear shoulder area. Now complete a Handcuffing Wrist Lock and tell them to bring the free hand to their back. Handcuff the free hand and the secured hand at the same time.

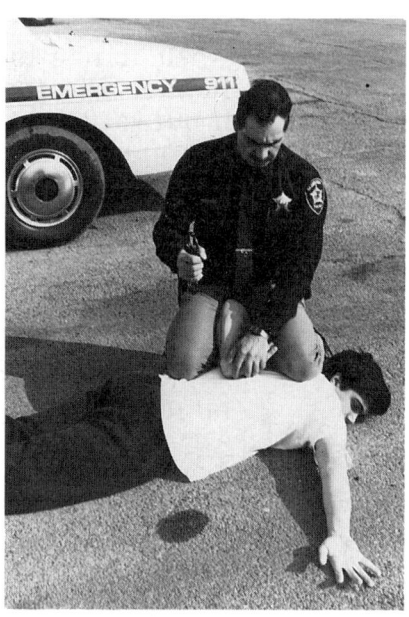 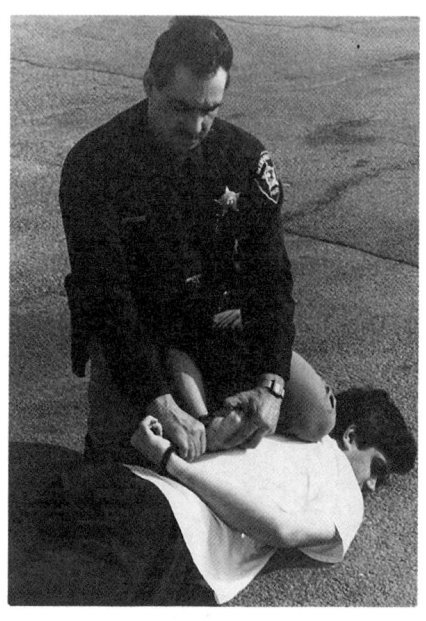

The officer approaches the subject carefully, completes a ground handcuffing wrist lock, and gets into position to handcuff him.

The officer handcuffs the subject in a stacking position.

Handcuffing the Resisting or Combative Subject

The number one rule is safety to the officer. As a 27 year veteran of the street, this author cannot emphasize enough the importance of the proper use of manpower when confronted with combative subjects. Police officers are not out there to spar and argue with subjects, and remember 50/50 on the street means you are losing. There are many law enforcement communities where backup officers may be many miles away, or in some cases, just not available. These are just a few techniques you can employ with resisting subjects.

> **Technique 1:** You have advised the subjects that they are under arrest but they refuse to cooperate. The left hand of a subject is up with a finger in your face.

Handcuffing and Officer Survival

(left) The officer grasps the subject's hand and gets his cuffs ready. (right) The officer places top cuff on the subject's wrist.

With your left hand grab the subject's raised hand and at the same moment apply the top handcuff to the subject's left wrist. Apply pressure downward, forcing the subject toward the ground. Apply an Armbar and Arm Lock, and bring the subject's free arm to the rear to complete the handcuffing.

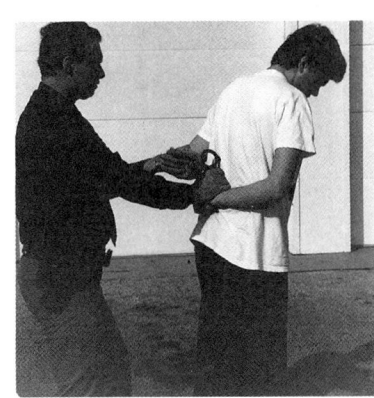

(left) Officer applies downward pressure forcing the subject to bend. (right) The officer applies second cuff in the stacking position.

▶ **Technique 2:** You have advised the subject of arrest and the subject responds by throwing a right punch at you. Using your left arm apply an Outside, Open Hand Block.

Once the block has stopped the punch, with the handcuffs in your right hand, apply the bottom handcuff to the subject's wrist. Now apply downward pressure on the grip portion of the cuff and rotate the handcuff which will immediately turn the subject around.

Grasp the subject's free hand to complete the procedure. Always double lock the cuffs.

The subject throws a right punch. The officer deflects the punch with his left hand and at the same time draws out his handcuffs.

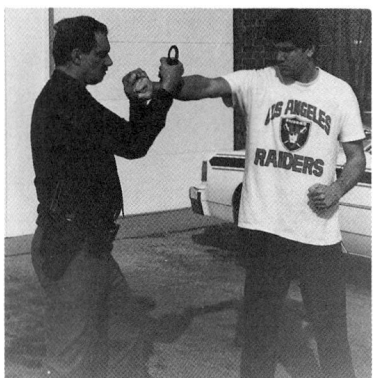 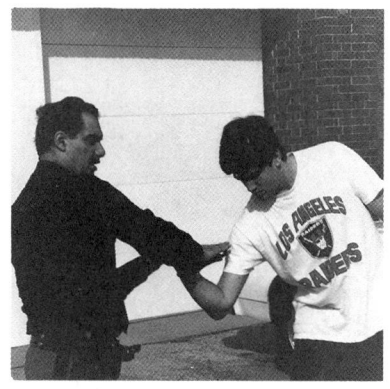

(left) The officer places the bottom handcuff on the subject. (right) The officer puts pressure on top of the handcuff which forces the subject downward.

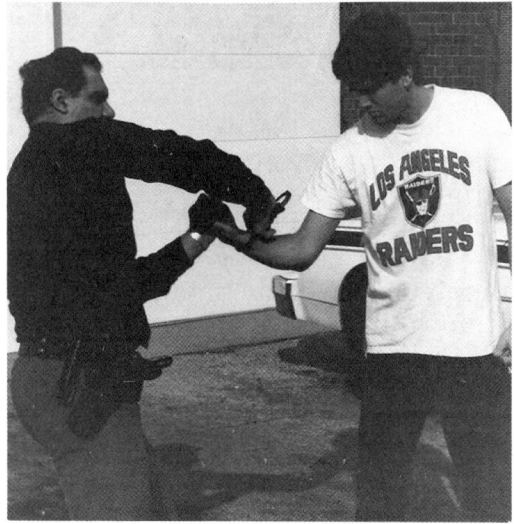

The officer changes his grip on the handcuff in order to turn the subject around for handcuffing the free hand.

Taking the Handcuffs Off Subjects

In all of these handcuffing techniques, it is essential to maintain control of the cuffs and subjects when removing the cuffs from them. Keep the subjects off balance. Have them bend forward as you remove the handcuffs. This is why the holes should be on the outside of handcuffed subjects.

Conclusion

This brief chapter on handcuffing has just touched upon some of the very basic techniques officers should know in order to better survive on the street. Handcuffing skills are like any other psychomotor skills in that these techniques **must** be practiced on a regular basis in order to maintain proficiency. Officers should review the basic handcuffing techniques and procedures every three months to insure continued improvement and efficiency in their use. The little discomfort officers may feel when practicing handcuffing is a small price to pay for proficiency in this essential tool of law enforcement. To survive on the street, officers must not neglect their handcuffing training. They should review the techniques often.

Special Thanks to Officer David Jenkins of the Glenview Police Department for taking the photographs for this chapter. Officer Jenkins is a man of many skills. He is a range instructor and a member of the regional area SWAT Team.

And a Special Thanks to Brian Truncale who agreed to endure some pain and discomfort for the photographs.

About the Author

Mr. Joseph J. Truncale has been a full time police officer for over 27 years and has worked in many areas of law enforcement including patrol, detective, juvenile, and tactical units. His special expertise is teaching psychomotor skills. He is a life-time student of the martial arts earning black belts in Karate, Judo, Jujitsu, and Kobudo. He has also studied other martial arts, such as boxing, wrestling, kick boxing, and several other Jujitsu styles. He is a recognized expert in police and martial arts weapons. He has written over 15 books and training manuals on defensive tactics and police weapons, and has over 100 articles and reviews published on various topics.

Mr. Truncale has instructed officers across the country at international seminars. He is a founding member of the American Society of Law Enforcement Trainers (ASLET), an International Instructor in the PR-24™ Police Baton, Straight Baton, Persuader Baton, and handcuffing and police defensive tactics. Besides working as a full time police officer, he has his own training and consulting company, Pro-Systems.

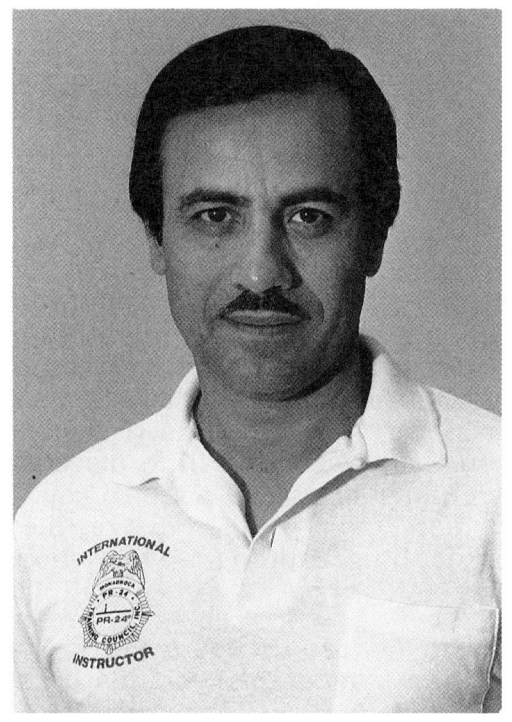

John P. Vazquez

Sergeant Vazquez is a 27 year veteran of the Elizabeth, New Jersey, Police Department. He has also been the Defensive Tactics' Coordinator for the Union County, New Jersey, Police Academy for the past 18 years. He is a former Platoon Leader and Trainer for the Union County Tactical Force in Union County, New Jersey.

Sergeant Vazquez is the Assistant Executive Director and a founding member of the American Society of Law Enforcement Trainers (ASLET). He is an International PR-24™ Instructor and Advisory Board Member to the PR-24™ Training Council. In addition, he is a National Trainer and Advisory Board Member to the National Law Enforcement Training Council (NLETC) and an Advisory Board Member to Police magazine.

Chapter 45

Crowd Confrontation Management

by John P. Vazquez

Introduction

The Centurion Guards during the Roman Empire knew the importance of the principle of "unity of effort." They also believed in a concept that was as important then as it is today; preparation.

The principles of unity of effort and preparation have surfaced time and again in response to emergency problems but oftentimes too late. The disorder of the sixties was a classic example. Many agencies went to great lengths to have their officers trained properly in crowd management. In the aftermath of the Los Angeles Riots in early 1992, these agencies are now looking for the expertise they previously enjoyed.

Today's centurions are aware of the potential for crowd involvement. They know what it takes to make a plan work. They also know, in order to insure success, the plan must be reinforced.

Other areas of concern are the luxuries of time and manpower. In larger cities, patrol units have been blitzed within seconds by people pouring out of projects and tenement buildings. The football term "blitzed," aptly describes the scenario confronting officers waiting for support. A system for spontaneous, small-group deployment would provide the time needed to evacuate or hold an area. This is possible with or without supervisory presence, as will be discussed.

The Disorder Platoon

Creating the Unit

To the administrator contemplating the formation of a Disorder Platoon, two important steps must be considered:

1.) **The training must be intense.** Like it or not, Disorder Platoon training is combat training. This involves hands on, active participation. Many administrators, in an attempt to save money, offer "piece meal" training. Officers watching videos and lecture formats by themselves will not do.

2.) **The training must be ongoing.** What you don't use, you lose! Therefore, training must be done consistently, not once a year. Repetition instills competence and competence breeds confidence. This is the essence of quality training.

Disorder Platoon Size

The strength of a Disorder Platoon is usually based on several factors, some of which is the size of the department, its jurisdictional responsibility, area population, and history of past occurrences. Its composition will be anywhere from two to four squads, depending on the number of officers allotted.

A squad generally has twelve officers which includes a squad leader and an assistant squad leader. The assistant's function is to assist the squad leader, at the rear, where he or she can coordinate special team operations, if needed.

Selecting Personnel

Officers who comprise the Disorder Platoon must understand the seriousness of their participation. They are all individual links of a chain which is only as strong as its weakest link. Therefore, they must all think and act as a unit.

Normally, the largest and fittest officers are selected to fill the ranks. This is to create as much psychological advantage, visually, as possible. However, today's agencies include female and minority representatives who are smaller in stature. Therefore, the emphasis should be towards coordinated skill development rather than visual impact.

Training Objectives

There are two major training objectives the administrator should focus on:

1.) Understanding the psychological, sociological, and cultural factors that may be underlying causes of the development of mobs.

Crowd Confrontation Management

2.) The development of an easily deployed unit capable of controlling or preventing outbreaks of violence.

Crowd control training, once instituted, must include all officers up to and including command personnel. Nothing is more frustrating to line officers than to be led by incompetents. In some agencies, the selection of Platoon Leaders is based on experience and ability rather than rank. This can be done without compromising the decision making powers of ranking officials and is sometimes advisable where lieutenants and captains have not had prior military experience.

Requisite Training

The following areas of knowledge should be inclusive for all members of Disorder Platoons:

- **Close Quarter Drilling:** The majority of officers today receive close quarter drilling at the police academy. The bad news is, that was probably the last time. Close quarter drilling is the process of moving individuals collectively from one position to an another. It develops timing, coordination, and discipline, which in turn creates a mechanism for unity of effort. Without close quarter drilling, it is difficult to develop an organization that will function as a unit. Drilling is probably the most overlooked of all skill development because of the assumption that it is too easy. Nothing could be further from the truth.

- **Physical Conditioning:** A well conditioned body should be the primary goal of all Disorder Platoon members, not only for the strength and stamina that is required, but also for the psychological edge created by the visual impact of physically fit personnel.

- **Tactical Formations:** The root of Crowd Confrontation Management is the ability to implement specially designed control formations. All officers should be well-versed in the various types of formations as well as their designated functions. It is also important that members understand their exact role within the control tactic and have a clear understanding of the department's overall plan for the prevention and control of violence.

- **Characteristics of Crowd/Mob Development:** An understanding of the sociological and psychological characteristics of crowd/mob disorders can assist in recognition of symptoms that may lead to problems.

- **Limits of Legal Authority:** Members must be aware of the scope of their legal authority with emphasis on limitations and responsibilities. Special attention must also be given to the topic of use of force and every precaution should be taken to avoid being provoked into violence. Therefore, each member must be indoctrinated in the importance of maintaining a level head.

- **Characteristics and Use of Specialized Equipment:** Each member must have a working knowledge of the various tools and weapons that may be used, such as tactical batons, gas masks, firearms, gas guns, etc. This will also provide proper alternatives if needed.

- **First Aid:** All members should be certified in First Aid, CPR, and Post Traumatic Stress Disorders.

The Origin of the Riot Law

The origin of the law dealing with riots has its roots in English Common Law. There was an act introduced in 1714 in response to those who were protesting the ascension of George I to the English throne. Unfortunately, there had to be twelve or more people present, and a magistrate had to read word for word the exact terms of this act, later to be called the "Riot Act."

American and British Law tend to view crowd disorders a little different from the rest of the world. We think of them as a breach of the peace, but a country like China views them as a resistance to authority. For this reason, our responsibility is always to the people we serve, not to those in authority.

Crowds vs. Mobs

A crowd has a general pattern similar to that of an individual. One of the main characteristics of a crowd is its awareness of the law and its willingness to abide by the principles of law and order.

A mob, however, will take the law into its own hands. It surfaces for a variety of reasons and usually does so as a remedy to a particular occurrence. The only sure way to prevent a mob from forming is to prevent the occurrence in the first place. This is often easier said than done.

Symptoms of Mob Formations

Usually the formation of a mob follows a recognizable process of

Crowd Confrontation Management

evolution. If it becomes apparent that one is forming, it can be prevented by inhibiting the process through planned intervention methods.

The process usually begins with a series of irritating events (i.e., police issuing too many traffic tickets). Then a traumatic event takes place (i.e., the arrest of a prominent citizen) and exaggerated rumors tend to surface about the event (i.e., the citizen died from police brutality) which creates frustration. When this occurs, people begin to congregate to vent their frustrations. This usually creates a chain reaction of emotion that makes the crowd less responsive to outside stimulus and more responsive to what is going on inside the crowd. At this point, the individual withers and the crowd takes over until finally overt behavior leads to violence and destruction.

During this process methods may be employed to inhibit the birth of a mob. For example, during the rumor phase, an anti-rumor squad of community leaders and police representatives could have been implemented to squash unfounded information.

Objectives at the Scene of an Unlawful Assembly

There are five basic objectives at the scene of an unlawful assembly:

1.) **Containment**
    Isolate the crowd from the rest of the community and monitor its behavior. Remove all sight seers from the area.

2.) **Dispersal**
    Give the order to disperse, but allow a realistic time for this to be accomplished. Direct them toward a previously designated avenue of escape. If formations are needed to facilitate dispersal, then use them. However, it should be noted that the use of formations is to control, not to punish.

3.) **Prevent Re-Entry**
    If a mob is allowed to re-enter an area, it can be more hazardous than before.

4.) **Arrest Violators**
    Usually the problem is solved the moment the trouble maker is arrested. However, when the decision is made to arrest, it should be done as expeditiously as possible. Units that remain at the scene with their rotating lights still activated attract unwanted individuals.

5.) **Establish Priorities**

    ☐ **Assess the Situation:** Monitor the rate of growth and the demeanor of the crowd through infiltration or on-scene observation. Determine the leaders, if there any, and note their descriptions. Be aware of anything that could be potentially hazardous to responding law enforcement officers.

☐ **Communicate Needs**: Be prepared. Let command officers know in advance what extra equipment may be required. Make necessary notifications to Emergency Management, Fire/Rescue, EMT, and Recall.

☐ **Be Flexible**: Create avenues of escape. Control drinking utensils or possibly consider closing liquor establishments to prevent the fueling of tempers. Don't operate with an outdated plan that won't allow for flexibility. It may be a shortcut to failure.

Control Formations

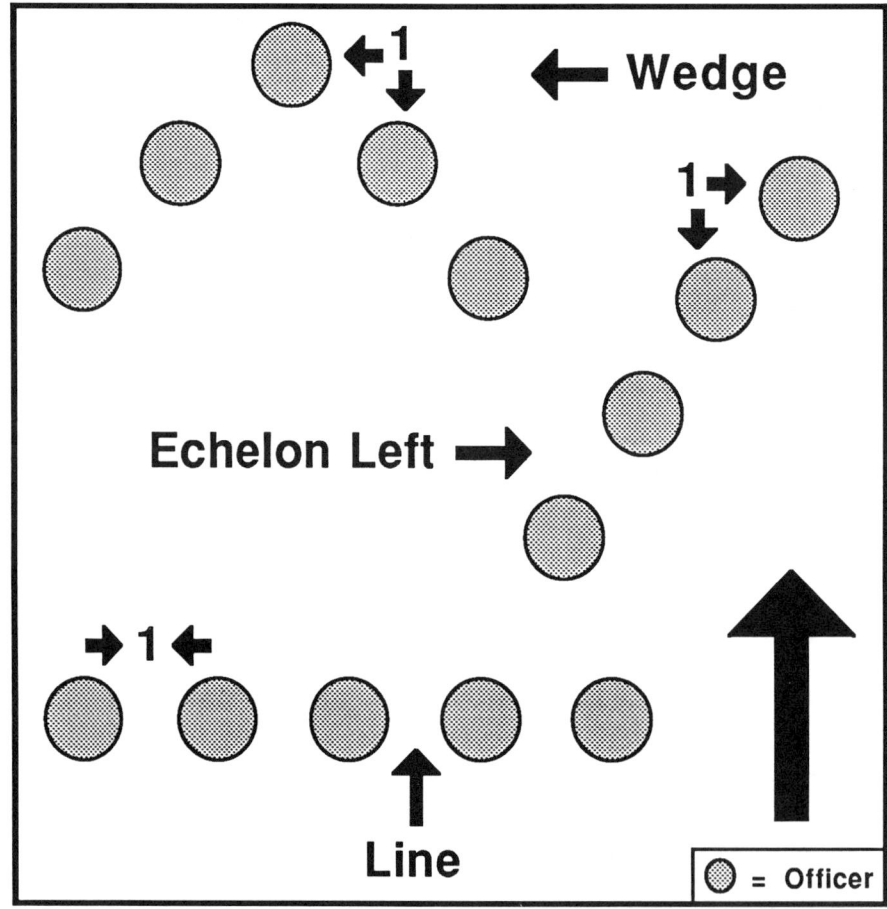

Figure 1: Fundamental Control Formations — Line, Wedge, and Diagonal (Echelon Left).

Crowd Confrontation Management

The fundamental control formations (see Figure 1 on page 428, Figure 2 below, and Figure 3 on page 430) are the Line, Wedge, and Diagonal (echelon left or right).

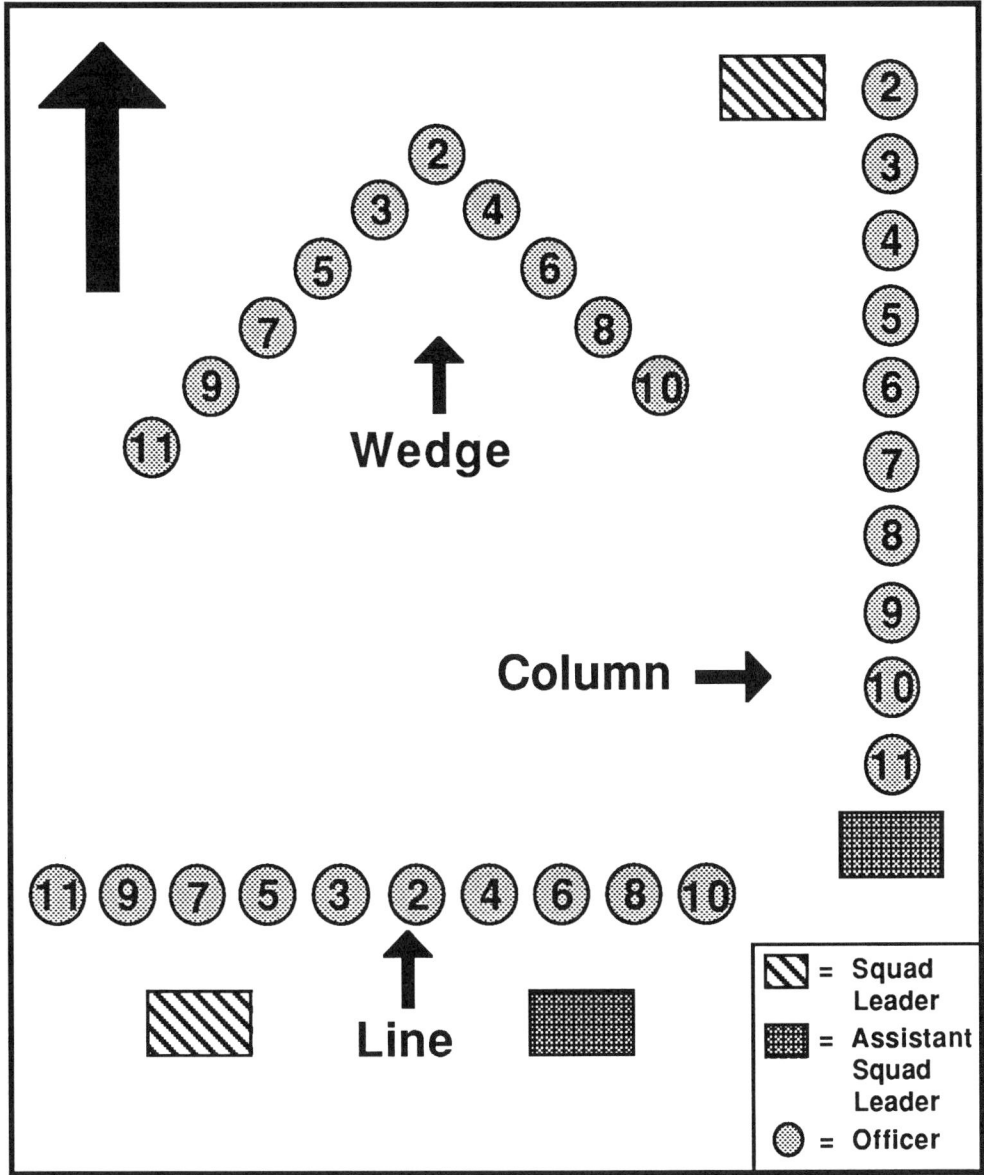

Figure 2: **Fundamental Control Formations — Line, Wedge, and Column.**

These formations were designed to provide a more accurate control of trained combat officers in the dispersal of crowds.

The difference between military and law enforcement concepts is that military combat formations were devised to destroy the enemy while the police mission is to dispel crowds with a minimum of casualties.

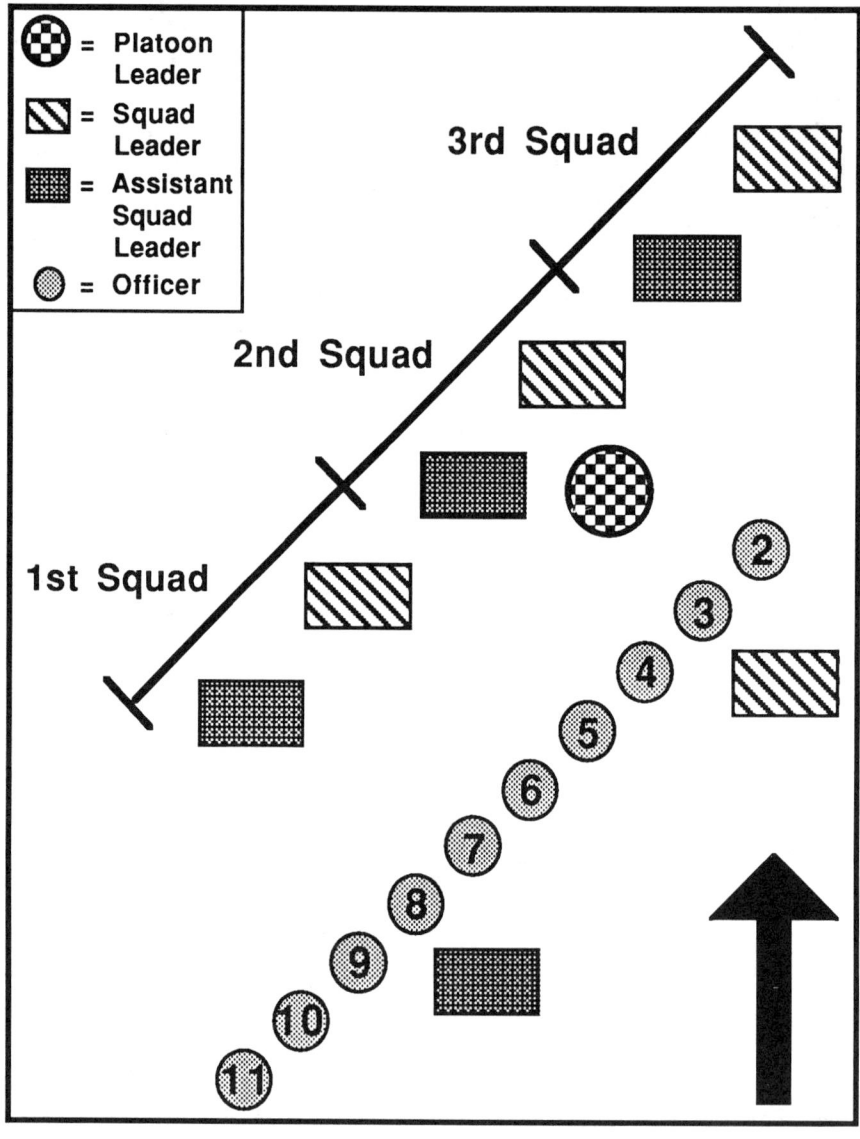

Figure 3: Fundamental Control Formations — Echelon Left.

Crowd Confrontation Management

Psychological Advantages

There are two basic psychological advantages to placing units into formations:

1.) When crowds observe the police moving as a unit it impresses them.

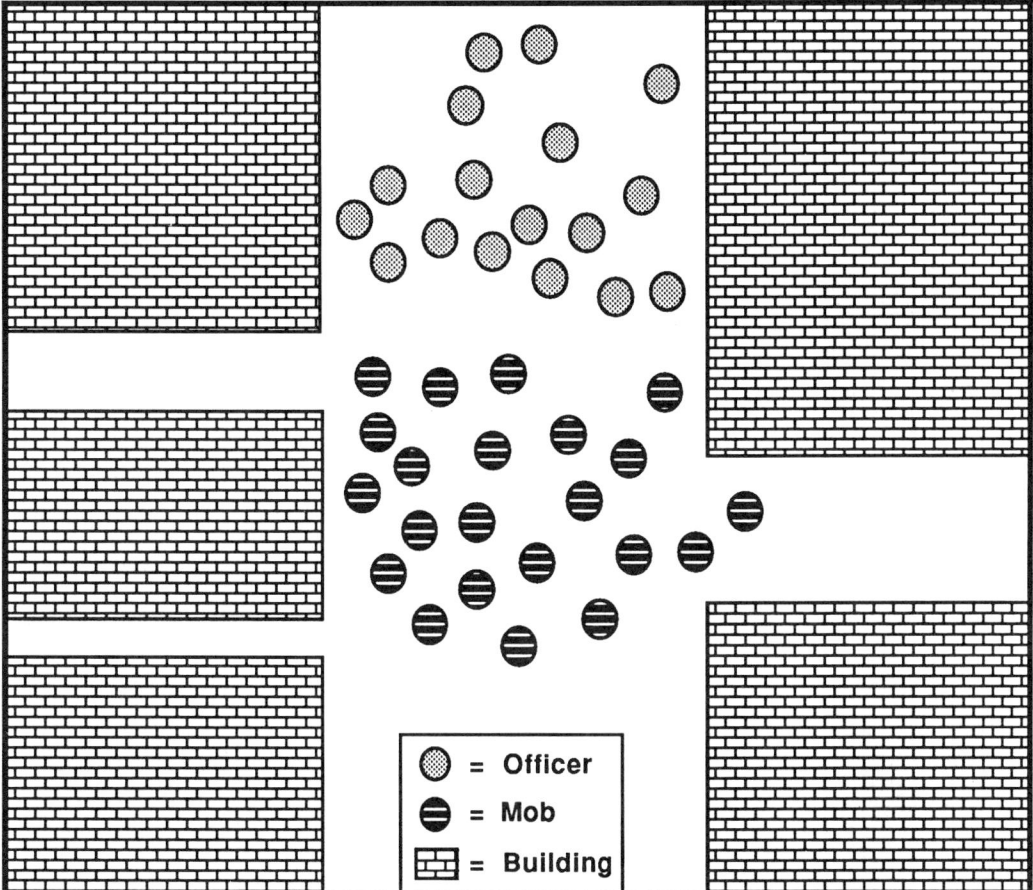

Figure 4: Police Moving as a Unit.

2.) When police officers are placed in a unit, it forces them to act as a unit rather than as individuals.

Functions of Formations

There is a specific purpose for design formation when dealing with crowd/mob disorders:

1.) The Line Formation is designed to move crowds out of, or into, an area. (see Figure 5 below).

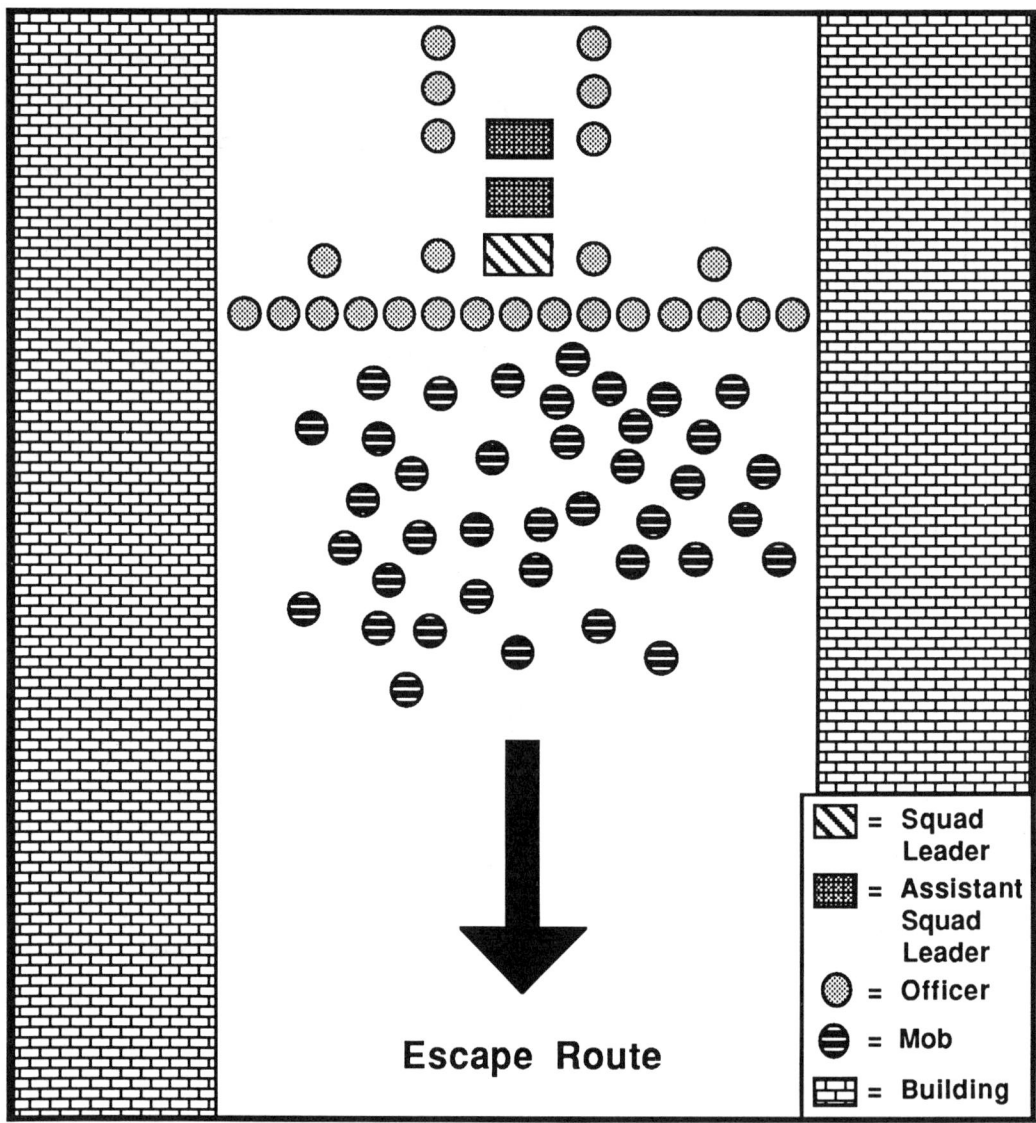

Figure 5: The Squad Line Pushes a Mob Back.

Crowd Confrontation Management

2.) The Wedge Formation is designed to divide the crowd in two, and to fragment it into a more manageable size (see Figure 6 below).

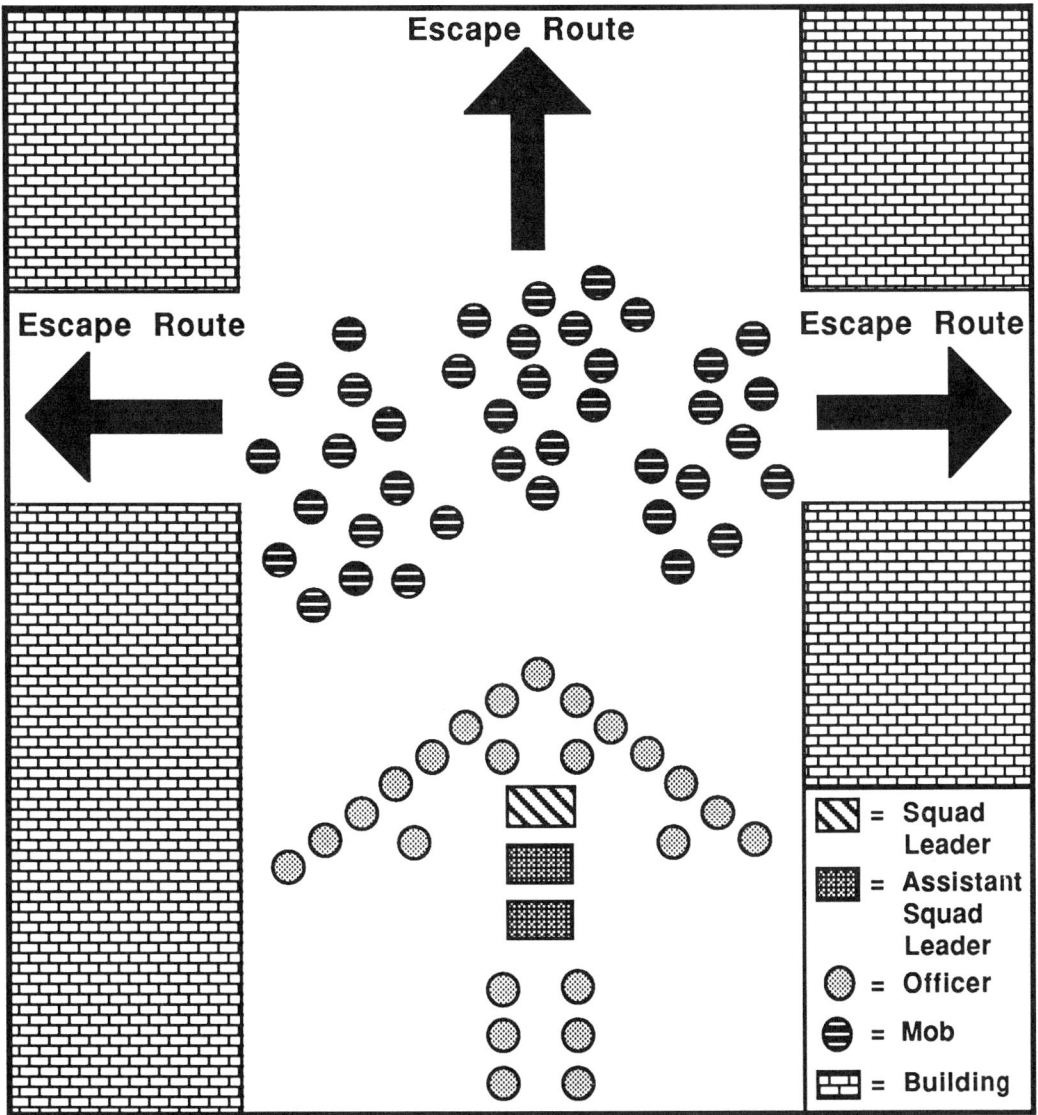

Figure 6: The Wedge Formation Divides the Crowd.

3.) The Diagonal or Echelon Left or Right Formation is designed to peel individuals away from a wall or fence. If an arrest team is trapped inside a doorway and surrounded by a hostile crowd, an echelon formation will assist in moving the crowd away from the doorway so the arrest team can be freed (see Figure 7 below).

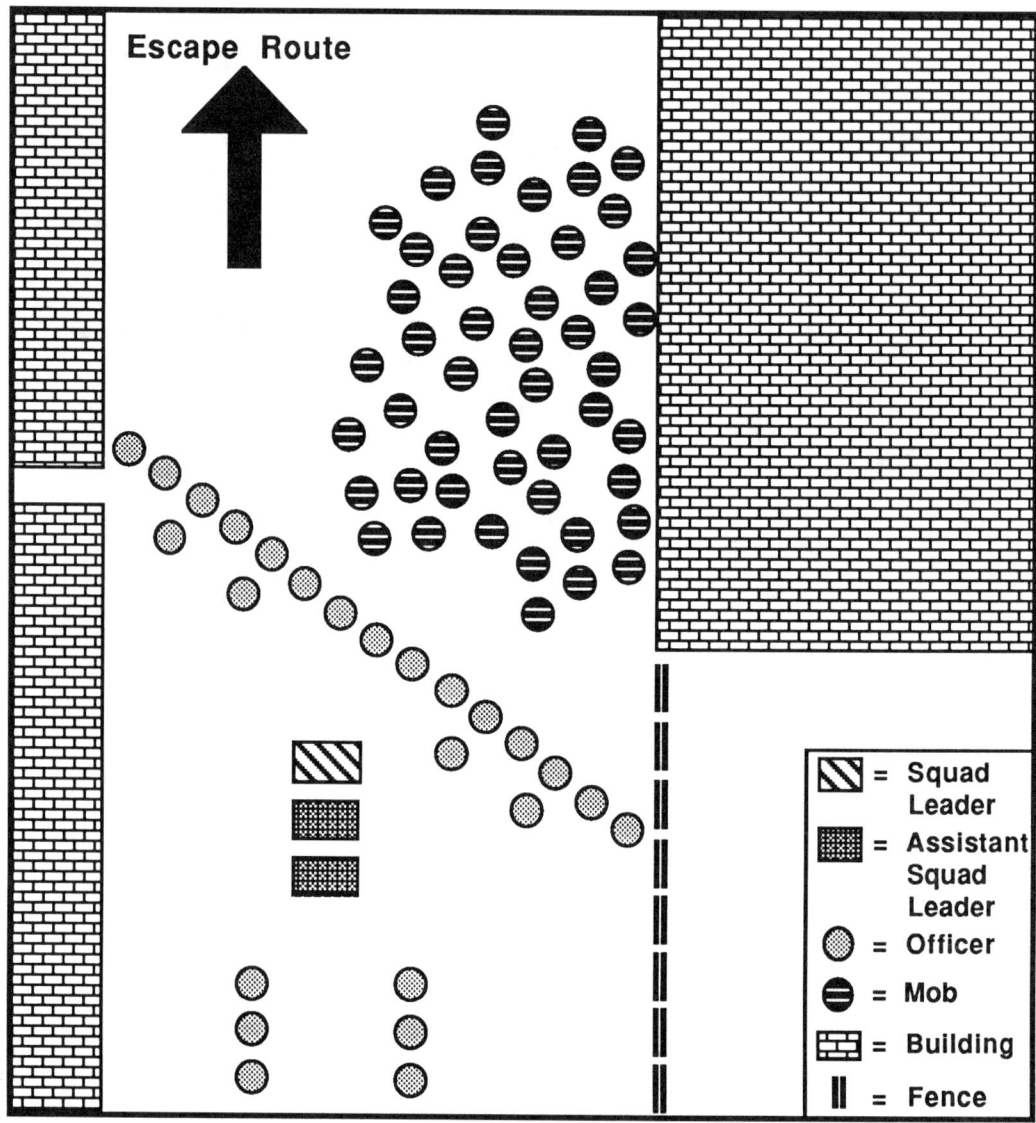

Figure 7: Echelon Right Formation

Mechanics of Assembling a Squad

When assembling squads, it is important to know that commands are usually given in two stages, preparatory commands and commands of

Crowd Confrontation Management

execution.

The standard commands are:

- **"Squad — Fall In."** All officers form a single line according to height with the tallest officer to the right.

- **"Squad — Count Off."** The first officer commences to count starting with the number two until all officers have been given a numerical designation.

- **"Squad — Fall In, Single File."** Officers fall in one behind the other in a column according to numerical designation.

- **"Squad — Fall In, Column of Twos."** Officers fall in two columns, side by side, with even numbered officers on the right and odd numbered officers on the left.

Interval and Distance

An interval is the lateral space between officers, and distance is the space between officers in a column. The interval and distance between officers is usually one pace or 30 inches.

Cadences

When marching in formation, the cadence is 120 steps per minute. When moving from an assembly to a formation, or from a formation back to an assembly, the cadence is 180 steps per minute or quick time.

Baton Positions

There are three basic baton positions:

1.) **Port Arms or High Port**: The baton is held at a 45 degree angle directly in front of the officer.

2.) **Safe Guard**: The baton is punched parallel to the deck (ground) pointing toward the crowd. The command, "Safe Guard" is given in one count.

3.) **On Guard**: The officer begins thrusting the baton towards the crowd in time with a stomp and drag cadence. The command, "On Guard" is given also in one count.

Staging the Disorder Platoon

There are four basic procedures to staging:

1.) Assemble at a point out of sight of the crowd/mob.
2.) Brief and issue necessary equipment.
3.) Assign numerical designations (count off).
4.) Report to the Commanding Officer.

Crowd Engagement

When the Commanding Officer has exhausted all means of persuading the crowd/mob to disperse, he or she will signal the platoon leader to march the Disorder Platoon into view. This is a last attempt to convince the crowd to leave. If this fails, he or she will direct the platoon leader to disperse the crowd. The platoon leader in turn, will communicate to the squad leaders which squads he or she intends to use and in what manner. This is based on the size of the crowd and its behavior.

Methods of Communication

There are several methods of communication used by the platoon leader to convey commands:

- Verbal Commands: Usually enhanced by the use of a bullhorn.

- Sound Signals: Predetermined signals with whistles or airhorns.

- Hand Signals: Predetermined signals with gestures.

Sometimes the noise of the crowd is so loud that all three methods may be used. This is especially true when something like smoke makes it difficult to be seen. Nevertheless, many platoon leaders tend to favor hand signals over all (see Figure 8 on page 437).

Crowd Confrontation Management 437

Figure 8: Hand Signals

Moving Into Formation

When the platoon leader selects a course of action, he or she turns toward the platoon and gives a command for a baton position, usually "Port Arms" or "High Port." He or she then signals the squad leaders and tells them what formation he or she wants, and whether it is of squad or platoon strength. The squad leaders in turn, look over their right shoulders and repeats these commands to the members of his or her squad.

The platoon leader then points to an area on the ground and yells, "Move." If he or she is not heard, the mere pointing of the finger will direct the members to move anyway. The squads that are used are told by their squad leaders to, "Follow me" and are directed to the area pointed to by the platoon leader. This is done at a very brisk pace or double time.

At the pointed to area, the #2 point man gets into his or her position so the others can construct the elements of the desired formation. The squads that are not used are told to, "Stand Fast," meaning, "Don't move, we're not going." Their function is "Squads in Support."

Support Squads and Special Teams

Support squads are usually designated according to need. Special teams work best if they are assigned to their own squad. The support squads may be used in:

- **General Support:** The squad marches in a column behind the formation, waiting to be assigned.

- **Lateral Support:** The squad creates parallel borders on each end of the formation to prevent the crowd from spilling behind the formation. It must be noted that all members designated as odd numbered form the border on the left, while all even numbered members form the border on the right. An exception is when two squads are used for lateral support. In this case, one squad will take one side and the remaining squad the other.

- **Close Support:** When members of the crowd appear to be squeezing between the officers in the formation, the support squad literally reinforces the original squad by filling in the spaces in the formation (see Figure 9 on page 439).

The squad assigned to special team duties may include:

1.) Arrest Team
2.) Gas Team
3.) Sniper Team
4.) Observer Unit
5.) Media Unit

Adjunct Units

Todays units have tremendous technology to assist in Crowd

Crowd Confrontation Management

Confrontation Management. Larger agencies have helicopters for observational assistance as well as mounted police to integrate crowd formations.

Some agencies have reported using K-9 Units with great success while others fear they create an image problem. It is interesting to note that K-9 handlers insist on being in front of the formations while they sweep the area with three dogs on 30 foot leads. This virtually makes the entire formation a support group used to secure an area. This also protects platoon members from innocent dogs who cannot tell the good guys from the bad ones.

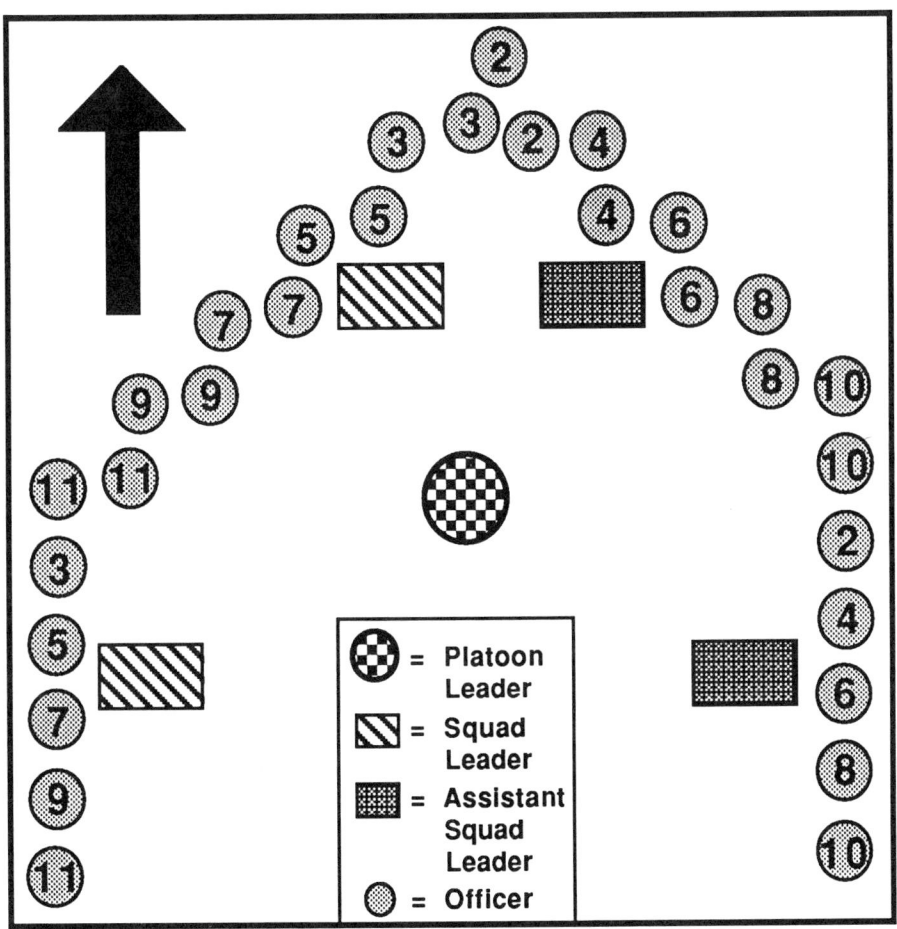

Figure 9: Platoon Wedge — Squads in Close and Lateral Support.

Execution of a Platoon Wedge

The execution of a three-squad platoon wedge may be done in several ways. The platoon leader forms a triangle over his or her head by touching his or her finger tips together. The verbal command is, "Platoon Wedge, First, Second, and Third Squads." Then pointing to an area, "Move."

The first squad to move is the second squad whose point person takes the point position at High Port facing the crowd.

All even numbered members take a position one step to the right and rear of the member in front. All odd numbered members take a position one step to the left and rear of the member in front. When the second squad has completed forming the wedge, the first and third squad just add onto it with the first squad adding on to the odd side, and the third squad adding on to the even side.

Another type of wedge formation is of squad size, but reinforced. The platoon leader assumes the same gesture as above, but says, "Squad Wedge First Squad, Second Squad in Close Support, Third Squad in Lateral support. Move."

This time the first squad takes the point position at the designated spot with odd numbers one step to the left and rear and even numbers one step to the right and rear. The second squad fills in the holes of the first squad with odd numbers to the left and even numbers to the right. Finally, the third squad creates lateral borders with odd numbers to the left and even numbers to the right.

Special Formations

The deployment of platoon and squad formations are varied and diversified. The formations should serve a purpose and be flexible enough to change. Many situations have been handled quite satisfactory with the basic three of Line, Wedge, and Echelon. However, it must be pointed out that many agencies have added other types for specific purposes. Some of these are:

1.) Crossbow Formation
2.) L Formation
3.) Inverted L Formation
4.) Diamond Formation

Crowd confrontation formations are only limited by the imagination.

Mini Formation

There are many instances when crowd confrontation is sponta-

Crowd Confrontation Management

neous and does not allow for the staging of an organized unit. This author recognized a need for a system that would allow officers to unify their efforts by organizing themselves into small units. This system has been shared for many years at the PR-24™ National Seminar held in London, Ohio.

The system basically works this way. If one or more patrol units find themselves being overwhelmed by a spontaneous crowd, or if a support unit notices that a hostile crowd is getting too close to an arrest team, one officer can designate himself or herself as a point person by yelling, "On Me" or "Team."

When this is done, the officer takes a position with a baton facing the crowd in either a Long Extended or On Guard position. A second officer can now take a position one step to the right and rear, or one step to the left and rear of the point person. If a third officer arrives, that officer takes whatever spot is left. What is now formed is a mini-wedge formation. All commands and functions are guided by the point person.

If a fourth officer arrives, he or she can protect the back of the wedge by creating a diamond. This fourth officer is entirely flexible to turn and do what he or she has to in order to protect the rear.

Once this system becomes familiar, officers are able to coordinate their efforts more efficiently by forming several mini-formations at the same time. The major goal is to have officers operating together as a unit to buy time and to effect a psychological advantage.

Patrol Operations

During emergency circumstances, squads are divided into eight or ten member teams by organizing them into two patrol vehicles four or five to a car. A squad leader drives one car and the assistant squad leader the other. All members will have counted off prior to entering the vehicles; odd numbers on the left side and even numbers on the right. An exception is when there is a fifth member sitting in the middle of the rear seat. The fifth member in car A is even, and gets out on the right side, and the one in Car B becomes odd, exiting on the left side. This balances out the formation. The squad leader always takes a position behind the formation while the assistant squad leader moves to the last position of the odd side.

Conclusion

During the sixties, in Union County, New Jersey, a plan was instituted to assist smaller communities by combining a percentage of all 21 agencies into one Tactical Force with county jurisdiction. This operated with great success until it dissolved from attrition. In the aftermath of the Los Angeles Riots, administrators are interested in bringing back the program. The principles of the "Old Centurions" once again remind us to get back to basics.

Crowd confrontation is an ever present dilemma. Therefore, systems designed to control it should be consistently reinforced. If we allow these training methods to erode, we will have to look for them down the road.

The solution to erosion lies in the principle of the three R's:

▰▶ **Replenish** what you have lost through attrition.

▰▶ **Reinforce** what you already have through training.

▰▶ **Refine** your plan of action to present day needs.

REMEMBER, WHAT YOU DON'T USE, YOU LOSE.

Biography

Ed Nowicki

Ed Nowicki is one of the nation's leading law enforcement trainers. In addition, he is the former Executive Director of the nation's largest law enforcement training association, the prestigious American Society of Law Enforcement Trainers (ASLET). A continuously sworn police officer since 1968, and a survivor of six separate shooting incidents, he began his law enforcement career with the Chicago Police Department, where he served for more than ten years. He has held the ranks of patrolman, detective, lieutenant, and Chief of Police with four law enforcement agencies.

Since 1981, Ed has been employed full time as a Police Training Specialist with Milwaukee Area Technical College and still serves part time as a sworn police officer for the Twin Lakes, Wisconsin, Police Department. He is an international trainer and has trained thousands of police officers. He is regularly featured as a speaker or presenter at a number of professional conferences. There have been articles written about him, and he has frequently appeared on television.

Ed Nowicki has been judicially recognized and declared an expert on police training and has received numerous awards for his work and contributions to law enforcement and law enforcement training. A widely published and respected author for various law enforcement publications, he serves as a contributing editor to *Law Enforcement Technology* magazine. He is one of two technical advisors for *Police* magazine, and he is an advisor to *The Police Marksman* magazine. In addition to *Total Survival*, he has written two other books. A former Municipal Judge, he holds a Bachelor of Science Degree in Criminal Justice and a Master of Arts Degree in Management.

Contact Information for the Authors

Albrecht, Steven F., Reserve Officer, San Diego Police Department, 1401 Broadway, San Diego, CA 92101, (619) 284-7514.

Armbruster, George, Chief Deputy, Lafayette Parish Sheriff's Department, P.O. Drawer 3508, Lafayette, LA 70502, (318) 232-9211.

Ayoob, Massad, Director of Lethal Force Institute, P.O. Box 122, Concord, NH 03301, (603) 224-6814.

Berry, Dean, Dean Berry Associates, Inc., P.O. Box 4490, St. Paul, MN 55104, (612) 222-4168.

Berry, Stan, 4653 Bryant Avenue, South, Minneapolis, MN 55409, (612) 822-9018.

Boyle, Michael F., Lieutenant, New Jersey Department of Environmental Protection, Central Region Office, R.D. 3, Box 386, Robbinsville, NJ 08691, (609) 259-3347.

Brave, Michael A., Account Executive and Senior Associate, Institute for Liability Management, 3006 Nimitz Street, Eau Claire, WI 54701, (715) 833-1125.

Bunting, Stephen M., Executive Director, American Society of Law Enforcement Trainers (ASLET), 102 Dock Road, P.O. Box 361, Lewes, DE 19958-0361, (302) 645-4080.

Burroughs, William E., Assistant Director of Training, SIGARMS, Inc., Corporate Park, Exeter, NH 03833, (603) 772-2302.

Casavant, Andrew J., President, Midwest Tactical Training Institute, 11311 S. Skunk Hollow Road, Mt. Carroll, IL 61053, (815) 244-2815.

Chandler, Dr. James T., 206 Twin Oaks Drive, Rochester, IL 62563, (217) 498-8889.

Chu, Douglas, Senior Instructor, Modern Warrior Defensive Tactics Institute, 711 N. Wellwood Avenue, Lindenhurst, NY 11757, (516) 226-8383.

Cirillo, Jim, 1211 Venetian Way, Panama City, FL 32405, (904) 271-4638.

Contact Information for the Authors

Clede, Bill, 272 Ridge Road, Wethersfield, CT 06109-1019, (203) 563-9555.

Collingwood, Dr. Thomas R., Director, Institute for Aerobics Research, 12330 Preston Road, Dallas, TX 75230, (214) 701-8001.

Donovan, Edward C., Executive Director, International Law Enforcement Stress Association, P.O. Box 3360, Plymouth, MA 02361, (508) 747-5746.

Dunston, Mark S., Director, North MS Law Enforcement Training Center, 1 Finney Lane, Tupelo, MS 38801, (601) 841-6400.

Fairburn, Dick, Chief of Police, Upton Police Department, P.O. Box 44, Upton, WY 82730, (307) 468-2475.

Farnam, John S., President, Defense Training International, Inc., P.O. Box 665, Niwot, CO 80544 (303) 530-7106.

Fortin, Neal, Inspector, Michigan Department of Agriculture, P.O. Box 30017, Lansing, MI 48909, (517)353-8130.

Fulton, Roger, President, Knight Management Corporation, P.O. Box 12035, Albany, NY 12212, (518) 456-6780.

Gordon, Kevin, Director, Crime Fighters Institute, 7 Industrial Drive, Suite 2, Cahokia, IL 62206, (618) 337-6722.

Grossi, David, Senior Instructor, Calibre Press, Inc., 666 Dundee Road, Suite 1607, Northbrook, IL 60062-2727, (708) 498-5680.

Hedden, Harvey V., Sergeant, Kenosha County Controlled Substance Unit, 1000- 55th Street, Kenosha, WI 53140, (414) 652-2621.

Jurasz, Dennis F., President, Dimensional Tactics Systems, Inc., P.O. Box 1306, North Tonawanda, NY 14120-9306, (800) 346-2625.

Klugiewicz, Gary T., Lieutenant, Milwaukee County Sheriff's Department, 821 W. State Street, Milwaukee, WI 53233, (414) 278-5135.

Lindell, Jim, President, National Law Enforcement Training Center (NLETC), 3238 Gillham Road, Kansas City, MO 64109, (816) 531-6419.

Lindsey, "Coach" Bob, Director of Security, Jefferson Parish President's Office, 1221 Elmwood Park Blvd., Suite 1002, Harahan, LA 70123, (504) 736-6434.

May, Jr., William A., Captain, Louisville Department of Public Safety, 1135 W. Jefferson Street, Louisville, KY 40202, (502) 587-3220.

McKinnon, Dr. Murlene E., CEO, MACNLOW Associates, 1116 Boulder Court, Lansing, MI 48917, (517) 323-0740.

McRoberts, David W., Lieutenant, Kenosha County Sheriff's Department, 1000 55th Street, Kenosha, WI 53140, (414) 656-7340.

Messina, Phil, President, Modern Warrior Defensive Tactics Institute, 711 N. Wellwood Avenue, Lindenhurst, NY 11757, (516) 226-8383.

Morrison, John, Detective Lieutenant, San Diego Police Department, 1401 Broadway, San Diego, CA 92101, (619) 531-2000.

O'Linn, Mildred K., Attorney, Franscell, Strickland, Roberts & Lawrence, 225 S. Lake Avenue, Pasadena, CA 91101-3005, (818) 304-7830.

Ouellette, Roland, President, R.E.B. Security Training, Inc., P.O. Box 697, Avon, CT 06001, (203) 677-5936.

Robinson, Tracy, Senior Instructor, Modern Warrior Defensive Tactics Institute, 711 N. Wellwood Avenue, Lindenhurst, NY 11757, (516) 226-8383.

Rossi, Guy A., Vice-President, Dimensional Tactics Systems, Inc., P.O. Box 1306, North Tonawanda, NY 14120-9306, (800) 346-2625.

Sanow Edwin J., Corporal, Benton County Sheriff's Department, 607 E. Sixth, Fowler, IN 47944, (317) 884-0080.

Sapp, Arthur N., Lieutenant, Colorado Springs Police Department, 224 E. Kiowa Street, Colorado Springs, CO 80903, (719) 632-6611.

Scotti, Anthony J., President, Scotti School of Defensive Driving, 11 Riverside Avenue, Suite 15, Medford, MA 02155, (617) 395-9156.

Smith, Larry, Independent Law Enforcement Training Specialist, Larry Smith Enterprises, P.O. Box 710141, San Diego, CA 92171, (619) 560-7394.

Smith, Terry E., Director of Training Standards, Monadnock PR-24® Training Council, Inc., P.O. Box 509, Fitzwilliam, NH 03447, (800) 258-5492.

Spaulding, David J., Sergeant, Montgomery County Sheriff's Office, 330 W. Second Street, Dayton, OH 45422, (513) 225-4673.

Contact Information for the Authors

Stover Brian J., Sergeant, Los Angeles County Sheriff's Department, 8838 E. Las Tunas Drive, Temple City, CA 91780, (818)285-7171.

Trautman, Neal E., President, Standards and Training, Inc., 135 E. Bahama Road, Winter Springs, FL 32708, (407) 699-4012.

Truncale, Joseph J., President, Pro-Systems, P.O. Box 261, Glenview, IL 60025, (708) 729-7671.

Vazquez, John P., Sergeant, Elizabeth Police Department, 1 Police Plaza, Elizabeth, NJ 07201, (908) 558-2109.

Suggested Reading

Albrecht, Steve. *Streetwork: The Way to Officer Safety & Survival.* Paladin.

Albrecht, Steve and **Morrison, John.** *Contact & Cover: Two-Officer Suspect Control.* Charles C. Thomas.

Ayoob, Massad F. *Fundamentals of Modern Police Impact Weapons.* Massad F. and Dorothy A. Ayoob, Police Bookshelf.

Ayoob, Massad F. *Gunproof Your Children/Handgun Primer.* Massad F. and Dorothy A. Ayoob, Police Bookshelf.

Ayoob, Massad F. *Hit the White Part.* Massad F. and Dorothy A. Ayoob, Police Bookshelf.

Ayoob, Massad F. *In the Gravest Extreme.* Massad F. and Dorothy A. Ayoob, Police Bookshelf.

Ayoob, Massad F. *The Semiautomatic Pistol in Police Service in Self-Defense.* Massad F. and Dorothy A. Ayoob, Police Bookshelf.

Ayoob, Massad F. *StressFire.* Massad F. and Dorothy A. Ayoob, Police Bookshelf.

Ayoob, Massad F. *StressFire II.* Massad F. and Dorothy A. Ayoob, Police Bookshelf.

Ayoob, Massad F. *The Truth About Self Protection.* Massad F. and Dorothy A. Ayoob, Police Bookshelf.

Berry, Dean and **Berry, Stan.** *Action Writing for the '90s.*

Berry, Dean and **Berry, Stan.** *Business Grammar & Style.*

Berry, Dean. *A Workbook of Writing Models.*

Berry, Dean. *The Officer As Writer.*

Chandler, Dr. James T. *Modern Police Psychology.*

Clede, Bill. *Police Handgun Manual.*

Clede, Bill. *Police Nonlethal Force Manual.*

Suggested Reading

Clede, Bill. *Police Officer's Guide.*

Clede, Bill. *Police Handgun Manual.*

Clede, Bill. *Police Shotgun Manual.*

Collingwood, Dr. Thomas. *The Aerobics Program for Total Well-Being.* M. Evans.

Dunston, Mark S. *Street Signs.* Performance Dimensions Publishing.

Fulton, Roger. *Common Sense Supervision.*

Marshall, Evan P. and **Sanow, Ed.** *Handgun Stopping Power, The Defenitive Study.* Paladin Press.

Nowicki, Ed and **Ramsey, Dennis A.** *Street Weapons.* Performance Dimensions Publishing.

Nowicki, Ed. *Supervisory Survival.* Performance Dimensions Publishing.

Nowicki, Ed. *True Blue, True Stories About Real Cops.* Performance Dimensions Publishing.

Ouellette, Roland. *Management of Aggressive Behavior.* Performance Dimensions Publishing.

Remsberg, Charles. *The Tactical Edge.* Calibre Press.

Scotti, Anthony J. *Emergency Driving for Police Officers.* Prentice-Hall.

Scotti, Anthony J. *Executive Safety and International Terrorism.* Prentice-Hall.

Trautman, Neal E. *A Study of Law Enforcement.*

Trautman, Neal E. *Law Enforcement In-Service Training Programs.*

Trautman, Neal E. *Law Enforcement - The Making of a Profession.*

Trautman, Neal E. *Law Enforcement Training.*

Trautman, Neal E. *Standards for Security and Law Enforcement Agencies.*

Trautman, Neal E. *50 Things Teens Can Do to Fight Drugs.*

Truncale, Joseph J., with **Johnson, Harriet,** and **Ramsey, Dennis.** *Persuader Defense Systems.* Pro-Systems.

Truncale, Joseph J. and **Connor, Gregory.** *Police Yawara Techniques.* University of Illinois Press.

Truncale, Joseph J. *PR-24™ Police Baton Advanced Techniques.* Monadnock.

Truncale, Joseph J. *The Use of the Monadnock Straight Baton.* Monadnock.

Truncale, Joseph J. *The Persuader Baton.* Monadnock.

Truncale, Joseph J. *The Rational Approach to Police Arrest and Control Techniques.* Pro-Systems.

Suggested Video Viewing

Baganz, Mark. *Courtroom Skills and Tactics.* Performance Dimensions Publishing.

Berry, Dean and **Berry, Stan.** *Report Writing and Writing Skills for Command Personnel.*

Collingwood, Dr. Thomas. *Fit for Duty.* Medina Productions.

Dunston, Mark S. *Street Signs: The Video.* Performance Dimensions Publishing.

Johnson, Eric. *Con Games and Con Artists.* Performance Dimensions Publishing.

Nowicki, Ed. *Interpersonal Communications Skills.* Performance Dimensions Publishing.

Nowicki, Ed and **Ramsey, Dennis A.** *Street Weapons: The Video.* Performance Dimensions Publishing.

Remsberg, Charles. *Surviving Edged Weapons.* Calibre Press.

Roemer, Paul. *Crisis Intervention.* Performance Dimensions Publishing.

Trautman, Neal E. *Law Enforcement Ethics.* Performance Dimensions Publishing.

Index

A

abnormal reaction   86
absenteeism   103, 118, 122
absorb   11, 183, 235, 269, 348, 377
absorption   236, 391
abuse of process   51
accessing weapon   313
accessories   40, 41, 47, 274
accident prone   121, 279
accountability   49, 250, 403
accreditation   407
accusation   151, 153, 160, 258, 394
acid   185
ACP chambering   137
action-reaction file tape   311
active voice   25
acute   118, 236, 287
Acute Pulmonary Edema   70
Adaptation Theory   59
adapter   246
additional verbal warning   205
adequate penetration   321, 323
adrenal compound   61, 62
adrenal dump   61, 62
Adrenaline   279, 299, 300, 312
AdvanTac Systems   43, 47
Adventurer's Outpost   47
aerobic power   102, 111

Index

Aerobics Program for Total Well-Being, The 118
aerosol 66-68, 71-73, 201, 313
affirmation 316
afraid 87, 93, 121, 138, 272, 401
age 106, 109, 112, 183, 185, 273, 286, 380, 394
aggression 62-64, 294-296
aggressive 14, 65-67, 80, 250, 289, 291, 292, 295-297, 312, 353, 354
agility 97, 102
agitation 293
AIDS 54, 151, 391
air 85, 116, 117, 173, 234, 236, 256, 314, 325, 349
airborne 66-68, 234
airhorn 436
alarm 79, 121, 169, 174
Albert J. Grazioli Award 330
alcoholism 84, 87, 105, 120
Alessi 16
alias 164
Allyn and Bacon 372
altitude 116
Alymyer 120
amateur 149
ambidextrous 377
American College of Sports Medicine 117
American Cop 399
American Detective 239
American Expeditionary Force 37
American Society of Law Enforcement Trainers (ASLET) 58, 222
American Way, The 397
ammo selection 319, 320
ammo test 319, 321
anaerobic power 102

anal sphincter   60
anarchy   154
anchor   255, 257
Anchor Books   248
Anderson, Lon   364
Angel of Death, The   186
anger   53, 54, 86, 241, 244, 295, 353, 364, 397, 404
ankle bracelet   128
anti-rumor squad   427
aperture   38, 138, 379
apparel   356
appeal   166, 283
appearance   85, 123, 163, 198, 204, 239, 249, 251, 252, 255, 256, 278, 282
Apple Blossom   65
Appleton   64
arbitrate   95
arbitrary   319
area of coverage   10
Arena   119, 155, 183, 187, 242, 272, 287
arithmetic   342
Arizona State University   120
armbar   417, 419
armed robbery   19, 91, 163
armpit   393
Arrest Team   433, 434, 438, 441
arrest and control   223, 387
arrogance   159, 256
Art of War, The   77
arteries   60
articulate   198, 201, 274, 275, 286, 287
artificial limb   394
as you were trained   91

Index

asphyxiant   236
asphyxiation   68, 70
Assault Rifle   133, 135-139, 376-379
assault vest   10
assembly   51, 380, 427, 435
Assets Protection   338
assistant squad leader   424, 441
assisted empty-hand tool   361, 362, 364, 365, 369, 372
assume the position   6, 202
Asthma   73, 105
at the corners   173
athletic   256, 276, 311, 317
atomic bomb   388
attack/kill zone   227, 228
attrition   441, 442
audible   17, 345
auditory exclusion   61, 62, 267
Austrian Steyr   134
autogenic breathing   63, 64
autoloader   14, 39, 143-148
autonomic nervous system   60
autopistol   39, 276
autopsy   325
Awerbuck, Louis   47

B

baby   96, 152, 153
baby-faced recruits   364
baby-faced trainers   364
backface signature   11
backward roll   304

bad life   86
badge   14, 19, 20, 100, 119, 122, 123, 187, 241, 400, 405
Baechle, T.   118
balance   96, 175, 207, 227, 228, 263, 275, 283, 284, 291, 301, 302, 304, 335, 361, 389, 390, 413, 421, 441
balance beam   336
Ball   139, 140
ball   130, 324, 328, 365
ballistic protection   9, 193
ballistic threat   11
ballistic vest   13, 14, 17
balloon   279
balls of feet   296
bar-arm   353
barrel   37, 41, 61, 92, 133, 134, 138, 139, 177, 212, 217, 218, 377-381
barrier   196, 365-368
baseball   356, 365-368
basketball-shaped   328
bastard   241
batter   365, 367, 372
battery   50, 51, 106, 122, 147
battle rifle   135, 136, 378, 379, 381
bayonet   37
bead sight   38
bedtime   349
beef   310
believability   245
Bellamy, R.F.   141
belligerent   297
belt   14, 15, 41, 201, 208, 225, 271, 273, 274, 276, 291, 298, 393, 421
belt buckle   393

Index

Benelli   39
Benny, Jack   295
Benson, Herbert   64
Beretta   39, 382, 383
beverage can   130
Beverly Hills Syndrome   54
Bianchi   16
Big bore   324
big game   140
binoculars   79, 235
biofeedback   122
birdshot   46
birth defect   73, 236
bizarre   152, 166, 391
Black Gangster Disciples (BGD)   126, 128
Black Hills Ammunition   139
black humor   152
Black   92, 230, 291
blade   38, 61, 200, 394
bladed   201, 226, 295, 296, 297
blindfold   268, 269, 271
Blindspot   242, 244
blitz   423
Blitz load   139
block   1, 62, 77, 93, 159, 181, 207, 212, 215, 219, 223, 226-228, 268, 300, 302-306, 322-328, 361, 364-368, 371, 373, 419
blood pressure   60, 73, 102, 105, 121, 158
blood vessel   60, 323
blouse   394
blowback operated   382
Blue Knight   154
blunt trauma   11, 327

Bo Brown   128
boat-tail   377
Bodily Changes in Pain, Hunger, Fear, and Rage   64
body armor   9, 11
body art   127
body composition   102, 107
body fat   106
body fluid   130, 131, 391
body language   204, 269, 289, 292
body mass   106, 107, 109
body mechanics   212
body signals   294
body weight   107, 110, 112, 337
bolt-action   133, 134, 139, 377, 378
bomb squad   186
boomerang   251
bowling pin   46, 279
box magazine   377
boxer stance   295
Boyce, R.   118
bra   394
brain   17, 59, 60, 88, 93, 121, 292, 311, 327
brake   340-343, 346
braking exercise   344
brass   129, 145, 309
brave   93, 96, 375
breathing   59, 60, 63, 65, 67, 121, 204, 295, 297, 299, 300
breeching lock   44
bribery   400
British Law   426
broad   197, 241, 315, 316

Index

Brobenzylcyanide 65
Brockart, J 118
brogans 15
bronchi 60
Broncho-Pneumonia 70
brotherhood 120, 399
brutal 210, 252
brutality 64, 397
buckshot 38, 41-44, 46, 133
buffered 43
building 71, 77, 80, 116, 122, 133, 152, 154, 169, 171-174, 180, 203, 223, 238, 244, 250, 252, 275, 354, 362, 423
building search 45, 75, 77, 169, 171-174, 176, 180, 183, 187
bullet-resistant 11
bulletproof 11, 299
bullet 14, 17, 26, 27, 32, 90, 92, 134, 138, 139, 145, 154, 318, 320-329, 388
bullhorn 436
bullshit detector 153
bunt 365-368
Bureau of Alcohol, Tobacco, and Firearms (B.A.T.F.) 41
burglary 33, 34, 160, 169, 172, 283
Burgoan, Judee K. 248
Burnett, C. 118
burn unit 88
burnout 84, 85, 89, 119-123, 157, 166
butane lighter 130
butt 380
butt cuff 41
buttock 304
button 62, 177
buttstock 41, 45, 380

C

cab-o-sil   67
cabbage   153
cadence   435, 436
Calibre Press   64, 84, 182, 207
California Department of Justice   141
California Peace Officers Killed in the Line of Duty Study   221
calisthenic   110, 112, 113
callous   120, 122
camaraderie   277, 279, 405
Cambridge University Press   248
Campain, J.   118
cancer   73, 102, 120
cane   394
canine   184
Cannon, Dr. Walter B.   59, 64
Canton v. Harris   184
canvas bag   267
capillaries   60, 65, 66
carbine   39, 137, 138, 140, 383
carcinogenicity   236
career development   97, 396, 406
cargo   233
carrier   15, 41, 46, 67
cartoon   99
cartridge   133, 135, 137, 138, 145, 379, 380, 381
case law   197, 199
casual space   246
Caucasian   291
Cayenne Pepper   66
CCI   325

Index

ceiling   236
Celotex   172
Centurion Guard   423
cerebral cortex   59, 60
certificate   99, 298
chain   3, 29, 283, 389, 410, 411, 424, 427
Chain Link Handcuffs   410, 411
chambered   46, 133, 135-139, 145, 147
Chapman, Ray   93
Cheathem, T.R.   248
checks and balances   404
chemical   65, 66, 68, 70-73, 121, 184, 236, 350, 385
Chemical Transportation Emergency Center (CHEMTREC)   236
chemistry lab   229
Chief Special   16
child abuse   83, 185, 186
chin   113, 292, 293, 301, 302, 304
chin-up bar   336, 337
China   260, 298, 426
Chinese National Television   298
Chloroacetophenone (CN)   65
Choate Machine & Tool Co.   40, 47
chronic   86, 121, 236
church   88, 253
Christensen, Larry B.   372
cigarette   167, 393
circle of life or death   224
Cirillo Drill   92
citation   1, 2, 28, 195, 278
Citizen Review Board   242, 287
city council   287
civil action   352
civil court   50, 153, 279, 282

civil damage 252
Civil Defense 235
civil forfeiture 49, 195
civil law 50
civil lawsuit 206
civil liability 50, 239, 407
civil litigation 49, 55, 75, 397
civil rights 186, 282
civil suit 282
civil tort 49
civilian concealed carry 321
clandestine 316
clarification 257
class 10, 117, 128, 132, 184, 203, 230, 273, 276, 337, 353, 364, 377
clergy 254, 255
Close Quarter Drilling 425
close support 438, 440
close-in confrontation 271
closed bolt 379, 383
clumsy 146, 261
coach 332, 363
coat 16, 67, 92, 274, 337, 392, 393
cocaine 125, 183
cocked 143, 146, 148, 174
Code of the West 187
coffee 167, 279, 309
collapsible stock 379, 380
collar 309, 392, 393
college professor 322
collision 17, 178, 340, 341
Color of the Day 18
color-coded scenario 92

Index

Colt   16, 20, 136-138, 143, 144, 146, 147, 310, 375, 379-381
Colt made all men equal   310
Column Formation   429
Combat Handguns   150
combat   11, 12, 37, 40, 41, 45, 47, 78, 81, 122, 142, 150, 182, 208, 260, 296, 363, 385, 424, 430
command authority   12, 152
command post   233
command presence   167, 199, 249,
Commando model   379-381
commerce   229
commercial   145, 367, 333, 334
commission   284
commitment   103, 310, 311, 399, 400, 404
committee   12, 57
communication   5, 15, 176, 178, 198, 239, 242, 244, 245, 247, 248, 364, 436
communication blindspot   242
communication skill   204, 242, 247, 316
compact   137, 265, 379, 382
competition   92, 157, 163, 274, 275, 277, 278
complacency   13, 331
compliance   53, 189, 196, 241, 247, 265, 351-354, 356, 358, 359
complaint   165, 244, 395
computer   85, 93, 94, 99, 164, 191
comradeship   400
concealed carry   15, 16, 20, 321
concealment   81, 91, 141, 172, 190, 195
concentration   70, 86, 116, 196, 236, 274, 277, 352
concrete   25, 332
condescending   241
confidence   44, 46, 47, 83, 93, 134, 144, 163, 251, 252, 257, 270, 277, 282, 291, 292, 301, 308, 310, 314, 316,

353, 395, 399, 424
confidential studies   319
confrontation   54, 144, 187, 198, 200, 203, 206, 209, 210, 223, 261-266, 268, 270-272, 281, 286, 299, 305-307, 309, 311, 314, 316, 331, 351, 361, 363, 374, 382, 383, 423, 425, 439, 440, 442
confrontational baton simulation   184
confrontational simulation   262, 307, 308, 310, 313
consensual encounter   199, 202
constitutional law   53, 316
consumers   398
contact and cover   7, 196, 202
contact officer   3-7, 202, 299, 309
containment   427
contamination   67, 145, 232, 234, 236
contempt   250, 256
contempt of cop   52
contraband   189, 387-389, 392-394
contradictory   207, 242, 252
conversion   51, 69, 339
Cooper Institute for Aerobics Research   101
Cooper, Colonel Jeff   38, 92, 101, 102, 118
Cops Behind the Badge   123
cop wear   15
cop killer   15
copper plated   43
cop   6, 7, 13-18, 20, 21, 99, 119, 153, 183, 185, 186, 189, 239, 398-401, 404, 405
Cor-Bon   322, 323
corner   80, 91, 172-174, 176, 179
coronary   101
correlation coefficient   321
corrosive   230

Index

cost   10, 87, 122, 123, 134, 225, 235, 275, 364, 377, 382, 383
cottage industry   38
cough   393
counselor   119, 185, 186
counterattack   262, 266, 269
countermeasure   207, 314, 317
Court of Appeal   285
court speak   206, 207
courtroom   142, 160, 201, 249, 251, 252, 255, 256, 266, 316, 363
cover officer   3-7, 180, 196
covert   141, 191
cowardice   281
cowboy   15
cowboy type hat   176
CPR   85, 426
crab walk   179
crack   125, 127, 129, 130, 131, 154, 175, 183, 249
crack pipe   130, 131
crash and burn   86
credible   99, 245, 249, 250, 258
Creek v. Wyoming   120
crime fighter   180, 181, 407
criminal procedure   53
crimped   145
Crips   126
crisis   18, 19, 21, 62, 63, 84, 85, 86, 88, 119, 122, 241, 375, 380, 383, 404
crisis intervention   205
crisis management   37
crisis rehearsal   309
Crockett, Thompson   73
cross-racial   53

Crossbow Formation   440
crossfire   202
Crowd Development   425
cruel and unusual punishment   51, 286
Cruise Missile   388
cruiser   17, 233, 341
crumple   300
Crunch, Crash, Bang Syndrome   146
crush (permanent) cavity   321, 328, 329
crutch   333, 394
crystalline   66
crystal   4, 65, 66
cultural ignorance   281
culture group   257
curb berm   273
curiosity   96, 126
curved   301
custom   10, 49, 52, 134, 282, 377
custom gunsmith   38
customer service   19, 163, 239
cyclic rate   382, 384
cylinder   39, 42, 43, 62, 145
cynicism   154, 166

D

D.O.T. Emergency Response Guidebook   231, 235
DARE   239, 244
dark glasses   292
darting eyes   292
data base   191
Davis Publishing Company   73

Index

Davis, Richard   17
dealer   125, 127, 129, 198, 376
debriefing   205
deck   85, 435
decock   146-148
decontamination   67, 68, 71, 236
dedicated   40, 151, 164, 221, 399
deep penetrator   322, 325
deep-cover   185
Dees, Connie   317
Def-Tec   73
defamation   51
defendant   28, 52, 55, 153, 161, 164, 283, 285
Defensive Shotgun, Techniques and Tactics, The   47
defensive stance   200, 201, 291
defensive tactic   4, 57, 58, 61, 62, 80, 183, 184, 187, 199, 202, 204, 206, 207, 213, 220, 263, 264, 266, 281, 288, 298, 309, 310, 311, 317, 352, 385, 409, 421, 422
defensively   302, 303
deflection   312, 377
degrease   68
dehydration   116
deictic movement   246
deliberate indifference   51, 52, 282
deliberately indifferent   49, 51, 52
deltoid   108
demeanor   19, 163, 239, 244, 249, 250, 256, 413, 427
denial of counsel   51
Department of Justice   141, 258, 283
department policy   198, 283
depersonalize   294
deployment   37, 66-68, 70-72, 77, 79, 81, 171-173, 179, 423, 440

depression   86, 121

deprivation   51, 282

deranged   71, 72, 157, 291, 293

desert patrol beat   379

Desmedt, John   395

despised   257

detective   2, 7, 16, 182, 239, 273, 274, 276, 277, 280, 298, 394, 421

detention   50, 199, 200, 202

diabetic   284

Diagonal Formation   428, 429, 433

diagonal deployment   172, 173

diagonal entry method   177, 178

Diamond Formation   440

diatomite   67

digestive organ   60

dignitary protection   382

dignity   49, 54, 157, 164, 165

dilate   60, 293

Diopter   378, 384

direction and documentation   275

disabled   289, 394

disabling   265, 353

disarming   3, 209-212, 216-221

Disarming With Wristlock Release   216, 219

Disaster & Emergency Services   235

discrimination   152, 153

disenchantment   400

dishonesty   397, 398

disinfectant foam   391

Disorder Platoon   423-425, 436

dispersal   68, 71, 427, 430

disperser   67, 68

Index

disposable handcuffs   413
distress   51, 249, 263, 294
disturbance   3, 96, 104, 169
disturbed   33, 34, 145, 219, 375
disturbing   257
dive roll   304
Dixie Cup   185
doctor   14, 92, 95, 105, 119, 122, 131, 151, 165, 278
domestic dispute   100, 240, 241, 246
dominant hand   212, 213
Donne, John   159
dose   68, 184, 236
dose response   236
Doubleday   248
double elbow lock   266
double jeopardy   53
double lock   389, 413, 415, 419
double talk   153
double time   438
double-action revolver   144-146
doughnut   167, 184, 309
down and dirty   206
downrange   274, 275
downwind   233
dress   14, 15, 17, 116, 128, 256, 394, 413
dried peas   267
drive   108, 152, 171, 180, 229, 234, 284, 312, 316, 339, 345, 348, 349, 380
driver   4, 28, 54, 119, 164, 191-195, 210, 229, 232, 245, 311, 339, 341, 343, 344, 346, 348
driver training program   344
Driving Under the Influence (DUI)   196
Driving While Intoxicated (DWI)   191, 196

Drug Crackdown   207
drug store   229
drug trafficking   129
drug war   129
drunk   99, 153, 193
dry fire practice   46
dry mouth   62
dual aperture   379
Dubrow, R.   118
duck walk   179
ducking   268
duct tape   301
due care   205
duffer   279
Dunton v. County of Suffolk   187
Dupont   11
dust   67
duties   3, 4, 25, 47, 49, 83, 85, 86, 98, 131, 161, 164, 165, 219, 223, 228, 258, 273, 318, 376-378, 398, 406, 438
duty belt   15, 16, 299, 302, 410
dynamic simulations   184

E

Earp, Wyatt   85
Eastwood, Clint   206
Echelon Left   428-430, 433
Echelon Right   434
economy of force   77, 78
economy of movement   303
ego   14, 270
elastic tissue   327

Index

Electronic Restraining Device (E.R.D.) 52
electronic   19, 52, 184
eleventh-hour decision   275
emblem   247
Emergency Medical Services (EMS)   229, 235
emergency call   345
emergency room   17, 391
emotion   25, 49-51, 55, 83, 84, 86-89, 103, 120, 157, 167, 183-187, 241, 294, 316, 331, 353, 375, 398, 399, 402, 427
empathize   351
employing governmental entity   52
empty stare   292
EMT   428
endearment   400
energy   1, 42, 60, 62, 103, 122, 184, 241, 264, 277, 305, 322, 327, 328
energy dump   328
English Amendment   286
English Common Law   426
environmental pathway   234
Epileptic   99
equality   241
ergonomic   38
Erickson, K.V.   248
Ericson, Dave   36
erode   442
escalate   54, 93, 166, 191, 207, 225, 233, 241, 246, 247, 286, 352, 354
escape route   5, 71, 173, 191, 193, 198, 200, 291, 293, 348
escort position   169, 170, 201, 354, 357, 358
establishing control   206, 207
estimate   134, 185, 200, 255, 283, 325, 381
ethical decision   397, 401, 402, 404

ethics   12, 87, 397, 401-406
ethnic group   291
euphemisms   153
evacuation   67, 72, 233
Evans, M.   118
evidence   3-7, 12, 28, 29, 33-35, 73, 85, 96, 125, 129, 161, 179, 183, 189, 196, 221, 247, 282, 387, 406
evil   20, 120, 128
exception   120, 166, 220, 272, 399, 438, 441
excessive penetration   321
executive   52, 153
exhaustion   121, 299
expanding bullet   139, 140, 325-327
expectation   119, 250, 332
Experimental Methodology   372
expert   57, 95, 100, 134, 137, 138, 142, 182, 184, 322, 326, 345
explosive   61, 230
exposure   66, 67, 70, 71-72, 96, 116, 161, 193, 232, 236, 258, 363, 371
extended magazine tubes   47
extortion   126
extraordinary   239, 267, 272
extreme   379
eye contact   239, 244, 245, 289, 291, 292, 294, 297
eye patch   271

F

Facade   242
face mask   131
facial expression   239, 245

Index

Fackler, M.L.   141
Failure to Expand: Federal 7.62 x 39 mm Soft Point Bullets   141
faith   20, 122, 154, 285, 405
falling   62, 93, 268, 301
false imprisonment   50, 51
fan   16, 267
fanny pack   18
fat   102, 106, 109, 129, 152, 325
fatal funnel   175
Father Time   184
father   395
fatty deposit   331
Faulkner Frisk, The   390
Faulkner, Sam   390
FBI Law Enforcement Bulletin   221
FBI National Academy   222
FBI, The Untold Stories   239
fear   18, 44, 53, 58, 59, 63, 64, 67, 79, 91-93, 120, 121, 174, 187, 249, 251, 255, 271, 294-296, 299, 301, 308, 331, 351, 439
Federal Bureau of Investigation (F.B.I.)   39, 42, 182, 202, 211, 222, 238, 281, 319, 321-323, 326, 330
Federal Civil Rights   49, 51-53
Federal load   139
Federal Order of Police (FOP)   15, 186
Federal Tactical Buckload   41
feet per second (fps)   42, 43, 322, 328, 339-343, 346
Fell, Richard and Wallace   120
felon   21, 95, 183
felony   3, 14, 16, 20, 125, 152, 183, 283, 284, 309
felony fliers   125
felony-in-progress   237
Felter, Brian A.   47

female   1, 2, 31, 33, 34, 108, 125, 128, 161, 393, 394, 424
fence   252, 283, 335, 336, 433
fetal position   302
Field Interview (FI)   3, 7, 193, 196-199, 201, 202, 316
Fifth Amendment Rights   151, 187
Fight-Flight Response   59-64, 121
fire department   159, 229, 234, 235
fire-fighting   234
Fire/Rescue   428
firearms' training   62, 90, 93, 95, 142, 184, 187, 221, 273, 275, 276, 278, 280, 309, 310, 320, 322, 401
firing reflex   44
First Aid   426
first person   24
first responder   231, 234
fish hook entry method   177
Fit for Duty   118
fitness assessment   104, 106, 109
fitness goal setting   104, 109
Five-O   128
fixed facility   234
fixed power scope   134
flammable   230, 233
flare   233, 235
flash-reactive target   279
flashlight   173, 176, 177, 179, 210, 278, 283
flat-footed   274
flechette   44
flexibility   17, 102, 107, 110, 113, 184, 352, 353, 390, 428
fluency   241
fluid   114, 116, 130, 131, 349, 391
fluid motion   263
fluid shock   265

Index

fluid-filled   327
flutters   333, 337
Flying Ford Takedown   199
flying ash can   325
folding stock   41
Folk Gang   128
follow-through   146, 263, 265, 402
following distance   340
food   128, 183, 234, 352
football   125, 423
force continuum   73, 199
force presence   4, 7
forearm   200, 201, 217, 219, 225, 226, 301, 365, 368, 369, 370
Forearm Leverage Release   216
forearm strike   314
forensic   12, 100, 323
Formal Analysis of Communicative Processes in Nonverbal Communication   248
Fortune 500   250, 338
Forward Spin   365, 366
fouling   379
Fourth Amendment   283-286
fourth generation   383
fragment   139, 324-326, 433
fragmentation   321, 324-326, 329
fragmentation and expansion   324
frangible bullet   326
Frequency of Physical Activity Exercise Capacity and Atherosclerotic Heart Disease Risk Factors in Male Police Officers   118
Fried, Bryan A.   372
friendliness   279
frisk   50, 130, 184, 197, 198, 202, 316, 387-395
Front Cross Grip   214, 215, 312

front sight blade   274
frontal assault   263
frustration   53, 54, 120, 121, 279, 398, 427
fulcrum   307
full synthetic stock   377
full-contact   256, 262
Fuller, Thomas   165
fumes   233
fun   15, 179, 273, 275, 277-279, 403
funeral   185

G

gang   1, 14, 125-128, 154, 257
garnisheeing   279
Garrity v. New Jersey   187
gas gun   426
gas mask   426
gas operated   134, 379
Gas Team   438
gases   145, 230
gauge   11, 37, 38
gauntlet   38
gear   38, 46, 60, 181, 274, 276
gelatin   139, 318, 320, 322-328, 379
General Adaptation Syndrome (GAS)   121
general support   438
generic standard   285
geometry   342
George I   426
gesture   161, 239, 246, 247, 289, 291, 294, 297, 436, 440
ghost ring   38, 378, 384

Index

gilt-edge accuracy   139
glazed stare   292
Glock   146, 309
glove   391
glycogen   60
glycogenolysis   60
goal oriented   353
Goal Oriented Training   266, 270
God   17, 93, 122, 249, 293, 331
goggles   131, 271, 276
golden rule   224, 402
golf   278
golf ball   303
Good Morning America   123
goose bumps   61
Goose Neck Come-A-Long   356
gossip   160, 161
governmental entity   49, 52
Government Printing Office   118
graffiti   126, 127
Graham v. Connor   283, 284, 286
grain   138, 139, 140, 321, 322, 324-326, 377
grappling technique   268
graveyard   276
gray area   316
gray twilight   155
greed   332, 397, 399, 404
Greener Double   37
Gregory, Richard   36
grenade   67
groin   148, 293, 295, 302, 305, 306, 393
groom   163, 256
groove   143-145

grossly inadequate   95, 96
groundfight   267, 268, 299, 301, 302, 306, 307
grunt speak   206
guardian   154, 337
Guidelines for Exercise Testing and Prescription   117
gun belt   15, 174
gun butt   201, 212, 219
gun mule   18
gunfight   91-93, 273, 276, 277, 279, 318-321, 327
gunmen   91, 92, 190
gun mounted lights   41
Gun Mounted Lights   47
gunpowder   275
Guns & Weapons for Law Enforcement   150
gunsmith   38, 138
Gute, D.   118

H

hair   61, 163, 179, 256, 309, 392
half-empty   86
half-full   86
Hall, Edward T.   248
hallucinate   293
hallucinogenic   198
hallway   153, 169, 176, 179, 210, 278
hammer   16, 143, 146-148, 214, 215, 274, 380
hand signal   6, 7, 436, 437
handcuff   6, 7, 20, 24, 31, 174, 202, 205, 273, 285, 300, 316, 355, 356, 387, 389, 390, 392, 409-421
handcuffing   3, 62, 205, 332, 354, 356, 391, 392, 409-415, 417-421

Index

Handcuffing Wrist Lock   417
handguard   37
Handgun Disarming Method   219, 220
Handgun Retention System   208-210, 212, 213, 218-221
Handgun Stopping Power   318, 325
handicapped   279, 394
handkerchief   92
haphazard   375
harassment   51, 152, 244
hardball   323, 324
Harper and Row   248
hashish   129
hazardous materials classifications   230
hazardous materials incident (HMI)   231, 232, 234, 235, 237
Hazardous Materials Incident Checklist   232
Hazardous Materials Incident Terms and Phrases   236
headlight   193, 348, 349
headline   281
health and medical screening   104
health risk reduction   102, 103
Healthy People 2000 Report   101
hearsay   161
heart and major vessels   323
heart rate (HR)   60, 63, 111
heat build-up   10
heat exhaustion   116
heat stroke   106, 116
heavy bag   267, 305
Heckler & Koch (H & K)   136, 377, 378, 383, 384, 381
helicopter   439
Hell   355
helper role   292
hepatitis   151

hero   151, 239
heroin   129
Hiatt, K.   118
Hibbard, Jack   372
Hidden Dimension, The   248
High Port   435, 437, 440
high beam   349
high cheek stock   377
high risk traffic stop   189-191, 196
hinged handcuffs   410, 411
Hispanic   291
hit potential   37, 39, 139
HIV   54
Hoekwater, Gene   248
holier-than-thou attitude   281
Hollywood   152-154, 173, 381
holocaust   119
Holt Rinehart and Winston   248
home defense   321
homicide   163, 164, 193
Homo sapiens   61
honesty   397, 403
Honor Guard   185
hormone   62
Horn Come-A-Long   358
hostage   71, 83, 84, 133, 229, 377
hostile   19, 37, 46, 157, 204, 241, 246, 352, 354, 371, 433, 441
hot line   186
hotshot   160
Howard Johnson's Hotel, New Orleans   375
Hubbard, Elbert   157
Human Aggression   64

Human Communication Research   248
humidity   116, 273
humility   271
humor   122, 152, 167, 168
hunger   59, 64
hustler   127
Hydra Shock   324
hygiene   356
hypodermic needle   130
hypoglossal nerve   353
hypothalamus   59

I

IACP, Police Standards Division   73
idealist   153
identification   124, 125, 127, 128, 233, 388
identifiers   15, 16, 128
ideographs   246
idiosyncrasies   242
ignition source   233
illustrator   246, 247
impact energy   322
impact weapon   73, 173, 361, 362, 372
Implementing Programs and Standards for Law Enforcement Physical Fitness   118
in-service   84, 95, 99, 186, 218, 396, 405, 406
incarcerate   128, 183
indecision   343
index   19, 106, 107, 109, 214, 215, 246, 295, 313
Indian Nations   53
inert   71, 313, 314

inertia 327
infantry soldier 378
infiltration 427
inflammatory 65
informant 127
infra-orbital nerve 353
ingest 130, 235
inhale 130, 235
initial verbal command 205
injury 51, 72, 76, 95, 103, 114, 116, 130, 133, 167, 186, 197, 198, 221, 223, 229, 264, 271, 284, 285, 296, 301, 304, 307, 326, 353, 391
inmate 388
inside position 169, 171, 172, 174, 201
insoluble 65
instinct 99, 244, 268, 277, 301, 302, 304, 308, 311, 373
insubordination 244
insulin reaction 284
integrity 55, 95, 185, 251, 397
interaction 141, 159, 241, 243-245, 248, 316, 351
internal regulatory system 60
International Association of Chiefs of Police (IACP) 118
International Institute of Stress 120
interpretation 25, 319
interrogation 199
intersection 341-345
interstate 229, 309
interval and distance 435
interview position 169, 170, 201
intimate zone 246
intimidate 241, 292, 294, 394
intoxicant 198
Introduction to Wound Ballistics 141

intrusion   199, 284

invalid   233

Inverted L Formation   440

invincible   11, 166

invisible deployment   171

irritant   65, 66

Ischemic Heart Disease and Acute Myocardial Infarction Mortality Among Police Officers   118

Isopropyl Alcohol   391

Israel Military Industries   381

Israeli Special Forces   381

J

jacket   2, 125, 139, 140, 201, 273, 276, 309, 322, 328, 376, 389, 392

jail   57, 164, 388

jam   379

Jefferson, Thomas   162

jello test   319

jerking eyes   292

JHP   138, 140, 322, 324-326

Johari Window   242, 243

Johnson four-part test   285

Johnson v. Glick   285

Johnson, Leonor Boulin   120

joint   105, 110, 144-146, 236, 299, 351, 352

Jones, Eugene   73

Jones, G.   118

Journal of Occupational Medicine   118

Journal of Trauma, The   141

judgment   56, 60, 96, 98, 121, 160, 166, 225, 241, 250, 251, 254, 287, 316, 398, 400, 405
Jujitsu   212, 421
jumping jack   333
jungle   379
jungle gym   336
Jurasz, Dennis   317
jurisdiction   13, 15, 19, 50, 54, 151, 196, 199, 234, 235, 261, 387, 424, 441
jury pool   282
justice system   23, 129, 258
juvenile   183, 257, 394, 421

K

K-9   72, 180, 330, 391, 439
Kansas City Police Department   210, 211, 212
Karate   212, 421
Kennedy, President John F.   164
Kentucky Bureau of Police Training   196
Kevlar   11, 46, 377
key   15, 28-30, 56, 65, 72, 78, 91, 97, 104, 160, 171, 180, 300, 311, 332, 352, 398
kick   268, 269, 293, 299, 300, 301, 302, 306, 307, 393, 421
kike   241
Kinesiological cue   201
Kinetic Energy   343
Kinetograph   246
KKK   154
Knapp, Mark   248
knee-buckle   327

knee   91, 107, 108, 113, 115, 135, 148, 179, 225, 228, 266, 269, 273, 289, 291,296, 300, 301, 303, 304, 327, 333, 337, 352, 392, 417

Knife Defense System   208, 221

Knoll, Don   273

knotted towel   365-368

knowledge of terrain   81

Kordite   271

Korea   381

Krueger, Freddie   173

Kubotan®   391

L

L deployment   179

L Formation   440

lack of self-confidence   353

lacrimation   236

lacrimator   65

lactose   67

lag time   278, 311

lambskin   131

landmark   283

LAPD SWAT   325

laser   41

Laser Products   47

laser rule   202

Lateral Vascular Neck Restraint System   208, 221

lateral support   438-440

laterally   303, 312

latex examination glove   391

latitude   257, 316

Law and Order   132, 316
law and order   426
Law Enforcement Assistance Administration (LEAA)   321
Law Enforcement Chemical Agents and Related Equipment   73
law enforcement code of ethics   406
Law Enforcement News   132
Law Enforcement Technology   316
law enforcement technology   9
Law Enforcement Television Network (LETN)   207
Law Enforcement Trainer of the Year Award   222
lay of the land   81
LC50   236
LD50   236
Lea and Feberger   117
leadership   398, 406
leap technique   175, 178
leather gloves   391
leg lift   333, 337
leg power   102
legitimate authority   54
Leite v. City of Providence   95
leprosy   278
less-than-lethal force   283
liability   49, 50, 52-54, 56, 57, 68, 76, 95, 145, 174, 186, 239, 282, 379, 407
life experience   88, 364
Lifeline® gym   315
lights   47
limitation   46, 47, 62, 63, 104, 272, 282, 332, 333, 337, 345, 426
limits of legal authority   426
Line Formation   432
lip   295, 296

Index

load   39, 42, 43, 133, 138, 139, 145, 233, 309, 322-326
local   1, 17, 119, 128, 134, 189, 229, 235, 236, 278, 322, 336, 364, 391
local sewer utility   235
local water company   235
locker room   206, 256, 314,
Loehr, James E.   311, 317, 372
long distance rifles   376
long gun   14, 44, 133, 136, 221
long term memory   309, 311
look-through stare   292
Lorenz, Konrad   64
Los Angeles Police Department   375
Los Angeles Riots   423, 441
loser   164, 278, 351, 398
low ready position   45
low shooter   278
Lower Forearm Strike   215, 219
lower back flexibility   102
loyal   158, 399
LSD   130
lubricant   145
lucrative   282
Luft, Joseph   242, 243
lung   66, 105, 325
lust   397, 399, 404
lying   33, 34, 61, 107, 108, 113, 115, 397, 398

M

MacKay, D.M.   248
madness   273, 280

magazine   40, 74, 134, 135, 139, 143, 146, 156, 166, 237, 260, 316, 338, 377, 379, 380, 382, 385, 386, 422

magazine tube   40, 41, 47

maggot   122

magic wand   362

magical powers   362

magically   313

magistrate   426

magnesium oxide   67

Magnum   13, 42, 137, 138, 140, 324, 325, 328

major leagues   367

malicious   53, 285

malicious motive   53

malicious prosecution   51

Malinowski, J.A.   141

malpractice   56

man overboard   85

maneuver   77, 78, 146, 202, 210, 215, 224, 339, 373, 411

manufacturer   11, 38, 40, 53, 134, 145, 232, 320, 325, 384

marijuana   129

marksmanship   47, 140, 141

Marlin   138

Marshall, Evan P.   318

Marsh, Jim   395

Marsh Speedcuffing Technique   391

martial arts   276, 295, 298, 421

martial arts master   269

martial arts stance   296

mass   77, 78, 106, 107, 109, 110, 111

mat   107, 304, 305

match grade ammo   377, 378

Material Safety Data Sheet (MSDS)   232

maximal heart rate   112

Index

McDonalds 183
Media Unit 438
medical check-up 104
Medina Productions 118
meditation 122
Mehrabian, Albert 240, 248
mental focus 311
mental illness 353
mental preparation 9, 11, 363
Mental Toughness Training for Sports — Achieving Athletic Excellence 317
mere exposure 363, 371
message 15, 18, 19, 159, 239, 240, 241, 242, 244, 245-248, 294
metallurgy 38
methodology 273, 280, 319, 323, 372
Methuen 64
Miami 6, 42
Micro-UZI 381
micropulverized 65-68
microscopic scrutiny 53
miles per hour (mph) 27, 70, 125, 339-346, 348
mini-baton 391, 394
mini-flashlight 391
Mini-UZI 381
Mini-Wedge Formation 441
minimum level of force 207
miraculous 91-93
Miranda 187, 195
mirror 130, 176, 346-348
Mirror Technique 175, 176
mirrored glasses 292
misdemeanor 1, 3, 152, 415

missile   44, 141, 326, 388
mission   1, 65, 67, 71, 133, 134, 137, 199, 258, 430
mistrust   241
Mob Development   425
Mob Formations   426
mobility   263
mobster   381
Modern Police Psychology   82
Modern Warrior Defensive Tactics Institute   264, 266, 298
Monadnock   58, 180, 202, 317, 360, 362-365, 367, 369-371, 373, 409, 410, 445
Monell v. Department of Social Services   282
monitoring   56, 111, 205, 276, 307
monkey bar   336
monk   269
morale   122, 407
Mossberg   38, 39
motherfucker   241
motion   72, 92, 107, 108, 110, 113, 114, 144, 263, 264, 276, 309, 352-357, 364, 365, 367, 391
motivation   117, 285, 286, 332
Motor Vehicle Accident (MVA)   186
motorist   341
mounted police   439
Mouse, Mickey   85
mouth   62, 63, 72, 87, 125, 145, 154, 235, 393
movement and surprise   76, 80
movie script   286
mucous membrane   65
multi-tasking   312
multiple assailant confrontations   261, 263-266, 268, 270
multiple assailants   261, 263-265, 267, 302, 306, 308
multiple shot bursts   46

Index

Murray   64
muscle   60, 62, 63, 88, 107, 110, 111-115, 121, 146, 267, 294, 311, 325
muscular endurance   107, 108, 112
mushroom   186, 324, 325
mutagenicity   236
mutant   154, 236, 256
muzzle   40, 42, 45, 137-139, 145, 146, 202, 263

N

name recognition   363
narcs   185
narcotics' trafficking   126
narrative format   23, 30
National Institute of Justice (NIJ)   11, 321
National Law Enforcement Training Center (NLETC)   220, 221
National Lawyer's Guild   283
National Rifle Association (NRA)   140, 141
National Tactical Officers Association   74
national accreditation process   407
NATO   134, 138
Neanderthal man   59
neck area   292
needle   130, 391
negative   40, 44, 55, 57, 84, 86-88, 121, 122, 241, 245, 246, 249, 250, 264, 282, 293, 299, 303, 311, 378, 388, 403, 410-413
negative discipline   303
negligent   44, 50, 52, 87, 119, 203
negligible   282
neo-Nazi   154

neon   256
nerve   61, 62, 212, 217, 265, 351-353, 372, 412
nerve motor points   352
nervous system   60, 61, 296, 327, 343
nervousness   249, 255, 257
network   88, 183, 185, 207, 257, 288, 396
neural shock   42, 327
neuromuscular reflexes   277
neutral position   302
newspaper   183, 260, 268, 301
Newsweek   123
NFL defensive linebacker   309
nickel-plated   92
nigger   241
night driving   348, 349
nightmare   126, 233, 309
nine millimeters (9 mm)   2, 10, 14, 137, 164, 273, 321-326, 382-384
nitrocellulose   67
no-brainers   84
non-aggressive manner   289
non-coercive   200
non-functional   313
non-lethal force option   184
non-muscular target   255
Nonverbal Behavior in Interpersonal Relations   248
Nonverbal Behaviors, Persuasion and Credibility   248
Nonverbal Communication   248
Nonverbal Communication in Human Interaction   248
non-verbal skill   199
non-word   257
notepad   278
Notice of Claim   186

Index

NRA Rifle Instructor Course   140, 141
nuance   286
Nyclad   324
nylon   33, 34, 41

O

obese   390
objective lense   134
obscuration   68
observant   195, 269
observation and monitoring   276
Observer Unit   438
obstacle   44, 202, 274, 275, 278, 337
occult   128
Ochlorobenzylidene Malononitrile (CS)   65
odor threshold   236
Of Human Interaction   248
offensive   77, 78, 209, 212, 218, 219, 302, 306, 308, 338, 373, 379
officer survival   2, 3, 9, 15, 17, 49, 58, 88, 182-189, 206, 207, 225, 229, 237, 311, 316, 317, 329, 361, 363, 409
Old West   310
oleo resin aerosol   313
Oleoresin Capsicum (OC)   65
Olin Super Match   322
On Aggression   64
On Guard   435, 441
on-guard stance   314
One Minute Drill, The   363
one hole   134
one plus rule   179

one-sided fighter   264
Onion Field, The   99
open bore   38
open choke   39
Oprah Winfrey Show   123
ordinance gelatin   318
organic   66, 230
organism   60
Oriental   291
Orwellian newspeak   153
ostrich effect   174
outlaw biker   391
outrider   19
Outside, Open Hand Block   419
Outstanding Citizens Award   330
over-penetration   138, 139
over-react   281
overload principle   112
overweight   104, 105, 167
oxidizing substance   230

P

pace   106, 268, 305, 406, 435, 438
pad   143, 144, 147, 306, 307
pain   17, 59, 61, 64-67, 105, 114, 117, 120, 121, 130, 179, 249, 265, 306, 353, 354, 357-359, 409, 411, 421
pain compliance   265
pain response   353
Paladin Press   318
Palm Down Gun Grab   217, 219

Index

palm 115, 200, 205, 214, 215, 217-219, 226, 247, 295, 354, 359, 389, 390, 411, 414, 417
panel discussion 281
paper target 46, 92, 93
Parabellum 137
paralyzed 394
parameter 56, 68, 70, 283
paramilitary 375, 406
paramount 71, 206, 223, 310
paranoia 87
paraphernalia 129, 131
parasympathetic branch 60
parkerized finish 377
particle 234
particulate cloud 65
partner 4, 14, 16, 55, 56, 88, 98, 108, 115, 125, 160, 174, 177, 179, 180, 196, 229, 243, 268, 280
pass-fail 275
passer-by 394
passive 25, 63, 245, 353, 354
past tense 24, 25
pastor 269
pat-down 1, 3, 5-7, 387
Patrol Rifle 133, 135, 137-140
pattern density 42, 43
paycheck 279
PCP 130, 210
peace sign 295
pebble 125, 129
Pecker, Woody Wood 257
pectoral 108, 335
peer counseling 83
pellet 39, 41-43, 67, 133

Penal Code section numbers   6
Penal Code   6, 183
penetration   43, 71, 138-140, 320-325, 329, 376, 379
pension   122, 130, 184
pepper   66
pepper popper   46
percentage fragmentation   320
perceptual distortion   61
perforate   326
perfunctory   275
peripheral vision   179, 195, 202, 304, 341, 345, 347
perjury   151
permanent (crush) cavity   321, 328, 329
peroneal nerve   353
perp   261, 325
perpetrator   16, 17, 20, 85, 95, 96, 401
personal space   289
perspiration   249
pessimistic   86, 120
Petratis, M.   118
petroleum jelly   271
phenomenon   209, 363, 366
Phil Donahue Show   123
phone pole   273
phosphate finish   378
physical conditioning   83, 84, 331, 425
physical exhaustion   120
Physical Fitness Capacity and Absenteeism of Police Officers   118
Physical Fitness Programs for Police: A Manual for the Police Administrator   118
physically fit   87, 104, 167, 353, 425
physics   77, 343
physiological readiness   102

Index

physiologically   59, 91, 265
piece meal   424
pig   15, 241
pipe   129-131
pistol   20, 39, 62, 92, 132, 135, 139, 149, 173, 276, 309, 378, 381, 385
pistol competition   92
pistol grip   41, 389
pistol sights   92
pitch   59, 241, 343, 372
pitcher   365, 372
pivot   216, 300
plainclothes   13, 15, 16, 18, 150, 260
plaintiff   95, 96, 207, 282, 284
plastic   130, 271, 274, 392, 411
plastic shell holders, slings   47
plump mushroom   324, 325
plywood   172
pocket   14, 16, 31, 130, 166, 200, 273, 274, 385, 388, 391-393
Pocket Pistols   385
poem   268
Point Blank   17
point man   176, 438
point of use incident   234
poison   204, 230
poker   301, 302
Police Chemical Agents Manual   73
Police Chief   118, 316
police chief   120
Police Locker   150
Police magazine   132, 315, 386, 422
Police Marksman The   74, 124, 132, 202, 315, 317, 386

Police Officer's Guide to Better Communication, The   248
Police Rights of Self-Incrimination   187
Police Shotguns and Carbines   47
Police Special   14
Police Stress Phenomenon   185
police academy   44, 84, 95, 132, 180, 208, 218, 288, 350, 364, 405, 422, 425
police backup   321
police brutality   15, 63, 119, 399, 427
police corruption   397
police periodicals   315
police pistol range   273
police shotgun   37-40, 42, 43, 47, 133
policy   11, 50, 52-54, 72, 139, 185, 186, 198, 274, 281-283, 287, 309, 339, 364
political climate   191
politician   53, 153, 159, 363
polymer   41
Popow v. City of Margate   95
popper plate   279
porous   391
Port Arms   435, 437
positive   2, 3, 46, 85, 87, 88, 98, 103. 104, 122, 126, 167, 179, 203, 219, 241, 244, 245, 258, 292, 293, 299, 304, 308, 310, 311, 351, 403, 405, 410, 411, 413
post-incident damage   55
Post Traumatic Stress Disorder   426
post-traumatic stress syndrome   87
posture   107, 201, 294
potassium chlorate   67
powder   67, 234, 275
Powers, Howard   247
power trip   152

Index

power-jacket hollowpoint   322
PR-24™   58, 180, 201, 202, 265, 288, 294, 317, 350, 360, 363-365, 367, 369-371, 373, 374, 386, 421, 422
PR-24™ Basic Course   363, 364, 371
PR-24™ National Seminar   441
practical accuracy   133, 138
practice baton   307
pre-emptor   313
pre-incident liability   53
precipitated   286
precision   133, 134, 140, 279
Prentice-Hall   47
preparation   9, 11, 85, 104, 257, 266, 331, 363, 423
President's Council on Police Fitness   118
pressure point   265, 317, 372
prestige   166, 398
priest   269
principles of conflict management   77, 81
prison   6, 15, 16, 20, 128, 165
prisoner   15, 20, 151, 205, 286
private sector   52, 163
private security   163
procedure   2, 6, 21, 24, 53, 68, 69, 75, 76, 83, 85, 98, 106-108, 111, 112, 144, 157, 164, 167, 180, 185, 187, 207, 211, 217, 218, 220, 282, 316, 319, 320, 322, 387, 389, 392, 393, 395, 404, 409, 412-415, 419, 421, 436
professional athletes   311
professional suicide   53
professional survival   183, 184, 187
professionalism   56, 162, 396, 399, 400, 405, 406, 408
progress-charted   275
project   96, 99, 241, 242, 258
projectile   11, 66-68, 71

promotion   98, 117, 120, 167
prone   2, 88, 121, 141, 180, 191, 279, 303, 305, 325, 392
pronunciation   257
prop search   388
prosecution   49-53, 55, 252
protect and serve   159, 162, 164, 168
provoke   164, 426
provocation   293
prowler   283
proxemic   239, 245
proximity   286
psychiatric break   87
psychological control   102, 103
psychological factor   11, 353
psychologically   91, 185, 265, 281, 304, 353
psychomotor skill   96, 184, 187, 203, 204, 223, 311, 421
psychosomatic illness   121
public address system (PA)   191, 192
public sector   163
public works department   235
public zone   289
pucker factor   60, 174
pull tab   128
pump   38, 39, 122, 138, 295, 299, 300, 312
pump action   38, 39, 138
pump-gun   37
punch   130, 187, 200, 227, 269, 293, 302, 304, 306, 315, 365, 366, 367, 411, 419, 420, 435
pupil size   293
purse   18, 283
pursuit   29, 50, 55, 85, 103, 104, 159, 164, 187, 191, 223, 342
pursuit driving   57, 83

Index

pushup   333-337
PVC pipe   303
Pyrotechnic   65-68, 70

Q

Quick Peek Technique   175
quick peek   80, 178, 200
quick time   435
Quik-Kuf Handcuffs   410-412, 415
quiver   249

R

rabbi   269
racial animus   54
racial slur   54
racism   129, 281
radar   15, 209
radio   1, 3, 5-7, 14, 15, 59, 85, 92, 121, 123, 158, 193, 197, 220, 237, 267, 300, 304, 306, 308, 309, 316
radio signal   6
radioactive   230
rage   59, 64, 295
railroad yard   229
Ranger   43, 182
rank   180, 273, 275, 399, 425
rapid eye movement (REM)   84
ratchet   389
rational thinking   67, 402
raw result   319, 320

razor blade   130, 391
re-entry   427
re-qualification   275
Reactionary Gap   224, 225, 227, 263
reactive target   279
reading the streets   125, 127
realism   46, 184, 276
realistic training   308
Rear Gun Hand Grip   214
reasonable suspicion   54, 184, 200, 387, 392
reasonableness   73, 283-287
recall   250, 327, 428
reckless disregard   53
recoil   40-42, 46, 143, 145, 379, 383
recoil buffer   379
recoil pad   40
recovered bullet diameter   320, 324, 326
recovering   268
recreation   101, 275, 277
recruit academy   275
redirect   67, 268, 306
reflective sunglasses   244
reflex   17, 19, 44, 91, 121, 220, 277
reframing   86
Regional Center for Criminal Justice   211
register   93, 147, 148, 191, 273
registration   191, 194, 195
regulator   60, 246, 247
reholster   147, 148
reinforce   6, 7, 15, 187, 199, 220, 271, 277, 311-313, 363, 405, 406, 423, 438, 440, 442
relationship   11, 75, 98, 157, 159, 162, 206, 223, 236, 246, 285, 353, 399

Index

Relative Incapacitation Index (RII)   321
Relative Positioning Concept   169, 172, 179
relative positioning   170, 201
relative strength   286
Relaxation Response, The   64
relevant   3, 184
religion   397
reload   16, 46, 145, 147, 273-275, 278, 279, 375
Remington   39, 43, 134, 136-139, 322, 376, 377
Remsberg, Charles   64
rendered-safe   274
repetition   62, 110-113, 257, 277, 311, 333, 334, 336, 424
repetitive physical practice   311
repetitive training   310
report   22-36, 39, 61, 98, 101, 123, 185, 206, 211, 219, 220, 223, 229, 234, 255, 286, 319, 409, 436
Republican National Convention   218
rescue   14, 15, 19, 233, 428
resistance   35, 71, 76-78, 81, 110, 112, 121, 143, 146, 148, 282, 283, 316, 389, 426
resting heart rate   112
restraint   20, 96, 129, 151, 170, 208, 221, 276, 277, 279
resuscitation   154
retaining strap   392
retaliation   53
reticle   134, 381
retractable stock   383
retrofit   40
Reverse Wrist Lock   354-356, 358
reverse funnel   302
reverse X entry method   177
review   6, 36, 81, 83, 85, 98, 117, 141, 173, 211, 242, 255, 256, 281, 285, 287, 307, 363, 365, 409, 421

revolver   14, 16, 18, 39, 62, 92, 138, 144, 145, 185, 273, 375, 385
rhythmic movement   246
Richmond, V.P.   248
ridged stability   263
rifle sight   38, 44
rifled slug   42, 44, 133
rifling twist   139
right stuff   83, 251
right to privacy   51
righteous   287
ring post front   378
Riot Act   426
Riot Law   426
riot control   68
risk aversion   77
ritualized combat   296
Road Warrior, The   154
Roaring 20's   381
Roberts, G.K.   141
robot   266
rock   125, 129, 130, 304
role model   3, 398, 403, 404
role play scenarios   184
roller-locked bolt system   383
roll   18, 114, 303, 304, 390
Roman Empire   423
romantic relationship   162
rookie   83, 160, 183, 187, 217, 273
Roosevelt, Theodore   155
rose-petal soup   153
roundnose   328

Index

round   10, 46, 69, 134, 138-140, 143, 147, 148, 172, 279, 380, 382
routine   6, 17, 47, 109, 112, 129, 131, 159, 165, 186, 189, 237, 271, 275
routine traffic stop   189, 196, 244, 304
rubber gloves   131
rudeness   244
Ruger   135, 136, 141
rule   5, 10, 26, 67, 84, 87, 96, 119, 120, 130, 138, 151, 158, 166, 179, 199, 202, 203, 223, 224, 232, 237, 242, 244-247, 251, 256, 261, 272, 278, 289, 294, 320, 341, 349, 402, 418
rumor   160, 161, 427
run-off water   234
Russian Short   138
Ryschon, K.   118

S

sadistic   152, 285
Safariland   41, 47
Safe Guard   435
safe speed   345
safety   5, 7, 9, 18, 19, 38, 66, 81, 85, 101, 116, 118, 143, 144, 146-148, 159, 160, 181, 193, 196, 198-200, 207, 217, 219, 223, 229, 232, 245, 247, 271, 278, 280, 319, 338, 354, 363, 380, 382, 388, 391, 395, 418
salary   262, 398
saline   235
salivary response   62
sanctified atmosphere   279
Sani-Fresh   391, 395
Satan   154, 293

saturate   65, 68, 71, 114, 186
scared   95, 272
scientific method   322, 323, 328
scoped rifle   79, 385
score   92, 99, 107-109, 185, 243, 275, 279, 317, 345
Scott, Foresman and Co.   248
scumbag   15, 19, 21
scrutiny   53, 282
search and seizure   184, 284, 316
search   3, 7, 29, 45, 51, 54, 75, 77, 125, 130, 131, 160, 165, 169, 171-174, 176, 179, 180, 183, 184, 187, 196, 197, 202, 211, 284, 316, 376, 387-389, 391-395, 400, 404, 413
seat belt   125, 192
Second Chance   17
secondary verbal command   205
secondary vision   292
secreted   121, 129, 393, 394
security   2, 5, 77, 78, 150, 154, 158, 163, 181, 202, 214, 217, 222, 297, 338, 396, 413
security holsters   16
Security Industry Product News   338
Security Management Magazine   338
security taps   201
seizure   51, 99, 105, 165, 184, 283-285, 316
select-fire   136
self-contained breathing apparatus   235
self-esteem   398
self-illuminating reticle   134
self-incrimination   51, 187
self-mutilation   128
self-tattooing   128
Selye, Dr. Hans   120, 121
semiauto qualification course   273

Index

semiautomatic   20, 375, 378, 379

seminar   9, 36, 82, 98, 142, 182, 186, 207, 208, 317, 337, 360, 421, 441

semiwadcutter   328

senior captain   273

Seven Principles of Officer Survival   225

sexism   281

sexual harassment   161

shaman   269

Shattered Badge, The   123

shell carrier   41, 47

shirt   15, 16, 18, 165, 256, 273, 393

shoe   15, 33-35, 104, 107, 116, 145, 163, 256, 271, 337, 393

shoot stimulus   279

short term memory   311

shot deformation   41

shotgun   14, 37-47, 71, 95, 133, 136, 137, 140, 141, 173, 174, 210, 375, 379, 385, 392

shotgunner   40

shot   6, 13-16, 18-20, 37, 41, 43, 45, 46, 79, 88, 92, 93, 133, 134, 136, 139, 141, 144-148, 151, 172, 179, 184, 209-211, 220, 221, 268, 274, 277, 279, 283, 299, 322-328, 378, 380, 382, 394

shoulder   2, 16, 37, 41, 71-73, 113-115, 151, 154, 176, 200, 201, 245, 269, 270, 285, 291, 309, 369, 384, 389, 390, 417

shoulder weapon   37, 71

shrink   186

shuffle step   263

shyster shark   279

Sick Policy   185

side-to-side bend   334, 337

sidearm   10, 14, 133, 137, 138, 143, 201, 220, 309, 312

sidesaddle   41, 47

Sierra   139, 322
SIGARMS Academy   73
significant other   88
Silent Language, The   248
Silent Passages   240
silhouette   176, 274, 313, 314
silica aerogel   67
simplicity   77, 78
simulated baton   305
simulated firearm   303, 305
simultaneously   42, 60, 212, 215, 239, 267, 308, 313, 352
sincere   187, 257, 399, 405
sing   268
single assailant confrontations   263
siren   89, 152, 191, 398, 345
sit-up   106-109, 113, 333, 337
sixth sense   131
size   39, 42, 68, 69, 71, 91, 96, 101, 129, 146, 267, 286, 293, 320, 327-329, 353, 379-383, 390, 424, 433, 436, 440
Skeeter   128
skepticism   15, 154
Sketch, H.   118
skill-building   275
skin   60, 66, 73, 93, 116, 295, 325
skinfold caliper   107
Skinheads   128
skirt   172, 394
slam dunk   206
slander   151
Slicing the Pie Technique   175
slide   19, 37, 46, 113, 143, 145, 147, 148, 180, 273, 358, 389, 391
slide action repeater   37

Index

slide-cocking autoloader   147
slide stop pin   147
slide-release lever   143, 146
sling   41, 47, 140, 141
slug   16, 38, 40, 42, 44, 46, 133, 256, 324
Smith & Wesson (S & W)   73, 350
smoke   17, 71, 92, 130, 234, 274, 349, 436
smokeable cocaine   129
smokey type hat   176
smoothbore   38-40
sniper   133-135, 137, 140, 141, 375, 378
Sniper Team   438
sniper rifle   133-137, 139, 376, 378, 379
sociological   424, 425
soft body armor   9, 10, 11, 46
softpoint   140-141
soil   234, 256
somnambulism   96
soot   145
soul   152, 154, 269, 310
sound signal   436
Southwestern Institute of Forensic Sciences (SIFS)   322
sovereignty   53
space   67-70, 148, 176, 199, 223-225, 227, 245, 246, 289, 293, 294, 343, 380, 435, 438
space age synthetic   380
Space, Time, and Distance   223-225, 227, 228
spalling   145
spatial   246
Special Weapons and Tactics (SWAT)   3, 47, 74, 75, 132, 133, 136, 186, 274, 277, 325, 375-377, 379, 385, 421
special interest groups   53
Special Weapons   385

specifically job related 184
specificity of training 333, 335
specimen 267
Spectra-Shield 11
speed 6, 15, 27, 60, 62, 63, 70, 89, 159, 191, 195, 274, 276, 325, 339-345, 349, 365, 366
SPEEDCUFFING, The Police S.A.F.E.T.Y. System 395
speedloader 16
speed-reloads 275
speedometer 339
Speer 325
spin 2, 159, 300, 305, 324, 326, 365, 366, 389
spine 59, 301
spirit 154, 155, 261, 270, 271, 272, 331, 363, 364
spray paint 126
Springfield 138
squad 1, 30, 88, 90, 171, 172, 176, 186, 189, 191-193, 195, 196, 223, 237, 280, 316, 330, 424, 427, 432, 434-441
squad leader 424, 436, 437, 438, 441
squads in support 438
squat 113, 301, 304, 332, 335, 337
stabilizing command 205
stacking handcuff method 411, 415-419
stairway 169, 179
stake-out 186
stamina 96, 310, 425
stance 45, 147, 158, 176, 200, 201, 291, 295, 296, 314
stand fast 438
Stanford Heart Disease Prevention Program 106
star-trekking 171
State Fire Marshal 234
statistic 10, 120, 209, 328, 365, 409
status 103, 117, 191, 245, 279, 398

Index

steal   20, 397, 398
steel plate   46
steering wheel   17, 193, 195, 346
STEL   236
Stephen Greene Press   317
step-drag   263, 264
step-up and down   334, 337
stereotypical   241
sterilize   148
Sterling   16
Steyr AUG   135, 380
stimulus response   311
stocks   47
stomach   91, 113, 121, 175, 205, 249, 303, 305, 354, 356, 357
stomp and drag   436
Storr, Anthony   64
strategy   75-81, 129, 225, 361
Street Survival series   84
Street Survival® Seminar   182, 207
Street Survival   207
street tactic   183
Stress and Physical Activity   118
Stress Disability   184
Stress in Law Enforcement   123
stress management   121-123
stress-feedback loop   63
stretch (temporary) cavity   321, 326-329
strike   39, 42, 62, 96, 137, 148, 160, 205, 215, 219, 235, 264, 265, 268, 291, 300, 304, 306, 314, 353, 361, 362, 371, 372
strike only implement   361
striking bag   267
stroll   256

Strong Leather   16
strong hand   212, 264, 265, 270, 291, 389, 390
strut   256
stuffed duffel bag   267
stun munition   72
subconscious   92, 93, 269, 311-313
submachine gun   376, 378, 381, 382, 383, 384
submissive   291
subsonic load   322
substance   129, 130, 197, 229, 230, 232, 233, 236
Sudden Infant Death Syndrome (SID)   186
Suki   199
superiority   241
supplemental weapon   313
supportive   244, 291, 296
surface   60, 65, 107, 116, 127, 134, 326, 249, 294, 301, 348, 365, 423, 426, 427
surprise   15, 16, 72, 76-80, 87, 160, 176, 189, 198, 201, 211, 294, 301, 302, 319, 324, 334, 337
surrender   92
survival mechanism   59-61, 63
Surviving Edged Weapons   207
sustained eye contact   244
swagger   256
SWAT Publications   47
Swearengen, T.   73
sweep   68, 70, 108, 265, 274, 279, 293, 439
swing   106, 216, 268, 274, 356, 365, 410
symbol   126, 231, 241
sympathetic branch   60, 61
symptomatic   66, 71, 72
synergism   236
synopsis   27, 28, 30, 31, 34

Index

synthesized 66
synthetic material 380
syringe 130

T

tachypsychia 61
tackle 122, 269, 299
Taco Bell 183
tactic of the week 314
tactical baton 426
tactical edge 72
Tactical Edge, The 64, 74, 207
Tactical Formation 425
tactical groundfighting 299, 304, 305
tactical response 83, 184, 224, 258
Tactical Shotgun Techniques 47
tactical unit 186, 421
tactile sense 195
tail-gunner 19
talk show 267
tape measure 255
target glance 292, 293
target heart rate (THR) 111, 112
tarnished 405
Task Force 185
tattoo 125, 127, 128
taxes 397
TB 73
Tear Gas Munitions 73
teeth 295, 296, 393
teeth clenched 294

telegraph   180, 264
telescopic sight   134
television   122, 123, 129, 152, 207, 233, 239, 257, 260, 288, 333, 334, 396
television anchor   257
television training   333
television viewer   282
tempo   241
temporary (stretch) cavity   321, 326-329
temptation policy   185
tenement building   423
Tennessee v. Garner   283
Teratogenicity   236
terminal   39, 132, 139, 140, 231
terminal performance   139
terrain   81, 277
Territo   120
territorialism   160
Terry stop   54
testimony   201, 249-252, 255-258
Texas Tower Incident, The   375
Texas Tower Sniper   79
textbook   396, 410
theatre   253
them vs. us mentality   281
third person   24, 36
Thomas, Charles C.   73
Thompson, General John T.   381
Thompson, The   381
Thorpe, Terry   73
threat level   9, 10, 11, 189
Threat Level I   10
Threat Level II   10

Index 515

Threat Level IIA   10
Threat Level III   10
Threat Level IV   10
Three R's: Replenish, Reinforce, Refine   117, 442
Three Rings of Safety, The   18, 19
three-bag exercise   268, 271
throw   126, 173, 195, 251, 307, 411
throw-dart   307
thumb   10, 67, 143, 144, 147, 200, 214, 215, 218, 247, 358, 390, 414, 415
Thumb Lock   415
Time   123
time equals distance   199
tissue   72, 114, 130, 141, 323-327
TLV   236
Tombstone Courage   11, 202
tone   204, 235, 241, 294, 309, 405
tongue   393
Top Cops   239
torque   389, 390
torso   39, 43, 45, 264, 321-324, 326, 328, 393
tort   49-51
torture   152, 249
total penetration depth   320
tradeoff   10
traffic   3, 153, 159, 166, 169, 189-196, 229, 231-235, 240, 241, 244, 245, 309, 340, 343, 345, 346, 348, 427
traffic cone   235
traffic violation   153, 195, 231, 309
Training Tips   150
transportation incident   234
trash can   273, 279
trauma   11, 50, 55, 84, 86-89, 96, 104, 141, 185, 327, 426

trench broom   37
trespass   51
triad of strength   331
triangle   179, 267, 268, 440
triangulation   179
Tribute — A Day On The Beat With America's Finest   330
triceps   108, 335
trick-bag   18
trigger   16, 44, 45, 83, 133, 143-149, 214, 215, 218, 279, 295, 353, 380, 382
trigger-cocking autoloader   145, 146, 148
trip throw   307
tritium insert   384
truck terminal   229
tuck   303, 304, 333
tuition   98
tunnel vision   61, 62, 147, 267
turret   274
TVI Journal   338
two second rule   341
Type L   322
Tzu, Sun   77

U

U.S. Border Patrol   319, 321, 322
U.S. Carbine   138
U.S. Coast Guard   225
U.S. Department of Health and Human Services   118
U.S. Department of Transportation   229, 231, 345
U.S. Marshal's Service   319, 321
U.S. Navy, Naval Station   141

Index

U.S. Navy Seal Team Six   322
U.S. Secret Service   319
U.S. Supreme Court   57, 184, 187
U.S. World & News Report   123
unconstitutional   49, 52, 166, 282
undercover   128, 182, 185, 186, 207
underwater weighing   107
unexpected   46, 62, 78, 272, 302, 388
UNISAF Publications Ltd.   338
uniform   13, 16, 18, 31, 37, 46, 81, 119, 227, 150, 154, 172-175, 181, 219, 241, 249, 252, 255, 256, 260, 274, 276, 336, 337
union contract   98
United Nations System   230
unity of command   77, 78
unity of effort   423, 425
University of Texas, Austin   375
unknown   93, 189, 193, 194, 196, 229, 242, 381
unknown risk traffic stop   189, 193, 194, 196
unsnap   211
upper body extender   108
upper body strength   62, 102, 108, 113, 115, 335, 389
upper rimmed glasses   292
use of force continuum   133, 184, 361, 372
UZI   304, 381, 382

V

vacuum   286
vapor cloud   233
variable scope   134
velocity   10, 42, 138, 140, 325, 328

Vena   120
ventilate   122
verbal command   175, 193, 202-206, 228, 284, 309, 436, 440
verbal skill   199, 352
verbal warning   205
verbalization   204-207, 297, 311, 353
vertical jab   315
Vesalius   59
vest   2, 9-11, 13, 14, 16, 17, 176, 194, 271, 274, 299, 337
vest saves   17
vicarious liability   186
Vice Lords   126
vice   186, 211
video   3, 22, 47, 54, 118, 206, 207, 243, 248, 267, 327, 330
video camera   251
Video Phenomenon   47
Vietnam War   37, 142
virus   391
viscera   60
visibility   79, 175, 179, 193, 341, 342
Vision, Wind, and Limbs   266, 308
visual imagery   122
visual stimuli   61
visualize   76, 179, 225, 265, 266
vital blow   306, 308
vital organ   302, 303, 327, 328
vital target   265, 306
vocal   62, 239, 241, 242, 244, 247, 322
vocal chord   62
volume   241, 327-329
volumetric   69, 70
volume of speech   294
vomit   66, 153

Index

vulnerable   83, 180, 189, 221, 245, 264, 265

W

waistband   195, 201, 392, 393
walker   336, 394
wall search   389
wallet   16, 33, 34, 195, 393
Wambaugh, Joseph   99
Warning Placard   231
warrior   154, 199, 252, 261, 264, 266, 267, 270-272, 298, 301, 304
warrior spirit   270, 271
Warsaw Pact round   136
water   65, 66, 72, 107, 116, 117, 139, 152, 229, 230, 234, 235, 279, 349, 392
waybill   233
Wayne, Jane   85
Wayne, John   85
weak hand   93, 212, 265, 270, 275, 389-391
weak leg   264
Weaponless Defense: A Law Enforcement Guide to Non-Violent Control   372
weapon retention   184, 187, 211, 218, 226, 312, 313
wearability   10
Weaver Stance   176
Wedge Formation   433, 440, 441
weight   10, 11, 69, 84, 104, 105, 107, 110, 112, 122, 140, 167, 185, 242, 251, 267, 269, 271, 274, 276, 291, 295, 296, 304, 325, 337, 377
weight lift   122
weight lifter   352
weight training   110, 276

welcoming committee 19
well-groomed 163
Wemmer, Rich 15
wheelchair 394
whiskey 310
whistle 273, 436
white flag 92
whites of the eyes 292
Whitman, Charles 79, 375
widow 395
Williams, M. 118
Wilson, Damon 73
Winchester 37, 43, 133, 134, 137-139, 322
window 10, 172, 174, 179, 195, 242, 243, 269
windshield 197, 349
wished 313, 362
wizard 362
wolf pack 261, 264, 265, 269, 272
wop 241
World War I 37
Wound Profile: Illustration of the Missile-Tissue Interaction 141
Wound Ballistics Review 141
wound value 323
wrap around entry method 177, 178
Wrist Twist 354-356
wrist 152, 174, 212, 216, 217, 219, 285, 352-359, 369, 389-391, 411-415, 417-419
wrist watch 174

X

X formation 177

Index

X pattern entry method   177

Z

yoga   122
Z Arm Control   359

10-codes   6
11-codes   6
+P   145, 321-325
99   128
911   14, 239

Other Books and Videos Available from Performance Dimensions Publishing

Con Games and Con Artists (Video): This program shows how some of the most popular confidence games are used on unsuspecting and trusting victims. Racine County, Wisconsin, Sheriff Eric Johnson, provides valuable insight into the methods and motivation of con artists.
ISBN: 1-879411-21-0. 27 minutes. $29.95.

Courtroom Skills and Tactics (Video): This video is meant to improve an officer's skills and abilities on the witness stand. Mark Baganz and John Livingston, two nationally known and well respected practicing attorneys, are featured. Meant for new and experienced officers alike, viewers are taken through a number of courtroom re-enactments that actually take place in a courtroom with an officer giving testimony. You have survived the streets, now learn how to survive the courts.
ISBN: 1-879411-16-4. 31 minutes. $29.95.

Crisis Intervention (Video): This program provides information on how to recognize and effectively intervene in a crisis situation. This program features Paul Roemer, a skilled and experienced hostage negotiator formerly with the Federal Bureau of Investigation. Viewers are also shown methods to de-escalate and resolve conflict that, if left unresolved, can lead to a crisis.
ISBN: 1-879411-20-2. 28 minutes. $29.95.

Interpersonal Communications Skills (Video): This video features one of law enforcement's most respected names, Ed Nowicki. This informative program shows how to use and recognize voice inflection, body language, and proper distance to enhance the interpersonal communications' process. Learn why some of the most effective law enforcement officers are also great communicators.
ISBN: 1-879411-19-9. 29 minutes. $29.95.

Law Enforcement Ethics (Video): This video emphasizes the value of ethics for today's law enforcement professional. Containing live footage and interviews, the program offers much needed "food for thought." Neal Trautman, Director of the National Institute of Law Enforcement Ethics, is featured.
ISBN: 1-879411-17-2. 28 minutes. $29.95.

Management of Aggressive Behavior (Book): This book was written by Roland Ouellette, a retired lieutenant with the Connecticut State Police and an expert on how to manage aggressive and violent be-

havior. This practical book contains 20 informative chapters that show how to recognize and manage aggressive behavior. Written in an easy to comprehend fashion with extensive photos.
ISBN: 1-879411-22-9. $14.95.

Street Signs (Book): Written by Mark S. Dunston, this is the most comprehensive identification manual ever written on symbols of crime and violence used by street gangs, hate groups, motorcycle gangs, prison gangs, and others as a secret method of communications. These street signs may be present in the form of tattoos, graffiti spray painted on walls, patches worn on clothing, or in many other ways. Street signs communicate a great deal about an entire group, or an individual group member. The *Street Signs* manual can be used alone, but it is best used in conjunction with *Street Signs: The Video* as a complete training and information package.
ISBN: 1-879411-13-X. 232+ pages. $14.95.

Street Signs (Video): This video visually dramatizes how many of the street signs shown in the book may put the uninformed at risk. Realistic and graphic portrayals will enlighten and amaze viewers. Although it can be used alone, this video is best used as part of a complete training and information package along with the book, *Street Signs*.
ISBN: 1-879411-12-1. 30 minutes. $29.95.

Street Weapons (Book): An identification manual for improvised, unconventional, unusual, homemade, disguised, and exotic personal weapons. *Street Weapons* is widely recognized as the most authoritative book ever written on these highly unusual weapons. This comprehensive manual contains hundreds of photos and drawings along with descriptions that clearly explain how these weapons can be used and carried covertly. Written by Ed Nowicki and Dennis A. Ramsey, two of the leading experts on these types of weapons. You will discover how a normal looking ring can turn into a deadly flesh tearing instrument, or how the stems to a pair of glasses can deliver deadly wounds. A companion to *Street Weapons: The Video*. Must reading for every law enforcement officer.
NOTE: This book will only be sold to law enforcement, security, corrections, or military personnel — proper identification required when ordering.
ISBN: 1-879411-11-3. 240+ pages. $19.95.

Street Weapons (Video): A companion to the book, *Street Weapons*. This fast paced video dramatizes the deadly potential of some of the weapons that are included in the book. Viewing this video should be mandatory for every law enforcement officer. Although this video can be used alone, it is most effective when used in cooperation with the book for a complete training and information package.

NOTE: This video will only be sold to law enforcement, security, corrections, or military personnel — proper identification required when ordering.
ISBN: 1-879411-12-1. 22 minutes. $29.95.

True Blue (Book): This critically acclaimed book contains "true stories about real cops." Written by one of the most respected law enforcement writers, Ed Nowicki, a twenty-four year law enforcement veteran who survived six shootings. *True Blue* contains an assortment of some of the most fascinating and compelling stories about the realities of being a law enforcement officer. This revealing book never lets up and will take you on a trip through the full range of human emotions. *True Blue* will have you uncontrollably laughing while reading one story and shedding tears while reading another. A provocative and sometimes shocking look into the extraordinary world of law enforcement. There's nothing quite like it!
ISBN: 1-879411-15-6. 255+ pages. $14.95.

Supervisory Survival (Book): Written by over 20 different authors, this book provides a unique perspective on how to survive the rigors of supervision. The list of authors contains some of the most well known and respected names in law enforcement. This books goes far beyond theory, it provides real and practical insights by experienced professionals. You've never seen a supervisory book like this. It is meant to be read by new, experienced, and aspiring supervisors.
ISBN: 1-879411-23-7. $17.95.

Why Not Save Time and Order Now with Your MasterCard or Visa? Call TOLL FREE 1-800-877-7413.

Order Form

Telephone Orders: Call 1-800-877-7413. Have your MasterCard or Visa ready.

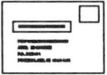

Postal Orders: Performance Dimensions Publishing, P.O. Box 502, Powers Lake, WI 53159-0502, U.S.A., (414) 279-3850.

FAX Orders: Fax your purchase orders to (414) 279-5758.

Quant.	Title	Price Each	Total
	Con Games and Con Artists (Video)	29.95	
	Courtroom Skills and Tactics (Video)	29.95	
	Crisis Intervention (Video)	29.95	
	Interpersonal Communications Skills (Video)	29.95	
	Law Enforcement Ethics (Video)	29.95	
	Management of Aggressive Behavior (Book)	14.95	
	Street Signs (Book)	14.95	
	Street Signs: The Video (Video)	29.95	
	Street Weapons (Book)	19.95	
	Street Weapons: The Video (Video)	29.95	
	True Blue (Book)	14.95	
	Supervisory Survival (Book)	17.95	
	Total Survival (Book)	24.95	
	Shipping & Handling (a flat charge for any quantity)		3.00
	Total Enclosed		$

☐ Please send FREE information about other books and videos when published.

☐ I would like to host a Seminar.

Method of Payment:
☐ Check   ☐ Money Order   ☐ MasterCard   ☐ VISA

If credit card: Card Number _____
Name on Credit Card _____
Signature _____ Expires _____

Send to my :   ☐ Work   ☐ Home

Name _____ Title _____
Agency/Company _____
Address _____
City _____ State _____ Zip _____
Agency/Company Phone ( ) _____
Home Phone ( ) _____

WHY WAIT? Call your order in to us RIGHT NOW! Call Toll Free at 1-800-877-7413